INTERVENTIONS: NEW STUDIES IN MEDIEVAL CULTURE
Ethan Knapp, Series Editor

Translating Troy

PROVINCIAL POLITICS IN ALLITERATIVE ROMANCE

Alex Mueller

THE OHIO STATE UNIVERSITY PRESS
COLUMBUS

Copyright © 2013 by The Ohio State University.
All rights reserved.

Library of Congress Cataloging-in-Publication Data
Mueller, Alex, 1973 –
Translating Troy : provincial politics in alliterative romance / Alex Mueller.
p. cm. — (Interventions : new studies in medieval culture)
Includes bibliographical references and index.
ISBN-13: 978-0-8142-1221-9 (cloth : alk. paper)
ISBN-10: 0-8142-1221-2 (cloth : alk. paper)
ISBN-13: 978-0-8142-9322-5 (cd)
1. English literature —Middle English, 1100 –1500 —History and criticism. 2. Trojans in literature. 3. Troy (Extinct city) —In literature. 4. Romances, English. I. Title. II. Series: Interventions : new studies in medieval culture.
PR275.T74M84 2013
820.9'001 —dc23
2012037640

Cover design by Laurence J. Nozik
Type set in Adobe Minion Pro
Text design by Juliet Williams
Printed by Thomson-Shore, Inc.

♾ The paper used in this publication meets the minimum requirements of the American National Standard for Information Sciences—Permanence of Paper for Printed Library Materials. ANSI 39.48–1992.

9 8 7 6 5 4 3 2 1

For Tiffany

CONTENTS

List of Illustrations	ix
Acknowledgments	xi

INTRODUCTION
    Translating Destruction into Alliterative Romance   1

ONE
    Genealogy: Trojan Historiography in England   19

TWO
    War: Reviving Troy   40

THREE
    Violence: The Corporeal Terror of the Roman Empire   81

FOUR
    Heraldry: Arthur's Roman Dragon   124

FIVE
    Territory: The Trojan Provinces of Britain   167

CONCLUSION
    Alliterating England   206

Works Cited	229
Index	246

ILLUSTRATIONS

FIGURE 1
    Glasgow University Library, Hunterian MS V.2.8 [*Destruction of Troy*],
    f. 1a. Table of Contents. Reproduced by permission of Glasgow University
    Library, Special Collections   13

FIGURE 2
    Admont, Stiftsbibliothek, Codex Admontensis 185 [Guido delle
    Colonne, *Historia destructionis Troiae*], f. 3b. Reproduced by permission
    of Admont Stiftsbibilothek   48

ACKNOWLEDGMENTS

> ergo age, care pater, ceruici imponere nostrae;
> ipse subibo umeris nec me labor iste grauabit;
> quo res cumque cadent, unum et commune periclum,
> una salus ambobus erit. (Virgil, *Aeneid,* 2.707–10)
>
> [Come then, dear father, clasp my neck. I will carry you on my shoulders; that load won't burden me. Whatever may happen, it will be for us both: the same shared risk, the same salvation.]

THIS SCENE in the *Aeneid,* when Aeneas offers to carry his father, Anchises, away from the smoldering ruins of Troy, has often come to mind as I have written this book. After all, this image of the legendary founder of Italy bearing forth the remnants of Troy offers a stunning synecdoche of *translatio imperii,* the translation of one empire into the birth of the next. Perhaps more significantly, though, I have personally felt a bit like an Anchises, who has been supported and carried forth by many virtuous Aeneases. While I would like to believe, as Aeneas suggests, that the many readers who offered advice and encouragement for this book did not consider their support to be burdensome, I feel nonetheless grateful to them for their willingness to shoulder some of the weight and risk of this project.

Among the many kind-hearted "translators," I owe my greatest academic and intellectual debt to Rebecca Krug, who tirelessly read and provided commentary for numerous drafts of chapters from beginning to end. Without her formative advice and enthusiastic dedication to my success, this project would not have reached its timely end. During the early stages of my research and writing, the community of medievalists in the University of Minnesota

English department and Center for Medieval Studies offered invaluable feedback that helped me establish the tenets of my core argument. In particular, I would like to thank Ana Adams, Matthew Desing, Ruth Karras, Stephanie Lohse, Andrew Scheil, John Watkins, and Ellen Wormwood, whose careful reading and constructive criticisms greatly strengthened the early versions of each chapter of this book.

As the book began to take shape, I also greatly benefited from conversations with conference participants in the Medieval Romance Society's "Death in Medieval Romance" (2006) and "Traveling Texts: Adaptation of Medieval Romance" (2011) sessions in Kalamazoo, the New Chaucer Society's "Reading Antiquity" (2006) session in New York City, the Medieval Academy's "Late Middle English Literature" (2007) session in Toronto, the Conference for David Benson (2010) at Harvard University, and the MLA Arthurian Discussion Group's "Biopolitics" (2011) session in Los Angeles. Of the many great scholarly friends I met in these venues, I want to single out David Benson, who offered early advice about the structure of the project that helped shape its scope and focus, and Michael Johnston, who consistently proved to be a wise interlocutor and incisive reader.

Much of this project relied upon direct access to manuscripts and their facsimiles, which was kindly facilitated by librarians at Glasgow University Library, the Hill Museum & Manuscript Library (HMML), and Admont Stiftsbibliothek. Without generous funding from an HMML Heckman Research Stipend and a University of Massachusetts Boston Joseph P. Healey Research Grant, this work would not have been accomplished. Moreover, support in the form of course releases from my department and dean at UMass Boston allowed me the precious time I needed to complete the writing of this book.

As this book approached its final stages, I profited enormously from wisdom kindly shared by Ian Cornelius, Stephanie Kamath, Christopher Leise, and Seth Lerer. Likewise, I cannot express my gratitude profusely enough to Malcolm Litchfield and Ethan Knapp at The Ohio State University Press, who nurtured this project to its completion through administrative support, timely responses to inquiries, and the procurement of invaluable reviews. These reviewers, Patricia Ingham and one anonymous reader, offered critiques and encouragement that improved my finalized manuscript beyond measure.

My family, both immediate and extended, has played an invaluable role in support of this book. I am grateful to my parents and my sister for their willingness to indulge my passion for medieval studies, even at an early age when knighthood seemed like a reasonable vocation. More recently, my in-laws have demonstrated a touching commitment to furthering my academic success, continually performing acts of generosity that I hope I can repay one day.

The last and most heartfelt expression of gratitude is reserved for my wife, Tiffany, whose patience and loving support of my work has never ceased to amaze me. Even while I was selfishly focused on the writing of this book, she gave me gifts I did not deserve, our two young girls, Harriet and Louise. Together, they have added a profound joy to my life that surpasses any I have ever known.

EARLY VERSIONS of parts of the book were previously published as "Corporal Terror: Critiques of Imperialism in *The Siege of Jerusalem*," *Philological Quarterly* 84.3 (Summer 2005): 287–310; "Linking Letters: Translating Ancient History into Medieval Romance," *Literature Compass* 4.4 (June 2007): 1017–29; and "The Historiography of the Dragon: Heraldic Violence in the Alliterative *Morte Arthure*," *Studies in the Age of Chaucer* 32 (2010): 295–324. I want to thank these journals for their permission to reproduce this material.

Introduction

TRANSLATING DESTRUCTION INTO ALLITERATIVE ROMANCE

TRY IF YOU CAN to forget the blind rhapsodist, the face who launched a thousand ships, the Trojan horse, wily Greeks, epic similes, rosy-fingered dawn, and dactylic hexameters. Imagine there are no gods pulling strings, intervening into human affairs, stirring up trouble, or resolving conflicts. And attempt desperately to cast from your mind that engaging *dramatis personae*: the incomparable Helen, the sulking Achilles, the bloodthirsty Hector, and the virtuous Aeneas.

Imagine instead an unremarkable Helen, a deceitful Achilles, a peaceful Hector, and a traitorous Aeneas. Consider what it must be like to hear a Trojan tale in alliterative verse, echoing throughout a hall filled with aristocrats hungry for ancient history, tales about their glorious ancestors, and, most of all, graphic violence. And as the story winds to its close, feel the air grow stale, detect gasps of despair as Troy falls, and sense the haunting presence of this destructive past.

Welcome to the Troy of medieval England. While most of us are familiar with the Troy story I have urged you to forget, that familiar tale of the theft of Helen and Greek revenge is only the sequel to a much longer tale that begins not only with a separate cast of characters, but also with an entirely different city of Troy. The Troy that falls at the hands of Agamemnon and his Greek army is a second Troy, rebuilt by Priam from the ashes of the first, which had been earlier lost by his father. While the fall of the second Troy occupies our cultural and literary imagination, the fall of the first Troy gripped medieval audiences, particularly a group of alliterative poets who composed romances in the north of England. These poets were uniquely attracted to the dark undercurrents of the tale that contained warnings about seeking martial prowess, translating imperial power to future generations, and promoting aristocratic exceptionalism. They were drawn to the foreknowledge gained from the consequences of imperial self-fashioning explored in episodes such as the following:

Jason and the sea-weary Argonauts seek respite on the shores of Troy. A Trojan lookout spies the band of Greeks and alerts the king of Troy, Laomedon, that invaders have landed. Neglecting introduction or parley, Laomedon summarily demands that the Argonauts depart immediately or prepare for battle. Hercules, the military strategist of the Greeks, becomes enraged by Laomedon's inhospitality and vows that they will return with a vengeance. And return they do.

After capturing the Golden Fleece in Colchis, the Argonauts land on the Trojan beach, this time with a formidable force, including the famed brothers Castor and Pollux. Hercules hatches their attack plan, which divides their host into two parties, one to guard the ships and the other to hide at the Trojan gate. Once Laomedon discovers the Greek band by the ships, he leads his army to meet them in battle. The Trojans experience temporary success, but while they are distracted by the mêlée, the second band of Argonauts, led by Hercules and Jason, clandestinely enter the city and sack it. Having learned that the city has been taken, Laomedon reverses his tracks and rallies his warriors to return to the city. The Trojans become trapped between the two bands and Laomedon is left to fight Hercules alone. Here is what unfolds, as told in the alliterative verse of one John Clerk of Whalley:

> . . . he come to þe kyng in a kene yre,
> Dang hym derffly don in a ded hate,
> Grippit hym grymly gird of his hede,
> Þrew it into þronge of his þro pepull;
> Þat moche sorowe for þe sight & sobbyng of teres,
> When þaire kyng was kylt . . . (1337–42)[1]

[He approaches the king in an intense fury, smites him dearly down with deadly hate, grips him grimly, cuts off his head, and throws it into a throng

---

1. John Clerk of Whalley, *The Destruction of Troy: A Diplomatic and Color Facsimile Edition, Hunterian MS V.2.8 in Glasgow University Library*, ed. Hiroyuki Matsumoto (Ann Arbor: University of Michigan Press, 2002). Future references to *Destruction* will be from Matsumoto's edition.

of his people; when their king was killed, there was much sorrow and shedding of tears at the sight.]

Laomedon's severed head becomes a visual marker, an heraldic assertion for the "sight" of the "pepull" of the destruction that will ensue. Once the "hede" of Troy has been toppled, the city and its inhabitants incur the wrath of the vengeful Greeks, who pillage the city, slaughter the men, and capture the women and children. So falls the first city of Troy.

This destruction of the first Troy is unknown to many of us for a number of reasons. First of all, the fall of the second Troy superseded this militaristic tale with a gripping Homeric tradition that fascinated postmedieval audiences with a compelling cast of characters including the incomparable Helen, the childish gods, the arrogant Achilles, and the crafty Odysseus. Secondly, the destruction of the first Troy cannot be found in the *Iliad* or the *Odyssey*—instead it was popularized in the Middle Ages through numerous translations of a Latin prose history known as the *Historia destructionis Troiae* composed by a thirteenth-century Sicilian judge named Guido delle Colonne.[2] Its credibility as a work of history was confirmed in 1412 when John Lydgate rendered it in Chaucerian iambic pentameter at the behest of Prince Henry in an attempt to bolster Lancastrian claims to noble lineage that reached back to ancient Troy.[3] While Lydgate's *Troy Book* enjoyed great acclaim among the aristocratic elite until the sixteenth century, once the Greek epics began to be translated into English, vernacular versions of Guido's *Historia* fell into relative obscurity.

Many English nobles believed that they were the inheritors of worldly power via the logic of *translatio imperii,* in which the destruction of one empire led to the birth of the next. While the destruction of Troy was lamentable, its imperial power arose, phoenix-like, once again in the form of the Roman Empire. And as Rome fell, Britain began its adolescence as a future imperial force that would strike fear in the hearts of their continental counterparts. Yet, when English aristocrats turned to Guido for indulgence of their fantasies, they found incisive critiques of their Trojan ancestors for

---

2. For the influence of Guido's *Historia* on late medieval England, see James Simpson, *The Oxford English Literary History, Volume 2. 1350–1547: Reform and Cultural Revolution* (Oxford: Oxford University Press, 2002); "The Other Book of Troy: Guido delle Colonne's *Historia destructionis Troiae* in Fourteenth and Fifteenth Century England," *Speculum* 73.2 (1998): 397–423; and Mary Elizabeth Meek's introduction to her translation, Guido delle Colonne, *Historia Destructionis Troiae* (Bloomington: Indiana University Press, 1974), xi–xxx.

3. John H. Fisher, "A Language Policy for Lancastrian England," *Proceedings of the Modern Language Association*, 107.5 (1992): 1168–80, at 1176.

their inhospitality, perfidy, and incompetence as well as a chilling prediction that the New Trojans will inherit destruction, not glory.

Guido's critical voice was attractive to a number of English readers, including the Northwest Midlands poet John Clerk of Whalley. He produced what has become known as the alliterative *Destruction of Troy*, one of several alliterative romances that were composed during the late fourteenth century in the north of England.[4] The most famous of these poems is *Sir Gawain and the Green Knight*, but other works, such as the alliterative *Morte Arthure* and the *Siege of Jerusalem*—comprising what Thorlac Turville-Petre calls the "bookish" set of alliterative romances—have recently begun to receive significant critical attention.[5] These four poems will serve as the focus for my analysis. Each are written within the tradition of chivalric romance, whereby the feats and conduct of individual knights (ancient, Arthurian, or otherwise) rise to the forefront of the action, which ranges from the placidly diplomatic to the excessively violent. Likewise, these romances perpetuate and in some cases enhance Guido's critiques of Trojan identity, attributes that distinguish these provincial histories from many popular *Brut* narratives that justified England's royal authority and national identity by claiming an ancestry that originates in ancient Troy and Rome. By ventriloquizing Guido, these alliterative romances express a deep-seated skepticism about the possibility of a sovereign English nation. Though these militaristic narratives are written to delight aristocratic readers with chivalric accounts of Hector's martial prowess, Vespasian's siege of Jerusalem, and Arthur's Roman conquest, they belie such martial fervor with graphic descriptions of violence, commentary on the suffering of innocent victims, and a preference for diplomacy that fail to satisfy expansionist sensibilities. The consistency of their northern dialects, metrical choice, and martial subject matter suggest that these romances emerged from a Trojan word-hoard of provincial skepticism toward aristocratic practice and claims to sovereignty. The unfortunate result of this dissent was their limited capacity to contribute to the canonical formation of English literary culture, which future readers placed on the shoulders of Chaucerian verse.

While many other alliterative poems, such as *The Wars of Alexander, Saint Erkenwald, Wynnere and Wastoure, The Awyntyrs off Arthure*, and even *The Parlement of the Thre Ages*, also express anti-aristocratic sentiment, it would be inaccurate to suggest that all alliterative poetry—not to mention all alliterative romances—operate as a coherent poetic program.[6] Their met-

    4. For more on the dating of *Destruction*, see chapter 2, note 1 and note 13; chapter 3, 94–99.
    5. Thorlac Turville-Petre, *The Alliterative Revival* (Cambridge: D. S. Brewer, 1977), 16.
    6. David Lawton, "The Diversity of Middle English Alliterative Poetry," *Leeds Studies in*

rical and thematic similarities, aggressive style, and northern provenance have proven to be attractive for the numerous critical attempts to establish the existence of an Alliterative Revival, a conscious and pervasive reproduction of Anglo-Saxon verse in the fourteenth century. What appears to be the almost obligatory nature of the alliterative pattern (aa/ax) has compelled critics to suggest that these texts represent a unified "revival" of alliterative verse that had previously fallen out of fashion after the eleventh century.[7] Since the late 1970s, however, many critics have challenged this theory by identifying the metrical and stylistic differences between Old and Middle English alliterative verse and noting the fallacy of basing a "revival" on surviving evidence, among other arguments.[8] Ralph Hanna has recently challenged the theory of revival by exploring the problems of prioritizing unrhymed long lines over its variations, which has led to a convenient exclusion of contradictory evidence.[9]

The trend against revivalist arguments was influentially begun by Norman Blake, who suggested in his review of Turville-Petre's *The Alliterative Revival* that arguments for an "alliterative school" pigeonhole evidence into a singular model, and accordingly do not account for the diversity and richness of the alliterative verse, fail to consider the possibilities of numerous revivals, and unnecessarily oppose alliterative and Chaucerian poetry.[10] When Chaucer's Parson admits, "I am a Southren man, / I kan nat geeste 'rum, ram, ruf' by lettre" (X.41–42), he marks alliterative verse as a northern genre, but this statement does not confirm the existence of a coherent and resurgent anti-Chaucerian school of poetics.[11] This characterization is

---

English 20 (1989): 143–72; "The Unity of Middle English Alliterative Poetry," *Speculum* 58 (1983): 72–94.

7. Turville-Petre's *The Alliterative Revival* is the most well-known study, but many previous critics had explored the legitimacy of this theory. For example, see J. P. Oakden, *Alliterative Poetry in Middle English* (Manchester: Manchester University Press, 1935), I.153, II.86–7; Dorothy Everett, "The Alliterative Revival," in *Essays on Middle English Literature*, ed. Patricia Kean (London: Oxford University Press, 1959), 46–96. For a recent examination of "Revivalist" literary history, see Randy Schiff's *Revivalist Fantasy: Alliterative Verse and Nationalist Literary History* (Columbus: The Ohio State University Press, 2011), 17–44.

8. See especially Ralph Hanna, "Alliterative Poetry," in *The Cambridge History of Medieval English Literature*, ed. David Wallace (Cambridge: Cambridge University Press, 1999), 488–512. See also Derek Pearsall, "The Origins of the Alliterative Revival," in *The Alliterative Tradition in the Fourteenth Century*, eds. Bernard S. Levy and Paul E. Szarmach (Kent, OH: Kent State University Press, 1981), 1–24; *Old and Middle English Poetry* (London: Routledge and Kegan Paul, 1977); and "The Alliterative Revival: Origins and Social Backgrounds," in *Middle English Alliterative Poetry*, ed. David Lawton (Cambridge: D. S. Brewer, 1982), 34–53.

9. Hanna, "Alliterative Poetry," 488–97.

10. N. F. Blake, "Middle English Alliterative Revivals," *Review* 1 (1979): 205–14.

11. Geoffrey Chaucer, *The Canterbury Tales*, in *The Riverside Chaucer*, ed. Larry Benson, 3rd ed. (Boston: Houghton Mifflin, 1987). Future citations of Chaucerian works refer to this edition.

far from treating alliterative verse "negatively and dismissively," as Turville-Petre suggests, and conversely may distinguish it as a particularly difficult and sophisticated literary form that the Parson does not possess the confidence to render. And it would be even more irresponsible to transfer this disapproving posture to Chaucer, who respectfully employs alliterative verse where it is most appropriate—in battle scenes in *The Knight's Tale* (I.2605–16) and *The Legend of Good Women* (635–48).[12] In characterizing previous critical attempts to denigrate and unify alliterative poetry, Randy Schiff aptly suggests that "the Alliterative Revival is a medievalist rather than a medieval phenomenon," which serves "to narrate the rise of Chaucerian protomodernity."[13] While it is tempting to imagine a distinct northern school of poetics opposed to Chaucerian verse, this supposition drastically simplifies the variety and depth of alliterative poetry and unnecessarily creates a division from Chaucer that is ultimately unproductive and unsustainable.[14]

Even though an oppositional relationship between Chaucer and alliterative verse cannot be convincingly maintained, I want to suggest that it is possible and useful to distinguish the "provincial" perspectives of alliterative poems. Previous critics such as Turville-Petre have turned to dialectical analyses to demonstrate that many of these poems have clear origins in the Northern provinces.[15] Building upon these linguistic analyses, I want to expand the "provincial" identity to include the historiographic perspectives of those who draw heavily upon Guido's Trojan history. In the opening lines of *Sir Gawain and the Green Knight,* the poet details the events of *translatio imperii,* in which Aeneas and his progeny "depreced *prouinces*" [subjugated *provinces*] (5–6), a characteristically dark illustration of the events that follow the destruction of Troy.[16] The *Gawain*-poet inherits this language from Guido's *Historia:* "Et nonnulle alie propterea *prouincie* perpetuum ex Troyanis receperunt incolatum" [And therefore some other *provinces* received from the Trojans a lasting settlement] (11).[17] As I will suggest throughout the

---

12. N. F. Blake, "Chaucer and the Alliterative Romances," *The Chaucer Review* 3.3 (Winter 1969): 163–69.

13. Schiff, *Revivalist Fantasy,* 2.

14. For one influential example of this "oppositional" theory, see J. R. Hulbert, "A Hypothesis Concerning the Alliterative Revival," *Modern Philology* 28 (1931): 405–22.

15. A. McIntosh, "A New Approach to Middle English Dialectology," *English Studies* 44 (1963): 1–11; Turville-Petre, *The Alliterative Revival,* 29–36.

16. The line numbers refer to *Sir Gawain and the Green Knight,* in *The Poems of the Pearl Manuscript,* ed. Malcolm Andrew and Ronald Waldron (Exeter: University of Exeter Press, 2002).

17. Guido de Columnis, *Historia Destructionis Troiae,* ed. Nathaniel Edward Griffin (Cambridge, MA: Mediaeval Academy of America, 1936). Future references to Guido's *Historia* are from this edition.

book, this reference to Trojan colonization highlights the westward proliferation of New Trojan provinces, which are marked by political perfidy, the death of innocent victims, and diplomatic division. As Patricia Clare Ingham has suggested, once this *translatio* becomes localized within Britain, regional contestations for sovereignty emerge between the Welsh and the English, who both claim King Arthur as their own.[18] The alliterative romances that embrace Guido's historiographic posture engage in what we might now call a postcolonial critique, recognizing the destructive work of imperial reason, which desires the establishment of centralized power at the expense of the marginalization of unsavory elements of empire-building, such as the collateral damage of war, the sacrifice of the innocent, and the subjugation of native inhabitants. Whereas postcolonial critics such as Dipesh Chakrabarty seek to "provincialize Europe" by decentering the historicist concept of a dominant western world, these alliterative romances provincialize Troy by interrogating the desirability of Trojan imperial inheritance.[19] By characterizing these romances as "provincial," I am not suggesting that they speak as outsiders to more dominant historiographies—in fact, they are intimately engaged with narratives typically associated with metropolitan sensibilities such as francophilia, chivalric fashion, noble genealogies, and the elevation of the status of the English language. For instance, if the *Gawain*-poet also composed *Pearl*, as most critics agree, his poetry demonstrates direct engagement with the Ricardian context of London through an increased reliance upon a French lexicon and an examination of courtly politics.[20] Transcending the limits of their regional locales, I consider these poems provincial inasmuch as they acknowledge and interrogate the doubtful practice of celebrating England's status as a Trojan province.

As a means to define the nature of provincial politics in alliterative romance, I have limited my analysis to a networked group of alliterative romances that share the following characteristics: 1) a reliance upon Guido's Trojan historiography; 2) Northern dialectical features and provenance; 3) critiques of chivalric practice and aristocratic claims to sovereignty; 4) metonymic relationships between the destruction of bodies and cities. As I will

---

18. Patricia Clare Ingham, *Sovereign Fantasies: Arthurian Romance and the Making of Britain* (Philadelphia: University of Pennsylvania Press, 2001), 21–50.
19. Dipesh Chakrabarty, *Provincializing Europe* (Princeton: Princeton University Press, 2007).
20. John Bowers, *The Politics of Pearl: Court Poetry in the Age of Richard II* (Cambridge: D. S. Brewer, 2001), esp. 81–82; E. V. Gordon, "French Element," in his edition of *Pearl* (Oxford: Clarendon, 1953), 101–6; Turville-Petre, "The 'Pearl'-Poet in his 'Fayre Regioun,'" in A. J. Minnis, Charlotte C. Morse, and Turville-Petre, eds., *Essays on Ricardian Literature in Honour of J. A. Burrow* (Oxford: Clarendon, 1997), 276–94.

suggest throughout this book, the skepticism of these romances is based on shared understandings of the relationship between natural and political bodies. In contrast to the logic that undergirds theories of sovereignty, such as *translatio imperii* and the transcendence of the body politic, which are based on a messianic redemption or resurrection of the political body (i.e. that of the empire or the sovereign), these alliterative romances highlight the finality of the death of the physical body and its inextricable connection to sovereign power.[21] That is, while aristocratic claims to sovereignty rely on an imperial authority that can be transferred via the destruction and subsequent redemption of a sovereign body, these alliterative poems reflect little faith in this fantasy, suggesting instead that the natural and political bodies cannot be separated and inevitably share the same fate. A useful analogy can be found in Michel Foucault's well-known exploration of biopolitics, in which the body is inextricably subject to mechanisms of power. As a way out of this bind, Foucault suggests a future in which the body may liberate itself from power through a "different economy of bodies and pleasures," a kind of jailbreak of sexuality from the binds of institutional authority.[22] Characterizing such a divorce is an impossible dream, Giorgio Agamben argues, "Like sex and sexuality, the concept of the 'body' is always already caught in a deployment of power. The 'body' is always already a biopolitical body and bare life, and nothing in it or the economy of its pleasure seems to allow us to find solid ground on which to oppose the demands of sovereign power."[23] For these alliterative poets, a ruling nobility justified by a redeemed Trojan bloodline represents a kind of hollow sovereignty that is "always already" marked by the corporeal violence and death that follow assertions of authority. In contrast to the optimism of *Troynovant*, these romances emphasize the lamentable fate of the physical body within such imperial ambitions.

The poems of my study realize this critique of biopower by envisioning the sovereign body as a metonym for the larger city or empire it rules. Turning back to the scene of Laomedon's beheading in John Clerk's *Destruction* as one example, we see that the dismemberment of the king leads directly to the destruction of the city. After Hercules tosses the Trojan king's head into the crowd of his people, the plundering of the city ensues, which forces the inhabitants to evacuate, leaving their possessions behind. And just as Her-

21. The seminal work on medieval theories of sovereignty is Ernst Kantorowicz's *The King's Two Bodies: A Study in Mediaeval Political Theology* (Princeton: Princeton University Press, 1997).
22. Michel Foucault, *History of Sexuality, Volume I: An Introduction,* trans. Robert Hurley (New York: Random House, 1978), 159.
23. Giorgio Agamben, *Homo Sacer: Sovereign Power and Bare Life,* trans. Daniel Heller-Roazen (Stanford: Stanford University Press, 1995), 187.

cules beheads Laomedon, "Grippit hym grymly gird of his hede" [grips him grimly, cuts off his head] (1339), the Greeks topple the first Troy, "Grippit vp the ground girdyn doun þe wallys" [dig up the ground, cut down the walls] (1376). Using the same collocation of "Grippit/gird" and "Grippit/girdyn" to describe the destruction of Laomedon and Troy, John Clerk alliteratively connects the fates of the sovereign and the city. As a challenge to the late medieval belief in the sempiternity of the king's body, the metaphor of the death of the natural body of the Trojan king leads directly to the death of the political body of Troy. While the future sovereigns such as Priam, Vespasian, and Arthur, who appear within the pages of these alliterative romances, make multiple attempts to redeem Troy through imperial inheritance, these efforts lead directly to more destruction and death. In this sense, Laomedon's severed head at the feet of his people is a cipher for what Agamben might call the "bare life" of New Troys, which will always be subject to the destruction from which they emerged.

This book contributes to recent scholarship that has departed from arguments about the unity of alliterative verse and embraced examinations of corporeality, violence, and fantasies of empire within these poems. Randy Schiff's recent book, *Revivalist Fantasy*, marks this decisive shift away from the tragic "rise and fall" narrative of the Alliterative Revival to uncover the nationalist desires that canonized Chaucer and relegated alliterative verse to the literary historical trash bin.[24] To complicate the assumed coherence of a singular revival, he analyzes the multiple "alliterative zones" that produced this verse and reveals the divergent agendas of the poems.[25] While Schiff's argument helpfully localizes the various and often divergent concerns of many alliterative poems, I seek to interrogate the shared topics of alliterative romance, such as military campaigns and the destruction of cities, which are remarkably cohesive and suggest a common interest in corporeal revivals—from the raising of the dead to miraculous healings—a thesis that has been pursued by Christine Chism.[26] Likewise, this book builds on the work of Geraldine Heng and Patricia Clare Ingham, who have analyzed the militarism in poems such as the alliterative *Morte Arthure* to establish romance as a repository for nationalistic fantasies.[27] Heng even goes so far as to suggest that romance serves as a means to reimagine crusade history and its

24. Schiff, *Revivalist Fantasy*, 7.
25. Ibid., 12, 74–83, 104–27.
26. Christine Chism, *Alliterative Revivals* (Philadelphia, University of Pennsylvania Press, 2002).
27. Geraldine Heng, *Empire of Magic: Medieval Romance and the Politics of Cultural Fantasy* (New York: Columbia University Press, 2003); Ingham, *Sovereign Fantasies*.

"unthinkable" and "undiscussable" bodily transgression, cannibalism, which emerges prominently in my discussion of the *Siege of Jerusalem*.[28]

However, no critic to date has noted how extensively the alliterative romances are invested in the topic of Trojan history. This lacuna is easily ignored because—with the obvious exception of John Clerk's *Destruction*—these poems do not set their scenes in ancient Troy. Rather, they invoke Troy explicitly through direct reference and implicitly through subtle connotation or imperial genealogy. Sylvia Federico has helpfully surveyed the figure of Troy in the works of Chaucer and his contemporaries, but her investigations are largely limited to Lancastrian London.[29] In great contrast to most of their metropolitan counterparts, the alliterative romancers of my study decentralize, rather than embrace, this figure of Troy as the paradoxical eastern origin of western authority. In each romance, the destruction of Troy haunts justifications of aristocratic identity, martial violence, and sovereign power.

Because of the deeply cherished connections between heritage and nobility, the alliterative romancers' investment in the figure of Troy becomes a full-scale critique of the Trojan politics largely embraced by the cultural milieu of the south. They resist the fashion of their metropolitan contemporaries, such as Geoffrey Chaucer and John Gower, to envision London as a "New Troy" or the last stop of *translatio imperii*, the translation of empire from Troy to Rome to Britain. Unlike their renowned alliterative cousin, *Piers Plowman*, the alliterative romances are defined by their vernacular engagements with Latin chronicles of militaristic enterprises. They translate Latin history into alliterative long lines that are well suited for the rhythm, pace, and spectacular violence of battle. This alliterative sensibility is expressed both through their consistency of meter and self-conscious revelations about the historical function of such formulaic verse. Based on the modest conditions and limited numbers of the manuscripts, their ambivalence about aristocratic sovereignty was not well received by or beyond their readership. Even though the audience is clearly imagined as aristocratic, the surviving manuscripts suggest that the readers ranged from clerics to educated country gentlemen.[30] It is striking that while *Piers Plowman* is extant in fifty-four manuscripts, most all of the alliterative romances survive in single copies. In fact, these poems resist the popularizing thrust of English romance and instead express great dismay at the clerical disenfranchisement endorsed by Langland and his contemporaries. Their lack of affinity with *Piers Plowman*

28. Heng, *Empire of Magic*, 2.
29. Sylvia Federico, *New Troy: Fantasies of Empire in the Late Middle Ages*, Medieval Cultures 36 (Minneapolis: University of Minnesota Press, 2003).
30. Turville-Petre, *The Alliterative Revival*, 40–47.

is demonstrated by their distinctive "provincial" politics that belie any revivalist sensibilities or fantasies of empire. Rather, these poems vernacularize their Latinate sources to express their hesitations about revivals of Troy to a lay audience with aristocratic pretensions. Readers expecting to hear glorious tales of their imperial ancestors would have been disappointed by the pessimism of these alliterative romances.

The sole surviving manuscript that contains the *Destruction* is a helpful case in point. It only takes a glance at Glasgow University Library's Hunterian MS V.2.8 to notice that the modest paper codex was obviously at some remove from an armigerous patron.[31] Its archaic vocabulary and alliterating units were so foreign to the Victorian scholar G. A. Panton that the description he sent to F. J. Furnivall in 1865 announced that the manuscript contained "[a] stately poem called the *Destruction of Troy,* wrote by Joseph of Exceter, who lived in the reign of King Henry the Second, from 1154 to 1189. In Old English verse."[32] This early editor of the manuscript not only misidentified the text and verse form, but also assumed it to be a work composed in the twelfth century. Without a precedent or an analogue, this Trojan history expressed through what appeared to be archaic Anglo-Saxon verse left Panton, and subsequent readers, at a loss.

To complicate matters further, the text itself suffered a loss at the seventh folio, one that proves to be provocative. As the poet details the achievements and personalities of each Argonaut, the description of Hercules is cut short and the manuscript proceeds into a latter point of Guido's second book, Jason's arrival at Colchis. Book II would have fascinated English readers since it is here that Guido both presages the destruction of the first Troy and tracks the city's influence upon the establishment of Rome and the Trojan heritage of Britain. Guido's account, however, does not include a glorious prophecy about the prestige and authority of the Trojan line. Instead, Guido recalls the origin of the strife between the Greeks and Trojans to Laomedon's dismissal of Jason and Hercules from the shores of Troy and then digresses to discuss the future ramifications of this inhospitable action, saying, "Propter quas tante cladis diffusa lues orbem terrarum infecerit" [On account of these things, a far-reaching plague of great destruction infected the whole world]

---

31. Cf. Linne Mooney, "Two Fragments of Lydgate's *Troy Book* in the Bodleian Library," *Journal of the Early Book Society* 4 (2001): 259–66, at 261; Lesley Lawton, "The Illustration of Late Medieval Secular Texts, with Special Reference to Lydgate's *Troy Book*," in *Manuscripts and Readers in Fifteenth-Century England: The Literary Implications of Manuscript Study* (Cambridge: D. S. Brewer, 1983), 41–69, at 52–54.

32. G. A. Panton, "Preface," in *The Gest Hystoriale of the Destruction of Troy,* G. A. Panton and David Donaldson, eds., Early English Text Society 39, 56 (New York: Greenwood Press, 1869 and 1874), vii.

(11). For post-Black Death readers who claimed the Trojans as ancestors, this pessimism about the destiny for New Troys would have been received with great discomfort or even indignation. Was the section's content too disagreeable for the English patron to tolerate?

While that question cannot be definitively answered, it is clear that the scribe of Hunterian MS V.2.8 perceived the missing section as noteworthy. The first folio lists an index of chapters and their descriptions inscribed with letters that are mostly consistent in size. Book II, which is almost entirely absent in the manuscript, is listed as "The ij^d boke: how the grekes toke lond vpon troy. CAWSE of the first debate" (Figure 1). It is important to note that the word "CAWSE" is noticeably large and bolded in comparison to the words of the other chapter descriptions. In fact, no other word or phrase in the table of contents, with the exception of the title and prologue, match the size of "CAWSE." While the *Destruction* contains the section that describes the Greeks arrival at Troy, it does not include subsequent text that would have included a discussion of the "CAWSE." The importance of the *lacuna* is confirmed if we turn to the lines preceding this missing section, which conclude a discussion of the life of Hercules and begin the story of one of the greatest imperialists of all time, Alexander the Great:

> The mighty Massidon kyng maistur of all,
> The Emperour Alexander aunterit to come:
> He wan all the world & at his wille aght. (313–15)

> [The mighty Macedonian king, master of all, the Emperor Alexander ventured forth. He conquered the world and controlled it at his will.]

A reference to one who conquered the world is an appropriate, albeit hyperbolic, convocation to a discussion of empire and praise of Alexander's ancestors, but here is where the *lacuna* begins—these lines end the folio and the text restarts on the next page with an account of Jason and the Argonauts' arrival at Colchis. Since the transition is so rough and the book is intact at this point, editors Panton and Donaldson not only concluded that folios are missing from an earlier manuscript, but also include in their edition the part of Guido's text which presumably would have been there. In fact, its absence may be the best testament to its importance.

To fill this void, I offer this book in an attempt to read medieval romance "against the grain" and open up new avenues of inquiry about its aristocratic, historical, and provincial nature.[33] Since these alliterative romances express

33. My method is informed by Gayatri Spivak's essay, "Subaltern Studies: Deconstructing

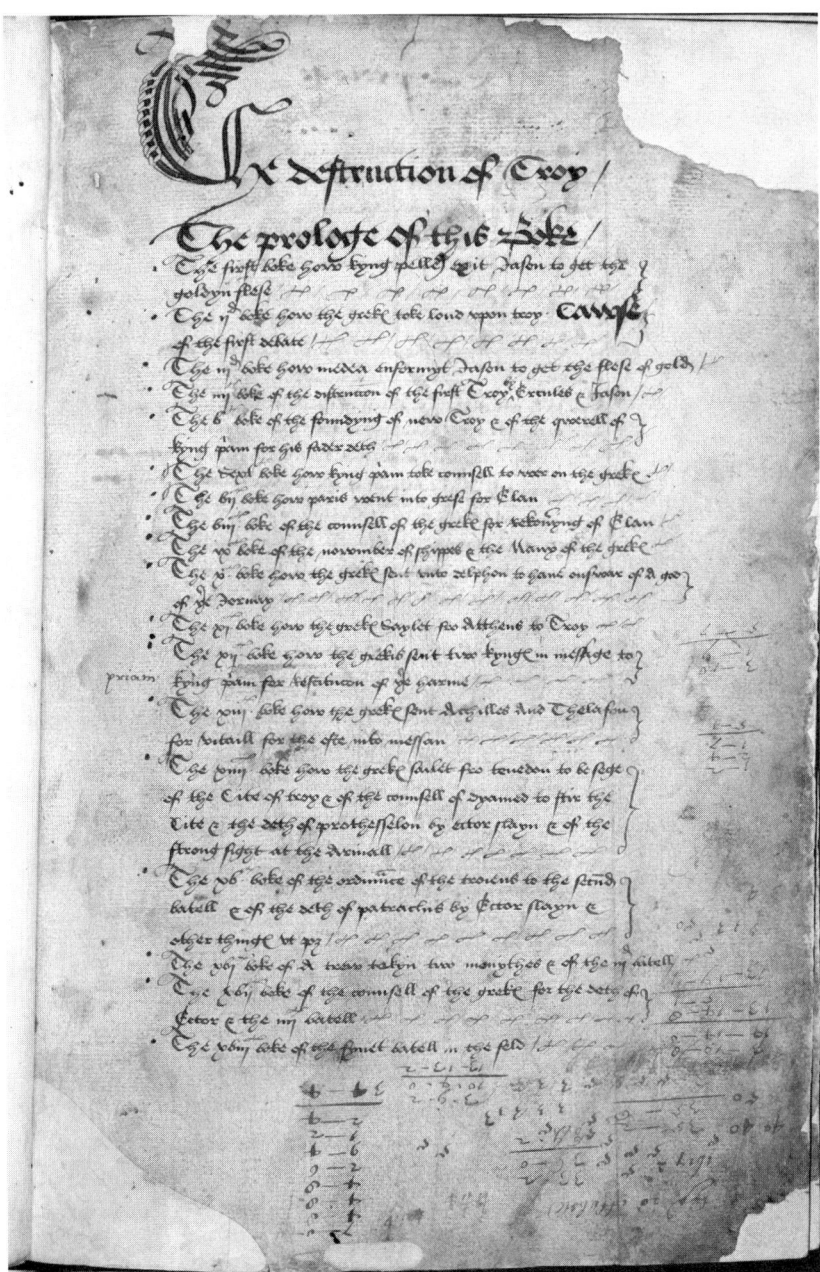

FIGURE 1. The table of contents, which emphasizes the "CAWSE" of the great debate. Hunterian MS V.2.8, f. 1a. Reproduced by permission of University of Glasgow Library, Special Collections

their regional Trojan politics through critiques of objects of chivalric value, my individual readings are structured around the following constituents of knightly identity: genealogy, war, violence, heraldry, and territory. And in keeping with the ancestral claims to nobility, the order of the chapters follows the itinerary of the *translatio imperii*, starting with Troy, continuing with Rome, and ending with Britain. I start with a survey of the historiographic landscape from which alliterative romance emerged, focusing on the genealogical concerns of two Latin books of Troy, the histories of Geoffrey of Monmouth and Guido delle Colonne. Moving into alliterative romance, I begin with the critiques of war that emerge in John Clerk's *Destruction of Troy*, continue with analyses of Roman violence in the *Siege of Jerusalem* and Arthurian heraldry in the alliterative *Morte Arthure*, and conclude with a reassessment of textual and geographic territories in *Sir Gawain and the Green Knight*. My readings of each poem are driven by the following questions: If medieval romances exemplify aristocratic ideals and justify royal bloodlines, why do these alliterative romancers characterize Britain's foundation as the product of treachery and destruction? What are the politics of alliterative invocations of Troy? And how do these writers indulge and subvert English fantasies of sovereignty through vernacular translations of classical history? As I have been suggesting, the answers to these questions supplement and interrogate current understandings of Trojan historiography in England, the genre of romance as cultural fantasy, the social function of literature, the relationship between metropolitan and provincial poetics, the unity of alliterative poetry, and the theory of the "alliterative revival."

I begin the first chapter, "Genealogy," by calling into question the pervasiveness of Galfridian historiography on English fantasies of empire through the analysis of the Guido-tradition that proves to be an attractive source for English romance. Scholars have attended to the alliterative *Destruction of Troy*, since it is a direct translation of Guido's *Historia*, but they have not fully accounted for the effect of the Guido-tradition on the other alliterative poems. These romances not only perpetuate a concern with the image of a destroyed Troy, but also contain anti-war themes and critiques of territorial expansion that they inherit from the *Historia*. Rather than expand upon the glorious genealogy from Priam to Aeneas to Brutus to Arthur, these poems treat Troy as a didactic and portable figure that represents the dire consequences of usurpations, sieges of cities, and the breaking of vows. Through these representations, Troy assumes characteristics of a body that experi-

---

Historiography," in *The Spivak Reader*, ed. Donna Landry and Gerald Maclean (New York: Routledge, 1996).

ences dismemberment, literally through diplomatic disagreement, sieges and looting, and metonymically through graphic descriptions of bodily mutilation inflicted upon the defenders and inhabitants of fallen cities. This metonymy is horrifically realized in the *Siege of Jerusalem,* in which the Roman extraction of gold from Jewish bodies prefaces the actual Roman looting of Jerusalem for its treasure. The beheadings of warriors, consumption of children, and disembowelment of besieged citizens represent or foretell the crumbling of towers, the enslavement of captives, and the liquidation of booty. Acts of treason drive and/or frame these narratives to serve as *exempla* that do not support aristocratic claims to sovereignty, but rather emphasize the eventual death and destruction of cities and bodies.

In chapters two through five, I track the influence of Guido's Trojan historiography on specific poems that comprise the genre of alliterative romance. I have selected John Clerk's *Destruction of Troy, The Siege of Jerusalem,* the alliterative *Morte Arthure,* and *Sir Gawain and the Green Knight* as representatives of this tradition because, in addition to their common formal, topical, and political sensibilities, they are indelibly marked by Guido's *Historia.* Chapter two, "War," focuses primarily on the alliterative translation of Guido's *Historia,* the late fourteenth-century *Destruction of Troy.* Its author, John Clerk of Whalley, negotiates between his roles as translator, historian, and alliterative poet to produce his account of the fall of Troy for English readers. According to Clerk, his translation of Guido's *Historia* provides vernacular access to historical truth that had not previously been available to his audience. By comparing Clerk's text with another translation of Guido's *Historia,* John Lydgate's *Troy Book,* I argue that Clerk's translational method, which he calls a "linking of letters," reflects his commitment to connecting a destructive past with an English present. The *Destruction* is an appropriate starting point, not only because of its status as a direct translation of Guido's *Historia,* but also because of its provenance in the Northwest Midlands, the residence of the *Gawain*-poet and the much contested origin of the Alliterative Revival. Furthermore, since the fall of Troy is the subject of the poem, the figure of Troy as both a city and body emerges with a historicity unparalleled in the rest of the alliterative corpus. If civil and corporeal fates are inextricable, as the *Destruction* suggests, then the exhumation and presentation of dead bodies revise history by establishing new narratives and genealogies of power. In all of the alliterative romances of this book, the dead wield authority that often leads to tragic consequences. The *Destruction* not only provides a graphic illustration of the revival of Hector's body, but also describes the construction of the New Troy in language that conjures up images of a ritual exhumation. These corporeal revivals are attempts to reassert lost power, but in the end, these undead bodies fail to regain authority and eventually inflict greater pain and death upon those they were supposed to protect. The embellishments of the destruction and resurrection of cities and bodies found in the *Destruction* reflect an enhanced pessimism about Britain's Trojan inheritance. Using Guido as its authority, the *Destruction* presents English readers with a narrative that in the very least is ambivalent about their Trojan identity, making readers privy to the war councils of their ancestor Priam, in which Homer's bloodthirsty Hector becomes a pacifistic diplomat who advises against war. By professing to tell the whole story from an accurate source, the *Destruction* asks readers to grapple with the complex and fractured nature of their Trojan ancestry and to ponder the value of an idealized New Troy in England.

The *Siege of Jerusalem* is the subject of chapter three, "Violence," not only because it may have been influenced by the *Destruction,* but also because it addresses the next stop for the *translatio imperii:* the Roman Empire. Critics have read the *Siege* as an unremarkable example of medieval antisemitism because of its perceived delight in the destruction of Jewish bodies. I want to suggest that these previous readings, while justified, have effaced the *Siege*-poet's critiques of war and imperialism. The *Siege*-poet modulates his antisemitic homily with a condemnation of the Roman Empire: the disciplined bodies are on display, creating a collective image that teaches its audience both the vengeance of God and the cruelty of Roman imperial siegecraft. Reinterpreting scenes in his sources that would normally incite virulent antisemitism in medieval Christians, such as Christ's passion, the flaying of Caiaphas, and the Jewish mother Maria's eating of her child, the *Siege*-poet transforms them into moments that exhibit the pitiable fate of the Jews and evince his disgust for the cruelty of the Roman conquerors. As the humanity of the besieged Jews grows, the newly baptized Romans, Vespasian and Titus, increasingly embody the surfeit of their pagan predecessor Nero by expressing exorbitant enthusiasm about their imperial stature and exacting excessive punishment of their enemies. Vespasian and Titus confront moral and corporeal dilemmas that efface their Christian identities, enhance their desire for power, and reflect their moral inferiority to Jews like Josephus. The result is an unexpected redirection in the poem's object of critique from the bodies of Christ-killing Jews to those of the bullion-hungry Romans. Through an analysis of these scenes of corporeal violence and their relationship to the historiography of the Northwest Midlands, I demonstrate that these illustrations of bodily dismemberment elicit sympathy for the Jewish victims and highlight the cruelty of the Roman conquerors.

Continuing to follow the itinerary of *translatio imperii,* chapter four, "Heraldry," addresses the alliterative *Morte Arthure,* a poem that not only establishes King Arthur as the inheritor of the Roman Empire, but also uses the *Siege* for one of its source texts. Whereas the *Destruction* exhibits ambivalence about Trojan historiography through its faithful adherence to Guido's text and the *Siege* questions Roman imperialism through illustrations of horrific scenes of violence, the *Morte* draws from an extensive catalogue of English, Latin, and French works to present a highly subtle and conflicted portrait of King Arthur. Capitalizing on the powerful ability of the alliterative line to illustrate the frenetic pace of battle, the *Morte*-poet continually draws on the Guido-tradition as a basis for his contention that the sacrifice of the innocent is inextricable from empire building. In the process, the *Morte*-poet engages in what I call "heraldic historiography" by attaching multiple meanings to recurring chivalric signs and symbols, made particularly manifest in the enigmatic sign of the dragon. Rather than bolstering hereditary claims to nobility, these heraldic devices attenuate martial fervor, obscure sovereign identities, emphasize the collateral damage of war, and reveal the danger of territorial expansion. By juxtaposing signs of empire with graphic scenes of evisceration and cannibalism, the relationship between heraldic assertions of royal authority and the extermination of innocent life becomes inseparable.

Chapter five, "Territory," is an examination of the most well-known alliterative romance, *Sir Gawain and the Green Knight,* and specifically its Trojan "frame," which rehearses a Trojan past that appears to bear no relevance to the present action of the Arthurian romance. The abrupt transition in genre from ancient history to playful romance highlights the disconnectedness of the aristocracy and their propaganda from the realities of empire formation. As a misappropriated symbol of glory, Gawain's girdle becomes a heraldic marker of the chivalric amnesia that obscures the images of a burning Troy, treasonous Aeneas, and the subjugation of provinces that surround the text. I want to suggest that this separation between Arthurian heraldry and infidelity is representative of the *Gawain*-poet's satiric use of historiographic and geographic borderlands as peripheral spaces that critique the central subjects of chivalry and "trawþe" in the romance. I focus on two such "margins." The first is the Trojan "frame," the first and last stanzas of the poem that operate as a textual border and historiographic lens through which we view the central action. The second is the topography of the Northwest Midlands and adjacent Welsh March, which serves as the "uncivilized" ground that Gawain treads in his journey to Hautdesert. Through an analysis of the historiography of the *Gawain*-poet's provenance in the Northwest Midlands and the intersections of Trojan and Anglo-Welsh geographies, I argue that the recitation of ancestry in the opening and closing stanzas highlights Britain's territorial violence, critiques the frivolity of the royal aristocracy, and displays a late-fourteenth-century provincial distrust of assertions of England's Trojan identity.

The conclusion synthesizes my examinations of alliterative poetry to identify these alliterative perspectives on war and interrogate the utility of the historical theory of the *translatio imperii et studii*. This "transferral of empire and learning" has been used to describe the pervasive medieval perception of the progression of history and knowledge that, for England, is based in the transfer of textual authority from the clergy to the lay aristocracy. I suggest that *translatio imperii* is fundamentally optimistic and providential in its design, which is in direct contrast to the remarkably pessimistic and retrospective conception of empire in these alliterative poems. If these poets were clerics who worked at the behest of aristocratic patrons, as the evidence suggests, these alliterative romanciers contributed in projects to which they were trenchantly opposed. Since these alliterative romanciers are not identifiable, I turn to the example of John Trevisa, whose translation projects and alliterative prose provide instructive analogues for the relationship between clerks and their employers and reaffirm the skepticism of these alliterative poets. Through a comparative reading of the Trojan text that held the greatest currency in the fourteenth and fifteenth centuries, Geoffrey Chaucer's *Troilus and Criseyde,* I more precisely identify the unique nature of these alliterative romances and their perspectives on the English aristocracy and England's imperial potential. For these poets, the larger consequence of the *translatio imperii et studii* is the disenfranchisement of the clergy and the destruction of innocent life.

ONE

Genealogy
TROJAN HISTORIOGRAPHY IN ENGLAND

THE HISTORIOGRAPHIC wilderness from which alliterative romance emerges resembles the forests and marches that Gawain traverses on his way to the Green Chapel. From Virgil to Augustine to Orosius, the landscape of *auctores* is familiar and unseemly, pleasing and harrowing, civilized and monstrous. Behind every tree and rock is Geoffrey of Monmouth, whose genealogical model of the *translatio imperii* is traceable in a vast number of consequent historical and literary works, including alliterative romance. His historiographic influence has gained so much recognition that Geraldine Heng has even claimed that "[b]y giving Britain a regnal genealogy extending back to the glories of ancient Troy through Brutus . . . Geoffrey's *Historia* [regum Britanniae] . . . supplies a foundational mythology irresistible to insular monarchs and virtually ensures that the *Historia*, issuing the foundational myth of Britain, will furnish the conditional matrix for imagining England as well."[1] While much of the English imaginary has a Galfridian heritage, many historiographers did not adhere to providential historiography or indulge fantasies of empire.

This chapter offers a challenge to the pervasiveness of the Galfridian historiography through the analysis of another popular historical tradition, that of Guido delle Colonne's *Historia destructionis Troiae*. Scholars of medieval romance have acknowledged the influence of Latinate historiographies, such

1. Heng, *Empire of Magic*, 66.

as the biblical Augustinian-Orosian paradigm that locates an origin in the Fall and undermines the optimistic logic of the *translatio imperii*. The critical attraction to Geoffrey's text, however, has created a body of scholarship that ultimately treats Galfridian history as the singular origin of late medieval Trojan genealogy and English romance. Even the title of Helen Cooper's definitive study of the romance genre in England, *The English Romance in Time: Transforming Motifs from Geoffrey of Monmouth to the Death of Shakespeare*, privileges a Galfridian origin, despite the minimal treatment of Geoffrey's *Historia* in the book itself.[2] This easily appropriated *Ur*-text, while attractive in its flexibility, does not fully account for the complexities of medieval romance and Trojan historiography after the twelfth century.[3]

THE BOOK OF TROY

Over the past few decades, medieval romance has become a fruitful site for the identification of nascent perspectives of English nationhood.[4] Central to this ongoing project has been Geoffrey's twelfth-century *Historia* because

---

2. Helen Cooper, *The English Romance in Time: Transforming Motifs from Geoffrey of Monmouth to the Death of Shakespeare* (Oxford: Oxford University Press, 2004). The bulk of her assessment of Geoffrey's "motifs" appears only on two pages, 23–24.

3. I must clarify a vital distinction here between the simplicity of the *Historia*'s imperial genealogical model and the complexity of Geoffrey's political purposes. While his specific political persuasions are difficult to identify, it is clear that his agenda is one that places Britain within the Roman line of imperial power. Except for those scholars who think that Geoffrey was not writing history at all—see J. E. Lloyd, *A History of Wales* 2 (London: Longmans, Green & Company, 1912), 528; Christopher Brooke, "Geoffrey of Monmouth as a Historian," *Church and Government in the Middle Ages*, ed. C. Brooke et al. (Cambridge: Cambridge University Press, 1976), 77–91; John Clark, "Trinovantum—the Evolution of a Legend," *Journal of Medieval History* 7 (1981): 135–51, at 143—most agree that the *Historia* is a legitimizing narrative of some kind. For a reading of its exaltation of non-monastic lifestyles, see Valerie I. J. Flint, "The *Historia Regum Britanniae* of Geoffrey of Monmouth: Parody and Its Purpose. A Suggestion," *Speculum* 54 (1979): 447–68. For its concern with the Anglo-Norman elite, see G. H. Gerould, "King Arthur and Politics," *Speculum* 2 (1927): 33–51, at 38; T. D. Kendrick, *British Antiquity* (London: Methuen, 1950), 9. For its attention to "cultural respectability" of the Welsh, see G. W. S. Barrow, "Wales and Scotland in the Middle Ages," *Welsh Historical Review* 10 (1980–1): 305; John Gillingham, *The English in the Twelfth Century: Imperialism, National Identity, and Political Values* (Woodbridge, U.K.: The Boydell Press, 2000), 19–39; Brynley F. Roberts, "Geoffrey of Monmouth and the Welsh Historical Tradition," *Nottingham Medieval Studies* 20 (1976): 29–40, at 40; Stephen Knight, *Arthurian Literature and Society* (New York: St. Martin's Press, 1983), 64–66.

4. The seminal article is Lee Patterson's "The Historiography of Romance and the Alliterative *Morte Arthure*," *Journal of Medieval and Renaissance Studies* 13.1 (1983): 1–32; reprinted as "The Romance of History and the Alliterative *Morte Arthure*," in *Negotiating the Past: The Historical Understanding of Medieval Literature* (Madison: University of Wisconsin Press, 1987), 197–230.

it blurs generic boundaries of romance and history, establishes a genealogy that connects the destruction of Troy with the birth of Rome and Britain, and justifies the sovereignty of the English aristocracy. Through the secular use of the *translatio imperii,* a prophetic model that promises future imperial glory for Britain, Geoffrey's text joins the *romans d'antiquité* in their exemplification of twelfth-century Norman-Angevin political ideology, which justified its nobility by claiming Roman and Trojan ancestry.[5] This Angevin propaganda is based on an optimistic rendering of *translatio,* a theory of the transfer of world power that originates in ancient Greek historiography and early biblical exegesis, in which the fall of Babylon leads to the birth and eventual destruction of future empires such as Persia and Macedonia.[6] Early Jews and Christians interpreted the dream visions in *Daniel* II and VII as the succession of world-empires that would end with the greatest of them all, that is, Rome.[7] By the ninth century, *translatio* began to be conceived as political concept in papal historiography that authorized the Pope's transfer of the Roman Empire to the German Holy Roman Empire. The *translatio* of Western Christendom reached its climax in the thirteenth century, when Innocent III endowed Charlemagne with Roman *imperium,* an action that asserted the papacy's pivotal role in such translations of power.[8] Geoffrey,

---

5. The *romans d'antiquité* are the Old French *Roman de Thèbes, Roman d'Enéas,* and *Roman de Troie.* See Paul M. Clogan, "New Directions in Twelfth-Century Courtly Narrative: *Le Roman de Thèbes," Mediaevistik* 3 (1990): 55–70, at 56–57; Robert Folz, *The Concept of Empire in Western Europe,* trans. S. A. Ogilvie (London: Edward Arnold, 1969). For the *translatio imperii,* see Werner Goez, *Translatio Imperii: Ein Beitrag xtlr Gedichte des Geschichtsdenkens und der politischen Theorien im Mittelalter und in der frühen Neuzeit* (Tübingen, 1958); Charles T. Davis, *Dante and the Idea of Rome* (Oxford: Clarendon Press, 1957); C. Stephen Jaeger, *The Origins of Courtliness* (Philadelphia: University of Pennsylvania Press, 1985), 263–64; H. Grundmann, "Sacerdotium, Regnum, Studium," *Archiv für Kulturgeschichte* 34 (1952): 5–21; H. Van den Baar, "Translatio Imperii Romani," *Analecta Gregoriana* 78 (1956): 45–47; Giovanna Angeli, *L'Eneas e I primi romanzi volgari* (Milan: Riccardo Ricciardi, 1971); Renate Blumenfeld-Kosinski, "Old French Narrative Genres: Towards the Definition of the *Roman Antique," Romance Philology* 34 (1980): 143–59, at 157–58.

6. Daniel Mendels, "The Five Empires: A Note on a Propagandistic Topos," *American Journal of Philology* 102 (1981): 330–37. Cf. J. W. Swain, "The Theory of the Four Monarchies Opposition History Under the Roman Empire," *Classical Philology* 35 (1940): 1–21; S. K. Eddy, *The King is Dead* (Lincoln: University of Nebraska Press, 1961), 16–35; D. Flusser, "The Four Empires in the Fourth Sibyl and in the Book of Daniel," *Israel Oriental Studies* 2 (1972): 148–75; L. G. Hartman, and A. A. di Lella, *The Book of Daniel* (New York, 1978), 31–33; H. Fuchs, "Zur Verherrlichung Roms und der Römer in dem Gedichte des Rutilius Namatianus," *Basler Zeitschrift für Geschichte und Altertumskunde* 42 (1943): 49–51; W. Baumgartner, "Zu den vier Reichen von Dan 2," *Theologische Zeitschrift* 1 (1945): 17–22; D. Winston, "The Iranian Component in the Bible, Apocrypha and Qumran," *History of Religions* 5 (1966): 189–92.

7. S. de Boer, "Rome, the 'Translatio Imperii' and the Early-Christian Interpretation of Daniel II and VII," *Rivista di storia e letteratura religiosa* 21 (1985): 181–218, at 182–83.

8. See Goez, *Translatio Imperii,* 137–88.

however, circumvents these ecclesiastical claims in his *Historia* and locates the origin of *translatio* in the destruction of Troy, whose fall spawns both the birth of Rome and Britain. This secularization of the theory has fascinated scholars because it is discernible in a vast number of historical and literary works, including romance. Critical perspectives on the *Historia*'s legitimizing influence as providing a matrix for English romance have been useful in characterizing late medieval conceptions of historical and royal authority, but their singularity has obscured other historiographies that critique such optimistic and linear models.

This emphasis on the "happy ending," which many romance plots provide, is by no means a feature that defines the genre. As Cooper notes, "The bulk of most romances . . . is devoted to the undergoing of hardship, and a surprising number . . . finally opt for a bleak fate over benevolent Providence."[9] Contributing to that "number" are the alliterative romances of this book. And while some of their critiques of providence may be traced to Geoffrey's *Historia*, I want to suggest that their emphasis on the "bleak fate" of New Trojans originates in another "Troy Book," Guido's *Historia*. Guido interrogates imperial translation by condemning the martial policy that causes the destruction of Troy and its Roman and British progeny. In Guido's *Historia*, Troy survives as a dismembered and tainted origin of Western civilization. Since Guido's *Historia* was so popular, proven both through its manuscript circulation (at least 150 manuscripts survive) and its status as a source that was translated into English three separate times in the space of fifty years, it deserves scholarly attention to account for its effect on the English imagination in the fourteenth and fifteenth centuries.[10]

Before proceeding further into a discussion of the nature and influence of the Guido-tradition, however, it is important to understand how Geoffrey's *Historia* emerged as the authority for Trojan historiography. The *Historia*'s popularity among medieval readers after the twelfth century is attested not only by its manuscript circulation, but also by the wide variety of vernacular texts such as Wace's *Roman de Brut*, and Laʒamon's *Brut* that used it as a source for their histories of Britain. Geoffrey articulates a common twelfth-century reception of Virgilian history, which traces the providential transfer of power from Troy to Rome to London, and sets the precedent for future British writers and rulers to lay claim to Trojan and Roman origins

---

9. Cooper, *The English Romance in Time*, 362.
10. See Sylvia Federico, *New Troy: Fantasies of Empire in the Late Middle Ages*, Medieval Cultures 36 (Minneapolis, University of Minnesota Press, 2003); C. David Benson, *The History of Troy in Middle English Literature: Guido delle Colonne's Historia destructionis Troiae in Medieval England* (Woodbridge, Suff.: D. S. Brewer, 1980).

in order to legitimize their ideologies and imperial designs.[11] The *Historia* engages in a reading and elaboration of Virgil's *Aeneid* that expresses enthusiasm for *imperium sine fine* that valorizes the Julian line and neglects the poem's melancholic critiques of Augustan Rome.[12] Understood this way, Virgil becomes an imperial patsy, merely controlling the action at his emperor's behest.[13] This uncomplicated interpretation of Virgilian politics prefers the potency of imperial prophecy to the extent that the dire fates of Pallas and Turnus are effaced and the legitimation of future empires is essentially left unquestioned. Likewise, Virgil's dramatizations of the threat that the Homeric Helen and her surrogates—Dido, Amata, Camilla, Juturna, and Lavinia—pose to the creation of empire are effectively ignored and ironically sacrificed for a singular focus on the genealogical power that inheres to Aeneas' founding of Rome.[14] Virgil's sympathetic portrayal of Dido—which has caused many to question an Augustan reading of the *Aeneid*—is left unacknowledged by Geoffrey and many twelfth-century readers.[15]

The twelfth-century *Roman d'Eneas* is a compelling example of this type of Virgilian reception: it effectively negates Eneas' culpability in the fall of Troy through a digression on the Judgment of Paris that blames the anger of Pallas and Juno as the sole cause for Trojan destruction. By suppressing Eneas' past and focusing on moral evaluations, the *Eneas*-poet reads the Roman imperial past as an Angevin present.[16] Geoffrey in the *Historia*

11. See Francis Ingledew, "The Book of Troy and the Genealogical Construction of History: The Case of Geoffrey of Monmouth's *Historia regum Britanniae*," *Speculum* 69.3 (1994): 665–704, at 669; for a discussion of the 217 extant manuscripts of Geoffrey's *Historia* see Julia C. Crick, *The 'Historia regum Britannie' of Geoffrey of Monmouth, 3: A Summary Catalogue of the Manuscripts* (Cambridge, Eng.: Brewer, 1989).

12. For darker reading of *Roma aeterna* in the *Aeneid*, see W. R. Johnson, *Darkness Visible: A Study of Vergil's Aeneid* (Berkeley: University of California Press, 1976), 1–22.

13. Michael Putnam, *Virgil's Aeneid: Interpretation and Influence* (Chapel Hill: University of North Carolina Press, 1995), 14.

14. Mihoko Suzuki, *Metamorphoses of Helen: Authority, Difference, and the Epic* (Ithaca: Cornell University Press, 1989), 92–149.

15. For a full analysis of the figure of Dido in the Middle Ages, see Marilynn Desmond, *Reading Dido: Gender, Textuality, and the Medieval Aeneid,* Medieval Cultures 8 (Minneapolis: University of Minnesota Press, 1994). For a discussion of Dido's reception from Ovid to Spenser, see John Watkins, *The Specter of Dido: Spenser and Virgilian Epic* (New Haven and London: Yale University Press, 1995); for a discussion that continues through John Dryden and John Long, see Richard F. Thomas, "Dido and Her Translators," in *Virgil and the Augustan Reception* (Cambridge: Cambridge University Press, 2001), 154–89.

16. Christopher Baswell, *Virgil in Medieval England: Figuring the Aeneid from the Twelfth Century to Chaucer* (Cambridge: Cambridge University Press, 1995), 200–20; Desmond, *Reading Dido*, 105–19; Lee Patterson, "Virgil and the Historical Consciousness of the Twelfth Century: The *Roman d'Eneas* and *Erec et Enide*," *Negotiating the Past,* 170–83. For a more detailed discussion, see Raymond Cormier, *One Heart One Mind: The Rebirth of Virgil's Hero in Medieval French Romance* (University, MS: Romance Monographs, 1973).

articulates this same authority of the Trojan genealogy for Britain through the prophecy of the Roman goddess Diana, who early in the text informs the legendary founder of Britain, Brutus, that he shall discover an island which

> fiet natis altera Troia tuis.
> Hic de prole tua reges nascentur, et ipsis
> Totius terre subditus orbis erit. (9)[17]

[shall be another Troy of your birth; here shall kings be born from your progeny, and through it the entire world shall be subdued.]

This vision of future subjugation of the world establishes Troy as an origin for empire and establishes worldly power that proved attractive to medieval monarchs and scholars ever since. Henry II in particular used Galfridian history as a means to bolster his own sovereignty and most likely sponsored Wace's translation of Geoffrey's *Historia*.[18] The court of Henry II also had a role in the production of Joseph of Exeter's *Ylias*, a Trojan epic based upon the legendary eyewitness accounts of Dares and Dictys, augmenting the text in the favor of the Angevins in England.[19] Such a courtly fashioning of this text may have been inspired by the ambivalence Joseph displays toward the Trojans.[20] By the thirteenth century, this type of historiography based on lineage inspired the composition and circulation of the *Histoire ancienne jusqu'à César*, a compilation of classical histories that begins with the Fall and continues throughout the ancient Greek, Trojan, and Roman civilizations.[21] Later in medieval England, Trojan historiography still enthralled royalty and nobility; for example, Edward II's Queen Isabelle possessed a manuscript titled *De bello troiano* and the youngest son of Humphrey of Bohun, Earl of

---

17. *The Historia Regum Britannie of Geoffrey of Monmouth, I: Bern, Burgerbibliothek, MS. 568*, ed. Neil Wright (Cambridge: D. S. Brewer, 1991). All citations from Geoffrey's *Historia* refer to this edition.

18. Patterson, *Negotiating the Past*, 199–210; Walter F. Schirmer and Ulrich Broich, *Studien zum literarischen Patronat in England des 12. Jahrhunderts* (Cologne: Westdeutscher Verlag, 1962), 27–203; Diana B. Tyson, "Patronage of French Vernacular History Writers in the Twelfth and Thirteenth Centuries," *Romania* 100 (1979): 180–222, 584; Reto R. Bezzola, *Les Origines et la formation de la littérature courtoise en Occident, 500–1200*, vol. 3, pt. 1 (Paris: Champion, 1963).

19. See A. K. Bate's editorial introduction to Joseph of Exeter, *Trojan War* (Wiltshire, England: Aris & Phillips, 1986), 21; Bezzola, *Les Origines de la littérature courtoise*, 2.327–34.

20. As A. G. Rigg notes, "In an age that was usually pro-Trojan, the *Ylias* is unusually neutral." *A History of Anglo-Latin Literature, 1066–1422* (Cambridge: Cambridge University Press, 1992), 102.

21. For a discussion of the *Histoire*, particularly within the context of a visual program obsessed with the death of Dido, see Desmond, *Reading Dido*, 119–27.

Hereford, was named Eneas.²² Claims for the linguistic importance of Troy were also made in 1394 when a writer in the court of the Duke of Brittany composed the *Chronicon Briocense,* which asserts that the British language was a diluted remnant of the ancient Trojan tongue.²³ There is no question that the glorious *Trinovantum* of Geoffrey's history captured the imaginations of monarchs and writers who sought to legitimize British imperial designs.

Nevertheless, Geoffrey's account has not been without its detractors. Medieval historians such as William of Malmesbury, Gerald of Wales, and William of Newburgh rejected its status as "history" based upon the assumption that Geoffrey's claim that his account originates in a Welsh *vetustissimus liber* was fraudulent.²⁴ Modern scholars have resurrected the *Historia* through the study of its manuscript circulation, its influence, and its participation in what scholars have labeled "imperial fantasies."²⁵ From this perspective, Geoffrey's *Historia* is irresistible in its tractability and portability—it seamlessly intertwines fantasy and history in a way that future readers, both medieval and modern, can consider the text both as an origin for romance and an account of serious historical significance. One word in particular, "fantasy," has become sovereign in a vocabulary widely employed in psychoanalytic readings of romance. Through the use of Lacan's theory of culture that connects the establishment of historical truth with pleasure, scholars such as Ingham and Heng trace the way the *Historia* indulges fictional genealogies that legitimize Britain's place within imperial world history.²⁶ Such scholarship has been insightful in establishing the *Historia*'s importance as a histori-

---

22. Juliet Vale, *Edward III and Chivalry: Chivalric Society and Its Context, 1270–1350* (Woodbridge: Boydell Press, 1982), 50; John Barnie, *War in Medieval English Society; Social Values and the Hundred Years War* (London: Weidenfeld and Nicolson, 1974), 101.

23. Michael Jones, "'Mon Pais et Mon Nation': Breton Identity in the Fourteenth Century," in *War, Literature, and Politics in the Late Middle Ages,* ed. C. T. Allmand (Liverpool: Liverpool University Press, 1976), 144–45.

24. Patricia Clare Ingham, *Sovereign Fantasies: Arthurian Romance and the Making of Britain* (Philadelphia: University of Pennsylvania Press, 2001), 21–32.

25. For more on Geoffrey's influence and the dissemination of his work, see Robert W. Hanning, *The Vision of History in Early Britain* (New York: Columbia University Press, 1966); Ingledew, "The Book of Troy and the Genealogical Construction of History"; Crick, *The 'Historia regum Britannie' of Geoffrey of Monmouth,* 3; for a treatment of the *Historia* as an "imperial fantasy" see Heng, *Empire of Magic,* 2. She characterizes the *Historia* as a text in which "historical phenomena and fantasy collide and vanish, each into the other, without explanation or apology, at the precise locations where both can be readily mined to best advantage—a prime characteristic of romance that persists henceforth."

26. Ingham, *Sovereign Fantasies,* 24–40. Heng does not work directly from Lacan, but uses this Lacanian conception of "fantasy" to identify the way Geoffrey's history works as a means of "cultural rescue" (18) in the horrific aftermath of the First Crusade. See *Empire of Magic,* 1–35.

cal text, explaining the imperial imagination of late medieval Britain, and making powerful generic connections between romance and history.

THE OTHER BOOK OF TROY

While psychoanalytic readings of historiography cross previously restricted boundaries of "history" and expand modern understandings of medieval historicity, they have often overlooked the significance of other non-providential histories. The elevation of the Galfridian tradition resulted in scholarship that posited Geoffrey's text not only as the origin of romance, but also as "*The* Book of Troy."[27] This reduction is convenient and often useful, but there are many romances and Trojan texts in the succeeding centuries that do not adhere to Geoffrey's version of the Troy story. I would suggest that the other, and arguably more important, book of Troy is Guido's *Historia*, which survives in approximately 150 manuscripts from the late thirteenth century and in three vernacular translations in the fourteenth and fifteenth centuries.[28] Even though it lacks modern scholarly attention, a thirteenth- or fourteenth-century English reader would have considered Guido's *Historia* to be the canonical work of Trojan history.

Guido's significance within the English historiographic landscape cannot be overstated. His vision of calamity for the inheritors of Troy, however, is markedly inconsistent with Diana's prophecy in Geoffrey's *Historia* and the "fantasy of the imperial origins of British monarchs."[29] The absence of a justification for empire in Guido's *Historia* must give us pause since this alternative history of the fall of Troy was widely embraced by many fourteenth-century English poets, including Geoffrey Chaucer. Before analyzing the Guido-tradition further, we should first establish Guido's place beside Geoffrey as a "British" historical authority. Since their titles and the works themselves deal with separate aspects of the Trojan heritage of Britain, we may wonder whether they should be juxtaposed at all. Whereas Guido exclusively treats the fall of Troy, Geoffrey follows Britain's Trojan heritage from Brutus' flight from Italy to the succession of British monarchs even after Arthur's death. However, Geoffrey continues a Virgilian history that is inextricably linked with a Trojan origin. Even Chaucer in *The House of Fame* jux-

27. Ingledew, "The Book of Troy and the Genealogical Construction of History."
28. C. David Benson, "'The Matter of Troy' and its Transmission through Translation in Medieval Europe," in *Übersetzung: Ein internationales Handbuch zur Übersetzungsforschung*, vol. 2, eds. Harald Kittel, Juliane House, Brigitte Schultze (Berlin and New York: Walter de Gruyter, 2007), 1337–40, at 1339.
29. Heng, *Empire of Magic*, 197.

taposes Guido and Geoffrey as authorities on the history of Troy. After listing the classical poets and historians, Homer, Dares, Dictys, and the enigmatic Lollius, he cites:

> Guydo eke de Columpnis,
> And Englyssh Gaufride eke, ywis;
> And ech of these, as have I joye,
> Was besy for to bere up Troye. (1469–72).[30]

It would appear at first that the index of *auctoritas* is hierarchical, since Chaucer proceeds from Homer to Dares and Dictys, but he interestingly transposes Guido and Geoffrey (*Gaufride*), placing Guido before Geoffrey. Even if the order of authority is not purposeful, Guido and Geoffrey are clearly juxtaposed as historians who translate or "bere up Troye." After all, the Latin meaning of *translatio* is "a bearing across," which is remarkably similar to Chaucer's characterization. In effect, Chaucer perceives both Geoffrey and Guido as Trojan translators, which reflects the inextricable nature of their relationship and establishes the likelihood that late fourteenth-century readers would have thought of Geoffrey when they thought of Guido (and vice versa) in the context of English and Trojan historiography and translation.

To understand the distinctions between the historical traditions of Geoffrey and Guido, we ought to attend to the scholarship that revived Geoffrey's claims to history. Frances Ingledew in his seminal article, "The Book of Troy and the Genealogical Construction of History: The Case of Geoffrey of Monmouth's *Historia regum Britanniae*," follows the work of Robert Hanning in arguing that Geoffrey's *Historia* represents a novel understanding of insular history in the later Middle Ages, which accepted the *translatio imperii* as the appropriate progression of power from civilization to civilization. It was, as Ingledew describes, a "return to Virgil" that was "at odds with the biblically oriented Augustinian-Orosian paradigm, which instead of claiming birth in Troy, confessed birth in the Fall."[31] By making this claim, Ingledew establishes Troy as the widely accepted historical origin of Britain after the twelfth century and consequently reads Troy as it appears in Galfridian contexts. Ingledew concedes that the British "Book of Troy is irreducible . . . to any single work," but contends that Geoffrey's *Historia* is "exemplary" because of its assumption of genealogical history and its remarkable dissemination

---

30. *The Riverside Chaucer*, ed. Larry D. Benson, 3rd ed. (Boston: Houghton Mifflin Company, 1987), 365. All citations from Chaucerian works refer to this edition.
31. Ingledew, "The Book of Troy and the Genealogical Construction of History," 666; Hanning, *The Vision of History in Early Britain*.

across Britain and the Continent.[32] By making this claim, Ingledew concretizes the same kind of qualified establishment of historiographic origin that Heng does with English romance.

In response, James Simpson contends that Ingledew errs, despite his qualification, in attributing the moniker "The Book of Troy" to Geoffrey's text, since Guido's *Historia* was also widely popular and known throughout Britain as the standard account of the fall of Troy. Simpson proceeds to track the influence of the Guido-tradition upon fourteenth- and fifteenth-century militaristic narratives, such as John Clerk's *Destruction of Troy*, John Lydgate's *Destruction of Thebes*, the alliterative *Morte Arthure*, Malory's *Works*, and *The Wars of Alexander*, that convey tragic messages about conquest, which differ markedly from the fantasies of their sixteenth-century successors.[33] While Simpson's correction is warranted and his attention to the Guido-tradition within the genre of tragedy identifies the vast differences between their histories, I want to suggest that Guido's *Historia* should also be considered a text of the Galfridian tradition. Simpson claims that Guido's *Historia* is "anti-Galfridian because it makes no serious play with the genealogical potential of the Troy narrative," which is certainly true in the large sense—Guido spares little space to describe the fate of the Trojan progeny and does not laud imperial progression—but Guido still addresses Trojan historiography in a distinctly Galfridian manner that confounds an impulse to posit Geoffrey as a straw man for Guido. Early in the *Historia*, Guido expresses an admiration of Alexander's imperialism as an introduction to the origin of the fall of the first Troy, which he locates in the story of Jason and the Argonauts and their voyage to search for the Golden Fleece. On their way to Colchis, where the Fleece resides, the Argonauts stop on the shores of Troy, which inspires Guido to meditate upon the implications of their arrival at this doomed city. He begins with his poignant reference to the "plague of great destruction," but then proceeds to the possible positive consequences of Troy's fall. He explains:

> vt ipsa Troya deleta insurexerit, causa per quam Romana vrbs, que caput est vrbium, per Troyanos exules facta extitit uel promota, per Heneam scilicet et Ascanium natum eius, dictum Iulium. Et nonnulle alie propterea prouincie perpetuum ex Troyanis receperunt incolatum. Qualis est Anglia, que a Bruto Troyano, vnde Britania dicta est, legitur habitata.

32. Ingledew, "The Book of Troy and the Genealogical Construction of History," 669.
33. See in particular Simpson's chapter, "The Tragic," in *The Oxford English Literary History, Volume 2: Reform and Cultural Revolution* (Oxford: Oxford University Press, 2002), 68–120, at 76.

[Though Troy itself was completely destroyed, it rose again, through which cause the city of Rome, which is the chief of cities, emerged, being built and enlarged by the Trojan exiles, by Aeneas, that is, and Ascanius his son, called Julius. And therefore some other provinces received from the Trojans a lasting settlement. Such is England, which we read was settled by the Trojan, Brutus, from whence it is called Britain.] (11)[34]

This passage operates in two ways that confound stark distinctions between Geoffrey's and Guido's histories. First, it relates the *translatio imperii,* in which the fall of one empire leads to the settlement of the next that we read not only in Virgil's *Aeneid* and Geoffrey's *Historia* but also in Otto of Friesing's *The Two Cities,* which may have been one of Guido's sources. Second, the comment, "[s]uch is England, which we read was settled by the Trojan, Brutus," indicates that Guido had read Geoffrey's *Historia,* since no other writer, including Otto, relates this unique story of the origin of Britain.[35] Guido was familiar with Geoffrey's popular theory of history and consistent with the Galfridian tradition.

If Guido would have ended his discussion of the *translatio imperii* here, he may have remained among the many inheritors and promoters of Geoffrey's prophetic emphasis on the recovery and redemption of failed empires. However, he continues his meditation upon the significance of the Argonaut's incursion and questions providence with a pessimistic thought: "Sed si tante proditionis causa fuerit subsequentis boni causa finalis humana mens habet in dubio" [But the human mind holds in doubt whether the cause of such a great betrayal was finally the cause of subsequent good] (12). This passage surpasses all others in its expression of Guido's ambivalence toward the foundation of New Troys. Guido refrains from outright condemnation of the *translatio imperii* by using the phrase "holds in doubt," but the word, "betrayal" (*proditio*) looms large and ultimately darkens the overall sense of the passage. At this point, it is unclear to which "betrayal" Guido is referring, but he hereby establishes, both in the destruction of the first Troy and in the rest of his history, that treason will be a theme that more explicitly emphasizes destruction over renewal. In fact, as we shall see, Guido's emphasis on *proditio* informs the characterization of Aeneas in *Sir Gawain and the*

34. All quotations of Guido's text are from Nathaniel Griffin's edition, Guido de Columnis, *Historia destructionis Troiae* (Cambridge, MA: Medieval Academy of America, 1936).

35. See Guido delle Colonne, *Historia Destructionis Troiae,* trans. Mary Meek (Bloomington, IN: Indiana University Press, 1974), 274–75. Meek suggests that Guido's knowledge of Geoffrey's *Historia* may have originated from his possible service in the retinue of Edward I. See Egidio Gorra, *Testi Inediti di Storia Trojana* (Turin: C. Trevirio, 1887), 102–3; E. Faral, *La Légende Arthurienne* (Paris: Champion, 1929), I:170–82.

Green Knight as "Þe tulk þat þe trammes of *tresoun* þer wroȝt" [the man who planned the plot of treason] (3).[36] Beginning and ending his discussion of the transfer of empire with the language of plague and betrayal, Guido responds to Geoffrey's *Historia* by suggesting that the *translatio imperii* may do more harm than good.

Guido's response may have been prompted by ambivalence about the fate of the Britons that can be found within Geoffrey's text. When Merlin offers his vision of the future to Vortigern, for example, his language is apocalyptic: "Montes itaque eius ut ualles equabuntur et flumina uallium sanguine manabunt. . . . Londonia necem .xx. milium lugebit et Tamensis in sanguine mutabitur" [For [Britain's] mountains and valleys shall be leveled, and the streams in its valleys shall run with blood. . . . London shall mourn the death of twenty thousand and the Thames will be turned into blood] (74, 78). While Diana's prophecy about the imperial glory of Britain looms large, Merlin's divination punctuates the violence that will result from the inevitable territorial conflicts. As Patricia Ingham points out, these dire visions emerge from a tradition of Welsh resistance to the triumphant future of Britain that the ruling Norman nobility would claim as their own.[37] On the one hand, a kind of Welsh optimism pervades Geoffrey's text via the "Breton Hope," which predicts a time when the native Britons would recover the island as their own (146). But on the other, the Bern and Harlech manuscripts include a retraction that appears to condemn this prophecy as nothing more than a fantasy of the oppressed: "Degenerati autem a Britannica nobilitate Gualenses numquam postea monarchiam insulae recuperauerunt" [The Welsh, once they had degenerated from the nobility of the Britons, never afterwards recovered authority over the island] (147).[38] These oppositional statements not only represent the complexity of what it meant to be "British," but also led Norman rulers to believe that the future glory could be exclusively theirs. More importantly, the recovery of Britain could then be cast into imperial time, which could take place in a distant era to come, after Geoffrey's history had been written.

In contrast to the vaticinative nature of Geoffrey's text, Guido questions the reliability of prophecy. Instead of hope, Guido prefers doubt (*dubio*) as a historiographic mode. While Guido's skepticism may be partly located in the Galfridian tradition, it also owes more to Orosius and Augustine, who ques-

---

36. All citations of the works of the *Gawain*-poet refer to *The Poems of the Pearl Manuscript: Pearl, Cleanness, Patience, Sir Gawain and the Green Knight*, ed. Malcolm Andrew and Ronald Waldron (Exeter, Devon: University of Exeter Press, 2002).
37. Ingham, *Sovereign Fantasies*, 36–37.
38. Ibid., 42–43.

tioned providential models for secular history. In his discussion of the Trojan inheritance of Rome, Orosius condemns the actions of Aeneas by stating:

> Paucis praeterea annis intervenientibus, Aeneae, Troja profugi, adventus in Italiam quae arma commoverit, qualia per triennium bella excitaverit, quantos populos implicuerit, odio excidioque afflixerit, ludi litterarii disciplina nostrae quoque memoriae inustum est.
>
> [Furthermore, in the few intervening years, the arrival in Italy (*Italiam*) of the Trojan fugitive (*Troja profugi*) Aeneas, which weapons (*arma*) he would shake, what sort of wars he would arouse over a period of three years, how many people he would envelop in hatred and afflict with destruction, have also been burned into our memories by elementary reading instruction.][39]

Despite his reverence for Virgilian vocabulary in these lines, echoing the opening lines of the *Aeneid* (Arma virumque cano, Troiae qui primus ab oris / Italiam fato profugus Laviniaque venit / litora), Orosius follows Augustine in tracking the negative consequences of Aeneas' wanderings on aspiring scholastic minds.[40] Neither Orosius nor Augustine promulgates a providential design for secular history, but they both admit the existence of a secular genealogy that reveals the failures of empire.

While Guido makes no attempt to situate the fall of Troy within a theology of history, his *Historia* exhibits the same adherence to imperial genealogy and pessimism about Trojan identity that we find in the works of Augustine

---

39. J. P. Migne, ed., *Patrologiae Cursus Completus*, vol. 31 (Paris, 1846), 731–32. This perspective of Aeneas follows Augustine, who rejected Virgil's history of Troy in his *Confessions*, but as Theodor E. Mommsen notes, more medieval historians read Orosius than Augustine. See his chapter "Orosius and Augustine," in *Medieval and Renaissance Studies*, ed. Eugene F. Rice, Jr. (Ithaca, NY: Cornell University Press, 1959), 348.

40. Although Augustine thought Aeneas' bellicosity was disturbing, he still found the emotive aspects of the *Aeneid* instructive. Sabine MacCormack suggests that Augustine "recalled the text of Vergil from an external vantage point and as a hostile critic and thus found nothing worthy of imitation in the wanderings of Aeneas. But that did not mean that Virgil's pathos was now lost on Augustine. It was in Virgil's footsteps that Augustine remembered his being 'inflamed' with diverse loves and rushing into sorrows, confusions, and errors, just as the characters in the *Aeneid* were inflamed with passions and rushed into conflict." *The Shadows of Poetry: Vergil in the Mind of Augustine* (Berkeley: University of California Press, 1998), 96–97. For examples of Augustine's sympathetic readings, see the following responses in his *Confessions* to the *Aeneid*: "exarsi . . . " (*Confessions* 2.1.1); "exarsi in pacem tuum" (*Confessions* 10.27.38); *Aeneid* 2.575, 5.172, 8.219, 7.445, 11.376; "inruebam in Dolores, confusiones, errores" (*Confessions* 1.20.31); *Aeneid* 2.383, 752, 3.222, 6.294, 9.355, 10.579. Citations from the *Confessions* refer to Lucas Berheijeni's edition in the *Corpus Christianorum. Series Latina* 27 (Turnholt, 1981). Citations from the *Aeneid* refer to *Opera*, ed. R. A. B. Mynors (Oxford: Oxford University Press, 1969).

and Orosius. We even discover a similar condemnation of Aeneas through the words of Hecuba:

> Ha nequam proditor, vnde a te procedere potuit tante crudelitatis impietas ut regem Priamum, a quo tanta magnolia suscepisti, tanto ab eo magnificatus honore, passus fueris interfectores eius ad eum ducere quem debuisti tua proteccione saluare? Prodidisti patriam tuam et urbem in qua natus fuisti et in qua fuisti tanto tempore gloriosus, ut eius ruinam aspicias et eius incendia uidere non horreas quibus fumat.
>
> [Ah, wicked traitor, how could you behave with such great evil and cruelty toward King Priam, from whom you have received such great possessions and by whom you have been exalted in great honor so that you could endure to guide the murderers to him, whom you should have saved by your protection? You have betrayed your country and the city in which you were born and in which you were famous for such a long time, so that you behold its ruin and you do not shrink from looking at the fires as it goes up in smoke.] (234)

Hecuba portrays Aeneas as one who not only caused the fall of Troy through treason, but also gazes upon its destruction without a scruple. Such a characterization is a far cry from the medieval idealization of Aeneas "bearing" or "carrying" the city of Troy to Rome, something that he does famously in the *Aeneid*, when he translates his father Anchises and his household gods away from the destruction and into Italy (2.634ff). In Guido's *Historia*, he tragically fails to fulfill his responsibility for "bearing" the city to its Roman glory and ultimately merits Hecuba's derision for his treason against the city and his sovereign in their time of need, a sentiment that epitomizes Orosius' lamentable message about Troy. For Guido, Aeneas carries with him the treason and subsequent destruction that will come to haunt his progeny.

Given the fact that the dominant version of history before the twelfth century emerged from the Augstinian–Orosian tradition, it is not surprising that its pessimism about the Roman Empire is still present in the thirteenth-century text of Guido and the subsequent texts he influenced. What is surprising, however, is the short shrift that scholars have given to the Trojan histories that do not adhere to the Galfridian historiographic model. Ironically, Guido's *Historia* suffers from the same problem that caused historians to question Geoffrey's claim of historical authority: fraudulent source citation. Since the late nineteenth century, modern readers have known Guido's stated intention to tell the truth in his prologue to be false because he fails to divulge the true source for his account of the fall of Troy. He claims to have followed the accounts of Dictys of Crete and Dares the Phrygian, when he actually bases his translation on Benoît de Sainte-Maure's *Le Roman de Troie*.[41] While Benoît's twelfth-century romance exerted a considerable influence on its own, Guido's translation of the *Roman*'s French octosyllabic couplets into Latin prose transformed his text into the canonical one. The pretense of the Latin chronicle genre helped Guido's text eclipse any claims to historical veracity that Benoît's text may have obtained. It is clear, however, that Guido's historiographic method has origins in what David Rollo calls Benoît's "spirit of skeptical analysis."[42] In his prologue, Benoît expresses admiration for Homer as a literary authority, but he eschews his account because of its historical inaccuracy.

> Mais ne dist pas sis livre veir,
> Quar bien savons senz nul espier
> Qu'il ne fu puis de cent anz nez
> Que li granz oz fu assemblez:
> N'est merveille s'il i faillit
> Quar onc n'i fu ne rien n'en vit. (51–56)[43]

[But his book does not tell the truth, for we incontrovertibly know that he was not born until a hundred years after the great army was assembled. It is hardly surprising that he was inaccurate, since he was never there and saw none of what happened.]

Like most medieval readers, Benoît rejects the fantasies of Homer and prefers another Trojan *livre*, that of Dares, both a "clerc merveillous" (99) and a Trojan war correspondent who claims to have recorded events he witnessed with his own eyes. Benoît characterizes Dares' book as authoritative, not only because it was believed to be a contemporary account, but also because it was discovered in the midst of academic research by yet another marvelous clerk named Cornelius, the nephew of the famous Roman historian Sallust (75–92). Benoît's clerical bias and careful treatment of the Trojan "authorities" represents what Rollo sees as a "skeptical" historiographic method in

---

41. Hermann Dunger, *Die Sage vom troyanischen Kriege in den Bearbeitungen des Mittelalters und ihre antiken Quellen* (Leipzig, 1869).
42. David Rollo, "Benoît de Sainte-Maure's *Roman de Troie*: Historiography, Forgery, and Fiction," *Comparative Literature Studies* 32.2 (1995): 191–225, at 212.
43. Benoît de Sainte-Maure, *Le Roman de Troie*, ed. Leopold Constans (Paris: Firmin Didot, 1904–12). All citations of the *Roman* refer to this edition.

which "the study of history is itself acknowledged as a historicized product of culture and takes as its primary object the self-conscious analysis of its own modes of production."[44] Guido's historiography of "doubt" follows this example, interrogating fantasies of empire as they were promulgated through an uncritical and unhistoricized belief in the redemptive power of the *translatio imperii*.

If Guido had divulged his real source, it is possible that we would be discussing the massive influence of Benoît's *Roman* upon Trojan historiography in England. Whereas medieval readers may have been forgiving of Guido's fraudulence, modern scholars have not been as merciful. Given the fact that Benoît's *Roman* is an amplification not only of Dares' *De Excidio Troiae Historia*, but also Dictys' *Ephemeris Belli Troiani*, both of which claim to be translations of Greek originals, to the eyes of many scholars, Guido's *Historia* is simply an irresponsible abridgement of a series of translations that only retains vestiges of the original.[45] Until 1964 only Egidio Gorra, Mary Meek, and Raffaele Chiàntera had attempted to study Guido's text as more than evidence of medieval plagiarism.[46] Since then, C. David Benson's book, *The History of Troy in Middle English Literature: Guido delle Colonne's Historia destructionis Troiae in Medieval England*, is the one exception among a wealth of scholarship interested in either the Trojan tradition or English poetry that closely tracks the pervasive influence of Guido's version of the fall of Troy in Britain. Even after the publication of Benson's book, Guido still has not garnered the scholarly attention he deserves. Ingledew, for instance, pays Guido little mind, despite the fact that the text he uses to introduce the historiographic importance of the Galfridian Trojan tradition, Sir Thomas Gray's *Scalacronica*, refers directly to Guido as the "gest de Troy."[47] Ingledew even places Guido's *Historia* within the scope of Virgilian tragic history that Augustine had rejected in his *Confessions*. In a discussion of medieval writers who revived Virgil, Ingledew claims, "[t]he distance traveled from Augustine in this respect is strongly apparent in Guido delle Colonne, *Historia destructionis Troiae*, . . . where Guido characterizes

---

44. Rollo, " Historiography, Forgery, and Fiction," 211–12.

45. Aristide Joly, *Benoît de Sainte-More et le Roman de Troie ou les Métamorphoses d'Homère et L'Épopée Gréco-Latine au Moyen Age* (Paris: F. Vieweg, 1870-1); R. M. Frazer, ed., *The Trojan War: The Chronicles of Dictys of Crete and Dares the Phrygian* (Bloomington: Indiana University Press, 1966).

46. Waller Bimster Wigginton, "The Nature and Significance of the Late Medieval Troy Story: A Study of Guido Delle Colonne's Historia Destructionis Troiae" (PhD diss., Rutgers University, 1964), iv–v.

47. Ingledew, "The Book of Troy and the Genealogical Construction of History," 666; Sir Thomas Gray, *Scalacronica*, ed. J. Stevenson (Edinburgh, 1836), 2.

the fall of Troy as a colossal and gratuitous misery and Troy's supersession by Rome as a redeeming consequence."[48] As I have demonstrated above, Ingledew's "redemptive" reading of Guido is not supportable—in fact, the opposite is the case. Guido's perspective of Troy's heritage as a "plague of great destruction" is consistent with Augustine's pessimism about the fate of secular empires.

Even a monograph on the subject of Troy in England, Sylvia Federico's *New Troy: Fantasies of Empire in the Late Middle Ages,* only refers to Guido's text tangentially and mischaracterizes its message and influence. While Federico acknowledges that the *Historia* was "extremely influential," she treats Guido's history as merely one of Chaucer's authorities on Troy and the basis for John Lydgate's *Troy Book*.[49] She then goes on to make a broad claim: "In the Troy stories examined in this book, we have seen that although Calkas, Antenor, and Aeneas are acknowledged as traitors, Helen and Criseyde take the blame for causing the destruction of Troy."[50] While it is certainly fair to characterize the *Historia* as a misogynistic text that callously treats women as currency in diplomatic negotiations, it is not accurate to claim that Guido blames Helen, or Criseyde for that matter, for the fate of the Trojans. In general, Guido equivocates in his discussions of whom to blame, but he places great emphasis on "the envious succession of the fates (*invidia series fatorum*)" (11), the inhospitality of Laomedon, and the vengeful anger of Priam as causes of "the plague of great destruction." Given Federico's cursory treatment of Guido, she may not have considered the *Historia* as one of "the Troy stories examined in this book." Even if that is true, she provides a brief analysis of Guido's "extremely influential" history that warrants elaboration.

THE NEW TROY AND GENEALOGICAL CLAIMS TO NOBILITY

The examples cited above are symptoms of a gap in scholarship that has far too often preferred the myth-making and fantastical Galfridian tradition to the sober and skeptical Guido-tradition in assessing the figure of New Troy in Britain in the later Middle Ages. Such invocations of Trojan origins were powerful political maneuvers, but we may call into question the notion that references to Troy were viewed as predominantly positive. As Lee Patterson has noted in *Chaucer and the Subject of History,* "[t]he location of historical authority in a single source naturally appealed to a medieval monarchy

---

48. Ingledew, "The Book of Troy and the Genealogical Construction of History," 672.
49. Federico, *New Troy,* 48.
50. Ibid., 145.

interested in promoting its own role as an exclusive source of political power, and the linearity of *translatio imperii* was convenient support for hereditary dynasties and genealogical claims."[51] Patterson rightly attributes much of Troy's glory to the influence of Geoffrey's *Historia*, and then proceeds to discuss the problems with the "linearity" that the *translatio imperii* demands. He then unapologetically declares Benoît's *Roman* as "the central document of Trojan historiography in the Middle Ages," a curious statement given the romance's seemingly nonhistorical nature, but both entirely consistent with his proclivity to read romance as historiography and technically accurate when we consider its status as the source for Guido's popular *Historia*.[52] Patterson even analyzes the texts of Benoît and Guido in depth later in the book and acknowledges the fact that this historiographic tradition places inexplicable catastrophe at the center of its concerns and "run[s] counter to, or subterraneously undermine[s], the uses of Trojan descent and *translatio imperii* in the service of secular interests."[53] Even though he recognizes this more pessimistic Trojan tradition as more pervasive and resistant to imperial designs, he still considers its role as legitimizing.

I find this conclusion unwarranted, especially since not all invocations of Trojan origins emerge from historical or literary contexts that depict Troy in a glorious light. In addition to literary texts such as John Gower's *Vox Clamantis*, which describes the fall of London as the New Troy, there is also the 1386 case of Nicholas Brembre, who was accused of having royalist ambitions, intending to rename London as "Parva Troia" or "Little Troy."[54] To Brembre's opponents, the desire for London to become another Troy was an

---

51. Lee Patterson, *Chaucer and the Subject of History* (Madison: University of Wisconsin Press, 1991), 92. See also R. Howard Bloch, *Etymologies and Genealogies: A Literary Anthropology of the French Middle Ages* (Chicago: University of Chicago Press, 1983); Gabrielle M. Spiegel, "Genealogy: Form and Function in Medieval Historical Narrative," *History and Theory* 22 (1983): 43–53.
52. Patterson, *Chaucer and the Subject of History*, 92.
53. Ibid., 123.
54. G. C. Macaulay, ed., *The Complete Works of John Gower: Volume 4* (Oxford: Clarendon Press, 1901). Future references to *Vox Clamantis* are from this edition; John P. McCall and George Rudisill, Jr., "The Parliament of 1386 and Chaucer's Trojan Parliament," *Journal of English and Germanic Philology* 58 (1959): 276–88, at 284. "Parva Troia" may have also vexed those who knew Virgil's "parvam Troiam" (3.349) at Buthrotum, a replica of Troy constructed by Helenus and other Trojans who fled the destruction of the Greeks in Book III of the *Aeneid*. The message of the replica is that Aeneas must not simply reproduce a new Troy, but construct something entirely different in Rome. David Quint identifies links between Virgil's description of Buthrotum's little Troy and the underworld in Book 11 of Homer's *Odyssey*. Read this way, *parva Troia* becomes a type of underworld that "reliv[es] a dead past." "Repetition and Ideology in the *Aeneid*," *Epic and Empire: Politics and Generic Form from Virgil to Milton* (Princeton: Princeton University Press, 1993), 58.

act of treason, not a glorious recognition of British heritage. Given the widespread influence of Benoît and Guido in late medieval England, the negative perspective of Troy by Brembre's enemies is unsurprising.

Likewise, if we turn to the fifteenth century and Christine de Pizan's treatments of Dido, we witness a Troy with a conflicted identity that calls into question its legitimizing authority. In *Le Livre de la Mutacion de Fortune*, Christine acknowledges the fact that the fall of Carthage was a necessary consequence for the promulgation of the Trojan imperial line (20599–606), but the destruction of Dido's great city inspires her to lament,

> Mais grant pitié fu de destruire
> Tel cite, qu'on veoit reluire
> En toute beaulté et richece,
> En force, en valour, en noblece. (20609–12)[55]

[But it was a great pity to destroy such a city, which could be seen to shine in complete beauty and wealth, in strength, in courage, and in nobility.]

Even though her source, the *Histoire ancienne jusqu'à César*, eliminates any mention of Dido in its strict adherence to an articulation of *translatio imperii*, Christine not only addresses the fate of Dido, but also meditates upon the negative consequence of Trojan treason. And by the time Christine composed *Cité des dames*, the tragic figure of Dido had developed into the central figure of her own Trojan historiography, which indicates her vested interest in expressing the darker side of empire.[56] Even if Christine did not read Guido's *Historia*, her treatments of Dido express ambivalence toward imperial fantasies that recognizes the victims of the elevation of the Trojan line.

Despite the acknowledged fact that the Guido-tradition had a significant influence upon the fourteenth- and fifteenth-century writers who addressed the subject of Troy, recent scholars have continued to read Troy as an origin of aristocratic and royal sovereignty without grappling with its fractured nature. The Galfridian tradition has therefore emerged as the authority on Troy since it was so wildly popular in the later Middle Ages and provides an attractive model in which Troy could become the inspiration for imperial fantasies.[57] Since the significance of Geoffrey's *Historia* in late medieval England is indisputable, recent scholars have not ventured beyond its her-

---

55. Christine de Pizan, *Le Livre de la Mutacion de Fortune*, ed. Suzanne Solente (Paris: A&J Picard, 1959).
56. Desmond, *Reading Dido*, 203–24.
57. Heng, *Empire of Magic*, 66.

meneutic shadow to explore the way alternative histories such as Guido's have influenced writers' interpretations of Troy. As this book demonstrates, an analysis of this marginalized tradition both complicates and illuminates the varied constructions of "New Troy" that poets and historians in the late fourteenth century perpetuated in order to understand the past, present, and future of England.

In the chapters that follow, I demonstrate that more than any other fourteenth-century corpus of English verse, the alliterative romances of the Guido-tradition demystify cultural and textual transfers of power from East to West that are embodied in the medieval notion of the *translatio imperii*— when one empire falls, a western empire takes its place. My investigation of Troy's status as an eastern origin for western culture and of widespread medieval obsessions with the East inform the way Troy, as a conquered figure, operates throughout these poems.[58] The heroes of these romances not only travel from Greece to Troy to Rome to Britain to enact cultural and imperial shifts, but also venture into the threatening, yet tantalizing, eastern locales of Africa and Jerusalem to engage in pilgrimages and conquer pagan territories.[59] Since perspectives on these geographical locations and their people vary widely, depicting Jerusalem in one text as a city of noble Jews and in another as a heathen stronghold of Christ-killers, I examine the way these alliterative romanciers theorize the East as a locus of paganism. Rome is the most complicated and compelling case: through these poems this city collectively serves as the means for Christian retribution and the father of Britain on one hand, and on the other the center of paganism and the threat of tyranny. By comparing the illustrations of Rome with those of Britain and the kingdoms of the Near East in alliterative romance, Rome emerges as an object of derision, not imitation. As Michael J. Bennett suggests, the *Gawain*-poet "wrote for a world which had been shattered," a sentiment which aptly characterizes the alliterative romanciers' ambivalence toward their imagined ancestry.[60] Instead of articulating a cycle of death and renewal, they suggest

58. Nicholas Birns, "The Trojan Myth: Postmodern Reverberations," *Exemplaria* 5.1 (1993): 45–78, at 50; Iain Higgins, *Writing East: The "Travels" of Sir John Mandeville* (Philadelphia: University of Pennsylvania Press, 1997).
59. Recent studies that have read these fantastical journeys and invasions through postcolonial theory have helpfully provided crusading contexts and defined premodern imperial desires that certainly influenced the composition of these poems. See Heng, "Warring against Modernity: Masculinity and Chivalry in Crisis; or, The Alliterative *Morte Arthure*'s Romance Anatomy of the Crusades," *Empire of Magic*, 115–79; Patricia Clare Ingham and Michelle Warren, "Introduction: Postcolonial Modernity and the Rest of History," in *Postcolonial Moves: Medieval through Modern,* ed. Ingham and Warren (New York: Palgrave Macmillan, 2003), 1–15.
60. Michael J. Bennett, *Community, Class, and Careerism: Cheshire and Lancashire Society*

that attempts to assert authority through the resurrection of a moribund past only perpetuate further destruction and suffering of the innocent. Their attempts to undercut these translations of power indicate that these alliterative poets perceived early constructions of English sovereignty as fundamentally fragmented, destructive, and unjustifiable.

---

in the Age of Sir Gawain and the Green Knight (Cambridge: Cambridge University Press, 1983), 231–35.

TWO

War

REVIVING TROY

THE SIGNIFICANCE of Guido delle Colonne's *Historia destructionis Troiae* to medieval England is best reflected by its English vernacular translations: the *Laud Troy Book* (c. 1400), John Lydgate's *Troy Book* (1420), and most importantly for this study, the alliterative *Destruction of Troy* (c. 1390).[1] The *Destruction* is of special interest because it is a translation of Guido's Latin prose into the English alliterative long line, a curious choice to the modern eye, but a relatively common one among alliterative poets. The only printed version of the *Destruction* that has ever been produced is the 1869/74 Early English Text Society edition, which was compiled by two Victorian

1. For a discussion of these translations, see C. David Benson, *The History of Troy in Middle English Literature: Guido delle Colonne's Historia destructionis Troiae in Medieval England* (Woodbridge, Suff.: D. S. Brewer, 1980). For the date of *Destruction*, see John Clerk of Whalley, *The Destruction of Troy: A Diplomatic and Color Facsimile Edition, Hunterian MS V.2.8 in Glasgow University Library*, ed. Hiroyuki Matsumoto (Ann Arbor: University of Michigan Press, 2002), iv. Any future references to *Destruction* will be from Matsumoto's edition. See also C. David Benson, "A Chaucerian Allusion and the Date of the Alliterative Destruction of Troy," *Notes & Queries* 219 (1974): 206–7; McKay Sundwall, "The Destruction of Troy, Chaucer's *Troilus and Criseyde*, and Lydgate's *Troy Book*," *Review of English Studies* 26 (1975): 313–17. Sundwall places *Destruction*'s composition after Lydgate's *Troy Book* based on the use of the word "reyne." Matsumoto points out, however, that the word is not unique and is actually a frequently occurring part of an alliterative unit. He suggests instead that the translation of this Troy text may be best considered within a context of Lancastrian nationalism, which would date the poem around 1400. See John H. Fisher, "A Language Policy for Lancastrian England," *PMLA* 107.5 (1992): 1168–80. For more on dating the poem, see note 13 and chapter 3, 94–99.

gentlemen, G. A. Panton and David Donaldson, who were particularly interested in identifying what they perceived as its Scottish origin.[2] Since they often regularized spelling and included doubtful, and sometimes inaccurate, readings of the manuscript, Hiroyuki Matsumoto created a diplomatic and color facsimile CD-ROM that more faithfully reproduces the sole surviving manuscript of the poem, Hunterian MS.V.2.8 in Glasgow University Library. Matsumoto also includes the name of the poet, John Clerk of Whalley, who was identified by Thorlac Turville-Petre in 1988.[3] The 2002 electronic edition attests to the need for this poem to be read in its manuscript form, since the size of the script, corrections, and evidence of truncation reveal a great number of interpretive curiosities. Therefore, I have primarily relied upon Matsumoto's edition and my own reading of the Hunterian MS V.2.8 *in situ* to track the poet John Clerk's use of his source and to argue that he undermines popular Trojan propaganda through a remarkably "historical" genre of poetic didacticism.

Contrary to previous scholarly findings, I want to suggest that a comparative reading of the Hunterian MS V.2.8, Lydgate's *Troy Book,* and Guido's *Historia* exhibits creative embellishments, divergences, and deletions, which reveal Clerk's prowess as both a poet and translator.[4] Through his negotiations from Latin to English and prose to poetry, Clerk manages to render his source accurately and alter sections strategically for both alliterative and

---

2. *The Gest Hystoriale of the Destruction of Troy,* ed. G. A. Panton and David Donaldson, Early English Text Society 39, 56 (New York: Greenwood Press, 1869 and 1874).

3. Thorlac Turville-Petre, "The Author of *The Destruction of Troy,*" *Medium Ævum* 57 (1988): 264–69.

4. For the contrary position see N. Jacobs, "Alliterative Storms: A Topos in Middle English," *Speculum* 47 (1972): 695–719; D. A. Lawton, "*The Destruction of Troy* as Translation from Latin Prose: Aspects of Form and Style," *Studia Neophilologica* 52 (1980): 259–70; John Finlayson, "Alliterative Narrative Poetry: The Control of the Medium," *Traditio: Studies in Ancient and Medieval History, Thought, and Religion* 44 (1988): 419–51. Finlayson summarizes the minority opinion: "These studies establish that, at the local level of story, [John Clerk] is concerned both to interpret his matter and to vivify it, rather than merely transliterate or paraphrase." "Guido de Columnis' *Historia Destructionis Troiae, The 'Gest Hystorial' of the Destruction of Troy,* and Lydgate's *Troy Book:* Translation and the Design of History," *Anglia* 113, no. 2 (1995): 141–62, at 143. Quotations from Guido's text are from Guido de Columnis, *Historia destructionis Troiae,* ed. Nathaniel Edward Griffin (Cambridge, MA: Medieval Academy of America, 1936). I will be using Griffin's edition of Guido's *Historia* as a basis for comparison with the awareness that this text is somewhat misleading since many of the apparent divergences of *Destruction* appear in other manuscript copies of the *Historia*. The variations I discuss in this chapter are inclusions or excisions that are so significant that they almost certainly did not exist in the other manuscripts that may have served as Clerk's copy of Guido. For a more detailed discussion of the copy of the *Historia* that may have served as the source for *Destruction,* see Gordon R. Wood, "A Note on the Manuscript Source of the Alliterative *Destruction of Troy,*" *Modern Language Notes* 67 (1952): 145–50.

thematic effects that differ from Guido's prosaic history. The result is a poem that effectively translates the figure of the destroyed Troy out of Latin and into the vernacular. Clerk both expands and reduces his audience by addressing his poem directly to an English audience—the "true" Troy is then accessed by those who are not Latin literate and at the same time made specifically relevant to late fourteenth-century England. To make his unsavory message about Britain's Trojan inheritance palpable, he manipulates alliterative tags to enhance the violence of war and to illustrate the tragic consequences of the revival of dead bodies and cities. Through graphic descriptions of Hector's death and pseudo-resurrection and the first Troy's destruction and reconstruction, Clerk revives a morbid Trojan past that enhances Guido's ambivalence about the *translatio imperii*.

This chapter is divided into four parts. The first focuses on a textual gap in the only surviving copy of the *Destruction*, an absence that is provocative to consider in identifying the way Clerk approached Guido's history. This lacuna is of great significance because it constitutes the end of Book I and beginning of Book II of Guido's *Historia*, which contain the references to the English inheritance of the Trojan "plague of great destruction." The second section addresses Clerk's translational method as a poet/translator/historian and offers an interpretation of his use of Guido to expand and specify his audience. Clerk's devotion to all of his roles not only highlights the high value he places upon alliterative poetry, vernacular translation, and the recording of history, but also proves his relative lack of originality to be entirely irrelevant to the value of his text. The third section addresses the role of the fates, Fortune, and human error through a discussion of Hector's anti-war speech and the invectives of Guido, Lydgate, and Clerk against the martial designs of Priam. Through a comparative reading, Clerk's *Destruction* emerges as the most critical of human culpability in the downfall of Hector and Troy. Hector's speech against war is the overwhelming ethical voice in the poem that urges readers to consider this Trojan failure as a historical exemplar of the dangers of martial designs. The fourth section focuses on Clerk's thematic use of death and revival. Read together, the resurrected figures of the slain Hector and destroyed Troy, body and city, reveal their metonymic relationship and suggest Clerk's condemnation of Britain's assumption of a New Trojan identity, a stance that differs from that of both Lydgate and Guido. The sections collectively demonstrate Clerk's interest in separating cultural and linguistic translation from aristocratic identity and Latinate authority in order to question idealizations of a New Troy.

THE *LACUNA* IN THE HUNTERIAN MS V.2.8

The most striking difference between the Hunterian MS V.2.8, which contains the *Destruction*, and extant copies of Guido's *Historia* is the absence of the end of Book I and the beginning of Book II, since this is the section that contains Guido's most direct interrogation of the transfer of empire. Recent editor Matsumoto and his Victorian predecessors, Panton and Donaldson, have already noted that this absence is a result of lost folios in the manuscript from which the Hunterian MS V.2.8 was copied, but no scholar to date has commented on the significance of this missing section.[5] What was included in the lost folios? While ultimately unanswerable, an understanding of the context of the missing section within *Destruction* and Guido's *Historia* highlights this historical tradition's resistance to the *translatio imperii*.

The Hunterian MS V.2.8 is an unassuming paper codex inscribed by the sixteenth-century copyist Thomas Chetham.[6] Many of the pages are worn and folios are missing, suggesting that this book was well used. John Clerk is not identified explicitly in the manuscript as the author of the poem—in fact, George Neilson in 1902 suggested that the mysterious poem was written by the infamous "Huchown of the Awle Ryale" as one of his many alliterative productions, including the *Siege of Jerusalem*.[7] This theory was rejected in 1988 when Thorlac Turville-Petre identified John Clerk of Whalley as the author of the *Destruction* through the discovery that the initia of the books spell "M. I[O]HANNES CLERK DE WHALELE." While this acrostic provided a name and place for the author, Turville-Petre could not specify which "John Clerk" wrote the poem since John Clerk was a common name in the area of Whalley in the late fourteenth and early fifteenth centuries.[8]

As I noted in the introduction, the gap in Clerk's text occurs at a pivotal point early in the narrative of Book II. At this moment, Guido breaks away from the Argonaut plot to meditate on the consequences of Laomedon's rash decision to threaten violence against the Greeks for daring to arrive on his

---

   5. The book is intact at this point, which supports the views of both editors that the gap existed in an exemplar. See Matsumoto, *The Destruction of Troy,* 316n; Panton and Donaldson, *The Gest Hystoriale of the Destruction of Troy,* 11.
   6. For a full manuscript description, see John Young and P. Henderson Aitken, *A Catalogue of the Manuscripts in the Library of the Hunterian Museum in the University of Glasgow* (Glasgow: James Maclehose and Sons, 1908), 309–10. For more on Chetham, see C. A. Luttrell, "Three North-West Midland Manuscripts," *Neophilologus* 42 (1958): 38–50.
   7. George Neilson, *"Huchown of the Awle Ryale," the Alliterative Poet* (Glasgow: James Maclehose & Sons, 1902).
   8. Turville-Petre, "The Author of *The Destruction of Troy,*" 264–69.

Trojan shores. Guido suggests that this action is the origin of a "plague of great destruction" that will infect future generations, including the New Trojans of England. A digression that examines the popular fiction of England's Trojan inheritance would have certainly caught the attention of readers such as Clerk, but since we have no immediate evidence to attest to this, we must turn to Guido's other known readers, Lydgate, and the anonymous author of the *Laud Troy Book*, in order to determine fourteenth- and fifteenth-century interest and use of this section of Guido's text. The *Laud*-poet ignores this section completely, which is unsurprising given his bellicose enthusiasm, but Lydgate sees Guido's digression as an opportunity to wander even further from the plot to explain the role that "gery Fortune" [fickle Fortune] (1.744) plays in inflicting destruction upon the world.[9] While Guido similarly refers to the intervention of "the envious succession of the fates" as a cause for Troy's fall, their role in the "plague of great destruction" is much less heavy-handed. Lydgate, on the other hand, elaborates on Troy's legacy by claiming that God interrupted the harmful course of events instigated by wily Fortune:

> For every wyght oughte to compleyne
> That lytel gylte schulde have swyche vengaunce,
> Except parkas thorugh Goddys purvyaunce
> That this mescheffe schulde after be
> Folwyng perchaunse of gret felicité. (1.806–10)

[For every man ought to complain that little guilt invites such vengeance, except perhaps through God's providence that this mischief should be followed afterwards by great felicity.]

According to Lydgate then, the providence of God works against Fortune in order to rectify a wrong and create a greater good. Lydgate continues by translating Guido's brief description of the *translatio imperii*, but amplifies the importance of each city involved in the transfer. Rome has now become not just the chief of all cities, but also of "passing famous worthinesse" (1.819). Likewise, Brutus is described as "passyngly famus" (1.832) and Britain is described as a "noble yle" (1.836). By including modifiers that glorify the

---

9. *Laud Troy Book*, ed. J. Ernst Wulfing (London: EETS, 1902); Benson claims the *Laud*-poet "is an exuberant story-teller whose racy style and obvious pleasure in the violence of the battle involve and excite the reader." *The History of Troy in Middle English Literature*, 67. John Lydgate, *Troy Book: Selections*, ed. Robert R. Edwards (Kalamazoo, MI: Medieval Institute Publications, 1998). All future references to Lydgate's *Troy Book* are to Edwards' edition.

new Troys and adding God's "purvyaunce" to Guido's nonprovidential history, Lydgate not only perpetuates the *translatio imperii,* but also bolsters its ability to supersede Troy's destruction. Given his tendency to amplify rather than compress Guido's text, it is especially curious that he fails to translate or comment upon Guido's pessimistic line, "Sed sit tante proditionis causa fuerit subsequentis boni causa finalis humana mens habet in dubio" [But the human mind holds in doubt whether the cause of such a great betrayal was finally the cause of subsequent good] (12).[10] Instead, Lydgate substitutes an elaboration of the Trojan genealogy:

> And thus whan Troye toun
> Eversed was and ibrought to nought,
> Ful many cite was ibilt and wrought,
> And many lond and many riche toun
> Was edified by th' ocasioun
> Of this were, as ye han herde me telle. (1.912–17)

[And thus when the city of Troy was overthrown and destroyed, many a city was founded and built, and many a land and many a rich town were edified by the occasion of this war, as you have heard me tell.]

Even though Lydgate generally remains faithful to Guido's historical account, his contention that "[f]ul many cite was ibilt and wrought" and excision of Guido's pessimism indicates a predilection for the furthering of the transfer of empire that runs counter to Guido's ambivalence. This is not to say that Lydgate's *Troy Book* is a triumphalistic poem through and through. In fact, as C. David Benson contends, Lydgate is more concerned with replacing "Guido's pessimism with practical advice" than bolstering English claims to empire.[11] Benson also characterizes Lydgate's references to Britain's Trojan heritage both in these lines and in his later description of Henry V as sovereign over "Brutys Albyoun" (5.3377) as historical fact.[12] It is certainly safe to assume that Lydgate, Clerk, and their contemporaries would have viewed their connection to Troy as part of truthful history, but Lydgate's endorsement of this transfer of power is nonetheless a rejection of Guido's critique of *translatio imperii.* Lydgate's reception of the missing section then sends at least two messages. First, its content as a whole, particularly the impe-

---

10. All quotations of Guido's text are from Nathaniel Griffin's edition, Guido de Columnis, *Historia destructionis Troiae* (Cambridge, MA: Medieval Academy of America, 1936).
11. Benson, *The History of Troy in Middle English Literature,* 123.
12. Ibid., 118.

rial genealogy, is attractive to English audiences and worthy of translation. Second, Guido's pessimistic coloring of *translatio imperii* does not suit the interests of Lydgate or his patron. Given Lydgate's embellishment and enthusiastic rendering of this section in the early fifteenth century, we must ask why this section is missing in Clerk's *Destruction*, which was most likely composed only twenty years beforehand.[13] While there are other portions of the poem in which lines are lost or compressed, no other missing section, which I estimate to be approximately three folios, matches the significance of this one.[14] No leaves are missing from the book, which indicates that the loss is the result of lost folios in an earlier manuscript. It is therefore highly probable that Clerk had included this section in his original composition of the poem and that it was either lost through copy error, overuse, or censorship. While copy error is a common reason for a missing section, the skipping of two or three pages would be an egregious error. Loss incurred through

13. Not all scholars agree that the *Destruction* is a fourteenth-century poem. In their attempts to explain the relationship between the *Destruction* and the *Siege of Jerusalem*, Ralph Hanna and David Lawton argue that the *Siege* must be an earlier poem than the *Destruction* since the *Siege* exhibits early circulation while the *Destruction* may have been composed as late as the 1530s. They argue for the *Destruction*'s belatedness based on Edward Wilson's claim that he discovered *the* John Clerk of Whalley who wrote the *Destruction*, a man who died in 1539. See Hanna and Lawton, eds., *The Siege of Jerusalem*, EETS OS 320 (Oxford: Oxford University Press, 2003); Wilson, "John Clerk, Author of *The Destruction of Troy*," *Notes and Queries* 235 (1990): 391–96. As Hanna and Lawton admit, this claim is not entirely compelling because, as Thorlac Turville-Petre notes, the name "John Clerk" is exceedingly common. See Turville-Petre, "The Author of *The Destruction of Troy*," 264–69. Yet, Hanna and Lawton still insist on the poem's lateness based on "the poet's wooden handling of the alliterative long-line" (xxxvi–xxxvii). Despite the difficulties that these questions raise in dating the poems, it is still likely that the *Destruction* is an earlier poem than the *Siege*. In addition to their common obsession with the synecdochic relationship between cities and bodies, Clerk's citation of Chaucer's *Troilus and Criseyde* dates the poem as early as the late 1380s and the *Siege*-poet's contribution to Ricardian crusading polemic (discussed in chapter 3) dates the poem to the late 1390s. Hanna and Lawton's insistence on the belatedness of the poem is ultimately unconvincing both because of Clerk's translational style and the evidence that points to the lateness of the composition of the *Siege*. Instead, I would attribute Clerk's "wooden" alliteration more to his dedication as a translator than to any imitative or derivative style. What scholars have perceived as Clerk's ponderous use of formulas and parataxis may indicate that he was an awkward stylist, not a nostalgic interloper of the alliterative tradition. The *Destruction*'s direct reference to Chaucer's *Troilus and Criseyde*, "Whoso wilnes to wit of þaire wo fir / Turne hym to Troilus . . ." [Whoever wants to know more of their woe turn to the *Troilus* . . .] (8053–54), dates the poem no earlier than 1385-6, leaving plenty of time for a late fourteenth-century composition. See E. Kölbing and Mabel Day, eds., *The Siege of Jerusalem* (Oxford: Oxford University Press, 1932), xxix; Benson, "A Chaucerian Allusion and the Date of the Alliterative 'Destruction of Troy,'" 206–7. Even though it is likely that it took a considerable amount of time for Chaucer's poem to be disseminated and read by Clerk, it is quite possible, given the geographical proximity of Clerk and the *Siege*-poet, that the *Siege*-poet would have had direct access to the *Destruction* before the 1390s, when Hanna and Lawton claim *Siege* was composed and circulated (xxxvii).

14. Panton and Donaldson, *The Gest Hystoriale of the Destruction of Troy*, 11.

overuse or censorship is especially compelling, because even a quick glance at one of the manuscript copies of Guido's *Historia* reveals the popularity of this section to its audience. For example, a reader who flips through Glasgow University Library's Koln 140 cannot miss the extent of the glosses that fill the margins. The importance of this section is reflected by scribal flourishes in other manuscripts as well. In Codex Claustroneoburgensis 746, held in the Klosterneuburg Stiftsbibliothek, a manicula (f.3a) points to the lines that relate *translatio imperii*. Codex Admontensis 185 of Admont Stiftsbibliothek even contains a manicula (Figure 2) that signals Guido's most pessimistic line "But the human mind holds in doubt whether the cause of such a great betrayal was finally the cause of subsequent good" (12). Since the glosses indicate that this part of Guido's text was well read and perceived as instructional, interesting, and/or controversial, it is probable that Clerk's readers turned to this section both to confirm their Trojan heritage and to interrogate aristocratic fantasies.

While we cannot uncritically support a reading of *Destruction* based on what has not survived, we would not do the "history" of Troy justice without following Clerk's textual clues, all of which indicate that this section was a part of the poem during its original composition. Even if this section were never a part of Clerk's original poem, we must consider why he might have excised this attractive historical content. All in all, the loss compels us to consider the fractured role Troy plays, not only within Clerk's version of the fall, but also within the late medieval English imagination.

THE LINKING OF LETTERS

Most scholars have ignored Clerk's poem precisely because it is a translation, and a fairly close one indeed.[15] Lydgate surpasses Clerk in the number and extent of his embellishments, expanding Guido's history to a colossal 30,000 lines that makes Clerk's 14,045, the longest of the alliterative genre, seem like a mere redaction.[16] If we turn to the prologues of each English translator, we gain insight into their differing perspectives on the appropriate way to treat their source texts. They both have to negotiate carefully between their roles of translator and poet: Clerk transforms Guido's Latin into alliterative formulae while Lydgate translates Guido's Latin into Chaucerian iambic pentameter. A comparison of the translational methods of Lydgate and Clerk

---

15. Benson, *The History of Troy in Middle English Literature*, 42–46.
16. Lois A. Ebin, *John Lydgate* (Boston: Twayne Publishers, 1985), 42.

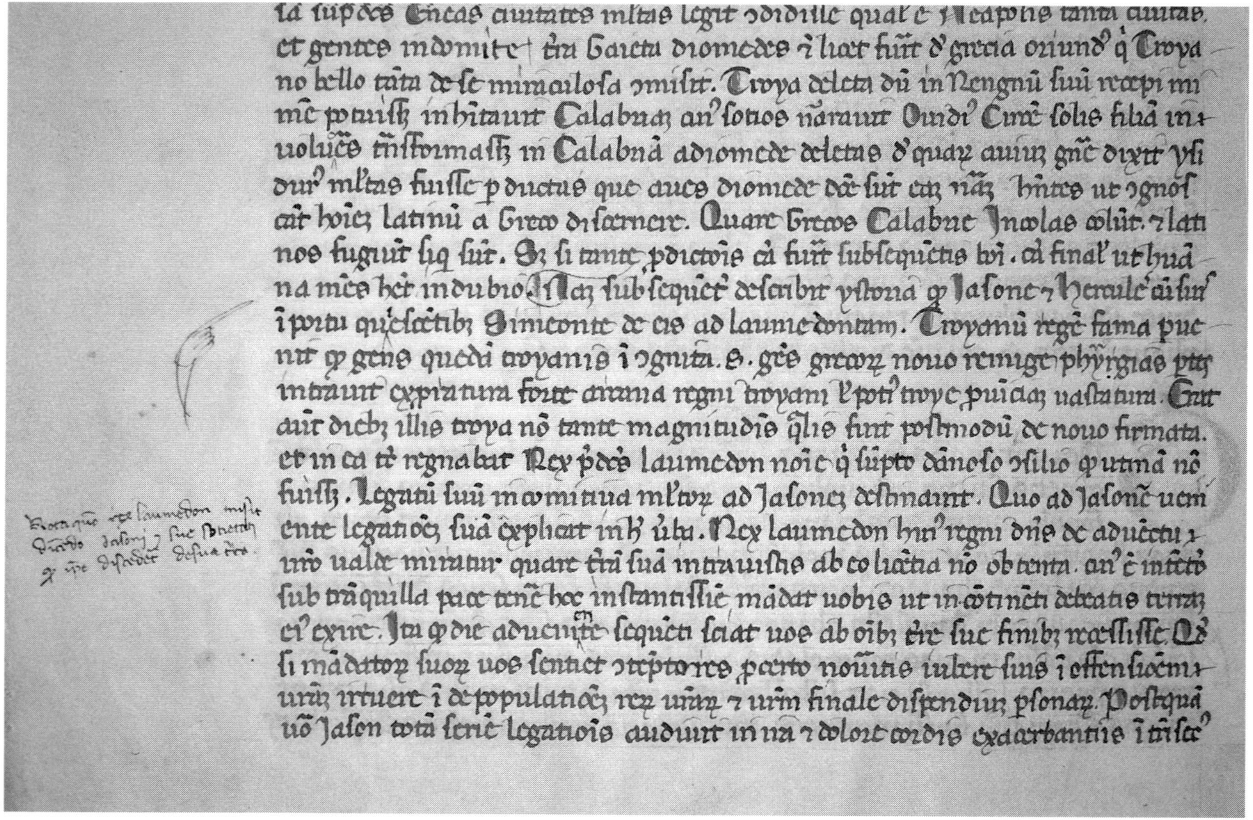

FIGURE 2. Codex Admontensis 185, f. 3b. Reproduced by permission of Admont Stiftsbibliothek

reveals the idiosyncratic ways they approach Guido's history. They both remain dedicated to the historiographic principle of providing Guido's history for English readers, but while Lydgate prefers to moralize the story and temper its pessimistic message through extensive digressions, Clerk presents the unsavory truth about England's destructive ancestors, eliminating and adding only what he deems necessary to contextualize Guido's history for an English audience.

If we turn to Clerk's prologue first, we find that he remains remarkably faithful to Guido's text. Clerk has the perplexing responsibility of acknowledging his source and interweaving his anonymous role in the translational history without digressing from Guido's own prologue. He does so by closely rendering Guido's version of the translational history of this particular Troy story, which begins with the two separate eyewitness accounts of Dares the Phrygian and Dictys of Crete and continues through a redaction by the Roman Cornelius Nepos, who ineptly combines the two versions (68–77). Clerk's fidelity, however admirable, has been the bane for scholars who pine for "original" texts. Upon close examination, however, Clerk proves to be much more than a mechanical translator. Clerk assumes the formidable job of not only rendering Latin into English, but also matching the sense of the Latin prose with English alliterative units, making his fidelity an impressive feat in the face of complicated linguistic and rhythmical circumstances. Because Clerk remains so faithful to his source, his original insertions are easy to identify. And despite Clerk's tendency to substitute several words of an alliterative unit and his criticism of Cornelius Nepos' brevity, most of Clerk's changes to Guido are compressions, eliminating details or digressions that are unnecessary for the telling of the history.[17] When Clerk dares to amplify passages, then, readers should take special note.

The first of the additions significant to an understanding of Clerk's view of Britain's Trojan heritage appears within the first five lines of the prologue. Before meditating upon stories lost from collective memory, as Guido does in his opening lines (3), Clerk begins with an invocation of God and an intention to tell "off aunters ben [t]olde of aunsetris nobill" (5) [of adventures told of noble ancestors]. Referring directly to noble ancestors whom aristocratic readers would expect to be the Trojans, Clerk perpetuates the genealogical construction of history elucidated so clearly in Geoffrey of Monmouth's *Historia regum Britanniae*. By beginning this way, Clerk explains the historical relevance this tale will have for its fourteenth-century readers and directly addresses Geoffrey's theory of history. Since Clerk refers

---

17. Lawton, "*The Destruction of Troy* as Translation from Latin Prose," 260.

to the Trojans as "nobill," the poem begins on an optimistic note that sounds more consistent with Geoffrey's than Guido's *Historia*. This added reference increases the importance of this account for his aristocratic readers and clarifies their connection to the events he is about to describe. By contrast, Lydgate writes specifically at the behest of his patron Henry V, calling him the ruler of "Brutys Albyoun" (104), a title that articulates more specifically the Trojan lineage of his regnal audience. Lydgate's history is also meant for other English readers both "hyghe and lowe" (111), but only so "[t]hat of the story the trouthe we nat mys / No more than doth eche other nacioun" (116–17). His translation is meant to laud Henry's rightful sovereignty and provide a history to all readers that has already been made known on the Continent. Clerk's sober addition for an audience of Britain's noble ancestors matches Lydgate's intention to reach readers "hyghe and lowe," but does not participate in imperial ideologies or competition with continental knowledge of the Troy story. Instead of elaborating upon the contribution of his text to established British historical chronologies, Clerk concisely specifies his audience and moves on.

After this addition, Clerk turns to Guido's justification for recording the truthful history of the fall of Troy. Guido goes into great detail about how stories are passed on and recorded by "faithful preservers of tradition" (*fidelia conseruatricia premissorum*) emphasizing the importance of "truth" (*ueritatem*) and a "faithful writing" (*fideli scriptura*) of the story of Troy (3). Clerk perpetuates this interest in faithful history by making several "truth" claims, beginning with the use of the word "[s]othe" in line 11, and then continuing with similar "truth" references throughout the prologue (lines 17, 36, 42, 51, and 94).[18] For both Guido and Clerk, their adherence to historical veracity distinguishes their accounts from writers who have skewed the truth according their own biases. Guido specifically condemns these mendacious recorders as "poets" (*poetice*) who attempt to disguise the truth through the use of "fictions" (*fictionibus*) (3–4).[19] Clerk, being a poet, qualifies this slightly by translating Guido's "poets" to "sum poyetis" (33), which allows him to maintain the emphasis on truth-telling and to deflect the damnation of all versifiers. This, seemingly minor, change calls our attention to the complicated

---

18. Matsumoto reads line 11 as "Soche stories" while Panton and Donaldson read "Sothe stories." A close reading of the manuscript indicates that either reading is possible, but the preponderant references to the truth of the stories make "Sothe" a more likely reading.

19. However, Guido does not argue that poetry contains no truth at all. For example, after his condemnations of famous epic poets, he claims that Virgil in his *Aeneid* "for the greater part . . . reported in the light of truth the deeds of the Trojans" [pro maiori parte gesta Troum . . . sub ueritatis luce narrauit] (4).

project that Clerk has undertaken: translating a truthful history not only from Latin to English, but also from prose to poetry.[20]

We may wonder, at the outset, if a medieval reader would believe it possible for Clerk to express the truth of history through poetry. According to our modern understanding of Aristotle's *Poetics*, history is particular and contingent, whereas poetry is universal and philosophical. Such a distinction implies an irreconcilable difference, but Aristotle qualifies this opposition by claiming that epic poetry draws on history in its thematic formulations.[21] Indeed the preeminent classicist Friedrich Nietzsche did not think that poets, especially Roman ones, could accurately represent history because of their inattention to particularities. In his discussion of translation in *The Gay Science*, he condemns the ancient Romans for recklessly appropriating Greek texts as their own. His invective is specifically directed at poet-translators, who "had no sympathy for the antiquarian inquisitiveness that precedes the historical sense; as poets, they had no time for all those very personal things and names and whatever might be considered the costume and mask of a city, coast, or a century."[22] Nietzsche's assessment could be accurately applied to Clerk's tendency to anglicize the Latin text, substituting English words and occupations for ones he did not recognize in Guido's Latin. Based on his readings of the ancient epic poets, Guido would have agreed with Nietzsche and accepted Aristotle's opposition of poets and historians.

However, since the *Poetics* was virtually unknown throughout the Middle Ages, and only accessible to the Latin West through translations of a tenth-century Arabic version and Averroës' commentaries, Aristotle's thoughts on poetry were primarily gleaned from his "scientific" works.[23]

---

20. It is important to remember that even though Guido claims to have followed the accounts of Dictys of Crete and Dares the Phrygian, Guido actually bases his translation on Benoît de Sainte-Maure's *Le Roman de Troie*. It is certainly possible that Clerk knew Benoît's *Roman*, but it is more likely that he believed Guido translated directly from Dares and Dictys. See Hermann Dunger, *Die Sage vom troyanischen Kriege in den Bearbeitungen des Mittelalters und ihre antiken Quellen* (Leipzig, 1869); Aristide Joly, *Benoît de Sainte-More et le Roman de Troie ou les Métamorphoses d'Homère et L'Épopée Gréco-Latine au Moyen Âge* (Paris: F. Vieweg, 1870–1); R. M. Frazer, *The Trojan War: The Chronicles of Dictys of Crete and Dares the Phrygian* (Bloomington: Indiana University Press, 1966), 3–15.

21. Timothy Hampton, *Writing from History: The Rhetoric of Exemplarity in Renaissance Literature* (Ithaca: Cornell University Press, 1990), 88–92.

22. Friedrich Nietzsche, *The Gay Science,* trans. Walter Kaufmann (New York: Vintage, 1974), 136–38.

23. E. N. Tigerstedt, "Observations on the Reception of the Aristotelian *Poetics* in the Latin West," *Studies in the Renaissance* 15 (1968): 7–24, at 7–8; Anton Baumstark, *Aristoteles bei den Syrern vom V.–VIII. Jahrhundert* (Leipzig: B. G. Teubner, 1900); Paul Moraux, *Les listes anciennes des ouvrages d'Aristote* (Louvain: Editions Universitaires de Louvain, 1951); Vito Maselli, "Tradizione e cataloghi delle opere aristoteliche," *Rivista italiana di filologia e istruzione classica*

Guido likely gained his perspective on poetry from Aristotle's *Metaphysics*, which demeaned poetry as merely a human invention and set below the divinity found in philosophy.[24] Even though both poetry and philosophy emerge from states of wonder and doubt, it is only philosophers, Aristotle contends, who transcend the ignorance of poetic fable and access truth.[25] Therefore, the Aristotelian idea in the *Poetics* that poetry is philosophical would have seemed fundamentally un-Aristotelian to Guido.

Also at work here is the medieval distinction between poetic and theological truth. The gold standard for truth was upheld by theological texts, which were true both at the literal and allegorical levels—in other words, they maintained their veracity in all senses. At the other end of the spectrum, poetry, or what Dante calls "favola," was literally false, despite any allegorical truth it may contain.[26] Guido condemns poets for writing stories that are false in the literal sense since such a commitment to falsehood entails "playing with" (*alludendo*) the truth and deluding audiences into thinking that they are reading the truth (1). The use of *alludendo* is especially disparaging because it implies that poetry is a frivolous activity. His invective is primarily directed toward Homer, who allegedly "eius ystorie puram et simplicem ueritatem in uersuta uestigia uariauit, fingens multa que non fuerunt et que fuerunt aliter transformando" [changed the pure and simple truth of his story into clever paths, touching on many things which did not happen and transforming those which did happen] (4). The most significant transformation was Homer's depiction of pagan gods fighting against the Trojans as if they were mortals.

Guido's charge against poets here is reminiscent of an episode in Plato's *Republic*, in which Socrates urges the poets of their republic against telling stories of gods acting impiously and warring against one another as they do in Homer's *Iliad* since such accounts blaspheme the gods and corrupt their hearers (378b–381e).[27] Socrates even addresses the subject of Troy, saying, "if anyone composes a poem about . . . the tale of Troy . . . we must require him

---

34 (1956): 337–63; Jaroslaus Tkatsch, *Die arabische Übersetzung der Poetik des Aristoteles*, I–II (Vienna: Holder-Pichler-Tempsky 1928–32); Rudolf Kassel, *Aristotelis de Arte Poetica Liber* (Oxford: Clarendon Press, 1965); Harry A. Wolfson, "Revised Plan for the Publication of a Corpus Commentariorum Averroïs in Aristotelem," *Speculum* 38 (1963): 88–104.

24. Ernst Robert Curtius, *European Literature and the Latin Middle Ages*, trans. Willard R. Trask (New York: Pantheon Books, 1953), 221.

25. James Simpson, "Poetry as Knowledge: Dante's Paradiso XIII," *Forum for Modern Language Studies* 25 (1989): 329–43, at 329.

26. Alex Preminger, O. B. Hardison Jr., and Kevin Kerrane, eds., *Classical and Medieval Literary Criticism: Translations and Interpretations* (New York: Frederick Ungar, 1974), 406.

27. All citations from Plato's *Republic* refer to Plato, *The Republic*, trans. Paul Shorey, The Loeb Classical Library (London: Heinemann, 1930).

to say that these things are not the work of a god" (380a). Homer's portrayals of the gods are false since the gods are inherently good, but Socrates does not claim that poets are inherently mendacious. In fact, he argues that they possess the capability to tell the truth since their accounts can have a profound effect on their readers (378b–e). Guido, on the other hand, presents Socrates' worse case scenario: he explains that the necessary consequence of these Homeric inventions was that other famous poets, such as Ovid "Cuius errorem . . . curiosius insecuti" [followed his (Homer's) error carefully] (4). Here Guido cleverly equates the commitment to fidelity of "preservers" with the diligence of poets, but unlike the "conseruatricia" who adhere to truth, poets remain faithful to "error."

As a poet then, how does Clerk maintain his intention both to translate the truth and to versify it through the alliterative long line? His main strategy to remain faithful to both roles is evident in the structure of his prologue. Rather than compare the *conseuatricia* with the *poete,* Clerk begins more generally and in the passive voice, which allows him to suspend any judgments about the writers of truths and falsehoods.

> So[th]e stories ben stoken vp & straught out of mynd
> And swolowet into swym by swiftenes of yeres
> ffor new þat ben now next at our hond
> Breuyt into bokes for boldyng of hertes
> On lusti to loke with lightnes of wille
> Cheuyt throughe chaunce & chaungyng of peopull
> Sum tru for to traist triet in þe ende
> Sum feynit O fere & ay false vnder. (11–18)

[True stories have been compiled, passed out of mind, or swallowed by forgetfulness through the passing of years because new things that have just happened are recorded into books to embolden hearts, are pleasant to look upon with lightness of will, and accomplished through chance and the changing of people. Some are truthful and credible, tried in the end, while some are invented completely and false underneath.]

The subjectivity of a poet or recorder is almost completely absent here—Clerk shifts the focus to the "stories" themselves and how they have been "swolowet" by the passing of time and "[b]reuyt" into books. Rather than blame the false tales on poetic deception, Clerk explains that after the intervention of "chaunce" and fickle human nature, "sum" remain "tru" and "sum" become "false." Clerk's refusal to translate Guido's blanket condemnation of all poets reflects his willingness to work against his source in order to further his poetic project and make the case that "sum" poets are capable of writing truthful history. As C. David Benson succinctly puts it: "Guido had distinguished false poets from true historians; the alliterative poet [Clerk] distinguishes true from false poets."[28] Of the English translators of the *Historia*, Clerk best defies Nietzschean accusations of recklessness, submits to Socrates' mandate, and most explicitly argues that "true" poets could also serve as historians. He maintains this focus on the truth throughout the poem, including his discussion of the fate of the Greeks long after Troy has fallen. Lydgate also qualifies Guido's condemnation of poets by claiming that, of the poets who rehearsed the history of Troy, "somme han the trouthe spared" [some have spared the truth] (259). Yet Lydgate unleashes an invective against those who have "transformed [the truth] in her poysy" [transformed the truth in their poetry] (262) that has no equal in the *Destruction*. Given their common selection of a poetic medium for the representation of history, it is clear that Clerk's contemporaries agreed that poetry could effectively express the truth.[29]

Despite their emphasis on the poet/historian dichotomy, medium mattered less than method to all translators of this Trojan historiographic tradition. Dares and Dictys emerge as the authorities, not because they wrote in prose, but because they obtained their accounts through first-hand experience. In his preface to Dares' *De Excidio Troiae Historia,* Cornelius Nepos claims that he translates word-for-word from Dares' account so that his audience may judge "utrum verum magis esse existiment, quod Dares Phrygius memoriae commendavit, qui per id ipsum tempus vixit et militavit, cum Graeci Troianos obpugnarent, anne Homero credendum, qui post multos annos natus est, quam bellum hoc gestum est" [whether they consider what Dares the Phrygian confided from memory to be more true, who lived and fought at the time when the Greeks contended against the Trojans, or believe Homer, who was born long after the war was over] (1).[30] In this view, Homer simply could not have related the truth because he was not present to record

---

28. Benson, *The History of Troy in Middle English Literature,* 37.

29. Ibid., 37–39. Benson contends that "[p]oetry and history may be judged antipathetic by both Guido and ourselves, but their union would have seemed perfectly legitimate in medieval England" (37). For a thorough explanation of Anglo-Saxon, Anglo-Norman, and Anglo-Latin expressions of "true" history through poetry, see M. Dominica Legge, *Anglo-Norman Literature and Its Background* (Oxford: Clarendon Press, 1963), 27–36. She gives the example of the poet-historian Gaimar who wrote his history of the English, *Estorie des Engleis,* in octosyllabic rhyming couplets, a verse form which he passed on to Wace and eventually Benoît, who ironically served as a poetic source for Guido's prose history.

30. *Daretis Phrygii De Excidio Troiae Historia,* ed. Ferdinand Meister (Leipzig: Teubner, 1873).

the facts. Dares and Dictys, on the other hand, claim to have witnessed the events and recorded their observations as diarists, thereby inscribing the truth in a way that neither Homer nor Virgil was capable of doing. Dictys establishes the veracity of his account by stating, "quae deinceps insecuta sunt, quoniam ipse interfui, quam verissime potero exponam" [I can relate the events that follow with utmost accuracy, since I myself experienced them] (13).[31] At this point in the prologue, Clerk distinguishes his alliterative version of the history through a reorganization of the textual chronology. Unlike Guido and Lydgate, who move directly into a condemnation of Homer and all poets, Clerk separates his discussion of Homer and "sum" poets who fictionalize the truth from his introduction by pausing to address the accounts that carry the most weight and interest for his audience. Here he privileges the "writing of wees þat wist it in dede, / With sight" [writing of men who knew it in deed, with sight] (23–24), a direct reference to the eyewitnesses Dares and Dictys, whom he will nominally authorize forty lines later. The language that Clerk uses to describe the unnamed Dares and Dictys originates in Guido's Latin, but his choice to invoke the truth-bearing characteristic of their accounts before identifying the truth-bearers privileges the empirical authority of their history over poetic mendacity.

If Clerk privileges eyewitness truth over literary medium, how then can we explain his use of an alliterative long line that complicates an accurate translation of the history? To answer this question, we should attend to the end of the stanza, where Clerk arrives at a curious conclusion that has perplexed readers. He claims that these eyewitnesses wrote:

>   of hom þat suet after
> To ken all the crafte how þe case felle,
> By lokyng of letturs þat lefte were of olde. (24–26)

[for those who followed afterwards so that they would know all the causes behind the events through the linking of letters that were left of old.]

While Clerk is directly referring to Dares and Dictys, who provided the account for the use of future generations, the reference to the "lokyng of letturs þat lefte were of olde" is difficult to decipher. The language that Clerk uses here has intrigued scholars of alliterative poetry because of the occurrence of a similar phrase in the prologue to *Sir Gawain and the Green Knight*,

---

31. *Dictys Cretensis Ephemeridos Belli Troiani Libri,* ed. Werner Eisenhut (Leipzig: Teubner, 1973).

which appears directly after a discussion of the fall of Troy and the Trojan heritage of Britain. The *Gawain*-poet claims that he will tell his story in a tongue,

> As it is stad and stoken
> In stori stif and stronge,
> With lel letters loken,
> In londe so hatz ben longe. (33–26)

[As it was set and established in a story stiff and strong, linked with true letters in our land for a long time.]

Like Clerk, the *Gawain*-poet makes reference to "letters loken" that he will utilize to transmit a tale, but it is not clear what these "locked letters" are. Malcolm Andrew and Ronald Waldron translate "lel letters loken" as "enshrined in true syllables," but concede that it could also mean "linked with true letters." The latter reading is especially provocative because it may either denote the precision of the meter or allude to the Anglo-Saxon tradition of the alliterative style.[32] If this line calls attention to the verse form, we could then argue for a linguistic and historiographic affinity between the *Destruction* and *Gawain* and cite these lines as evidence for a particular alliterative interest in the fall of Troy.

Unfortunately, we cannot make that claim. As Norman Blake has forcefully argued, the consistency of alliterative meter is "too arbitrary an organizing principle" for a coherent literary movement, especially since the content of the alliterative poems varies so widely.[33] More recently, Randy Schiff has identified the "artificial extraction of texts" that is required to fashion evidence for Revivalist arguments about the self-conscious use of the verse form.[34] Rather than speculate about what these lines say about the poetic medium of their Anglo-Saxon predecessors, I want to suggest that these lines refer to the translation or "linking" of Trojan and British history.[35] To do

---

32. Malcolm Andrew and Ronald Waldron, eds., *The Poems of the Pearl Manuscript: Pearl, Cleanness, Patience, and Sir Gawain and the Green Knight* (Exeter: University of Exeter Press, 2002), 31–36n.

33. N. F. Blake, "Middle English Alliterative Revivals," *Review* 1 (1979): 205–14, at 206.

34. Randy Schiff, *Revivalist Fantasy: Alliterative Verse and Nationalist Literary History* (Columbus: The Ohio State University Press, 2011), 36–44, at 36.

35. This metrical reading has been attractive to scholars of alliterative poetry such as Turville-Petre and Chism because it calls attention to a Middle English alliterative long line that is both aesthetically striking and encourages the reader to make aural and interpretive connections between individual words in each line. Hence, the reader must "link" the "letters" of the line in order to appreciate their consonance and ponder the significance of their juxtaposi-

so, we must read these lines in an entirely different way. Derek Pearsall is another critic who warns against making too much of these lines as evidence of a continuous or revived alliterative tradition, but his claim that Clerk's "lokyng of letturs" is directly derived from his source is not entirely accurate. The closest reference to any "locking of letters" in Guido's prologue is in his description of Ovid, who "in multis libris suis utrumque contexuit" [bound both of these [truth and falsehood] together in his many books] (4). For Guido, poets deceive their readers by "locking" or "binding" the truth with fiction, a sentiment that Lydgate translates into his own text by claiming that Ovid "poetically hath closyd / Falshede with trouthe" (299–300). The only other "locking" to which Lydgate refers is the consonance of truth that he applies specifically to the accounts of Dares and Dictys (315–16), but he places little emphasis on the phenomenon of their invariation. When Clerk refers to "locking," he is neither discussing Ovid, who appears in his prologue more than twenty lines later, nor implying the confluence of truths and lies. Instead, he uses this "locking of letters" to conclude the first section of his prologue in a way that differs significantly from the texts of Guido and Lydgate. As I suggested above, Clerk restructures his prologue so that he can preserve the reputation of "sum" poets and introduce his versified history. This strategy suspends discussion of specific writers such as Ovid and shifts the focus to the importance of transmitting forgotten tales to future generations. In so doing, Clerk cleverly introduces Dares and Dictys without mentioning them by name—he views their credence as truth-tellers, rather than their *auctoritee,* as noteworthy. The "lokyng" may then be read in a variety of ways that suit Clerk's project. First, the "lokyng" may be the "securing" of the true account, which may have been performed by Dares and Dictys in the act of writing what they had witnessed. But since he does not specify them here as Lydgate does, Clerk may be referring to his own "securing" of

---

tion. The use of this poetic form has traditionally been attributed to the "Alliterative Revival," which has led Turville-Petre and Chism to speculate that the emergence of these poems may be evidence of an attempt to create a "classical" genre of English poetry that looks back to earlier Anglo-Saxon poetry. See Chism, *Alliterative Revivals,* 16–20; Turville-Petre, *The Alliterative Revival* (Cambridge: D. S. Brewer, 1977). However, scholars have not uniformly embraced such an understanding of the phenomenon of alliterative poetry in the late fourteenth century. Derek Pearsall, advises against reading these obscure references to "linked letters" as an indication of the continuity or revival of alliterative poetry in the later Middle Ages since there is little evidence to support it. Rather, they may simply be conventional expressions that authorize old tales expressed through any medium and may not refer to their meter at all. Pearsall similarly rejects the connection between the similarity between the lines in *Gawain* and *Destruction* by claiming that Clerk's line is simply "imitated" from Guido's prologue. See "The Alliterative Revival: Origins and Social Backgrounds," in *Middle English Alliterative Poetry and Its Literary Background,* ed. David Lawton (Cambridge: D. S. Brewer, 1982), 34–53, at 43.

the truth through the act of translation, which makes the history available to a large audience. Second, the "lokyng" may also mean "locking" or "linking," which may refer either to the combination of the accounts of Dares and Dictys by Guido, or to Clerk's own text that "links" the Latin Trojan history to an English poetic tradition.[36] This reading is corroborated by a direct reference to Dares and Dictys, who "wrote all þe werkes wroght at þat tyme / In letturs of þere langage as þai lerned hade" [wrote all the works made at that time in letters of their language as they had learned] (58–59). The "letturs" that they used to record their "werkes" are most likely those same "letters" that were "linked/locked." As James Simpson aptly notes, "the combined accounts of Dictys and Dares are a guarantee of truth."[37] Read this way, the "lokyng" is a combining that also "locks" or ensures that the truth will be revealed. Finally, the "lokyng" could signify a "looking" or a retrospection that "hom þat suet after" had to do in order to understand and pass on the truth about the fall of Troy. This reading alters the grammatical subject slightly, so that the "lokyng" is performed either by the transmitters of the tradition such as Guido or Clerk or any future reader of the texts that record the tale.

All these readings that denote a "securing," "linking/locking," and "looking," place an emphasis on an accurate, well-preserved, and rhetorically humble translation of the truth about Troy. While it is tempting to read the "lokyng" as a reference to a continuous or revived tradition of alliterative poetry in England, we should restrain our desire to make too much of a "classical" English tradition with very little evidence to support it. Instead, I suggest that we read this "lokyng of letturs" as a "translating of words/accounts." Understood this way, the specific use of the word "lokyng" carries multiple meanings that encompass translation—after all, Clerk has to take special care both to link his words together to create effective alliterative units and to establish the truth about Troy through a translation that remains faithful to Guido. Clerk then secures these accounts in a way that Plato would have certainly endorsed. As a poet he translates the truth both linguistically and historically through the use of interlocking lines that serve a didactic purpose for future generations. Unlike some poets who link truth with falsity,

---

36. Of course it was neither Guido nor his source Benoît, but a Latin redactor who "linked" the accounts of Dares and Dictys. Benoît and Guido thought this Latin text was one written by Cornelius, nephew to Sallust, since the account begins with a letter that commences, "Cornelius Nepos to Sallustius Crispus" [Cornelius Nepos Sallustio Crispo], but it may in fact have been Joseph of Exeter's *De Bello Trojano*. For a more detailed explanation, see Mary Meek's introduction to her translation: Guido delle Colonne, *Historia destructionis Troiae* (Bloomington: Indiana University Press, 1974), xix.

37. James Simpson, *The Oxford English Literary History, Volume 2. 1350–1547: Reform and Cultural Revolution* (Oxford: Oxford University Press, 2002), 86.

Clerk locks this Latin "eyewitness" account into an English alliterative word hoard that can be translated truthfully to future British generations. In doing so, Clerk promulgates Guido's version of the Troy story and rejects the poetic mendacities of Virgil and Homer. Clerk's "locking" encourages the English reader to view his poem not as a fanciful epic, but a work of sober history that privileges truth over entertainment.

Clerk's commitment to both his poetic project and a faithful translation of Guido is so thorough that it periodically causes him to make some infelicitous decisions in the creation of his text. For example, in the lines preceding the "lokyng" line, Clerk amplifies Guido's comment on the transmission of great stories—"Vigent . . . pro gestorum magnitudine continuata recordia dum preteritorum in posteros sermo dirigitur" [continuous records flourish on account of the greatness of the deeds, as long as the discourse of what is past is distributed to posterity] (3)—not only because Clerk needs space in the text to mollify Guido's contempt for poets, but also because Guido's content is too brief to match the length of alliterative long lines. He then repeats the tag "most out of mynd" in line 10 with "straught out of mynd" in line 11. As Lawton notes, such glaring poetic mistakes should not lead us to condemn Clerk as a poet, but rather should serve as "an index of his high respect for Guido, and of his seriousness as a translator."[38] Even though Clerk may not completely succeed in composing a precise and rich poem in English verse, his negotiation between poetry and prose still secures a faithful translation of the Troy story.

After postponing and deflecting Guido's contempt for poets and establishing his authorial identity as a poet-translator, Clerk finally turns to the specifics of the Troy story and how he intends to provide the "truth of the matter" without rhetorical flourishes for a vernacular reading audience. The separation between the stanza that ends with the "lokyng of letturs" and the following stanza is clearly marked in the manuscript with a new rubric and large bold letters that begin the first line, "Now of Troy . . . " (27). It is only at this point that Clerk turns to the subject of his poem and joins Guido in a condemnation of false poets. The translation remains very close until both Guido and Clerk make the transition from false to true accounts. Here we witness the tension between Latin prose and vernacular poetry—while Guido legitimizes his history through writing in Latin, Clerk deemphasizes the authority of Latin and again reverts to generalities to avoid direct contradiction of Guido. Guido claims that his text ensures "ut fidelium ipsius ystorie uera scribentium scripta apud occidentales omni tempore futuro uigeant

---

38. Lawton, "*The Destruction of Troy* as Translation from Latin Prose," 263–64.

successiue, in vtilitatem eorum precipue qui gramaticam legunt, ut separare sciant uerum a falso de hiis que de dicta ystoria in libris gramaticalibus sunt descripta" [that the true accounts of the reliable writers of this history may endure for all future time hereafter among western peoples, chiefly for the use of those who read grammar books, so that they may know how to separate the true from the false among the things which were written of the said history in grammar books] (4). What Guido fails to clarify in this prolix sentence is that those "grammar books," which fail to provide the whole truth, are the instructional texts that are filled with the work of the epic poets, Homer, Ovid, and Virgil, who combined both truth and falsity in their Latin poems.[39]

Guido's history is then intended for a reading audience who values the truth-telling power of Latin prose. Lydgate, in trying to render Guido's Latin into English, cannot escape Guido's Latin and finally is forced to admit failure. As noted above, Lydgate claims early on to translate not only for Henry, but also for the "hyghe and lowe" in order that the story of Troy would be known in English as it had already been known in French and Latin on the Continent. Yet, Lydgate's devotion to a vernacular telling of this history is tempered by his anxiety about his fidelity to the Latin text. He not only praises Guido's Latinity, but also prays that God help him remain faithful to the text (372–84), a sentiment that continues throughout the prologue and first book, until he experiences a kind of translation anxiety in Book II. At this point, his pen had begun to "quake and tremble" (145) because he fears that his patron Henry "[m]y making rude schal beholde and rede" (148). He feels he cannot reproduce Guido's rhetorical color and is reduced to decide that since "in ryme Ynglysch hath skarseté . . . I ne can / Folwen Guido" (168–70) and "I leve the wordis and folwe the sentence" (180). On one level this is an example of the "modesty topos," but it is not long before Lydgate's "modesty" becomes an admission of the inadequacy of English to match Latinate diction.

Despite Lydgate's desire to exalt the English language, this translational crisis indicates that he feels that English cannot match the rhetorical complexity and sonority of the Latin language. This forces him to shift his fidelity from the Latin rhetoric to the historical ideas of Guido's text. He now calls on Clio, the muse of history, to help him with his historical project (178–79), which effectively transforms his text from a translation to a moralistic tale that Pearsall has called "a homily first, an encyclopedia second, and

---

39. Thirteenth- and fourteenth-century readers would have most likely only known Homer from a rudimentary Latin translation. See Benson, *The History of Troy in Middle English Literature*, 3.

an epic nowhere."[40] Lydgate essentially admits what Talal Asad would call the "inequality" of English within the medieval hierarchy of languages, and accordingly crumbles in the face of Latinate authority.[41] By contrast, Clerk neither cowers nor relinquishes his translational project to provide the history of Troy for an English audience. While he acknowledges Guido's preference for Latin by relating that "wise men haue written the wordes before / Left it in latyn for lernyng of vs" (31–32), the rest of his references to language are more general and functional for the purposes of his narrative. To establish Guido's account as the authority, he does not refer to its Latin prose, but instead claims that of all the histories of Troy, Guido's is "þe text euyn" [the correct text] (51). Clerk treats Dares and Dictys in a similar manner; since Guido never mentions the language they used to compose their diaries, Clerk characterizes their "werkes" as written "[i]n letturs of þere langage as þai lerned hade" (58–9).[42] Given his goal of "lokyng" or translating letters for readers who neither know Latin nor possess memory of past historical events, the use of letters from "their language" privileges the vernacular and inclusive narrative that he intends to provide for a lay aristocratic audience.

An examination of Clerk's prologue, its divergences from Guido's *Historia*, and its similarities and differences to Lydgate's *Troy Book* lead to four conclusions. First and foremost, Clerk is a faithful translator who prefers compression and only embellishes when necessary. His fidelity to his source indicates that he makes no attempt to mitigate Guido's pessimism about the consequences of the fall of Troy and therefore translates the warning against imperial designs for fourteenth-century English readers. Second, Clerk cleverly restructures his narrative and plays with shades of meaning in order to further his alliterative poetic project. This means that he often reverts to repetitive phrases to maintain both poetic subjectivity and historical fidelity. Third, vernacular poetry can appropriately and accurately express Guido's Latinate "eyewitness truth" about historical events. His manipulation of Guido's invective against poetry preserves the reputation of "sum" poets who

---

40. Derek Pearsall, *John Lydgate,* Medieval Authors: Poets of the Later Middle Ages (London: Routledge and Kegan Paul; Charlottesville: University Press of Virginia, 1970), 129.

41. Talal Asad, *Genealogies of Religion* (Baltimore: Johns Hopkins University Press, 1993), 189–93. See also Christopher Baswell, "*Troy Book:* How Lydgate Translates Chaucer into Latin," in *Translation Theory and Practice in the Middle Ages,* ed. Jeanette Beer (Kalamazoo: Medieval Institute Publications, 1997), 215–37. Baswell still views the *Troy Book* as successful in its imperial designs and contends that Lydgate's use of Chaucer's English in the narrative "produces another kind of national contest that is parallel with the militant national contests of Trojans and Greeks, British and French: a linguistic contest to succeed Guido's Latin with an English eloquence that is nonetheless as laureate as its predecessor" (226).

42. Since Guido never combined Dares and Dictys accounts and instead translated Benoît's *Roman,* he may not have known the language in which they wrote.

work to tell the whole truth and resist the trifles of Homer, Ovid, and Virgil. Fourth and most importantly, as a quintessential poet-translator, Clerk amplifies the importance of translation, not only of language, but also of the message that the translation bears. "By lokyng of letturs," Clerk employs a new language (English) and a challenging mode (alliterative poetry) in order to reach a new audience. Without the establishment of the veracity of Clerk's historical method, we sense that he fears that his romance may not be read as history at all. In other words, his fidelity and dedication to "locking" this account are attempts to define his poem as a serious work of translation and history that has the capability to critique contemporary strains of imperial historiography.

HECTOR'S HESITATIONS

Having established the salient characteristics of Clerk's alliterative project and his translation theory, we may now examine the historical didacticism in the Troy story itself. In the words of Lydgate, I now "leve the wordis and folwe the sentence" of the *Destruction* to demonstrate the way this text functions as an historical exemplar. This forces us to ask the following question: if Clerk remains faithful to Guido and specifies a particular English audience interested in alliterative poetry and Trojan historiography, which historical ideas does the *Destruction* uniquely express? To understand Clerk's perspective on England's Trojan identity, we should attend to the causes that he attributes to the fall of Troy. While the exhumation of Troy and the vivification of Hector that I describe later in the chapter provide compelling images of doom, the most pacifistic parts of the poem are found in the dissension within the Trojan war councils. Unlike the *Aeneid*, wherein gods manipulate events and the destiny of the Trojan line seems to be transparent, Clerk's *Destruction* illustrates a martial world that is almost completely determined by the will of military councils.[43] Within the councils, we hear the declamations of the great Trojan heroes Hector, Troilus, and Aeneas and the most direct arguments against war, which allow us to discern the heightened agency of humans in the *Destruction*. In comparison, Lydgate's *Troy*

43. Of course, the *fatum* of Virgil's Aeneas is not as clear as it seems. Virgil shows great sympathy for those who suffer the pain caused by Aeneas' adherence to his destiny (i.e. Creusa, Dido, and Pallas) and it is clear that Aeneas himself does not understand his fate. When he observes his future on Vulcan's shield, he does not comprehend its significance ["rerumque ignarus"]. See Virgil's *Aeneid*, in *Opera*, ed. R. A. B. Mynors (Oxford: Oxford University Press, 1969), 8.730. See also Mihoko Suzuki, *Metamorphoses of Helen: Authority, Difference, and the Epic* (Ithaca: Cornell University Press, 1989), 144–49.

Book illustrates a world in which Fortune plays an enhanced role in causing a human tragedy that can only be redeemed through God's "good" providence. Providence assumes an empire-engendering potential for Lydgate that has no equivalent in Clerk's *Destruction*. The absence of providence for Clerk is precisely the point—humans cannot anticipate that martial investments will yield imperial benefits.

In the words of Clerk's Hector at the first war council, the Trojans suffer from not being able to perceive "the fer end what may fall after" (2246). This prophetic problem of failing to perceive one's destiny pleads for what Virgilian providence seems to provide: a certain future of imperial glory.[44] This providential theory of empire is most clearly articulated in Book VI of the *Aeneid*, when Anchises describes to Aeneas the transmigration of souls from Elysium into the future bodies of the founders and defenders of the Roman Empire:

> Nunc age, Dardaniam prolem quae deinde sequatur
> gloria, qui maneant Itala de gente nepotes,
> inlustris animas nostrumque in nomen ituras . . . (756–58).[45]

> [Come now, what glory shall follow hereafter the Dardan race, what children of the Italian clan shall remain, illustrious souls and heirs in our name . . .]

Examined uncritically, this ethereal transfer of power, in which an imperial spirit inhabits new bodies across time, provides hope and a justification for Roman sovereignty that is notably absent in the texts of Clerk and Guido. Lydgate's Hector, however, has a Virgilian ring to him: he exalts "good providence," but claims that "I hold it no prudence / To Fortune, ful of doubilnes" (2300–1). Even though the council agrees to acquiesce to Fortune's "doubilnes," Lydgate propagates a providential design that contains the potential for heroic souls to transmigrate from oblivion to glory. Clerk's Hector instead laments the absence of such providence; whereas Virgil's Aeneas is constantly nudged on by his fate, the *Destruction*'s Priam and his realm are essentially left to their own devices to determine the future of Troy.

44. By using the adjective "Virgilian," I am not claiming that the *Aeneid* and its imperialism can be read in any singular way at all. Instead, I refer to the Galfridian reading of Virgil that appropriates the *Aeneid*'s imperial genealogy for its own political ends (see my discussion in chapter 1, 20–26).

45. As clear as this vision seems, it is important to note that when Aeneas later leaves Anchises in the Underworld, he passes through the ivory gate of false dreams. Suzuki, *Metamorphoses of Helen*, 144.

This is not to say that fate plays no part in the *Destruction*, but a comparison of the role of fate within Guido's and Lydgate's texts reveals Clerk's enhanced attribution of human error to the fall of Troy. As I mentioned earlier about the missing section of Book I and II in the *Destruction*, Guido attributes blame for the "plague of great destruction" to both "the envious succession of the fates" and Laomedon's inhospitality. However, the role of the fates for Guido is minor and vague, especially in comparison to Virgil, and the brunt of the blame is placed on the actions of the military leaders such as Priam, who are the object of periodic invective throughout the narrative. After Antenor's diplomatic mission to Greece fails and Priam organizes a council of war, Guido halts the progression of the narrative briefly to reprove Priam's boldness and lack of self-control in pursuing war against the Greeks: "Set dic, rex Priame, quis fatorum casus infelix ad tante infelicitatis audaciam tue quietis animum instigauit ut frenare proprios animi motus tui, licet non sint in hominis potestate, per matura consilia minime potuisses, ut, dum licetbat, abstraheres ab iniquis consiliis pedem tuum, et dum licebat, sciuisses tuas preteritas dissimulare iacturas, que per tot annorum curricula forte poterant obliuione deleri?" [But, say, King Priam, what unhappy accident of the fates incited your peaceful heart to such unfortunate audacity, so that you were not able in the least to curb the unique impulses of your heart by mature counsels (although, these impulses are not in the control of man), so that while it was permitted, you might have withdrawn from evil counsels, and while it was permitted, you would have known how to disguise your past losses, which perhaps through the course of so many years could have been obliterated by forgetfulness?] (56–57). The uncertain dynamic between fate and human agency that Guido expresses here somewhat lessens the poignancy of his reprisal and confuses his message. Even though Guido acknowledges that the "fates incited" Priam to action and that these "impulses are not in the control of man," he expects that Priam should have been able to restrain his passion, avoid bad advice, and cover up his mistakes. In other words, "Even though you could not have prevented it, you should have."

To modern readers this reproof seems ridiculous and reflects what C. David Benson calls Guido's "inability to find God's guiding hand or any other logic in the ruin and carnage of the Trojan War."[46] Guido knows about the imminent destruction of Troy, but fails to express in clear terms the nature of providence and freewill. In his translation, Lydgate amplifies the confu-

---

46. C. David Benson, "'O Nyce World': What Chaucer Really Found in Guido Delle Colonne's History of Troy," *The Chaucer Review* 13.4 (1978–79): 308–15, at 310.

sion by claiming that the fault lies in "infelicité," "trouble," "hap," "destyné," "hateful influence," "sodeyn sort," "fortune graceles," "chaunce unhappy," "willful lust," and "fonnyd hardynes" (1797–804). Despite his variation of causes, Lydgate characteristically turns to "providence" to which Priam has been "[d]irked and blind" (1812). Thus, Lydgate doubly remains faithful to Guido's confusion and the presence of Virgilian providence, which naturally leads to even more frustrating interpretive ambiguity.

There is no such equivocation in Clerk's translation. Instead of trying to lay blame upon both the fates and Priam, Clerk directs the attack upon Priam:

> But say me sir kyng what set in þi hede
> What wrixlit þi wit & þi wille chaunget
> Or what happont the so haastely þi with hardnes of wille
> To put þe to purpas þat pynet þe aftur
> What meuyt the with malis to myn on þi harme
> And to cache a counse to combur þi selue rewme
> With daunger and drede of a dede hate
> ffor a lure þat was light & of long tyme
> Þat wold ȝepely haue bene forȝeton in yeres a few. (2059–67)

[But tell me sir king, what controlled your mind, what overcame your wit and changed your will, or what happened to you so hastily with a willful eagerness to put you to the purpose that you regretted afterwards? What moved you with malice to bring trouble to yourself and to accept counsel to harm yourself realm with danger and dread of a dire hate for a minor crime from a long time ago that would quickly have been forgotten in a few years?]

Clerk deftly avoids the discussion of the role of the fates through the employment of a strategy that has become his *modus operandi* in his translation of Guido: the obfuscation of the grammatical subject. To remain faithful as a translator, Clerk does not contradict his source and only cuts references to the fates so that Guido's question, "what unhappy accident of the fates incited your peaceful heart?" becomes a coupling of alliterative tags: "But say me sir kyng what set in þi hede / What wrixlit þi wit & þi wille chaunget?" Clerk's reversion to generality about "what" incited Priam's war mongering allows him to remain consistent with Guido while at the same time to alter slightly the object of the invective to the "malis" of the Trojan king that causes him "to cache a counse to combur þi selue rewme." Here an examination of Chetham's manuscript yields some interesting findings about this mystifying line.[47] I have quoted Matsumoto's diplomatic text above to show how the reading of the manuscript leads to at least two different readings. Rendered literally, the line means "to accept counsel to harm your self realm." Chetham most likely crossed out "selue" and wrote in "rewme," but we will never know whether "rewme" was in his copy text or was an addition by him or another reader because Clerk's translation of Guido at this point in the passage is relatively loose. Guido makes references later in the invective to the broader implications of the decision to go to war, but here they are less heavy handed than they are in *Destruction*. Clerk continues to criticize Priam by contending that "þi fall was so fuerse with so fele other" [your fall with so many others was so fierce] (2083), which continues the charge that Priam's actions will not only harm him "selue," but also his realm and future generations to come. In contrast to Virgil's providential model and Guido and Lydgate's oblique notions of the authority of the fates and providence, Clerk creates a martial world in which tragedy is driven not by the machinations of fate, but by human error. Clerk's emphasis on human fallibility is why the treason of Aeneas and Antenor, instead of the treachery of the Greeks, looms as the most significant cause of the fall of Troy.

In all of the texts, the argument against war falls on deaf ears and Troy's destruction commences. Guido, Lydgate, and Clerk all effectively urge for reasonable approaches to war, but a comparative reading reveals that the *Destruction* emerges as a raw expression of human freewill. Clerk's Trojan history then does not deride the "doubilnes" of Fortune or throw up its hands in cosmologic confusion, but rather directs its polemic at its human audience. To make the message palpable, Clerk continues the attack upon martial designs through the figure of Hector and his response to his father's proposal to attack the Greeks.[48] While this greatest of Trojan heroes acknowledges the need to avenge the rape of Hesione and the destruction of the first Troy, he proceeds to beg Priam:

Consider to our cause with a clene wit
Let our gate be so gouernet þat no grem follow
Ne no torfer be tyde ne no tene after

---

47. Panton and Donaldson read the first part of the line as "to cache a connse" and consider "connse" to be a corruption of "comse," which means "beginning," but a close look at the manuscript indicates that the word could also be the "counse" or "counsel" of Matsumoto's text. Given Guido's emphasis on mature and evil "consilia," "counse" is the preferable reading.

48. This folio of the manuscript is especially worn, possibly indicating its interest or value to its readers.

Ouer lokes all lures to the last ende
What wull falle of þe first furth to þe myddis
Sue forth to þe secund serche it within
And loke to þe last end what lure may happyn.
Hit is no counsel to encline ne to calle wise
Ne not holsom I hope þat hedis to þe first
And for ses not the fer end what may falle after. (2237–46)

[Consider our cause with a clear mind. Let our conduct be so guarded that no grief will follow, neither harm nor injury will be incurred afterwards. Examine all losses that will occur by the end, what will happen in the beginning onwards to the midway point. Proceed forth to the next effect, search it within, and look to the very end what destruction may follow. It is not wise or prudent advice to follow, I think, to attend to what happens first and not foresee the far end or what may happen afterwards.]

Through this bold speech, Hector implores Priam to consider not only the short term rewards or consequences, but also "the last ende," which signifies the future ramifications of their warlike endeavors. The repetitive emphasis on the "ende" in this passage not only encourages the reader to consider the destructive end of the Trojans but also originates singularly in Hector's multiple references to the "end" (*fine*) of their war with the Greeks in Guido's text (59–60), which is an instructive alteration to his unacknowledged source, Benoît de Sainte-Maure's *Le Roman de Troie*. In Benoît's romance, Hector also speaks these words of caution about "la fin" (3804), but only after Antenor ardently urges the same message:

Quar ço nos diënt li autor:
Qui grant chose vueut envaîr,
La fin a qu'il en deit venir
Deit esguarder, se il est sages,
Que n'en vienge honte e damages. (3646–50)[49]

[For this is what authorities tell us: whoever wishes to attack a great thing, if he is wise, will examine the conclusion at which he ought to arrive so that he does not bring about shame and harm.]

---

49. Benoît de Sainte-Maure, *Le Roman de Troie*, ed. Leopold Constans (Paris: Firmin Didot, 1904–12).

By having Antenor remain silent and Hector speak these wise words of caution, Guido makes the sentiment more authoritative. After all, Antenor becomes an insidious traitor while Hector dies valiantly for a cause he supports only through his loyalty to his father. Given this shift, the Guido-tradition posits Hector as the tragic hero of the history, who represents the fall of reason that haunts the imperial ideology, not only of the Trojans, but also of their progeny.

Other characters such as Cassandra and Helenus support Hector's hesitations, but their speeches are swallowed up by the cacophony of Trojan voices that praise the war effort. Paris and Troilus both urge for war and their support of Priam sways the council in favor of Paris' expedition to Greece, thereby continuing the progression of events that lead to the destruction of Troy. Hector eventually joins the fray with the rest of the Trojans and becomes so caught up in his bloodlust that even his wife Andromache's nightmare about his death cannot convince him to refrain from battle. As soon as it seems that his chilling words are forgotten, Achilles treacherously slays him, which elicits an outpouring of Trojan grief that is embodied in Hector's pseudo-resurrected body seated in his tomb. Hector's death is the beginning of the end of Troy, and the many lines devoted to the description of his tomb remind us of his wise counsel that urged Priam to consider the consequences of war.

EXHUMING TROY

As I will suggest throughout the book, careful attention to death and resurrection is characteristic of the alliterative romances of the Guido-tradition. Christine Chism has argued a similar point, even going to so far to imply that alliterative romances writ large serve to "animate British history by reviving past bodies," citing the examples of the giant of St. Michael's Mount, Sir Priamus, and even the Green Knight.[50] These "revivals" of characters who refuse to die serve as a clever conceit for the Revivalist claim about a moribund verse form that is resurrected in the fourteenth century, but as Blake and Schiff have suggested, such arguments place undue weight on alliterative poetry as a coherent genre.[51] Yet, Chism's contention that the alliterative romances invoke "the past to reinforce or challenge contemporary ideologies" certainly applies to Clerk's project, which weakens the triumphalistic

---

50. Chism, *Alliterative Revivals*, 6.
51. Blake, "Middle English Alliterative Revivals," 205–14; Schiff, *Revivalist Fantasy*.

force of the *translatio imperii* both through the animation of dead bodies and through the revived and dismembered figure of Troy.[52] Through a comparative analysis of the death and pseudo-resurrection of Hector and the destruction and reconstruction of the First Troy in both the *Destruction* and Lydgate's *Troy Book,* Clerk's rendering of these events emerges as uniquely damnatory of the exploitation of Trojan heritage of Britain as a legitimizing tool.

While Chism acknowledges that alliterative romances interrogate historical notions of linearity, she does not consider the figure of the destroyed city of Troy that fractures the coherence of these narratives. She characterizes the more substantial romances (*Sir Gawain and the Green Knight, The Wars of Alexander, The Siege of Jerusalem,* and the alliterative *Morte Arthure*) as engaging in the message of "caveat imperator," but because she does not consider the influence that the *Destruction* or the Guido-tradition exacts on these poems, she does not attend to the historiographic problems they pose.[53] As I demonstrate, the resurrections that occur in the *Destruction* transcend benign interrogations of the *translatio imperii*—they reveal how each invocation of Trojan historiography awakens a dangerous past that exposes the destructive implications of imperial desires. The half-dead figure of Troy adds a pessimistic coloring to these alliterative romances that does more than admonish—it condemns.

The clearest example of a "revived body" in the *Destruction* is that of Hector, who is treacherously slain from behind by Achilles and then memorialized by Priam in a morbidly iconographic monument. To understand Clerk's representation of the revival, we should first turn to Lydgate's exegetical version of Hector's death in Book III. Rather than dwell on the unscrupulous Achilles in Guido's text, Lydgate shifts the focus to the avarice of Hector. Instead of emphasizing Hector's prowess in battle, Lydgate homilizes upon the deadly consequences of coveting. After slaying a Greek king, Hector strips the armor of this dead warrior, leaving his back vulnerable to Achilles' spear. This inspires Lydgate to lament

> But out, allas, on fals covetyse,
> Whos gredy fret—the whiche is gret pité—

52. Chism, *Alliterative Revivals,* 9, 30–33. See Simpson, *Reform and Cultural Revolution,* 78; W. R. J. Barron, *English Medieval Romances* (London: Longman, 1987), 112–17. Simpson contends that Barron incorrectly categorizes *Destruction* as a romance. Even though *Destruction* exhibits few characteristics of French romance, I suggest that we read it as a historical romance— its analogues would not only be Geoffrey's *Historia*, but also *The Wars of Alexander,* the *Siege of Jerusalem* and the alliterative *Morte Arthure*.
53. Chism, *Alliterative Revivals,* 31.

> In hertis may nat lightly staunched be.
> The etyk gnaweth be so gret distresse
> That it diffaceth the highe worthines
> Ful ofte sythe of thies conquerours
> And of her fame rent aweie the flours.
> Desyre of havynge in a gredy thought
> To highe noblesse sothly longeth nought;
> No swiche, spoillynge, nor robberie
> Apartene not to worthi chivalrye:
> For covetyse and knyghthod, as I lere,
> In o cheyne may nat be knet yfere;
> For kouthe it is that ofte swiche ravyne
> Hath cause ben and rote of the ruyne
> Of many worthi—whoso liste take hede—
> Like as ye may now of Hector rede
> That sodeinly was brought to his endynge
> Only for spoillynge of this riche kyng. (3.5354–72)

[But curses, alas, on false avarice, whose greedy gnawing—which is a great pity—may not lightly be assuaged in hearts. This desire causes such great distress that it disfigures the high worthiness very often experienced by these conquerors and rends away the flowers of their fame. The desire for possessions or covetous longing does not truly belong in high nobility; no such stealing, spoiling, or robbery appertains to worthy chivalry: for avarice and knighthood, as I understand them, may not be knitted together in a chain; for it is known that often such greed has been the cause and root of the ruin of many worthies—whoever wishes take heed—such as you may now read about Hector who suddenly was brought to his ending just for despoiling this rich king.]

These lines, entirely unique to Lydgate's version, more than simply provide material for those inclined to patristic exegesis and reading Troy's fall as a result of deadly sin. They give Hector a character flaw of imprudence, which taints his admirable anti-war declamation, desecrates the memorial that Priam erects for him, and reduces his status as the symbol of Trojan glory. Clerk, on the other hand, eschews this homiletic mode and reproduces faithfully the sequence of events that he finds in Guido's text. Hector dies through no sin of his own, but through the treachery of Achilles, which leaves his reputation as a virtuous warrior intact.

Hector's innocence at the moment of his death possesses symbolic significance, but his pseudo-resurrection garners more interest for Clerk since it translates further destruction. After describing the excessive mourning and fainting that ensues after the procession of Hector's dead body, he turns to the construction of his tomb. This is a natural sequence of events within the metonymy of the body as a representation of the city, since the city serves as what Henri Lefebvre calls a "guardian of civic unity" that "binds the living to the dead just as it binds the living to one another."[54] Monuments to the dead contain the civic chaos that ensues from the death of one of its members, particularly one such as Hector, a potential Trojan monarch. Hector's funerary structure is far from conventional, however. Instead of enclosing his body in the privacy of a crypt that would allow the body to decay away from the human eye, Priam pursues a ghastly public alternative:

> Then priam the prise kyng prestly gert come
> Maisturs full mony & men þat were wise
> He fraynet at þo fre with a fyn wille
> How the korse might be keppit in his kynd holl
> ffresshe vndefaced & in fine hew
> As a lede vpon lyue likyng to se
> And not orible ne vgly of odir to fele. (8726–32)

[Then Priam the prized king quickly summoned skilled artisans and wise men. With great eagerness, he asked the men how the corpse might be kept in its natural state, fresh, undefaced, and in a fine hue, just as a live man were to appear, and not horrible, ugly, or of a foul odor.]

Priam's consultation with Trojan undertakers reflects a desire to revive Troy's greatest hero and maintain the power that he wielded as a "lede vpon lyue." As Troy's greatest warrior, Hector is a metonym for the prowess of Troy and remains its martyr even until the final lines that list the warriors he killed in battle. Allowing his body to putrefy would seemingly foretell the decay of the city. In order to accomplish the impossible task of reviving the dead flesh, the architects of the tomb engage in what James Simpson cleverly characterizes as "macabre engineering."[55] They construct an elaborate monument that includes a tabernacle adorned with pure gold and fine stones, a walkway for

---

54. Henri Lefebvre, *The Production of Space,* trans. Donald Nicholson-Smith (Malden, MA: Blackwell, 1991), 235.
55. Simpson, *Reform and Cultural Revolution,* 89.

observers, a golden image of Hector, and even the seated body of Hector himself (8733–73).

> Þan þo maisturs gert make amyddes his hed
> A hole þurgh his horne pan hertely by craft
> There in put was a pipe with a prise ointment
> Of bavme & of balsamom þat brethed full swete
> With oþer maters mynget þat most were of strenght
> Conseruatours by craft þat cointly were made. (8774–79)

> [Then the artisans made in the center of his head a hole through his skull eagerly by skill; therein was placed a pipe containing a noble ointment of balsam that smelled very sweet, mixed with other elements, which were of a strength cunningly fashioned by the undertakers' craft.]

The detail of the embalming and the translation of Guido's "uertice" (177) to the Anglo-Saxon kenning "horne pan," meaning "skull" or "horn pane," invites us to read Hector's body as a coroner would, following the route of the vivifying liquid from his head down to his feet as if through an x-ray or autopsy.[56] This description of the course of the "lycour" that enlivens Hector's flesh and the illustration of the additional adornments that the death ministers add to his tomb continue for another thirty-nine lines (8780–818), a detailed digression that has no equal in the rest of the poem. The effect is the invocation and establishment of Hector's presence as a vivified fragment of Troy's glorious past for all to witness.

Yet, this decryption of Hector's body subverts the representative power of the body politic. In the case of most funerary monuments, as Lefebvre suggests, such civic architecture "produces living bodies" and the "animating principle of such a body, its presence, is neither visible nor legible as such, nor is it the object of any discourse, for it reproduces itself within those who *use* the space in question, within their lived experience."[57] For the Trojan people, Hector's presence is eerily visible, collapsing the metonymic distance between the city and the body. Rather than represent the transcendence of

---

56. The later Middle English equivalent "braynne-panne" is used by Sir Thomas Malory in both martial and "crime-scene" contexts. Its suitability for the description of battle is shown after Launcelot rescues Gwenyver from the fire, in which he "smote sir Gaherys and sir Gareth upon the brayne-pannes" (1178.2). The latter use, which recalls Hector's "autopsy," would seem to fit a modern crime scene investigation. Tristram is identified by the gap in his sword, which is consistent with the fragment that was "founde in the braynne-panne of sir Marhalte" (389.26). Eugène Vinaver, ed., *The Works of Sir Thomas Malory* (Oxford: Clarendon Press, 1967).

57. Lefebvre, *The Production of Space*, 137.

the body politic in the manner of a funerary effigy, his enlivened body is a testament of his death and an historical exemplar of the horrors of war that is reaffirmed in the listing of the dead at the end of the poem. By contrast, Lydgate is not satisfied to leave his hero as a fixture in a living monument. Instead, he follows Chaucer's *Troilus and Criseyde* in stellifying his hero, whereby Hector's "soule" (5749) leaves this temple to enjoy the "joie and blisse above the sterris clere" (5752).[58] This implies that his presence can no longer be found in the tomb, but in the heavens, an image that is strikingly similar to the Virgilian transmigration of souls. Whereas Lydgate's Hector becomes a glorious constellation for future observation and imitation, Clerk's revived Hector carries with him the presence of the past and the potential for future horror on earth. He now sits, like a saint's body preserved for pilgrims who seek spiritual healing, as a martyr who spoke the truth about war and paid dearly for it.

Hector's specter, in the manner of the Green Knight's head, also terrifies onlookers in the *Destruction* and inspires bellicosity. Priam and his architects defy the putrefaction of Hector's body and postpone their own destruction, but not for long. A death ritual for Hector at his tomb becomes the occasion for the encounter between Achilles and Hector's sister Polyxena, which inspires a love-struck Achilles to beseech the Greeks to cease their siege in return for Polyxena (9089–400). Here, as is often found in medieval romances such as *Yvain and Gawain* and Chaucer's *The Knight's Tale,* a knight woos a woman over the corpse of his adversary.[59] In this case, the sight of Polyxena prostrate in front of Hector's body, "sittyng full hoole"

58. Chaucer describes Troilus "As he that was withouten any peere, / Save Ector, his tyme, as I kan heere . . . / And whan that he [Troilus] was slayn in this manere, / His lighte goost ful blisfully is went / Up to the holughnesse of the eighthe spere, / In convers letyng everich element; / And ther he saugh with ful avysement / The erratik sterres, herkenyng armonye / With sownes ful of hevenyssh melodie." See *Troilus and Criseyde* in *The Riverside Chaucer,* ed. Larry Benson, 3rd ed. (Boston: Houghton Mifflin, 1987), 5.1803–4, 1807–13.

59. And in each case, the living knights grieve: Ywain grieves after watching the translation and Palamon actually participates in the rite, wearing the adornments of a mourner (2882–84). See Mary Flowers Braswell, ed., *Sir Perceval of Galles and Ywain and Gawain* (Kalamazoo: Medieval Institute Publications, 1995), 869–74. Such lamentation for an enemy is a convention of romance that is especially well illustrated in the death ritual of Darius in the alliterative poem *The Wars of Alexander.* See Hoyt N. Duggan and Thorlac Turville-Petre, ed., *The Wars of Alexander* (Oxford: Oxford Univ. Press, 1989), 3449. As Alexander observes Darius' funeral, he "as a barne gretis," a ritual that he performs at the death of all his enemies. Chism argues that his tears allow him to move past the death of an honorable adversary and prepare himself to battle another enemy. Enemies like Darius possess hero status, even in the eyes of Alexander, and a proper ritual of honor allow them "to be mourned more cleanly; dead heroes do not haunt as powerfully as dead victims." Thus, by participating in the grief, winning knights move from battle to battle without carrying the guilt and consequences of dishonoring their defeated foes. See *Alliterative Revivals,* 143.

(9118), wounds Achilles and restrains his bloodlust. His lovesickness even causes him to grieve as Polyxena does at the feet of the enlivened Hector. Just as "teris . . . trickilt on her [Polyxena's] tryet chekes" (9133), "terys on his [Achilles'] chekes / Ronen full rifely" (9209–10). While these similar phrases equalize the two characters in their grief, the tears of Polyxena only "trickle," while those of Achilles "run abundantly." Thus, Hector's revived body serves as the catalyst for a wounding that causes even more significant damage upon Achilles' martial identity than he had inflicted on Hector in defeating him on the battlefield. However, this transformation from Greece's greatest warrior to swooning lover only temporarily encumbers Hector's slayer and stalls the martial intentions of the Greeks. As Simpson notes, Polyxena's "grief at Hector's death initiates a terrible and determinant pattern of violence and recrimination . . . [that] . . . can only finally be resolved by her sacrifice, which ends the Trojan war by allowing the Greeks to return, to their own disasters."[60] Her death is intimately connected not only with Achilles' tomb, upon which she is slain by Achilles' son Pyrrhus, but also with the artificially revived Hector, whose half-dead presence haunts the rest of the narrative and dooms all, both Trojans and Greeks, to destruction.

The preserved Hector serves as the clearest, but not the most poignant, example of a "revived body" in the *Destruction*. When Priam returns to the ruins of the first Troy that his father Laomedon had ruled, he "[s]egh the buyldynges brent & beton to ground" (1518) and bewails the horrific sight so intensely "þat all his wongys were wete for weping of terus" (1520). As the first Trojan mourner of the poem, Priam's example becomes the basis for the many future descriptions of grief. Clerk commonly uses the image of the tears on the faces of the grief-stricken for hyperbolic effect. For example, after Hector, Deiphobus, and Troilus have all been slain, Paris weeps so profusely, that his tears "[o]uer flowet his face fell on his brest / With streamys out straght þurgh his stithe helme" (10661–62). The fates of these heroes and the city they defend are intimately connected, and the grief crescendos from Priam's first gaze on the ashes of the first Troy until the final destruction of the new city. Priam's sorrow over the fallen city is the exemplar for other scenes of the mourning, indicating that we should understand Priam's object of weeping to be not only an incinerated city, but also a dismembered body that he desperately hopes to revive.

Clerk may have assimilated this notion of the "city as a body" from Virgil's *Aeneid*, a text to which he refers directly three times (49, 1492, 12914). At the end of the description of the fall of Troy, Virgil describes the destroyed

---

60. Simpson, *Reform and Cultural Revolution*, 94.

Troy, which is embodied in the decapitated Priam, as "ingens litore truncus, / auulsumque umeris caput et sine nomine corpus" [a monstrous torso on the sea-shore, a head torn off the shoulders and a body without a name] (2.557–58). According to the imperialistic reception of Virgil, the fragmented parts of Troy are dispersed seeds that germinate to become a Roman empire that will fully bloom under Caesar Augustus, but for Clerk, such raisings of the dead do not lead to life and imperial power, but instead to death and greater destruction. In the *Destruction,* Priam attempts to revive Troy in a way that prefigures his later embalming of Hector: he commissions masons, miners, and architects to resurrect the destroyed city. Even the language Clerk uses to describe the rebuilding evokes a ritual exhumation of a dead body. Clerk explains how the workers "[s]erchit vp the soile þere þe Citie was" (1533), which indicates that digging took place. The use of "serchit vp the soile" is especially evocative because it refers doubly to digging and searching, two actions that go hand in hand in exhumation. Interestingly, there is no such grave digging vocabulary in Guido; he merely recounts how the workers "amotis ruderibus et ruinosis locis purgatis" [removed the debris and cleared the ruins] (46), which characterizes the first Troy more as detritus to be removed than a body to be preserved. Lydgate's version is fairly similar to Clerk's, but too architecturally specific to be rendered as an exhumation. The digging that occurs is given a purpose: "To make sure the fundacioun" (537). Lydgate uses several lines to describe the removal of the ruins and the building of the new wall, which reflects his interest in the details of the New Troy's construction. By contrast, Clerk's divergence from his source here prepares his readers for Priam's further futile attempts to "revive" Troy, including his refreshment of Hector's flesh through a constantly flowing embalming liquid and his final attempts to resist the Greeks and the treason of Aeneas and Antenor.

Clerk is more interested in revealing to his audience of Trojan inheritors how these attempted resurrections ultimately fail than how they temporarily succeed. Even though Priam effectively digs up the ashes of Troy and "byld vp a bygge towne of þe bare vrthe" (1534) to reestablish Trojan power, his newly erected city suffers even more complete destruction than its predecessor did. Clerk reminds the audience of their Trojan ancestry by calling Priam's realm a "new Troye" in the title to the fifth book despite the fact that his source reads "magne Troie" or "great Troy" (43) in the title and "secunde Troye" in the text of the book (46). Using the term "new Troye" reaffirms Clerk's familiarity with Geoffrey's *Historia,* which describes Brutus' search of the island for the site of the city that Diana had promised. On the land adjacent to the river Thames, "Condidit itaque ciuitatem ibidem eamque Troiam

Nouam uocauit. Ex hoc nomine multis postmodum temporibus appellata tandem per corruptionem uocabuli Tinouantum dicta fuit" [he founded the city and called it New Troy. It was known by this name for many ages thereafter until at last, through corruption of the name, it was called Trinouantum] (14).[61] While the "new Troye" in his title is more evidence that Clerk knew Galfridian history, it also suggests that he was aware of the contemporary uses of the term. During the reign of Richard II, at the Smithfield tournament held in October 1390, the Crie des Joustes proudly refers to London as "la neufe troy," which serves as one of many examples of appropriations of Trojan identity.[62] Another late fourteenth-century alliterative poet, the anonymous author of *Saint Erkenwald* uses the same label for London: "Now þat London is neuenyd hatte þe New Troie, / þe metropol and þe mayster toun hit euermore has bene" (25–56).[63] On the surface, this statement expresses an enthusiastic acceptance of the *translatio imperii* and a subsequent optimism about Troy's future that is absent in *Destruction*, but the fact that the *Erkenwald*-poet calls London a "New Troie" suggests that Clerk may have used the same label to evoke "London" to establish an insular Trojan geography in the minds of his readers.

The doomed New Troy of the *Destruction* possesses added significance when juxtaposed with the New Troy that appears in John Gower's contemporary Latin poem, *Vox Clamantis*. Gower's first book, written in response to the 1381 Rising, describes a dream he had:

A dextrisque nouam me tunc vidisse putabam
Troiam, que vidue languida more fuit:
Que solet ex muris cingi patuit sine muro,
Nec potuit seras claudere porta suas. (1.879–882)[64]

[On my right I then thought I saw New Troy, who was weak in the habit of a widow. Ordinarily surrounded by walls, it lay open without a wall, and the gate could not shut its bars.]

---

61. The *Historia Regum Britannie* of Geoffrey of Monmouth, I: Bern, Burgerbibliothek, MS. 568, ed. Neil Wright (Cambridge: D. S. Brewer, 1991).
62. F. H. Cripps-Day, *The History of the Tournament in England* (London: Quaritch, 1918), xli–xlii; Sheila Lindenbaum, "The Smithfield Tournament of 1390," *Journal of Medieval and Renaissance Studies* 20 (1990): 1–20; Juliet R. V. Barker, *The Tournament in England, 1100–1400* (Woodbridge: Boydell, 1968), 100.
63. Ruth Morse, ed., *Saint Erkenwald* (Cambridge: D. S. Brewer, 1975).
64. For a discussion of Gower's composition of Book One in response to the 1381 rising, see Eric W. Stockton, ed., *The Major Latin Works of John Gower: The Voice of One Crying and The Tripartite Chronicle* (Seattle: University of Washington Press, 1962), 11–32.

Using the image of a powerless Troy as a representation of London's vulnerability to revolt, Gower envisions a city that does not bear the trappings of empire, but rather lies exposed and ripe for plunder. Clerk's New Troy, on the contrary, has walls and fortifications aplenty, which he describes in detail for 153 lines (1535–1687), but the effect is not to boast New Troy's indestructibility. Instead, Clerk's tone is nostalgic:

> Was neuer sython vnder son Cite so large
> Ne neuer before as we fynd fourmyt in vrthe
> Nonso luffly on to loke in any Lond out. (1538–40)

[There was never since under the sun a city so large; never before would we find one so formed on earth nor one so lovely to look on in any land.]

Clerk not only reminds his readers of the New Troy's reformation from its grave in the "vrthe," but also contends that no future city will match its size or beauty. The mention of "never sython" is a brief moment of providence that prophesies the inability of future cities to match the glory of Troy. According to the *translatio imperii*, Troy's hereditary cities are Rome and, more significantly for Clerk's audience, London. This accords with the fate of this beautifully constructed New Troy, which the Greeks invaded

> And the bildynges bete doun to the bare erthe
> All the cite vnsarkenly þai set vppon fyre
> With gret launchaund lawes into the light ayre
> Wroght vnder wallez walt hom to ground
> Grete palis of prise put into askys
> With flames of fyre fuerse to be hold. (12005–10)

[and beat the buildings down to the bare earth. All of the city they fiercely set on fire with great launching strokes into the light air, toppled walls to the ground, reduced the great palace of renown to ashes with flames of fire fierce to behold.]

Clerk sends the ominous message that cities attempting to match Troy's glory will return to ashes in the end. Excising Guido's condemnation of the savagery of the Greeks (234), Clerk emphasizes the culpability of the Trojans themselves. His ire is directed instead at Aeneas and Antenor, whose homes have been spared, interjecting, "anger hom betyde!" [may they suffer for it!] (12015). Like Gower, Clerk is disgusted by the way Troy has been left without fortifications and rendered defenseless. The vulnerable city is literally beaten back down into the earth from which it had arisen and fire consumes what has been left standing.

As Simpson observes, these scenes are consistent reminders of how diplomacy has failed and "history is held in the balance by purely human passions and decisions."[65] Such an emphasis on human culpability emerges throughout the narrative, but most memorably after the Trojans fail to heed the advice against war.

> Hade the counsell ben kept of the knight Ector
> And the Ernyst speche Eftward of Elinus the Bysshop
> Cassandras care considret with all
> With the prophesy of Protheus put into hertys
> Troy with þi toures hade bene a toune noble
> And wond in his weile to the worldes ende. (2711–16)

[Had the counsel of the knight Hector been heeded, and afterwards Helenus the Bishop's earnest speech and Cassandra's fear considered as well, with the prophecy of Proteus taken to heart, Troy with its towers would have been a noble city, and would have dwelled in its wealth until the world's end.]

While Clerk never denies the power of divine providence, he crafts a world in which humans are the diplomatic agents of their own prosperity or demise. Unfortunately, Clerk's New Troy assumes the guise of the undead and tragically perpetuates the "plague of great destruction" to which it eventually succumbs.

A "DESTRUCTIVE" CONTRIBUTION TO TROJAN HISTORIOGRAPHY

The treatment of Hector's death and his tomb is emblematic of Clerk's perspective of the entire history of the Trojans. Rather than view Hector's death and Troy's fall as an opportunity for a rebirth or stellification that will spawn future heroes and empires, Clerk sees the destruction of Troy as an event of lamentable tragedy and loss. At the end of his history, following the example of Dares, Dictys, and Guido, there are no expressions of hope for future

---

65. Simpson, *Reform and Cultural Revolution*, 88.

generations, only the epitaphs of the dead and the ones they slew in battle. We find a compelling analogue in the treatment of Hector by Christine de Pizan, who by 1400–1 had begun to assume a position that was antithetical to many optimistic renderings of the Troy narrative.[66] Christine developed an increasingly pessimistic perspective of Hector that is reflected in her three representations of this Trojan hero in *Epistre Othea, Le Livre de la Mutacion de Fortune*, and *Cité des dames*.[67] In the last of her Hector narratives, *Cité des dames*, he is already dead, and his tomb is the macabre spectacle and catalyst for consequent devastation and death that we find in the *Destruction*.[68] As Lorna Jane Abray aptly notes, "Christine spoke of Hector not to praise him, but to bury him, to close the door on his elaborate tomb before his awe-inspiring corpse betrayed yet more of the living to their doom. Troy to her, like original sin, was a poisoned inheritance and Hector just another old Adam to be transcended."[69] Like Clerk, Christine contends that Hector's heroism has expired and any imitation of his martial prowess unnecessarily revives a contaminated Trojan line that should be left dead and buried.

Such a morbid ending did not suit the tastes of Lydgate, who eliminates the listing of the slain and substitutes a conclusion in which he identifies himself, lauds his patron Henry V, and pays homage to Chaucer. Since Lydgate was working from a source in Guido who was ambivalent about imperialism, his *Troy Book* naturally expresses hesitations and anti-war invective, but its approval of the *translatio imperii* is made manifest in its praise of Henry V. Lydgate not only names him "protector of Brutis Albyoun" (5.3377) and "[o]f Normaundie the myghti conquerour" (5.3381), but also goes on to make many references to his heritage that entitles him to rule in both England and France (5.3381–416). For Lydgate, the fall of Troy serves as an exemplar more for the mutability of worldly things and the consequences of sin than for the tragic consequences of war. Clerk, by contrast, makes no attempt to moralize or justify territorial expansion at the end of his poem and instead remains faithful to Guido's ending, which seals the tomb, so to speak, on Troy's glory.

66. *Oeuvres poétiques de Christine de Pisan*, ed. Maruice Roy (1896; repr. London: Johnson, 1975), 39; Judith L. Kellogg, "Christine de Pizan as Chivalric Mythographer: *L'Epistre Othea*," in *The Mythographic Art: Classical Fable and the Rise of the Vernacular in Early France and England*, ed. Jane Chance (Gainesville: University of Florida Press, 1990), 100–24, especially 109–11.
67. Lorna Jane Abray, "Imagining the Masculine: Chistine de Pizan's Hector, Prince of Troy," in *Fantasies of Troy: Classical Tales and the Social Imaginary in Medieval and Early Modern Europe*, eds. Alan Shepard and Stephen D. Powell (Toronto: Centre for Reformation and Renaissance Studies, 2004), 136–43.
68. See *Book of the City of Ladies*, trans. Earl Jeffrey Richards (New York: Persea, 1982), 47–51.
69. Abray, "Imagining the Masculine," 147.

Both the specter and unheeded counsel of Hector cast Troy's authority as an origin of empire buried in the soil. Though Troy's glory is not translated, something is passed on hereditarily. There are multiple references throughout the poem not only to British inheritance, but also to consequences that will affect future generations, presumably in the form of Guido's "plague of great destruction." The *Destruction of Troy* then translates to its English readers what it advertises: destruction. As I demonstrate in the following chapters, we witness this message not only in this poem, but also within other surviving alliterative romances that incorporate Trojan history in their narratives.

THREE

Violence
THE CORPOREAL TERROR OF THE ROMAN EMPIRE

IN HIS influential essay "The Critique of Violence," Walter Benjamin suggests that violent actions must be evaluated "within the sphere of means, themselves, without regard for the ends they serve."[1] As Giorgio Agamben points out, this moment in Benjamin's essay is informative for the relationship it establishes between sovereignty and law because it identifies violence as "a pure medium" and "a means that . . . is considered independently of the ends that it pursues."[2] Benjamin and Agamben's definition of violence, which eliminates its justificatory value, offers a useful characterization of one late-medieval English poet's representation of the corporeal violence inflicted on Jews in the first-century Roman siege of Jerusalem. The Jewish bodies that appear in the late fourteenth-century alliterative romance, *The Siege of Jerusalem*, are afflicted by a kind of violence that demands attention to the violence itself, not its "necessity" within salvation history. While the christological "ends" of such violence are the supersession of the old Judaic law and the punishment of Jews for their "crime" of crucifying Christ, the *Siege*-poet consistently diverts attention from this purpose to critique violence as

---

1. Walter Benjamin, "Zur Kritik der Gewalt," in Rolf Tiedemann and Hermann Schweppenhäuser, *Gesammelte Schriften*, vol. 2, pt. 1 (Suhrkamp, 1921), 179; translated by Edmund Jephcott in *Selected Writings, Vol. 1, 1913–1926*, ed. Marcus Bullock and Michael W. Jennings (Cambridge: Harvard University Press, 1996), 236.
2. Giorgio Agamben, *State of Exception*, trans. Kevin Attell (Chicago: University of Chicago Press, 2005), 61.

a means divorced from its end. The violated Jewish bodies possess no value or rights within the operation of Roman sovereignty over Jerusalem and are accordingly reduced to what Agamben calls "bare life."[3] As extinguishable entities, these Jewish *corpores* assume a didactic power that modulates this antisemitic homily with a condemnation of Roman imperialism: the disciplined bodies are on display, creating a collective image that teaches its audience both the vengeance of God and the cruelty of Roman imperial siegecraft.[4]

The *Siege* is primarily known as a vitriolic invective against the Jews for crucifying Christ that delights in describing scenes of excessive violence.[5] With the notable exceptions of Christine Chism, Randy Schiff, and Suzanne Yeager, few scholars have been able to avert their gaze from the horrifying fate of the Jews in the poem to acknowledge the complex investigations of Roman imperialism that emerge through these disturbing scenes of corporeal malady and dismemberment.[6] This chapter explores the way that the *Siege*-poet treats the bodies of the Jews and Romans as sites of anxiety-producing indeterminacy and recasts them as objects of both punishment and compassion. When the poem's scenes of corporeal violence are read as didactic in nature, it becomes clear that the graphic details of these scenes are a manifestation of a pessimistic martial discourse that fails to delight, but rather

---

3. Giorgio Agamben, *Homo Sacer: Sovereign Power and Bare Life* (Stanford: Stanford University Press, 1998).

4. I accept Gavin Langmuir's definition of antisemitism as an irrational form of anti-Judaism. Therefore, I use the adjective "antisemitic" to characterize the psychopathological discourse that colors the *Siege*-poet's illustrations of the Jews. Also, the fact that this poem was composed after the twelfth century, when Langmuir claims such antisemitism began, suggests that its composition originated from the tradition of Christian accusations of Jewish ritual murder, blood libel, and host desecration. See Langmuir's *Toward a Definition of Antisemitism* (University of California Press, 1990); Anna Sapir Abulafia, ed., *Religious Violence between Christians and Jews: Medieval Roots, Modern Perspectives* (New York: Palgrave, 2002), xvi.

5. For an assessment of scholarship that focuses on the antisemitic aspects of the poem, see Elisa Narin van Court, "*The Siege of Jerusalem* and Augustinian Historians: Writing About Jews in Fourteenth-Century England," *Chaucer Review* 29, no. 3 (1995): 227–48. Derek Pearsall condemns the poem as a "model of a decadent poetic" in *Old and Middle English Poetry* (London: Routledge & K. Paul, 1977), 169. A. C. Spearing similarly decries its "horrible delight in the suffering of the Jews," in *Readings in Medieval Poetry* (Cambridge: Cambridge University Press, 1987), 167, 172. More recently, Ralph Hanna claims that the poem contains "cheerfully sanctioned violence" in "Contextualizing *The Siege of Jerusalem*," *Yearbook of Langland Studies* 13 (1999): 109–21, at 110.

6. Christine Chism, *Alliterative Revivals* (Philadelphia: University of Pennsylvania Press, 2002), 181–88, at 181; Randy Schiff, "The Instructive Other Within: Secularized Jews in *The Siege of Jerusalem*," in *Cultural Diversity in the British Middle Ages: Archipelago, Island, England,* ed. Jeffrey Jerome Cohen (New York: Palgrave-Macmillan, 2008), 135–51; Suzanne Yeager, "The Crusade of the Soul in *The Siege of Jerusalem*," in *Jerusalem in Medieval Narrative* (Cambridge: Cambridge University Press, 2008), 78–107.

instills a deep, emotionally overwrought ambivalence about the horrors of war and empire-building. The sympathy for the Jews that the *Siege*-poet interjects directs attention to the cruelty, imperial intentions, and internal division of a Roman Empire that had been fictively recast as newly Christian. Ultimately, the relentless succession of scenes of violence demands that readers question the martial ethics not only of the superseded pagan Roman Empire of Nero, but also of constructions of empire based on the logic of Christian "justice" embodied in the converted Titus and Vespasian.

As hard as they may try, however, Titus and Vespasian are unable to shed their Old Roman imperial identities. Even after the virtuous Jew Josephus heals his crippled body, Titus cannot control the wrath against the "Christ-killers" in exacting the siege that he has inherited from his father Vespasian, who is continually described as "wroþe" [angry] (371), "wode wedande wroþ" [furious raging wildly] (385), and "wroþ as a wode bore" [angry as a wild boar] (781) in his confrontations with his Jewish enemies, an emotion that is in direct contrast to the Jews who talk "mekly" [meekly] (338) and fight as "ferce men & noble" [fierce and noble men] (867).[7] The *Siege*-poet's compassionate characterization of the Jews is unique given his sources in Flavius Josephus' *Jewish War* and Ranulph Higden's *Polychronicon,* which describe the Jews as filled with "impetuosity and unbridled rage" (6.159)[8] and "furor cum temeritate" (429).[9] Through new interpretations of these scenes, the *Siege*-poet attributes the Jewish rage in his sources to the vengeance of Vespasian, which he consequently translates to Titus when he grants him control of the siege. The translation of power is inextricably linked to the same kind of vengeance that infects Priam after the death of Laomedon and the destruction of the first Troy.

  7. All citations from the poem refer to *The Siege of Jerusalem,* ed. Ralph Hanna and David Lawton, EETS OS 320 (Oxford: Oxford University Press, 2003).
  8. All references to *Jewish Wars* are from Flavius Josephus, *The Jewish Wars,* trans. H. St J. Thackeray (Cambridge: Harvard University Press, 1928; rpt. 1990); E. Narin van Court, "The *Siege of Jerusalem* and Recuperative Readings," in *Pulp Fictions of Medieval England: Essays in Popular Romance,* ed. Nicola McDonald (Manchester: Manchester University Press, 2004), 151–70, at 157. Until Hanna and Lawton's study of the *Siege*-poet's use of Josephus, scholars had assumed that the *Siege*-poet either used the fourth century loose Latin translation of Josephus attributed to one "Hegisippus" or did not have access to Josephus at all. See E. Kölbing and Mabel Day, eds. *The Siege of Jerusalem* (Oxford: Oxford University Press, 1932), xxi. Hanna and Lawton identify a closer translation of Josephus by Rufinus of Aquileia (fl. ca. 385–410) that survives in over two hundred manuscripts and contains multiple parallel passages to *The Siege of Jerusalem.* See Hanna and Lawton, *The Siege of Jerusalem,* xl–lv.
  9. Future citations of the *Polychronicon* and John Trevisa's Middle English translation refer to Ranulph Higden, *Polychronicon, Together with the English Translation of John of Trevisa and an Unknown Writer of the Fifteenth Century,* eds. Churchill Babington and Joseph R. Lumby (London: Longmans, Green, and Co., 1869). Trevisa translates this phrase as "woodnesse and folye." See Narin van Court, "The *Siege of Jerusalem* and Recuperative Readings," 157.

Titus and Vespasian, as representatives of a Christian Roman Empire, would have held a unique significance for a late fourteenth-century English audience because they serve both as the imperial predecessors of England and as the human hands of divine vengeance. The extensive illustrations of Roman siegecraft and glorified annihilation of a heathen Jerusalem have even led Malcolm Hebron to claim that poem "emphasizes the heroism of the Romans and the exotic strangeness of the defenders."[10] While I believe this reading can be supported, this chapter argues the opposite, claiming that the heroism of the Romans is undercut by intimate and sympathetic depictions of Jewish corporeal destruction. At times, it may appear that the *Siege*-poet "cheerfully sanction[s]" the violence the Romans inflict upon the Jews, but his overall perspective of Christian imperialism is more ambivalent than it seems.[11]

This interrogation of imperialism is remarkable because it runs counter to the dominant ideology of empire in the Middle Ages, that of the *translatio imperii*. Rather than adhere to this optimistic model of imperial translation, the *Siege*-poet draws on the skeptical historiography of John Clerk's *Destruction of Troy*, Guido delle Colonne's *Historia destructionis Troiae*, and William of Newburgh's *Historia rerum Anglicarum*. In making his own mark on this historical tradition, the *Siege*-poet interrogates the logic of empire-formation, which requires the destruction of one empire for the birth of the next, and accentuates the synecdochic relationship between cities and bodies. By treating the bodies of Jewish victims and Roman conquerors as irredeemable casualties of imperialism, he articulates what Agamben has characterized as the biopolitical nature of the sovereign body, which inflicts corporeal violence to assert power.[12] Agamben's theory of sovereignty originates in the ancient Roman law that posited criminals as *homines sacri*, a label that accorded them a contradictory status as both sacred and profane. In other words, the *homo sacer* may not be sacrificed, yet he may be killed by anyone with impunity.[13] This ambivalence of the sacred eliminates any divine or civil value for the criminal and reduces him to the status of "bare life."[14] Such an evacuation of criminal life makes all humans potential *homines sacri* and subject to unsanctionable killing by state or sovereign authorities. Furthermore, if the sovereign is, as Carl Schmitt influentially suggests, "he who

---

10. Malcolm Hebron, *The Medieval Siege: Theme and Image in Middle English Romance* (Oxford: Clarendon Press, 1997), 124.
11. Hanna, "Contextualizing the *Siege of Jerusalem*," 110.
12. Agamben, *Homo Sacer*, 78–89.
13. H. Bennett, "Sacer esto," *Transactions of the American Philological Association* 61 (1930): 5.
14. Agamben, *Homo Sacer*, 8.

decides on the state of exception," sovereignty is an entity that exists outside of the law.[15] Decisions about life and death then endow the sovereign with political power, establishing a sphere that Agamben calls "that of the sovereign decision, which suspends law in the state of exception and thus implicates bare life within it."[16] Within the eyes of a Christianized Roman Empire, Jerusalem and all of its inhabitants are subject to extermination that is justified outside of both messianic and secular law. The *Siege*-poet's critique of this reduction of the Jewish body to "bare life" reflects an awareness of the insidious operations of sovereignty and casts skepticism on historiographies that emphasize a redemptive optimism about the destruction of cities and the imperial glory of Rome.

CHRIST AS *HOMO SACER*

The most compellingly didactic figure that articulates pessimism about empire throughout the *Siege* is the mutilated body. Christ's scourging begins this motif, setting the inimitable example of a body that is both sacred to the faithful and criminal to his persecutors. As Sarah Beckwith notes, Christ's body, both in the late medieval passion and Eucharist, was "the very meeting place of the sacred and the profane" that acknowledged both his human and divine nature.[17] For modern anthropologists, the destroyed human body of Christ represents the paradox of the *homo sacer*. As Agamben points out, over time the Latin term *sacer* came to signify both sacrality and criminality, creating an ambivalence of the sacred that had been previously noted by Freud, among others. But in his examination of the phenomenon of *homo sacer*, Agamben suggests:

> What defines the status of *homo sacer* is therefore not the originary ambivalence of the sacredness that is assumed to belong to him, but rather both the particular character of the double exclusion into which he is taken and the violence to which he finds himself exposed. This violence—the unsanctionable killing that, in his case, anyone may commit—is classifiable neither as sacrifice nor as homicide, neither as the execution of a condemnation to death nor as sacrilege. Subtracting itself from the sanctioned forms of both

---

15. Carl Schmitt, *Political Theology: Four Chapters on the Concept of Sovereignty*, trans. George Schwab (Chicago: University of Chicago Press, 2005), 5.
16. Agamben, *Homo Sacer*, 83.
17. Sarah Beckwith, "Making the World in York and the York Cycle," in *Framing Medieval Bodies*, ed. Sarah Kay and Miri Rubin (Manchester University Press, 1994), 254–76, at 254.

human and divine law, this violence opens a sphere of human action that is neither the sphere of *sacrum facere* nor that of profane action.[18]

This "double exclusion" refers to the location of the *homo sacer* outside both human and divine jurisdiction, which attributes a liminality to the body that obscures its status as distinctly sacred or criminal. Agamben connects the structure of this violent *sacratio* of the victim with what he calls the "sovereign sphere," which is the political space wherein the sovereign subject has license to take human life without declaring the act as homicidal or sacrificial. This leads him to conclude that, "[t]he sacredness of life, which is invoked today as an absolutely fundamental right in opposition to sovereign power, in fact originally expresses precisely both life's subjection to a power over death and life's irreparable exposure in the relation of abandonment."[19] The quintessence of sovereign or imperial power is therefore the violence it may inflict on human life. Read this way, Christ's body, in its subjection to Roman sovereignty, possesses no individual right to life or sacrificial power and instead serves as the first casualty of Roman imperialism in the poem. The emphasis on Christ's corporeal destruction invites readers to dwell on his human, expendable nature in addition to his spiritual transcendence and central role in providential history.

Most critics will acknowledge that the fourteenth-century environment, which Eustache Deschamps described as an "age of tears, of envy, of torment, . . . [an] age of decline nigh to the end," may have contributed to the pessimism that runs through the extensive illustrations of bodily violence and digressive expressions of moral outrage.[20] Yet, few modern readers of the *Siege* are willing to acknowledge the genealogy of destruction that this poem reaffirms. Michael Livingston notes this "dark" perspective of the poem, but insists that the *Siege*-poet believed that "the downward spiral of society would end, finally and inevitably."[21] To prove this point, he turns to the poem's articulation of divine providence, which begins and ends with a visitation of Christ.[22] Even though the poem begins with a visit from Christ, it is a macabre vision, in which Christ is bloodied with scourges. In fact, the Christ who appears is a tortured and mutilated body:

---

18. Agamben, *Homo Sacer*, 82–83, 78–80.
19. Ibid., 83.
20. See Michael Livingston, ed., *The Siege of Jerusalem* (Kalamazoo, MI: Medieval Institute Publications, 2004), 30; Carter Lindberg, *The European Reformations* (Oxford: Blackwell, 1996), 24.
21. Livingston, *Siege of Jerusalem*, 30.
22. Ibid., 30–36. See in particular Livingston's helpful visual aid, "Figure 2: Structure of *Siege of Jerusalem*."

A pyler py3t was doun   vpon þe playn erþe,
His body bonden þerto   [and] beten with scourgis:
Whyppes of quyrboyle   [vm]bywente his white sides
Til al on rede blode ran   as rayn [i]n þe strete. (9–12)

[A pillar was placed down upon the plain earth, his body bound to it and beaten with scourges: whips of leather beset his white sides until blood ran on them as rain in the street.]

Such scenes of Christ's passion in the late fourteenth century were commonplace, but in this poetic context, Christ's scourged body serves both as the catalyst for future destruction and as an emblem of the corporeal violence that runs throughout the poem, just as his "blode ran as rayn [i]n þe strete" (12). The blood of the crucified Christ marks all in its path, from Titus' facial lesion (30–32) to the Eucharistic sacrifice of Maria's child (1081–88), both healing and destroying those it affects.

Likewise, if we expect "Christ's second visitation" at the end of the poem, we are bound to be disappointed.[23] After the Romans have obliterated Jerusalem and then sowed the land with salt (1295), they collect their booty and head home:

Whan alle was demed and d[on]   þey drow[en] vp tentis,
Trossen here tresour   and trompen vp þe sege.
Wenten syngyng away   and han here wille forþred
And hom ridden to Rome;   now rede ous oure Lord. (1337–40)

[When all was said and done they drew up their tents, packed up their treasure and trumpeted up the siege. Having had their will, they went away singing and rode home to Rome. May our Lord guide us.]

Presumably, Livingston reads the last half-line of the poem, "now rede ous oure Lord" (1340) as the path to Christ's second coming, which he claims, "lies just beyond the end of the poem," but such a stock ending surely carries less eschatological weight.[24] In fact, Livingston aptly notes that these lines describe a return to Rome, both physically and spiritually, which recognizes the path of the imperial line more than a fulfillment of prophecy.[25] Very little of this passage exhibits Christian optimism—rather it focuses on the trea-

23. Ibid., 35.
24. Ibid.
25. Ibid.

sure obtained and the gleeful singing of the soldiers as they return home. I suggest that we read this "joy" within the context of previous events, which are the destruction of the temple, the selling of the Jews, and the suicide of Pontius Pilate. Even if we read these events as divinely sanctioned and the consequence of Christian supersession, the ending stanza does not reaffirm the justice of these acts. Instead, the Romans ride away with an ill-gotten profit of imperialism established through an arrogant display of violence.[26]

FLAYING JEWS AND IMPERIAL SIEGECRAFT BY PROXY

Christ's spiritual transcendence in the passion sequence is modulated by his role as *homo sacer*, which posits his mutilated body as just one of the many casualties of Roman imperialism. As an object of corporeal punishment, Christ's body is surprisingly equated with the bodies of Jews, which are also scourged and crucified for their crimes.[27] An unforgettable instance of antisemitic corporeal violence is the flaying of Caiaphas and other Jewish clerics, an act that the *Siege*-poet describes as an antitype of Christ's passion and crucifixion:

> Domesmen vpon de[y]es demeden swyþe
> Þat ech freke were quyk fleyn þe felles of clene;
> [Firste] to be on a bent with blonkes todrawe
> And suþ honget on an hep vpon heye galwes,
> Þe feet to þe firmament, alle folke to byholden,
> With hony vpon ech [half] þe hydeles anonynted;
> Corres and cattes with claures ful scharpe
> Foure kagge[d] and knyt to Cayphases þeyes;
> Twey apys at his armes to angren hym more
> Þat renten þe rawe flesche vpon rede peces.
> So was he pyned fram prime with persched sides
> Tille þe sonne doun s[yed] in [þe] somere tyme. (697–708)

[The judges upon the dais quickly decide that each man would be flayed alive, cleaned of their skin; first to be drawn upon a field by horses, and

---

26. See also Chism, *Alliterative Revivals*, 181–88.
27. For more on these scenes of mutilation, see Roger Nicholson, "Haunted Itineraries: Reading *The Siege of Jerusalem*," *Exemplaria* 14, no. 2 (2002): 470–84; Hanna, "Contextualizing *The Siege of Jerusalem*," 109–21; Chism, "Profiting from Precursors in *The Siege of Jerusalem*," *Alliterative Revivals*, 155–88.

then hanged all together upon a high gallows, with feet to the sky for everyone to behold, the skinless anointed with honey upon each side, four dogs and cats with sharp claws caught and latched to Caiaphas' thighs, two apes[28] at his arms to torment him further that rent the raw flesh to red pieces. Thus was he pained from prime with pierced sides until the sun set in the summer sky.]

While such attention to the detail of the punishment may express antisemitic odium against Caiaphas and his fellow priests, there is more than sadistic hate going on here. This juridical act is performed with a pedagogic objective in mind—the revered clerics are not simply flayed, but flayed publicly, for "alle folke to byholden," which implies that all who observe the fate of their bodies will learn not to betray their allegiance to Rome. Vespasian intensifies this lesson by ordering the bodies to be burnt "into browne askes" (720) and their remains to be blown back over the walls of Jerusalem. He even takes his message a step further, beseeching his soldiers to cry out to the Jews, "Ther is doust for your drynke!" [There is dust for your drink!] (723) and "bidde hem bible of that broth for the bischop soule" [beseech them to imbibe that broth for the bishop's soul] (724). By having his men desecrate the remains of the priests and force the Jews to drink in their ashes, Vespasian orders the besieged to become cannibals. This cannibalism is a parody of the passion and the Eucharist: Caiaphas is tortured, executed, and consumed in a way that both meets and exceeds the violence of Christ's crucifixion. Like Christ, Caiaphas is pierced in his side (707), but the Romans amplify his suffering by having him drawn (699) and rent by dogs, cats, and apes (703–6). Caiaphas and his fellow priests' bodies are burnt into ashes to prevent any possibility of bodily resurrection and then they are literally, without any divine act of transubstantiation, fed to the living Jews. Whereas the Eucharistic wine is

---

28. Livingston reads "apys" as "apiece," which is plausible reading, but I prefer Hanna and Lawton's reading of "apes." While attaching apes might seem an excessive and ridiculous detail, I want to thank Tim Stinson, who is working on an electronic edition of the poem, for identifying the source for this in the *Bible en François*. See *La Vengeance de Nostre-Seigneur: The Old and Middle French Prose Versions*, 2 vols., ed. Alvin Ford, Studies and Texts 63, 115 (Toronto: Pontifical Institute of Mediaeval Studies, 1984–93). In describing this scene the *Bible* has, "Puis le fist atachier as cuisses a deus cheannes de fer, deus chiens et deus chaz et deus singes touz vis . . . " (116). The *Siege*-poet seems to keep the two apes (*singes*) of his source text. See also the Middle English prose translation of the *Bible*, edited by Phyllis Moe in *The Middle English Prose Translation of Roger d'Argenteuil's Bible en françois: Edited from Cleveland Public Library, MS Wq091.92–C.468*, Middle English Texts 6 (Heidelberg: Winter, 1977). This translation postdates the *Siege*, but that translator also rendered *singes* as *apis* (85). Stinson notes that the exemplar for this translation does not survive, but its appearance in the translation adds further support for the movement from *singes* to *apys*.

the catalyst for Christian communion, this cannibalistic dust is a catalyst for Jewish destruction. As Heather Blurton suggests, such representations of cannibalism enact "the too literal incorporation of one body into another. It is, however, precisely this metaphoric range—of incorporation, of the annihilation of the body and thus of identity—that lends cannibalism its utility as a metaphor for representing the dissolution of political as well as fleshly bodies."[29] Moreover, the forced consumption of the remains of their own high priests suggests that their religious and political fates will coalesce into a singular act of self-destruction.

At the same time that the *Siege*-poet establishes these Jews as antitypes of Christ, their dispersed remains symbolize the diaspora that the destruction of Jerusalem will effect. The *Siege*-poet sums up the nature and message of their death:

Þus ended coursed Cayphas   and his clerkes [twelf],
Al tobrused myd bestes,   brent at þe laste,
In tokne of tresoun   and trey þat [þ]e[y] wroȝt
Whan Crist þrow h[ere] conseil   was cached to deþ. (725–28)

[Thus ended the lives of cursed Caiaphas and his twelve priests, completely mangled by beasts, and finally burned, as a token of the treason and trouble that they caused when Christ was put to death through their counsel.]

Here the *Siege*-poet identifies "tresoun" as the sin that Caiaphas and the twelve clerics committed through their "conseil."[30] Through the use of these terms, the *Siege*-poet characterizes Caiaphas and the clerics as treasonous counselors for their role in convincing Pontius Pilate to inflict Roman punishment for a false cause. Their crime of deceptive "conseil" would have been subject to the Old Roman rite of *sacratio* in which the criminals would have been declared *sacer*.[31] Caiaphas and the clerics then join Christ as *homines sacri*, paying the ultimate price of their subjection to the Roman Empire. The more significant consequence of their misdeed is the ensuing destruc-

---

29. Heather Blurton, *Cannibalism in High Medieval English Literature* (New York: Palgrave MacMillan, 2007), 8.

30. The phrase "tokne of tresoun" is strikingly similar to the "token of vntrawþe"(2509) in *Sir Gawain and the Green Knight*. Gawain also sees his "token" as a didactic symbol, one which represents his treason against Bertilak. See *The Poems of the Pearl Manuscript: Pearl, Cleanness, Patience, and Sir Gawain and the Green Knight*, ed. Malcolm Andrew and Ronald Waldron (Exeter: University of Exeter Press, 2002).

31. Agamben, *Homo Sacer*, 85.

tion of their holy city, an obliteration that is intimately connected to the fate of their bodies.

If we follow the "flaying" motif throughout the poem, we discover that the death of the Jewish clerics parallels the imperial ascendancy of Vespasian and reaffirms what Agamben calls "the inseparability of the *imperium* from a power of death."[32] No figure of Roman history better embodies the association between empire and death than Vespasian's predecessor, Nero. After falling out of favor with the Roman people through his executions of Peter, Paul, and Seneca, and his burning of the city of Rome, Nero commits suicide, leaving the imperial throne vacant for a successor (897–900). After a series of botched emperorships, Vespasian is called to the seat, which raises a chivalric dilemma regarding the "breaking of truth." Vespasian had vowed to destroy Jerusalem and enact what he perceived as God's vengeance for the Jewish killing of Christ. He is, in the eyes of a Christian audience, also fulfilling the scriptural prophecy (Matthew 24:2), which would seemingly bind him to his task. Yet, Sir Sabyn of Syria beseeches Vespasian to break his vow and assume the imperial throne, using the following "flaying" logic: "For as fers is þe freke atte ferre ende / Þat of-fleis þe fel as he þat foot holdeþ" [The man at the far end who flays off the skin is as fierce as he who holds the foot] (991–92). The language used here describes men engaged in breaking a deer, whereby one flays from the "ferre ende" and the other holds the foot steady. Through this distich, Sir Sabyn makes the argument that Vespasian's chivalry and his attention to his vow to obliterate Jerusalem will remain intact even if his agency will reside at a geographical extremity, that is, Rome. By comparing the siege to the hunt, Sir Sabyn speaks to the sensibilities of an aristocratic audience who perceive hunting and hawking as staples of chivalric life. This flaying motif contributes to a larger pattern of hunting and hawking in the poem that David Lawton has characterized as "turning violence into the recreation of honourable men."[33] Vespasian agrees with this logic and leaves his son Titus to hold the foot steady, thereby privileging his own imperial stature to a fulfillment of Christian prophecy.

This means that Vespasian no longer has to be in the dirty business of repressing the Jews—the demands of the Roman Empire call him to exact the fate of Jerusalem callously from afar. As Hanna aptly puts it, "the total action of the poem is constituted by the displacement through which torn flesh blandly gets transformed into Vespasian's heroic resolve and by the rule

32. Ibid., 89.
33. Lawton, "Titus Goes Hunting and Hawking: The Poetics of Recreation and Revenge in *The Siege of Jerusalem*," in *Individuality and Achievement in Middle English Poetry*, ed. O. S. Pickering (Woodbridge, UK: D. S. Brewer, 1997), 105–17, at 117.

of agency through which such resolve animates cooperative underlings to perform 'enobling' acts of racial violence."[34] For Hanna and many readers, Vespasian's translation of power is presented to a late fourteenth- and early fifteenth-century audience as an act of good faith, which would support such imperial governance by proxy. To justify this reading, Hanna points to the poem's reception in the south by the scribe Richard Frampton, who in the 1410s copied the *Siege* into the manuscript now known as Cambridge University Library (CUL) MS. Mm.v.14. Hanna believes that Frampton worked for a "Lancastrian ménage" in London, not only because of recorded payments from the Duchy of Lancaster or Henry IV, but also because of the Roman road between the Duchy center at Pontrefract in West Yorkshire and Lancaster that runs right by the monasteries at Whalley, Sawley, and Bolton, the probable sites for the poem's composition.[35] He further suggests that Sir Sabyn's flaying argument speaks to an issue of governmental agency that brought about the Lancastrian assumption of the English throne in 1399. In short, Hanna views the poem and its support of monarchical proxies as "arguments justifying usurpation and regicide" that would have been important subjects of discussion within the Ricardian and Lancastrian courts.[36]

Speculating even further, Hanna suggests that the *Siege*-poet's fascination with flaying the flesh of Jews may have been easily assimilated by Lancastrian readers who inflicted similar religious violence upon Lollards who rejected the doctrine of transubstantiation. In the absence of Jews who had been expelled in 1290, the Lollards "materialized the *corpus Christi*" and suffered the displaced cruelty of "Christian xenophobia."[37] Given the poem's compo-

34. Hanna, "Contextualizing *The Siege of Jerusalem*," 109–11. The breaking of the deer is explained in detail in *The Parliament of the Three Ages*, 75–78: "I raughte the righte legge byfore, ritt it þeraftir, / And so fro legge to legge I lepe thaym aboute, / And þe felle fro þe fete fayre I departede / And flewe it doun with my fiste faste to the rigge" [I grasped the right leg first, ripped it next, and thus from leg to leg I moved quickly around them, and I separated the skin clean from the feet, and flayed it down with my fist quickly to the backbone]. See Thorlac Turville-Petre, *Alliterative Poetry of the Later Middle Ages: An Anthology* (Washington D.C.: Catholic University of America Press, 1989), 73; for his treatment of the flaying scene, see 168–69.

35. Hanna, "Contextualizing *The Siege of Jerusalem*," 115–18. Hanna also suggests a more direct route for the poem to reach a Lancastrian audience through Thomas, sixth lord of Clifford, and knight under Richard II (118). See also George E. Cokayne, *The Complete Peerage* 3 (London: St. Catherine's Press, 1910–59), 292; Chris Given-Wilson, *The Royal Household and the King's Affinity: Service, Politics and Finance in England 1360–1413* (New Haven: Yale University Press, 1986), 282. Ad Putter objects to the localization of the poem in this region on dialectical grounds. See his review of Hanna and Lawton's edition of *Siege* in *Speculum* 81.2 (April 2006): 524–26, at 525 and his introduction with Judith Jefferson and Myra Stokes, *Studies in the Metre of Alliterative Verse*, Medium Aevum Monographs 25 (Oxford: Society for the Study of Medieval Languages and Literature, 2007), 11–12.

36. Hanna, "Contextualizing *The Siege of Jerusalem*," 118–19.
37. Ibid., 119–20.

sition near York, the notorious location of the 1190 pogrom, it is likely that the *Siege* is a product of an environment of antisemitism.[38] It is also plausible, I believe, to envision flayed Jews as flayed Lollards in the midst of virulent religious intolerance that led to Arundel's Constitutions in 1409.[39] That said, Hanna's argument rests on a reading of the *Siege,* and specifically CUL MS. Mm.v.14, that praises the imperialism of Vespasian and justifies xenophobic violence, a reading that I wish to call into question.

THE *SIEGE* AND THE GUIDO-TRADITION

I begin by considering the manuscript context of CUL MS. Mm.v.14, which establishes a literary relationship between the *Siege* and the Guido-tradition. As I will demonstrate, their juxtaposition in the manuscript represents their larger thematic commonalities and fascination with the destruction of war, which undercuts rather than justifies imperial and martial violence. To do so, we should start with an examination of the contents of this fascinating early fifteenth-century codex:

I. Folios 2^r–139^v: Guido delle Colonne's *Historia destructionis Troiae.*
II. Folios 140^r–85^r: the prose *Historia de preliis Alexandri Magni.*
III. Folios 187^r–206^v: *The Siege of Jerusalem.*[40]

Even though the manuscript is primarily intended for the Latin reader, it has a particularly "alliterative" flair, not only because of the presence of the *Siege,* but also because the Latin texts are sources for two other alliterative poems, the *Destruction of Troy* and the *Wars of Alexander.* Given the subjects and languages of these works, the audience of this manuscript was deeply interested in Greek and Roman history and the Latin prose and alliterative English used to express it. The juxtaposition of Latin historical texts to English alliterative romance, and specifically Guido's *Historia* to the *Siege,* compels us to revisit scholarship that has established the *Siege's* relationship to the Guido-tradition and its contemporary alliterative romances.

38. Ibid., 114.
39. See Nicholas Watson, "Censorship and Cultural Change in Late-Medieval England: Vernacular Theology, the Oxford Translation Debate, and Arundel's Constitutions of 1409," *Speculum* 70.4 (1995): 822–64.
40. For a full manuscript description, see Hanna and Lawton, *The Siege of Jerusalem,* xix–xx. For a recent discussion of other manuscript contexts of the *Siege,* see Michael Johnston, "Robert Thornton and *The Siege of Jerusalem,*" *Yearbook of Langland Studies* 23 (2009): 125–62.

We should first address the work that has established a compositional relationship between the *Destruction* and the *Siege* since they exhibit undeniable similarities in poetic vocabulary and structure. Scholars are divided on the relationship between the *Destruction* and the *Siege*, some claiming that the *Siege*-poet borrowed from the *Destruction*, and some claiming that the *Destruction* borrowed from the *Siege*. Mary Hamel, following the work of Mabel Day, argues that the *Siege* uses the *Destruction* in a way that transcends the stock formulas of alliterative verse, which Ronald A. Waldron had previously identified in an analysis of several Middle English alliterative poems.[41] They reveal unquestionable correspondences of ideas, images, versification, word choices, and collocations.[42] Given the irrefutable similarities not only between individual lines such as "Merked montayns and mores aboute" (*Siege* 730) and "All merknet the mountens & mores aboute" (*Destruction* 7350), but also between the overall structures and sequences of the lines, there is evidence of dependence that is difficult to dismiss even with arguments about the formulaic nature of alliterative verse. Hamel goes even further to claim that the *Siege* borrowed from the *Destruction* since there could be no other source for these lines in the *Siege* than the *Destruction*'s relatively faithful rendering of Guido's *Historia*. This argument, she claims, is augmented by the fact that the author of the alliterative *Morte Arthure* used both the *Siege* and the *Destruction* extensively.[43] If we accept this argument, it would appear that we are able to establish not only a relationship of dependence between the two poems, but also identify the *Destruction* as a source for the *Siege*.

Unfortunately, the correspondence between the two poems is not as certain as we might hope. In studying the dialect and date of the *Siege*, editors Ralph Hanna and David Lawton conclude that the *Siege* not only is earlier

---

41. Mary Hamel, ed., *Morte Arthure: A Critical Edition* (New York: Garland Publishing, 1984), 54–55; Kölbing and Day, *The Siege of Jerusalem*, xxvi–ix; Ronald A. Waldron, "Oral-Formulaic Technique and Alliterative Poetry," *Speculum* 32.4 (1957): 792–804. Waldron characterized *Destruction* as particularly conventional in its use of formulas, which meet rhythmical and alliterative demands in a way similar to the oral-formulaic structure of Old English. This conclusion that all the poems emerge from a common tradition seemingly confounded attempts by scholars to ascertain dependency between texts and devalues what appear to be original contributions by alliterative poets.

42. They focus in particular on the correspondences between lines 729–37 of the *Siege* and lines 7348–56 in the *Destruction*.

43. Hamel, *Morte Arthure*, 54–55; Kölbing and Day, *The Siege of Jerusalem*, xxvi–xxvii; George Neilson also identified a number of "borrowings" to claim that the same author wrote both *Destruction* and *Siege*, but scholars have since refuted this claim. See Neilson, "*Huchown of the Awle Ryale,*" *the Alliterative Poet* (Glasgow: James MacLehose & Sons, 1902), 282–88. See Livingston's helpful summary of the arguments about *Siege*'s date, provenance, and source material in his introduction to *Siege of Jerusalem*, 8–13, 21–30.

than the *Destruction* in its composition, but also may have no direct relationship to Clerk's poem. They identify Barnoldswick, West Yorkshire, as the home of the *Siege*-poet, which would link him with Clerk geographically since Clerk comes from nearby Whalley, a town which lies approximately twelve miles to the west of Barnoldswick.[44] Based on these identifications, these poets lived closer together than poets of any other two extant alliterative poems, which might indicate that they even knew one another and had access to each other's work. Hanna and Lawton use this evidence not to demonstrate a relationship of dependence, but instead to argue that their proximity may show "their reliance upon a specific local tradition of alliterative verse, a common word-hoard and poetic grammar more closely related than simply a general 'alliterative tradition.'"[45] Yet, they qualify their claim by acknowledging, "direct borrowing may not be so easily dismissed."[46]

And if we consider, as Mary Hamel and Roger Nicholson have, the crusading context that must have influenced the *Siege*-poet's intense fascination with the Holy Land, it is likely that the *Siege* emerged from knowledge of the crusade that was organized by Richard II and Charles V in 1396.[47] While the *Siege*-poet's crusading fervor could have been gleaned from his late-antique source text, the *Vindicta Salvatoris*, the decision to translate this tale of the destruction of Jerusalem for English readers suggests a currency for its compositional moment in the late fourteenth century. A Ricardian campaign could have provided the motivation for such a poem since the crusaders had formidable opponents and obstacles ahead of them. The crusade began against the Ottomans, who were threatening Constantinople, and was expected to continue against the Mamluks, who had occupied Jerusalem since 1279. Of course this last gasp at crusade never reached the Holy Land since the Ottomans overwhelmed the crusaders at Nicopolis.[48] However, since the *Siege*-poet could have never comprehended the finality of this event, it is not surprising that crusading ideology emerges in the living,

---

44. Hanna and Lawton, *The Siege of Jerusalem*, xxxvi; Turville-Petre, "The Author of *The Destruction of Troy*," *Medium Ævum* 57 (1988): 264–69.

45. Hanna and Lawton, *The Siege of Jerusalem*, xxxvi. Such an argument is both distinct from and reminiscent of Waldron's oral-formulaic thesis, but for the purposes of this discussion, its contention for the existence of the "word hoard" does the same work as Waldron's: it dispels attempts to identify borrowings and moments of originality. See also Turville-Petre, "The Author of *The Destruction of Troy*," 267.

46. Hanna and Lawton, *The Siege of Jerusalem*, xxxvi.

47. Hamel, "*The Siege of Jerusalem* as a Crusading Poem," in *Journeys Toward God: Pilgrimage and Crusade*, ed. Barbara N. Sargent-Baur (Kalamazoo: University of Michigan Press, 1992), 177–94; Nicholson, "Haunted Itineraries," 447–84.

48. For a full account of this crusade, see J. J. N. Palmer, *England, France, and Christendom, 1377-99* (Chapel Hill: University of North Carolina Press, 1972), 180–210.

breathing form it does in the poem. In fact, Nicholson suggests that the *Siege* may be, at least in part, a result of a polemical tradition that had campaigned for crusade throughout the 1390s. This polemical context is best represented by Philippe de Mézières in his *Epistre au roi Richart* in 1395. This letter to Richard expresses anxiety about the increasing power of the Islamic Turks and the threat they pose to Christian imperialism. At this point, the Turks had defeated the Christian troops at Thessalonika in 1387 and Kosovo in 1389, and had begun to broach the borders of Christendom.[49] Charles V added to this fervor with a letter to Richard II, stating that the outcome of their 1395 campaign was to "succor our fellow Christians and to liberate the Holy Land."[50] Such a goal accords with Phillipe's desire for a crusade and clarifies the ultimate object of the campaign to be the liberation of Jerusalem.

If the *Siege* is read with this crusade polemic in mind, the attention it pays to the chivalry of Titus and Vespasian in besieging Jerusalem recalls contemporary expeditions to regain the Holy Land. It is also appropriate that the site of Titus' conversion to Christianity is Bordeaux, the location of a 1395 peace accord between the English and French; a negotiating agreement from the conference even claimed that this diplomatic action would allow "Christendom [to] be saved from the malice and evil onslaught of the infidels who are attempting to destroy and annihilate it in various areas."[51] The outright obliteration of Jerusalem that occurs in the *Siege* represents this kind of aggressive response to threats against Christian dominion. It is then geographically consistent for Titus to embark from Bordeaux on a crusade to avenge the death of Christ by the Jews. Given the pervasive nature of this crusade polemic throughout England during the 1390s, it is quite probable that the *Siege* was a product of this discourse later in the decade, after the composition of the *Destruction*. And when the remarkably similar vocabulary, linear structure, and imagery are also factored into the equation, it is quite likely that the *Siege*-poet used the *Destruction* as a source. Such a rela-

---

49. Nicholson, "Haunted Itineraries," 463–64. For more on Philippe de Mézières see G. W. Coopland, ed., *Philippe de Mézières: Letter to King Richard II* (Liverpool: Liverpool University Press, 1975). For the crusading fervor in late medieval texts, see Christopher Tyerman, *England and the Crusades, 1095–1588* (Chicago: University of Chicago Press, 1988), 304ff; Denys Hay, *Europe in the Fourteenth and Fifteenth Centuries* (London: Longman, 1989), 280; Hamel, "*The Siege of Jerusalem* as a Crusading Poem," 179; Chism, "*The Siege of Jerusalem*: Liquidating Assets," *Journal of Medieval and Early Modern Studies* 28 (1998): 309–40.

50. Nicholson, "Haunted Itineraries," 464–65. Palmer also agrees that the "ultimate destination was to have been Jerusalem itself." *England, France, and Christendom,* 205, 242–44. Richard II also sent a letter of support for his half-brother Robert Holland, who was negotiating with Sigismund of Hungary in 1394, which indicates a military expedition to Hungary and Jerusalem. See Tyerman, *England and the Crusades*, 263.

51. Cited by Palmer, *England, France, and Christendom*, 182, 203.

tionship of dependence would explain their common didactic program of dismembered cities and bodies that undercuts the discourse of imperialism.

Even if we were to concede that the *Siege* is not directly dependent upon the *Destruction*, it is still evident that the *Siege*-poet drew from Clerk's source, Guido's *Historia*. Despite their attempts to relegate the *Destruction* to the mid-fifteenth century, Hanna and Lawton admit that the *Siege* and the *Destruction* share generic affinities, particularly in their attention to chronicle history.[52] This assertion is supported by CUL MS. Mm.v.14, which contains one of the nine extant copies of the *Siege* and is bound with Guido's *Historia* and the *Historia de preliis Alexandri Magni*. Since the Latin texts are historical in nature and the same hand inscribed all three works, it can be inferred that the intended audience of this manuscript was learned and deeply interested in Greek and Roman history.[53] This means that the scribe and audience most likely considered the *Siege* a history—and possibly the same kind of history as Guido's *Historia*. This volume contains multiple glosses in English and Latin in handwriting of several different scribes, which indicates that these historical texts were of great interest to their audience over an extended period of time.[54] Even though not all of the manuscript contexts for the *Siege* limit its genre as history, it is clear that its compliers often juxtaposed it with learned works that reflect its historical and theological significance.[55]

In addition to a generic affinity, the *Siege* also shares a particular rhetorical technique with Guido's *Historia*. As Nicholas Jacobs points out, the *Siege*-poet drew from Guido's *Historia* in his use of *amplificatio*. In addressing what had previously been thought to be a specifically alliterative topos, Jacobs analyzes the spectacular storm sequences that appear in many of the alliterative poems, especially the *Siege*, the *Destruction*, and *Patience*, in order to demonstrate that their accounts originate in classical models.

---

52. Hanna and Lawton, *The Siege of Jerusalem*, xxxxvii–xxxxviii; Pearsall, *Old English and Middle English Poetry*, 162–69; Hanna, "Alliterative Poetry," in *The Cambridge History of Medieval English Literature*, ed. David Wallace (Cambridge: Cambridge University Press, 1999), 488–512.

53. Bonnie Millar, *The Siege of Jerusalem in Its Physical, Literary and Historical Contexts* (Dublin: Four Courts Press, 2000), 25; G. Guddat-Figge, ed., *Catalogue of the Manuscripts containing Middle English Romances* (Munich: W. Fink, 1976), 109. Guddat-Figge observes that the *Siege* is not as thoroughly decorated in gold, blue, red, and white illuminations or initials as the Latin histories, possibly because the illuminator did not think that the *Siege*'s Middle English deserved decoration.

54. Millar, *The Siege of Jerusalem in Its Physical, Literary and Historical Contexts*, 25. She notes the following names on the Ms.: *Arthur Maynwaring 1567* f.1^r; *Robert Cotton* in Greek f.1^r, f. 207^r; *Richard Broyes* f. 208^v; *Edwardus Savage Capillanus* f. 208^v; *Johannes Redmayn* f. 208^v; *Johannes Kyngsinn of Endbern* f. 208^v; see *A Catalogue of the Manuscripts preserved in the Library of the University of Cambridge*, iv. repr. (Cambridge, 1980), 320–21.

55. For a full discussion of its historical, theological, crusading, and alliterative manuscript contexts, see Millar, "The Manuscript Contexts of *The Siege of Jerusalem*," 15–41.

Because of the large number of shared borrowings that exist in the *Destruction*, Jacobs also admits the possibility that the other alliterative poets could have developed their storm narratives through their readings of the *Destruction*, but Jacobs eventually concludes that Guido's *Historia* is the more likely source because of its popularity throughout England in the late fourteenth century and the unique correspondence between the storm descriptions of Guido and Clerk. Since Guido's extensive storm scenes are not found in his own French source, Benoît de Sainte-Maure's *Le Roman de Troie*, it is evident that Guido was influenced by a Latin rhetorical tradition that he received through his knowledge of classical literature. While it is possible that the alliterative poets learned the technique of *amplificatio* from rhetorical manuals, it is not likely, especially since the printed manuals do not suggest storm descriptions as instances for elaboration.[56] Instead, Jacobs suggests that Guido's *Historia* was their source for this type of rhetorical embellishment—after all, Guido's extensive influence in the later fourteenth century is manifested in the three English translations, which were completed within the period of fifty years.[57] We cannot then arrive confidently at the conclusion that the *Destruction* had a direct influence upon the *Siege*, but given the *Siege*'s linguistic, structural, and rhetorical correspondences to both the *Destruction* and Guido's *Historia*, we can establish the *Siege* as a poem that belongs to the Guido-tradition.

While scholars such as Hamel and Jacobs have addressed the *Siege*'s connection to Guido and Clerk's texts in terms of language and style, they have not acknowledged larger thematic similarities, such as a pervasive ambivalence towards imperialism that manifests itself in the *Siege*'s graphic descrip-

---

56. Nicholas Jacobs, "Alliterative Storms: A Topos in Middle English," *Speculum* 47 (1972): 695–719, at 695–703. For the content and influence of rhetorical manuals, see Derek Pearsall, "Rhetorical *Descriptio* in *Sir Gawain and the Green Knight*," *Modern Language Review* 50 (1955): 129–34; E. Faral, *Les arts poétiques du xiie et du xiiie siècle*, Bibliothèque de l'École des Hautes Études 238 (Paris: É. Champion, 1923); John of Garland, *Poetria*, ed. G. Mari, *Romanische forschungen* 13 (1902): 883–965; Gervais of Melkley, *Ars poetica*, ed. H. J. Gräbener, *Forschungen zur romanischen Philologie* 17 (Münster, 1965).

57. Jacobs, "Alliterative Storms," 704. However, Jacobs does not readily dismiss a relationship between the *Destruction* and the *Siege* and even proceeds to identify characteristics that are shared by the *Destruction*, the *Siege*, and *Patience*. He observes that their respective storm scenes all contain: (1) an elaboration on the height and depth of the waves; (2) a distinction between the dark clouds and the lucent storms; (3) the loss of the gear and rigging of the ship; and (4) the appeals to the gods or saints. Since nearly all these thematic correspondences that appear in the *Siege* and *Patience* also appear in the *Destruction*, it is possible that the *Destruction* was the medium through which the alliterative poets obtained knowledge of Guido's meteorological amplifications; however, given many elements in Guido's *Historia* that correspond to alliterative poems other than the *Destruction*, most notably the names of the winds, Jacobs concludes that it is not likely that the *Destruction* was the channel of transmission for the topos (704–12).

tions of the dismemberment of cities and bodies. Given the *Siege*-poet's tendency to draw on Guido's meteorological themes, it is not surprising that he would also translate Guido's destructive figure of Troy into his treatment of the Romans. Even more intensely than the *Destruction*, the *Siege* meditates on the destructive consequences of treason, which, contrary to many derisive readings of this poem, reflects the evils committed by the Roman imperialists and connects their fate to that of their Trojan ancestors. The *Siege*'s juxtaposition to the *Historia* in CUL MS. Mm.v.14 suggests that its audience may have been one that interrogated, rather than simply accepted and promulgated, the value and consequences of imperial endeavors.

TITUS AND THE BIOPOLITICAL NATURE OF SOVEREIGNTY

If we also consider the way the *Siege*-poet presents the flaying maxim and Vespasian's decision to become Roman emperor within the poem itself, it becomes clear that Vespasian's imperial desires ultimately trump his original vow and belie readings that do not perceive the poem's critique of Vespasian's actions. By using the "flaying" language in this way, the *Siege*-poet connects the fate of the Jewish clerics with the fate of hunted deer and characterizes the Romans' treatment of the Jews as inhuman. For many readers of the poem, this dehumanization of the Jews is part and parcel of a larger accepted antisemitic tradition and would therefore seem unexceptional. However, as these scenes of Jewish dismemberment accumulate to a state of frenzy, the *Siege*-poet expresses compassion for the fate of the Jews. As I will demonstrate, the juxtaposition of the "flaying" scenes with a later questioning of these acts undermines what would otherwise be a glorious occasion for empire. Even by assuming the imperial throne, Vespasian cannot escape his culpability in the cruelty of the siege that he governs through his newfound inheritance, one that has a history, in the words of the *Destruction*'s Hector, of not being able to anticipate what horrid things will happen at "the fer end" (2246).[58]

The larger context of the flaying maxim supports this reading. Later in the poem, the *Siege*-poet continues his use of bodily violence and malady through Titus' corporeal response to news of his father's imperial ascendance. The joy that overtakes him is so overwhelming that his body betrays his enthusiasm:

---

58. John Clerk of Whalley, *The Destruction of Troy: A Diplomatic and Color Facsimile Edition, Hunterian MS V.2.8 in Glasgow University Library*, ed. Hiroyuki Matsumoto (Ann Arbor: University of Michigan Press, 2002).

And Titus for þe tydyng ha[þ] take [so] mychel ioye
Þat in his synwys soudeynly a syknesse is fallen.
Þe freke for þe fayndom of þe fadere blysse
With a cramp and a colde cauȝt was so hard
Þat þe fyngres and feet, fustes and ioyntes
Was lyþy as a leke and lost han here strengþe,
Becroked aȝens kynde and as a crepel woxen. (1027–33)

[Titus took so much joy from the news that a sickness suddenly struck his limbs. Because of his gladness about his father's happiness, he was gripped with a cramp and a chill so intense that his fingers and feet, fists and joints were as limp as leeks and lost their strength. Against nature he grew crooked and walked like a cripple (or dwarf).]

Articulating a dialectic of imperial desire and illness that threatens the capacity of the Romans to sustain their siege against Jerusalem, the natural and political bodies of sovereignty become inseparable within the figure of Titus. This scene also belies the modernity of Foucault's biopolitics, which insists that "modern man is an animal whose politics calls his existence as a living being into question."[59] Here a decidedly premodern figure embodies the inextricable relationship between what Agamben calls "bare life" (*zoē*) and poltical life (*bios*), in which the physical body of Titus reacts somatically to transformations in the imperial life of Rome.[60] The image of Titus as a "crepel," which according to the *MED* could refer both to a "cripple" and "dwarf," suggests a deflation of imperial power and descent to a death-like state that can only be remedied through the reduction of superfluous "ioye."[61] In his unnatural sickness, Titus possesses neither the physical nor imperial power that Vespasian bestowed upon him.

As Chism has argued, this moment "threatens the poem's trajectory towards a new Christian empire by introducing a premature ending, a Christian/Roman empire that has not fully assimilated the profits from the

---

59. Michel Foucault, *History of Sexuality, Volume I: An Introduction,* trans. Robert Hurley (New York: Random House, 1978), 143.

60. Agamben, *Homo Sacer,* 1–8.

61. In most instances, "crepel" refers to "cripple." For a standard example, see *Cleanness*: "Þay ben boþe blynde and balterande cruppelez" (103). For the more obscure "dwarf" definition, confer the *Catholicon Anglicum*: "A Crepyll: hic tantillus [cp. A Dwarghe: hic tantillus]" in S. J. H. Herrtage and H. B. Wheatley, eds., *Catholicon Anglicum: An English-Latin Wordbook,* EETS 75 (1881; reprint 1987); Millar, *The Siege of Jerusalem in Its Physical, Literary and Historical Contexts,* 89. She even claims that Titus experiences a "symbolic death."

destruction of both its predecessors."[62] When Chism refers to "predecessors," she naturally means Old Rome and Jerusalem, but given the *Siege*'s place in the Guido-tradition, we should add Troy. This is not to say that readers would literally perceive Troy to be a city that stands transparently behind Rome and Jerusalem, but only that the figure of the crippled Titus represents the dangers of imperial translation that Guido's fractured figure of Troy embodies. While it is possible to read Troy as the pagan ancestor of Nero's Old Rome and completely separate from the New Roman Christendom, Titus' unnatural enthusiasm for the news of his imperial lineage indicates that he cannot fully divorce himself from the Old Roman destructive desire for power. Acting as the proxy for the sovereign body of his father, Titus' corporeal reaction represents the inseparability of the sovereign's body from the physical body. Understood this way, the excessive zeal of the political body overwhelms Titus' physical body and confounds any separation of Roman imperial desire and Christian retribution. If Vespasian's preference for imperial authority and translation of power to Titus were to go unquestioned, we might embrace readings of the poem that legitimize the casualties of empire, but this is clearly not the case.

Failing to purge his imperial heritage and fantasies and to escape the limitations that his body has imposed upon him, Titus seeks help from his Jewish enemies, who prove to be superior both in virtue and reason.[63] Titus sends for Josephus, who is not only a Jewish cleric and defender of Jerusalem, but also the historian who wrote *The Jewish War,* an account of the siege that is sympathetic to the Romans. The choice to have a Jew provide counsel in such a medical matter not only violates medieval canon law, which forbids Christians to consult Jewish physicians, but also defies the predominant medieval Christian perception of the relationship between Jews and the body.[64] As Anna Abulafia suggests, since Jews refused to accept the orthodox teaching that God retained his divinity after assuming human form, "they were viewed by these Christians as lacking spiritual qualities and being dominated by their bodies."[65] A situation in which a Christian emperor, who

---

62. Chism, *Alliterative Revivals,* 182.
63. Narin van Court, "The *Siege of Jerusalem* and Recuperative Readings," 162.
64. James Brundage, "Intermarriage between Christians and Jews in Medieval Canon Law," in *Sex, Law, and Marriage in the Middle Ages* (Aldershot, Hampshire: Variorum, 1993), XIII: 25–40, at 27; Raymond of Penyafort, *Summa de paenitentia,* eds. X. Ochoa and A. Díez, Universa bibliotheca iuris, vol. 1.4.3 (Rome, 1976), col. 277; Geoffrey of Trani, *Summa super titulis Decretalium* (Aalen, Scientia Verlag, 1968), X.5.6; Johannes Teutonicus, *Glossa Ordinaria* to the *Decretum* (Venice, 1605), C.28 Q.1 c.13 v.*percipiat.*
65. Abulafia, "Bodies in the Jewish-Christian Debate," in *Framing Medieval Bodies,* 123–37, at 126.

cannot secure a Christian remedy for his body's revolt, consults the reason of a Jew would have been perceived by many medieval readers to be implausible, to say the least. But when we consider the bodily nature of the cure, it is clear that Titus is the one ruled by his body. Josephus obtains safe passage to Titus' bedside, where he presents a man whom Titus hates more than any other on the earth.

> Whan Tytus saw þat segge   sodeynly with eyen,
> His herte in an hote yre   so hetterly riseþ
> Þat þe blode bygan to [b]red[e]   abrode in þe vaynes
> And þe synwes resorte   in here self kynde.
> Feet and alle þe fetoures,   as þey byfore were,
> Comyn in here owen kynd. . . . (1049–54)

[When Titus saw that man suddenly with his eyes, his heart rose so furiously in a hot rage that his blood began to pulse in his veins and his sinews were restored to their old strength. His feet and all his features were as they had been before, revived to their natural state. . . .]

The mere sight of this man inspires such "hote yre" (1050) that his blood resumes its course and revives his limbs to their former strength. Detailing the course of the blood as it restores his features not only reminds us of Clerk's account of the pouring of balsam through Hector's dead body in an attempt to revive his body to an illusory living state in the *Destruction*, but also articulates the relationship between superfluous wrath and healing. An excess of joy is therefore balanced by an excess of anger to resurrect Titus' lifeless body back to its "owen kynd" and his status as "kyng" (1054).[66] If this miracle is read according to the principles of patristic exegesis, it is curious to say the least. Not only does the *Siege*-poet offer no real explanation of this cure by wrath, but also he significantly alters his source, the *Legenda Aurea* of Jacobus de Voragine, in retelling it.[67] Jacobus continually denies the apocryphal miracle's significance and only recounts it because his own source includes it. Also, Jacobus specifically identifies this hated "segge" as Titus' slave and offers the explanation of the cure that opposites have the power to cure one another. In the *Siege*, the man who inspires such hatred is undoubtedly a Jew, since Josephus brings him from the city. This substitution attri-

---

66. Millar, *The Siege of Jerusalem in Its Physical, Literary, and Historical Contexts*, 89.
67. Jacobus de Voragine, *Legenda Aurea*, ed. T. Graesse (Dresden, 1846), 301. For a discussion of the *Siege*-poet's alterations of the *Legenda*'s account, see Millar, *The Siege of Jerusalem in Its Physical, Literary, and Historical Contexts*, 72.

butes the cure entirely to Jews and "God of his grace" (1055) and leads to a scene of forgiveness between Titus and his enemy. Titus then offers Josephus a reward for his efforts, which Josephus rejects, choosing instead to return promptly to Jerusalem.[68] These alterations reveal the *Siege*-poet's admiration of benevolent Jews such as Josephus, who repress their own hostilities in offering compassion to an enemy.

Even though the details of Josephus' cure of Titus highlight the usefulness of the Jews to the triumphal narrative, this compassionate experience only tempers Titus' enthusiasm about his father's imperial status. After Titus is healed, he returns to his martial task with a renewed vigor, unlike previously in the poem when he and his soldiers emotionally withdraw from the siege, taking up chivalric activities such as hunting and hawking (885–93). This earlier movement away from the horrors of their military campaign recalls Vespasian's decision to break his vow and assume the emperorship, which again demonstrates the Romans' preference for the security of their empire over adherence to Christian vengeance. Bonnie Millar notes, "This indicates a change in them, how they are raised above the problems of siege warfare, and separates them from the city where Mar[ia] is driven through the madness of hunger to eat her own child, representing the breakdown of social identity and order."[69] The Romans' retreat into the pleasures of imperial excess is in direct contrast to the starving Jews, who arise to the forefront of the narrative directly after the resurrection of Titus' body.

Instead of causing forgiveness and peace, Josephus' act of mercy unleashes the destruction that accompanies the revival of sovereign power. Like Hector's vivified corpse in the *Destruction*, Titus' healed body enacts further destruction that begins the line following Josephus' return to the city:

> Bot alle forsakeþ þe segge   and to þe cite ȝede
> With condit as he come—   he kepiþ no more.
> [And] Tytus segyþ þe toun   þer tene is on hande
> For hard hunger and hote   þat hem is bylompyn. (1065–68)

[But the man left them all and went to the city, with safe conduct as he had arrived, he kept nothing more. And Titus besieged the town where woe was at hand, for painful and intense hunger had wracked them.]

---

68. Jacobus de Voragine, *Legenda Aurea*, 301. Josephus' refusal to accept an award is an original contribution to the story by the *Siege*-poet. According to the *Legenda*, "Titus et servum in sui gratiam et Josephum in sui amicitiam recepit" [Titus accepted the slave into his favor and admitted Josephum into his friendship], but a reward is not mentioned.

69. Millar, *The Siege of Jerusalem in its Physical, Literary, and Historical Contexts*, 89.

Both the visual and aural similarities between "segge" (man) and "segyþ" (besieged) invite us to read the abrupt transition between the miracle and the final days of the siege together, suggesting that Titus' consequent actions are contemptible. The phrase "forsakeþ þe segge" and its proximity to "segyþ þe toun," encourage us to imagine Titus as one who "forsakeþ þe sege (siege)" just as Josephus had forsaken all gold and jewels he had been offered for his services. Using the same grammatical positioning two lines later, the *Siege*-poet reverses the syntax so that attention is directed to Titus' identity as a cruel military commander, who callously "segyþ þe toun." The introduction of such evocative aural and visual correspondences between "segge" and "sege" demarcates a clear line between the lesson of forgiveness and imperial vengeance. Having learned nothing from the Jewish "segge," the healed Titus continues the siege with renewed vigor.

Like his father before him, Titus' cruelty forces the Jews to revert to unnatural consumption and cannibalism, actions that inspire the *Siege*-poet's sympathy. As Blurton suggests, the threat of cannibalism is especially poignant because "cannibalism is not simply a destructive act: rather it is an act that targets the fundaments of identity."[70] For the *Siege*-poet, these desperate acts may potentially be performed by anyone, even a nobly born and loving mother. After forty days of no food and water, the *Siege*-poet reports that the Jews must resort to drinking their own tears, and eating their shields and shoes (1071–76). To amplify the horror of the siege, the *Siege*-poet describes the fate of a woman Maria, whose hunger deludes her into roasting and eating her own child:

> On Marie, a myld wyf,   for meschef of foode,
> Hire owen barn þat ȝo bare   brad on þe gledis,
> Rostyþ rigge and rib   with rewful wordes,
> Sayþ, 'sone, vpon eche side   our sorrow is alofte:
> Batail aboute þe borwe   our bodies to quelle;
> Withyn h[u]nger so hote   þat neȝ our herte brestyþ.
> Þerfor ȝeld þat I þe ȝaf   and aȝen tourne,
> Entre þer þou [o]ut cam,'   and etyþ a schouldere. (1081–88)

[One Maria, a noble woman, out of hunger for food cooked on coals her own child that she bore, roasted its back and its ribs with rueful words, saying, "Son, our sorrow has surrounded us on all sides: a battle outside the city to slay our bodies; within a hunger so intense that it nearly bursts our

---

70. Blurton, *Cannibalism in High Medieval English Literature*, 8.

hearts. Therefore give back the life that I gave you. Turn about and enter the body you came out from." And she ate a shoulder.]

The reference to a "myld" or "noble" woman accentuates the supposedly uncharacteristic nature of her behavior and emphasizes the depths of despair that have driven a gentle woman to commit such a base act. More importantly, the invocation of the name "Marie" and the expression of her sorrow connect her suffering with that of the Virgin Mary when she watched the crucifixion of her son Jesus.[71] Given the Virgin Mary's image as the quintessential mother who nursed the savior of humankind, devout Christians would have been disturbed by the perversity of the scene. The reference to the Virgin Mary juxtaposed with the eating of a child, invites us to read this Maria as a monstrous version of Christ's Mary, who is transformed from the bearer and nurturer of Jesus into a desperate cannibal, who justifies her right to the consumption of his body by claiming that he will return to her stomach from whence he came. The Eucharistic nature of this cannibalism is even more explicit than Vespasian's earlier order to blow the ashes of Caiaphas and the other flayed Jewish clerks over the walls of Jerusalem for the living Jews to drink. By demanding that the Jews "bible" (724) or drink the powdered remains of the priests and then later reducing Maria to the eating of the shoulder of her child, the *Siege*-poet highlights the contaminated Eucharistic structure behind these antitypical acts. In these cases, no transubstantiation is necessary or desired—the ritual is raw in its literality and evokes the horror of those that discover Maria's sacrilege.[72] To medieval Christians, cannibalism was the most heinous crime one could commit because the act confused bodily identities and posed a problem for the last days when the bodies of the faithful would be reunited.[73] To make matters worse, it is the

---

71. Compare also Geoffrey Chaucer's *Prioress's Tale*, in which similar "pitous" language is used to describe the sorrow of the mother of the "litel clergeon" who is ritually sacrificed by Jews (593–624). See *The Riverside Chaucer*, ed. Larry Benson, 3rd ed. (Boston: Houghton Mifflin, 1987).

72. Chism, *Alliterative Revivals*, 161. For the literary history of Maria's cannibalism, see Merrall Llewelyn Price, "Imperial Violence and the Monstrous Mother: Cannibalism at the Siege of Jerusalem," in *Domestic Violence in Medieval Texts*, eds. Eve Salisbury, Georgiana Donavin, and Merrall Llewelyn Price (Gainesville: University Press of Florida, 2002), 272–98. Price suggests that Josephus may have created this cannibalistic Maria, since his *Jewish Wars* contains the earliest account. However, the starving mother motif originates in 2 Kings 6:28, in which a Samarian woman and her neighbor devour her son with the agreement that they will eat the neighbor's son the following day. Unfortunately for the Samarian woman, the neighbor hides her son the next day, breaking their agreement (273).

73. C. Walker Bynum, *The Resurrection of the Body in Western Christianity, 200–1336* (New York: Columbia University Press, 1995), 31–33.

most vilified Other, the Jew, who violates the innocent body of a child, which conjures images of other antisemitic allegations, such as child abuse, host desecration, and well-poisoning that were common after the twelfth century.[74] The image of a Jew devouring a child specifically plays on the Christian fear of Jewish ritual cannibalism, made famous at the German monastery at Fulda where Jews were accused of murdering five boys and drawing their blood for religious or medicinal purposes.[75] As Miri Rubin observes about such xenophobia, "The Jew came to carry all of the pent up anxiety, shame and fear which Christians harboured about themselves, their bodies, their God, their doubts, their desires."[76] Because of the horror of bodily fragmentation and the innocence of the Christ-like infant, its dismemberment and consumption strikes a ghastly note for the Christian reader.

In describing this episode, however, the *Siege*-poet does not use Maria's cannibalism to condemn the Jews. Instead, he alters his sources and provides sympathetic commentary through eyewitness testimony, another hallmark of the historiography of the Guido-tradition. The *Siege* contains one of the earliest versions in English of this infamous tale of Maria's cannibalism and primarily depends on Josephus' account; however, the *Siege*-poet also draws from Hegesippus' fourth-century Latin redaction of the *Jewish War*, which uniquely includes Maria's claim that her child return to her womb.[77] Yet, instead of translating Hegesippus' condemnation of "factum Mariae, quod cuiusvis barbari atque impii mens perhorrescat" ["the deed of Maria, at which the mind of even the barbarian and the impious would shudder"], the *Siege*-poet offers no moral evaluation of Maria's act and emphasizes the pitiable nature of her state through a revised account of the eyewitnesses of

---

74. Gavin Langmuir, "Thomas of Monmouth: Detector of Ritual Murder," *Speculum* 59 (1984): 820–46; R. P. Hsia, *The Myth of Ritual Murder* (New Haven: Yale University Press, 1988); Miri Rubin, "Desecration of the Host: The Birth of an Accusation," *Studies in Church History* 29 (1992): 169–85; "The Person in the Form: Medieval Challenges to Bodily 'Order,'" in *Framing Medieval Bodies*, 100–22, at 108; J. Trachtenberg, *The Devil and the Jews* (New York: Jewish Publication Society of America, 1943), 97–108; C. Ginzburg, *Ecstasies: Deciphering the Witches' Sabbath* (New York: Pantheon Books, 1991), 33–68.

75. Langmuir, *Toward a Definition of Antisemitism*, 264; *Annales Ephordenses* in *Monumenta Germaniae Historica, Scriptores* (Hanover, 1826–1934), 16:31; *Annales Marbacenses* in *Monumenta Germaniae Historica*, 17:178.

76. Rubin, "The Person in the Form," 108.

77. Price, "Imperial Violence and the Monstrous Mother," 279. Price contends that since the *Siege*-poet emphasizes the place "þer þou [o]ut cam" rather than Hegesippus' "redi fili in illud naturale secretum in quo domicilio sumsisti spiritum" [return, son, into that natural mystery in which place you took up the spirit], the *Siege*-poet transforms Hegesippus' "womb-stomach conflation" into "a vagina-mouth conflation, suggesting a connection between the motif of the devouring mother and castration anxiety. See also Barbara Creed, *The Monstrous-Feminine: Film, Feminism, Psychoanalysis* (London: Routledge, 1993), 109.

this horror.[78] After smelling the roasting meat, starving Jews storm through her door, demanding their share. When she offers them a piece of her son they recoil in horror:

[Forþ] ey went for wo wep[ande sore]
And sayn, 'alas in þis lif how longe schul we dwelle?
ȝit beter were at o brayed in batail to deye
Þan þus in langur to lyue and lengþen our fyne.' (1097–1100)

[They went away from this woe, weeping sorely and saying, "Alas, how long shall we endure in this life? It would be better to die from one blow in battle than to live in anguish this way and prolong our end."]

Far from rejoicing in their plight, the *Siege*-poet expresses ambivalence for the dire fate of the Jews in reproducing their sympathetic laments. This is in contrast to his source Josephus, who precedes this scene with a barbarization of his fellow Jews, claiming that they consume feces and other "food" that even the lowest of animals would reject (5.571). Instead of following his sources that emphasize the perversions of the Jews, the *Siege*-poet transforms the episode's effect from disgust to desperation. In the manner of the *Kiddish ha-Shem* or Sanctification of God's Name, they decide to sacrifice all who do not possess the strength to fight.[79] According to the *Vindicta salvatoris*, twelve thousand Jews slay one another to claim the glory of their own defeat, but in the *Siege*, it is characterized as a mercy killing.[80] By creating a more desperate fate for the Jews, the *Siege*-poet does not paint their deaths as unjustified, but rather condemns the manner of their deaths. Titus amplifies his power as an instrument of God to a level of imperial cruelty that transcends the ethics of Christian vengeance. The decision to kill themselves also intimately connects Jewish cannibalism and suicide in a way reminiscent of

---

78. For a more extensive discussion of Hegesippus' account, see Price, "Imperial Violence and the Monstrous Mother," 275–76.

79. Narin van Court, "*The Siege of Jerusalem* and Recuperative Readings," 160; Kenneth Stow, *Alienated Minority: The Jews of Medieval Latin Europe* (Cambridge: Harvard University Press, 1992), 116–18. According to rabbinic commentaries, *Kiddush ha-Shem* obeys the order of Leviticus 22:32, which requires self-immolation for divine sanctification.

80. "Melius est nobis ut nosmetipsos interficiamus, quam dicant Romani quod illi occidissent nos et fecissent super nos victoriam. Et extraxerunt gladios suos et percusserunt se, et mortui sunt numero duodecim millia hominum ex ipsis" [It is better that we should destroy ourselves than the Romans say that they had struck us down and had obtained victory over us. And they drew forth their swords and pierced themselves, and twelve thousand people died]. For the text of *Vindicta salvatoris* see Constantin Tischendorf, ed., *Evangelia apocrypha* (Leipzig: Mendelssohn, 1876), 477; 471–86.

their earlier consumption of the ashes of Caiaphas and his fellow priests, a crime which had been directly preceded by seven hundred Jews who "slow hemself for sorrow of here clerkes" (714). Here again, grief, not a desire for glory, instigates self-immolation.

Both their refusal to satisfy their hunger and their desire to die honorably elevates their virtues and reminds us of the temperance and grace of Josephus that directly precede Maria's pitiable cannibalism. Through the juxtaposition of Jewish mercy and suffering, the actions of the Romans in the figure of Titus are called into question. Titus receives the grace of God through Josephus, but refuses to grant a truce to the Jews who have been reduced to eating their clothes and their children (1110). It is only when Titus hears about the dead being thrown over the city walls because of the lack of burial ground that he finally breaks down and shows remorse:

> Whan Titus told was þe tale,   to trewe God he vouched
> Þat he propfred hem pes   and grete pite hadde. (1155–56)

> [When Titus was told this tale, he vowed to true God that he had offered them peace and had great pity for them.]

His grief at the Jewish suffering commences the sixth and final passus of the poem, which prepares readers for the lamentable obliteration of Jerusalem. As the events unfold and the Roman besiegers are confronted with the sight of the emaciated bodies of the Jews, the sympathy expressed for the fate of the besieged increases. Titus makes his way into the city, smelling the dead corpses and viewing those who had become reduced to "[n]o gretter þan a grehounde to grype on þe medil" [no greater than a greyhound to grip around the middle] (1252). Even though Titus "tarieþ noȝt" [did not delay] (1253), the *Siege*-poet interrupts the narrative to lament that it "was pite to byholde" [was a pity to behold] (1247). The humanity of the Jews also swells—whereas they are normally characterized as the infidel, the Jews now become "[w]ymmen" (1147), "ladies" (1249), "[b]urges" (1251), and "peple" (1247). Even though the *Siege*-poet ultimately sanctions their destruction, he cannot refrain from expressing what Elisa Narin van Court has called "the humanizing impulse" that mollifies the antisemitism of the narrative and condemns the imperial resolve of the Romans.[81]

To consolidate his sympathy for the Jews and his ambivalence about Roman imperialism, the *Siege*-poet attends to the fate of Sir Sabyn of Syria,

---

81. Narin van Court, "*The Siege of Jerusalem* and Recuperative Readings," 163.

the soldier who earlier used the flaying motif to persuade Vespasian to embrace his imperial seat. As the Romans cease their siege and storm the city, Sir Sabyn and Domitian begin an assault of the walls. Sir Sabyn ascends the ladder and slays six Jews, before the seventh bests him:

> Þe seueþ hitteþ on hym   an vnhende dynte
> Þat þe brayn out brast   at boþ noseþrylles,
> And Sabyn ded of þe dynt   into þe diche falleþ. (1202–4)

[The seventh hit him with such a hideous strike that his brain burst out through both nostrils, and Sabyn, dead from the blow, fell into the ditch.]

The numerologically significant seventh debrains Sir Sabyn and sends his body to the ditch where the other rotting bodies lie. It is important to note that the *Siege*-poet does not describe the specific fate of any other character and that Sir Sabyn is the only Roman captain to be killed. When we juxtapose this scene with Sir Sabyn's earlier imperial logic in his advice to Vespasian, the strike to his head becomes a blow to imperial reason. Unlike his source Josephus, who distinguishes Sir Sabyn from the other soldiers as exceedingly thin with blackened skin, the *Siege*-poet does not emphasize his eastern heritage and instead associates him with the future Roman emperor Domitian in their assault upon the walls.[82] Sir Sabyn's violent death then serves as a Roman portent of doom that reminds readers of the biblical prophecies and visions of the sword and heavenly army that had appeared three years prior, spelling the judgment of Jerusalem.[83] By recalling them in the aftermath of Sir Sabyn's death and in the midst of Titus' ire, the *Siege*-poet does not, as Chism suggests, "separate the invaders from the victims."[84] Instead the fates of the conquering Romans are conflated with the conquered Jews. The *Siege*-poet never wavers in exacting what the audience would have perceived as a justified punishment of the Jews, but complicates a clear opposition between the besiegers and the besieged to critique Roman imperialism.

From the scourged *corpus Christi* to the brainless Sir Sabyn, the *Siege*-poet inserts horrific illustrations of mutilated, dismembered, and revived bodies into his alliterative narrative not to delight bloodthirsty readers, but rather to emphasize the indiscriminate corporeal damage that inheres to

---

82. Millar, *The Siege of Jerusalem in its Physical, Literary, and Historical Contexts*, 67.
83. For a discussion of the way the *Siege*-poet uses his sources in presenting these prophecies, see Millar, "The Role of Prophecy in the *Siege of Jerusalem* and its Analogues," *The Yearbook of Langland Studies* 13 (1999): 153–78.
84. Chism, *Alliterative Revivals*, 180.

martial assertions of imperial sovereignty. The alliterative long line is an appropriate choice, not only because of its adaptability to historical themes, but also because of its ability to replicate the violence and frenetic pace of battle. As Thorlac Turville-Petre observes, alliterative romanciers such as the *Siege*-poet "realized how wonderfully alliterative verse, with its repeated emphasis on the stressed syllables, evoked the energy of a violent battle or a storm at sea, and some poets seize on every opportunity for a display of this sort. *The Siege of Jerusalem* is mainly taken up with endless descriptions of battles. Individually they are fairly powerful, but together they quite overwhelm the story."[85] The relentless succession of scenes of dismemberment and corporeal malady are so vivid and dominant that the poem reads as if it belongs to an unrecognized genre of medieval horror. Through these horrific images, the *Siege*-poet obscures the message of Christian vengeance and submits the imperialism of the Romans to scrutiny. Attention is consistently directed to victimized bodies, which exhibit a corporeal didacticism that privileges compassion over vengeance. While a providential structure is certainly evident throughout the poem, its articulation of salvation history is frequently interrupted by dismembered bodies, which express a message that strives against enthusiasm about martial endeavors, Roman imperialism, and antisemitism. Because of their status as "bare life" within the Roman sovereign sphere, the bodies of Caiaphas, his clerks, Maria, and her son are equalized with Christ as casualties of imperialism. By eliminating the sacrificial nature of Christ's crucifixion and reminding the audience of his identity as a Jew, this corporeal didacticism belies the providential nature of the salvational poetic that emphasizes the redemption of Christ's sacrifice. Without a christological justification for such violence against Jews, the destruction of Jerusalem becomes merely an object the expanding Roman Empire may consume.

AUGUSTINIAN HISTORIOGRAPHY

As tempting as it might be to reduce the *Siege* to a singular product of the skeptical Guido-tradition, its thematic complexity and tentative providentiality reflect the influence of a variety of theological and historical discourses. The *Siege*-poet's reluctance to embrace Jewish suffering may have been influenced by the Augustinian teaching that urged the preservation of Jews as the witnesses to Old Testament law. Based on manuscript evidence, the

---

85. Thorlac Turville-Petre, *The Alliterative Revival* (Cambridge: D. S. Brewer, 1977), 100.

poem was likely composed at Bolton Priory, which would make the *Siege*-poet an Augustinian canon who would have been conversant not only with a large number of Latin histories such as Guido's *Historia* and Ranulph Higden's *Polychronicon*, but also the Augustinian doctrine of toleration that was expressed through texts such as William of Newburgh's twelfth-century *Historia rerum Anglicarum*.[86] These histories vary widely in their subject matter and scope, using genealogical modes of history, arguing for the preservation of the Jewish people, and questioning the validity of Geoffrey of Monmouth's popular version of British history. Scholarly studies have already traced the influence of Higden and Newburgh upon the *Siege*, but they have not commented on the significance of this anti-Galfridian strain upon the poem. As the following analysis indicates, the *Siege*'s place within the Guido-tradition suits this Augustinian historiographic context.

We should begin our investigation of local anti-Galfridian sentiment with the Augustinian canon William of Newburgh since his *Historia* is the most intimately connected with local Yorkshire history and expresses a sympathetic perspective of Judaism.[87] Like the *Siege*, William's chronicle contains explicit accounts of violence against Jews, but his subject is not the Roman siege of Jerusalem in 70 C.E. Instead, William records the pogroms that occurred in Yorkshire in 1190, including both specific details of the riots and his own opinions about the necessity of preserving the Jewish race as physical representations of Christ's sacrifice (316–17).[88] Even though William considers Jews to be the treacherous crucifiers of Christ, he also criticizes their barbarous treatment at the hands of avaricious English Christians (308–9; 312; 313). In his account of the massacre at York, he cites Psalm 59:12, which commands, "Ne occidas eos, nequando obliviscantur populi mei" [Slay them not, lest my people forget] (316). This central passage to the Augustinian doctrine of toleration is the basis for the claim that Jews should be preserved as living witnesses of the Old Testament law. Jeremy Cohen urges, however, "One ought not to characterize Augustine as an advocate of Jews and Judaism," since he did not stray from the standard patristic

---

86. Hanna, "Contextualizing *The Siege of Jerusalem*," 115–16. Bolton Priory owned both a copy of *Siege* and one of its sources, the *Bible en françois*. See Moe, *The Middle English Prose Translation of Roger d'Argenteuil's Bible en françois*. For more on the Augustinian doctrine of toleration, see Narin van Court, "*The Siege of Jerusalem* and Recuperative Readings," 164–65; "*The Siege of Jerusalem* and Augustinian Historians," 227–48; Chism, *Alliterative Revivals*, 156–60.

87. William of Newburgh, *Historia rerum Anglicarum* in *Chronicles of the Reigns of Stephen, Henry II, and Richard I*, ed. Richard Howlett (London: Longman, 1856). All future references to William's *Historia* are to this edition.

88. Narin van Court, "*The Siege of Jerusalem* and Augustinian Historians," 239. See also R. B. Dobson, *The Jews of Medieval York and the Massacre of March 1190*, Borthwick Papers 45 (York: St. Anthony's Press, 1974).

exegesis that supported their diaspora.[89] In following Augustine, William still expresses an anti-Judaic xenophobia, but he contextualizes the York pogrom with the siege at Masada (318–9), providing a frame that redirects his ire onto the persecuting Christians. He draws on Josephus' *Jewish War* to describe the way the Jews in Clifford Tower slay themselves in avoidance of capture by the Christian townspeople, which increases his sympathy for the Jewish victims and compels him to condemn the Christian murderers. William even shockingly suggests, "Et de his quidem, quos ita plusquam belluina illa confecit immanitas, incunctantur dixerim, quia si in petitione sacri baptismatis fictio defuit, ejus nequaquam effectu fraudatos sanguis proprius baptizavit. Sive autem ficte sive non ficte sacrum petierunt lavacrum, inexcusabilis est execranda illa crudelitas lanistarum" [With regard to these persons, whom savage excess executed thus, if there was no fiction in their petition for holy Baptism, I will assert, without hesitation, that their own blood baptized them, and by no means were robbed of its efficacy; but whether they sought the holy font with deception or without deception, the cruelty of those murderers is to be execrated without excuse] (321–2).[90] Here, William not only illustrates the baptismal power of their sacramental death, but also upbraids the actions of the Christians who enacted the pogroms. This defense of besieged Jews within the context of the Roman siege of Masada and William's use of Josephus translates almost seamlessly into the ideologically modulated antisemitism that we find in the *Siege*.

The *Siege*-poet, likely an Augustinian canon from Yorkshire as well, would have been familiar with the doctrine of toleration and Newburgh's history, which explains not only his disgust for antisemitic violence, but also his distrust of imperialistic enthusiasm. The consummate historiographic tradition that reflects the potential for global sovereignty emerges from Geoffrey's popular *Historia*, since it articulates the genealogical power of empire from the fall of Troy through the prophecies of Merlin. However, historians such as William of Malmesbury and Gerald of Wales rejected Geoffrey's claims to historical accuracy and attacked the existence of his anonymous Welsh source.[91] One of the central figures of this anti-Galfridan historiography was none other than William of Newburgh.

89. Jeremy Cohen, *Living Letters of the Law: Ideas of the Jew in Medieval Christianity* (Berkeley: University of California Press, 1999), 67–145, at 67.
90. For more on Newburgh's condemnation of Christian cruelty, see Narin van Court, "*The Siege of Jerusalem* and Augustinian Historians," 239–44; Nancy Partner, *Serious Entertainments: The Writing of History in Twelfth-Century England* (Chicago: University of Chicago Press, 1977); Antonia Gransden, *Historical Writing in England c. 550 to c. 1307* (Ithaca: Cornell University Press, 1974), 265.
91. Patricia Clare Ingham, *Sovereign Fantasies: Arthurian Romance and the Making of Britain* (Philadelphia: University of Pennsylvania Press, 2001), 21–32.

In the preface to his *Historia*, William launches an invective against the "ridicula figmenta" (11) of Geoffrey, contrasting his ridiculous fictions to his truthful sources in Bede and Gildas, who make no attempts to embellish the glory of the Britons and unashamedly relate the, sometimes embarrassing, truth of the English people. Gildas in particular emerges as admirable in his truth telling: "nec veretur, ut verum non taceat, Brito de Britonibus scribere quod nec in bello fortes fuerint, nec in pace fideles" [Nor is the Briton (Gildas) afraid, so that as a result he keeps quiet about the truth, to write about the Britons that they were neither courageous in war, nor faithful in peace] (11). William's praise of the guileless historiography of Bede and Gildas is strikingly similar to Guido's admiration of the eyewitness accounts of Dares and Dictys, which he claims adhere to "ueritatem" [truth] and "fideli scriptura" [faithful writing] (3).[92] The similarities continue as William commences his philippic against Geoffrey; he not only accuses Geoffrey of inventing fictions, but also derides him for praising the Britons above the Macedonians and the Romans (11).[93] Guido likewise criticizes Homer, Ovid, and Virgil for inserting "fictionibus" [fictions] (3-4) into their epic histories, which then caused future generations to receive a contaminated version of the fall of Troy. Using the examples of poor historians, both William and Guido distance themselves from historiography that blends truth with invention.

William then proceeds into a much more amplified invective than can be found in Guido—he launches a full-scale attack on Galfridian historiography, critiquing especially the prophecies of Merlin and the outlandish accounts of King Arthur's conquests (12-17). As he concludes his assault, William sarcastically asks, "An alium orbem somniat infinita regna habentem, in quo ea contigerunt, quæ supra memoravit?" [Does he dream of another world possessing countless kingdoms, in which the circumstances he has recounted took place?] (17). This charge against Geoffrey for indulging imperial fantasies positions his own history as one that will remain not only faithful to the truth, but also critical of British attempts to match the empire of the Romans. Given the fact that William was a historian who followed the Augustinian-Orosian paradigm, his reluctance to accept Geoffrey's new secular history is no surprise.[94] For the *Siege*-poet, the historical perspective he obtained from

---

92. Guido de Columnis, *Historia destructionis Troiae*, ed. Nathaniel Edward Griffin (Cambridge, Massachusetts: Mediaeval Academy of America, 1936). Textual citations refer to this edition.

93. "At contra quidam nostris temporibus, pro expiandis his Britonum maculis, scriptor emersit, ridicula de eisdem figmenta contexens, eosque longe supra virtutem Macedonum et Romanorum impudenti vanitate attollens."

94. Francis Ingledew, "The Book of Troy and the Genealogical Construction of History: The Case of Geoffrey of Monmouth's *Historia regum Britanniae*," *Speculum* 69.3 (1994): 665-704, at 666; Robert W. Hanning, *The Vision of History in Early Britain* (New York: Columbia University

both William and Guido provided him with a suitable basis for his ambivalence about the birth of the Christian imperialism that he relates in his account of the fall of Jerusalem. With this historical context in mind, we are hard pressed to read the *Siege*-poet's graphic descriptions of mutilated bodies as merely an indulgence in a "decadent poetic" and instead are urged to see these gruesome images as representations of the unsavory consequences of war and empire.[95]

Another of the *Siege*-poet's sources, Higden's *Polychronicon*, corroborates his skepticism of Galfridian historiography. While Higden draws on Geoffrey's *Historia* extensively in producing the English portion of his universal history, he expresses doubts about the veracity of King Arthur's conquests in a manner strikingly similar to that of William: "Gaufridus dicit se mirari quod Gildas et Beda nullam de Arthuro in suis scriptis fecerunt mentionem; immo magis mirandum puto cur ille Gaufridus tantum extulerit, quem omnes antiqui veraces et famosi historici pœne intactum reliquerunt" [Geoffrey states that he wonders why Gildas and Bede made no mention of Arthur in their writings, but I think it should be wondered why Geoffrey praised him so much, whom all ancient authorities and famous historians left untouched] (5.334, 336).[96] His invocation of Gildas and Bede is reminiscent of William's invective, a reference that was not lost on Hidgen's English translator John Trevisa, who seems, at first glance, to be a staunch defender of Galfridian historiography.[97] After translating Higden's doubts about Geoffrey's historical accuracy, Trevisa interrupts the narrative, insisting, "Here William telleþ a magel tale wiþ oute evidence; and Ranulphus his resouns, þat he meveþ aȝenst Gaufridus and Arthur, schulde non clerke move þat can knowe an argument, for it followeþ it nouȝt" (5.337). Trevisa attacks both Higden and William in an ardent attempt to defend Galfridian historiography, which not only attests to Geoffrey's continuing popularity throughout the later Middle Ages, but also represents a larger move to suppress such skepticism about Arthur's existence and his continuation of empire.

Furthermore, Higden's doubts about Geoffrey's veracity may be evidence of a particularly northern interpretation of British history, since Higden wrote the *Polychronicon* at nearby St. Werburgh's in Chester. Since it began to be circulated among nearby monasteries as early as 1340, it had a wide

---

Press, 1966).

95. Pearsall, *Old and Middle English Poetry*, 169.

96. For more on Higden's use of Geoffrey in the writing of British history, see John Taylor, *The Universal Chronicle of Ranulph Higden* (Oxford: Clarendon Press, 1966), 44–45; T. D. Kendrick, *British Antiquity* (London: Methuen, 1950), 14.

97. As I demonstrate in the sixth chapter (208–18), Trevisa's defense of Geoffrey is most likely inserted to please his patron, Lord Berkeley.

influence throughout the region, and one copy, British Library MS Harley 3600, even ended up at Whalley Abbey, the residence of John Clerk.[98] Clerk may have even obtained the idea for concealing his name in the flourished capitals of each of his chapters from Higden, who disguised his name in the same way.[99] Since the *Siege*-poet was most likely a neighbor of both Chester and Whalley, it is reasonable to suggest that both the *Destruction* and the *Polychronicon* served as local historiographic influences for his perspective on imperialism.

When we consider the collective influence of Guido, Clerk, William, and Higden, it becomes clear that the *Siege*-poet contributed to historiography that sought truthful accounts of British deeds and questioned imperial fantasies. While this analysis of William's *Historia* and Higden's *Polychronicon* does not prove the composition of the *Siege* at Bolton, it strengthens the previous suggestions by Ralph Hanna, David Lawton, and Elisa Narin van Court that the *Siege*-poet wrote and disseminated his work from this region. Furthermore, the existence of anti-Galfridian invective within these texts reinforces the *Siege*-poet's assimilation of a skeptical discourse that interrogates English hereditary claims to empire. When the *Siege,* a poem replete with horrifying and sympathetic depictions of violence against Jews, is read within the context of the Augustinian doctrine of toleration and the repudiation of imperial designs, it is difficult to interpret the Roman siege of Jerusalem as a providential inevitability carried out with the enthusiastic sanction of the poet.

ROME AS TROY

Having argued for the *Siege* as a poem that strives against Galfridian historiography and embraces the Guido-tradition, I conclude this chapter by addressing a potential objection to my claim that the poem engages in the debate of *translatio imperii:* the apparent absence of the figure of Troy.

98. Hanna and Lawton, *Siege of Jerusalem,* xxxv; Taylor, *The Universal Chronicle of Ranulf Higden,* 105–9, 152–59.
99. Turville-Petre, "The Author of *The Destruction of Troy,*" 264–65. Just as the initial letters of each chapter of *Destruction* spell "Maistur Iohannes Clerk de Whalele," the initial letters of the first sixty-six chapters of *Polychronicon* spell "PRESENTEM CRONICAM CONPILAVIT FRATER RANULPHUS CESTRENSIS MONACHUS" ("Brother Ranulph, a Cisterian monk, compiled this present chronicle"). Turville-Petre also notes that the *Speculum Curatorum* uses the same naming method and that the end of *Ars Componendi Sermones* contains a note that states, "littere capitanee huius artis syllabatim inuicem tantum sonant Ars Ranulphi Cestrensis" ("These capital letters by the method of alternating syllables are consistent with the method of Ranulph, the Cistercian").

As pervasive as the popular knowledge of Trojan historiography was during the fourteenth century, we may ultimately wonder if the readers of the *Siege* would have so intimately associated the fates of Troy and Rome. And even if they did, would they have related the fall of Troy and Rome with the destruction of Jerusalem? To resolve these doubts, we should return to Guido's text. First of all, despite the fact that his *Historia*, both by virtue of its title and content, is indelibly concerned with the figure of Troy, it also reflects a prominent interest in the figure of Rome. This is no real surprise, since the logic of the *translatio imperii* demands that the Roman Empire subsume its destructive past in order to create imperial glory, so much so that the very fact that Troy was never really an empire is entirely forgotten in the later Middle Ages. Since the linearity of the translation of power demands a constant movement forward, from destruction to rebirth, and the Roman Empire looms large as having achieved the penultimate western imperial fantasy, Britain's claim to a Trojan origin becomes an allegory for a genealogical claim to Rome.[100] To invoke Troy is to invoke Rome, and vice versa.

But just as Roman glory sheds imperial light upon Troy, the destroyed figure of Troy provides a faulty architectural model for Rome. This is demonstrated most clearly when Guido describes the construction of the New Troy and the river Xanthus that runs through it. He naturally compares its layout to that of Rome: "Ad huius itaque fluminis instar ordinates extitit Tyber Rome, qui, per medium Rome erumpens, per Troyanum Heneam ad similtudinem Troye factam vrbem Rome geminas discinxit in partes" [The Tiber at Rome was arranged in the image of this river, which, running through the middle of Rome, divided into two parts the city of Rome made in the likeness of Troy by the Trojan Aeneas] (48–49). Here Guido identifies Aeneas as a kind of mimetic Aristotelian architect. Aeneas does not simply establish the Trojan origin of Rome by virtue of his heritage—he consciously builds a third Troy in the image of its predecessor. Guido's use of "image" (*instar*) and "likeness" (*similtudinem*) spell doom for Rome, because it is the

---

100. Nicholas Birns, "The Trojan Myth: Postmodern Reverberations," *Exemplaria* 5.1 (1993): 45–78, at 53. Drawing on Harold Bloom's *The Anxiety of Influence*, Birns contends that this dislocation is not only a "diachronic anxiety" whereby claims to Trojan ancestry are attempts to avoid "the inverse dialectic between *imperium* and *ecclesia* . . . and avert a fate like Rome's," but also a "lateral anxiety" that essentially erases the significance of eastern rivals such as Byzantium and Islam. Bloom, *The Anxiety of Influence* (New York: Oxford University Press, 1973). See also Geraldine Heng, *Empire of Magic: Medieval Romance and the Politics of Cultural Fantasy* (New York: Columbia University Press, 2003), 17–61, 115–79. Heng similarly suggests that Rome in Geoffrey's *Historia* and in the alliterative *Morte* actually represents twelfth-century Constantinople within the context of the First Crusade.

same Aeneas who callously watches Troy burn to the ground through his treasonous negotiations with the Greeks later in the *Historia*.

Guido's articulation of the architectural aesthetic of mimesis marks a clear divergence from Aeneas' role as the founder of Rome in Virgil's *Aeneid*. In Book III of the *Aeneid*, Aeneas and his band of fleeing Trojans arrive on an island that has been inhabited by Trojan refugees such as Andromache and Helenus. Here at Buthrotum, Aeneas witnesses a replica of Troy (*parvam Troiam*) that includes all of the architectural details of the former Troy, including Pergamum and the Xanthus. Yet, Virgil takes pains to show that Aeneas is not satisfied with the *imitatio* before his eyes, and that he will construct a Rome that will prove to be more than a simple reproduction. As Aeneas prepares to leave, he declares,

> effigiem Xanthi Troiamque uidetis
> ... si quando Thybrim uicinaque Thybridis arua
> intraro gentique meae data moenia cernam,
> cognates urbes olim populosque propinquos
> ... unam faciemus utramque / Troiam animis. (497–505)[101]

[A copy of Xanthus and Troy you see. . . . If ever I enter the Tiber and Tiber's neighboring fields and observe the city-walls granted to my race, at that time, of our sister cities and neighboring peoples . . . of these two we shall make one Troy in spirit.]

The use of the word "cernam," which I translate as "observe," literally means "separate," implying a distinction between the city-walls of Rome and those he has witnessed of Troy and its effigy. He also establishes that they will only be Troy in spirit (*animis*), which reflects his desire to carry on the soul of Troy, without translating its image. This distinction holds the utmost importance because Aeneas' Rome can only assume its imperial power through a genealogy that must exorcise its destructive past. As David Quint notes, "with its parade of replica Troys—each successively and more explicitly revealed to be a place of death—the fiction of Book 3 insists that this future can only be reached if the Trojans relinquish their past and its memories, if they can escape from a pattern of traumatic repetition."[102] This avoidance of repetition is an avoidance of architectural imitation, since deathly reconstructions of Troy cannot escape nostalgia of the previous model of Troy.

---

101. See Virgil, *Opera*, ed. R. A. B. Mynors (Oxford: Oxford University Press, 1969).
102. Quint, "Repetition and Ideology in the *Aeneid*," in *Epic and Empire*, 61.

Instead of encouraging an evasion of the past, Guido emphasizes the *instar* and *simultudinem* of Troy and Rome, which effectively reproduce the destructive cycle of building new Troys that begins with Priam and continues with Aeneas. Guido amplifies the accuracy of the reproduction by identifying common characteristics of each city: division and contamination. The Xanthus, which divides Troy into two parts, not only provides sustenance, but also eliminates waste through subterraneous tunnels (48).[103] By constructing the Tiber in a similar manner, Aeneas translates these same characteristics to Rome, which prove to contain more than architectural significance. The image of a city divided with sewers that force contamination underground becomes a metaphor for the divisive war councils and the secret treason of Antenor and Aeneas. This is a far cry from the copy of the Xanthus in Virgil's *Aeneid*, which is described as a drying brook (*arentem rivum* [350]), a clear indication of its infertility and harbinger of Troy's irreproducibility. Instead, Aeneas is called to the Tiber, which will transcend the image of the Xanthus and spawn imperial growth that cannot be achieved through the reproduction of a doomed city. By departing from Virgilian architecture and having Aeneas construct Rome based on this faulty model of Troy, Guido inscribes a destructive subtext into the image of Rome, one that would historically divide and conquer its imitations.

Clearly the *Siege*-poet and his readers would have received ample justification for connecting the fates of Troy and Rome from Guido or Clerk's Trojan historiography, but would they have perceived the destruction of Jerusalem and its inhabitants to be prophetic for the fate of the Roman Empire? To answer this question, I have identified two interrogations of imperial propaganda that the *Siege* shares with the *Destruction*: the logic of the *translatio imperii* that requires the destruction of one empire in order to spawn the construction of another; and the synecdochic relationship between bodies and cities. In the same way that Clerk articulates the fall and rise of New Troys, the *Siege*-poet imagines the beginning of a Christian empire through the destruction of Jerusalem and the return of the soldiers to Rome. While the *Siege*-poet certainly asserts the power of the Roman Empire, he does so in a way that confounds stark differences between Romans and Jews, bodies and cities. The *Siege*-poet blurs distinctions through the accumulation of scenes that describe the destruction of bodies and the grief of the besieged. And just like its alliterative relative, the *Destruction*, the fate of the bodies and cities are intimately connected thematically and linguistically. The bodies of

---

103. "Hic etiam fluuius per meatus artificiose compositos et subterraneas caharactas per latentes ductus aquarum neccessaria fecunditate decurrens ciuitatem ipsam ordinates incursionibus mundabat, per quarum lauacrum congeste immunditie purgabantur."

the besieged Jews are not only obliterated, but also liquidated in the same way as the city itself.

The most powerful example of the *Siege*-poet's equation of the Jewish body to the city of Jerusalem occurs in the final days of the siege in a manner reminiscent of Aeneas and Antenor's treasonous negotiations with the Greeks in the *Destruction*. As the starving Jews await their impending destruction, many resort to eating the only object of value they have left: their gold. After Titus accepts their surrender and cedes their passage out of Jerusalem, a few Roman soldiers realize that these Jews have hidden their treasure in their stomachs:

[With]outen leue of þat lord   ledes hem slowen,
[G]oren euereche a gome   and þe gold taken,
Fayn[er] of þe floreyns   [þan of] þe frekes alle. (1170–72)

[Without asking permission of their lord, the men slew them, goring every one of them to extract the gold, more delighted with the money than with all the men themselves.]

In their greed, the Romans liquidate the Jewish bodies' gold, forcing a violent expectoration of wealth. This is the macabre antithesis of Maria's cannibalism—instead of a return to the stomach, it is a withdrawal from it. Shortly afterwards, the Romans seek greater monetary extractions from the city itself, which "Telle couþe no tonge þe tresours þat þey founden" [no tongue could tell of the treasure they found] (1274). Despite the disclaimer, the *Siege*-poet describes the treasure the Romans pillage in great detail, emphasizing the Roman avarice and demonstrating a keen interest in the wealth of Jerusalem (1254–80). The special attention the *Siege*-poet gives to the gold of the Jews may have also been the result of the "bullionism" or drain of gold and silver bullion after 1350 as well as the famine and debts that Bolton Priory suffered in the early fourteenth century.[104] In any case, these bullion fantasies intimately connect the fate of the bodies of the Jews with the city of Jerusalem in a manner undeniably similar to Aeneas and Antenor's treason against Troy. For the money of the Greeks, they sacrifice the body of their king Priam and the great city that they had previously called their own.

Likewise, the Romans destroy and burn the city in a manner that mirrors not only their earlier mutilation and cremation of Caiaphas and the other

---

104. Chism, *Alliterative Revivals*, 175; Ian Kershaw, *Bolton Priory: The Economy of a Northern Monastery, 1286–1325* (Oxford: Oxford University Press, 1973), 171–83.

Jewish priests, but also the fall of Troy in Clerk's *Destruction*. The Romans dismember the city, tearing down its "[p]elours" (1269) and "walles" (1282), and also burn every last vestige of the temple and town, reducing it to "poudere" (1284). This language recalls the torture and burning of the Jewish priests, who were eventually transformed into "browne askes" (720) and blown back into the city as "powdere" (722) for the inhabitants to drink. The reduction of the city to ashes is also found in the *Destruction* when the Greeks "[gr]ete palis of prise put into askys" (12009), a phrase that links the fate of the Troy and Jerusalem. As Malcolm Hebron notes, literary illustrations of the sieges of Troy and Jerusalem are often very similar because, "[a]t the heart of the vision of besieged Troy of Jerusalem is the idea of a purging experience, a painful rite of passage in which a great cultural or spiritual change is effected."[105] For Clerk and the *Siege*-poet, purgation requires human casualties and a physical return to dust through burning and beating. In the *Siege*, Titus orders, "Doun bete þe bilde, brenne hit into grounde" [the buildings beaten down, burned to the ground] (1264) and Jerusalem is later "doun betyn and brent into blake erþe" [beaten down and burned into the black earth] (1292) just as Troy in the *Destruction* is "bete doun to the bare erthe" [beaten down into the bare earth] (12005). The linguistic and syntactic similarities between these descriptions reaffirm the relationship of dependence between the two poems, and also suggest a greater thematic similarity of a return to dust, which gestures towards the transience of these imperial endeavors. Not only do bodies assume their place in the ground in the listing of tombs at the end of the *Destruction*, but also the cities themselves take a residence in the earth, which prevents their imperial translation. Titus even punctuates the impossibility of translation by commanding that his soliders plow the ground and sow it with salt. After this is done he declares, "Now is þis stalwourþe stede distroied foreuere" [Now this stronghold is destroyed forever] (1294–96). By sowing the ground with salt and declaring that this city will never rise again, Titus both literally ensures that the Jews will no longer have a homeland and paradoxically sterilizes the salvific authority to be gained from it. Given the Roman heritage in Troy and the eternal nature of destruction proclaimed through the words "distroied foreuere," the *Siege*-poet cleverly amplifies the language of the destruction of Troy to prophesy the doom to come for the Roman Empire.

Since the *Siege* shares the amplificatory rhetoric, corporeal didacticism, and historiographic perspective of the Guido-tradition, it is no surprise that it also promulgates the Trojan "plague of great destruction." Yet, inasmuch as

---

105. Hebron, *The Medieval Siege*, 135.

this chapter seeks to identify the *Siege*-poet's assimilation of Clerk's alliterative style and Guido's imperial pessimism, it must not be said that the *Siege* is despairingly "imitative."[106] I would suggest, in the words of Michel Foucault, that a reading of *Siege* defies attempts to "distinguish the original from the repetitive" in its interweaving of theological and historical source material and unique embellishments.[107] As much as the *Siege*-poet focuses his efforts on the destruction of Jerusalem, he cleverly inserts accounts of the burning of Rome (900) and the casting of Vitellius' body into the Tiber (948) that both reflect Rome's complicity in the fall of Jerusalem and highlight the dangers of architectural *imitatio*.

Especially instructive is the *Siege*-poet's connotative use of the name Sir Sabyn, which appears throughout the narrative as a name that refers to two separate characters. The first "Sir Sabyn" is Titus Flavius Sabinus, Vespasian's brother, who meets his end at the hands of the emperor Vitellius.[108] This murder incites the fraternal vengeance of Vespasian, who tortures and executes Vitellius by dragging him through the streets of Rome, disemboweling him, and then casting him screaming into the Tiber (939–48). As a conclusion to Vitellius' imperial life, the *Siege*-poet remarks,

> Seuen monþes þis [segge]   hadde septre on hande,
> And þus loste he þe lyf   for his luþer dedes.
> Anoþer segge was to seke   þat septre schold haue,
> For alle þis grete ben gon   and neuer agayn tournen. (949–52)

> [Seven months this man held the scepter in his hand, and thus lost his life for his terrible deeds. Another man was to seek that scepter, because all the great men were gone and never again returned.]

While the passage suggests that another "segge" would seek the throne, it is clear that any "grete" possibilities have left the scene. This skeptical tone is accentuated by the brevity of Vitellius' reign, a mere seven months, which suggests that periods of peace will be brief. Moreover, the circumstances of Vitellius' death provide a linguistic structure for the second "Sir Sabyn," who appears shortly afterwards as the Syrian advisor to Vespasian who advises him to rule by proxy. The conflation of the two Sabyns is marked not only by their closeness to Vespasian, but also by their violent deaths and the numero-

---

106. Pearsall, *Old and Middle English Poetry*, 169.
107. Michel Foucault, *The Archaeology of Knowledge and The Discourse on Language*, trans. A. M. Sheridan Smith (New York: Pantheon Books, 1972), 14.3
108. See Livingston's note on line 939, *The Siege of Jerusalem*.

logical instruction they provide about the interrelation between cities and bodies. As a kind of resurrected brother of Vespasian, the second Sir Sabyn shares Vitellius' fate of being undone by the number seven: Vitellius dies in his seventh month as emperor and Sir Sabyn dies at the hands of the seventh warrior at the walls of Jerusalem (1202).

Furthermore, their corpses both inhabit architectural spaces, a river and a ditch, designed to keep contaminates from infecting inhabitants of the city. According to Guido, Aeneas constructed the Tiber in imitation of Troy's Xanthus, but instead of revealing how the Tiber remains separate from the sewers, the *Siege*-poet figuratively connects Vitellius' contamination of the famed Roman river with the diseased ditch and the stinking canal that carry poisoned air and water into Jerusalem.

> Suþ dommyn þe diches   with þe ded corses,
> Crammen hit myd karayn   þe kirnel[e]s alle vnder,
> Þat þe stynk of þe ste[w]e   myȝt strike over þe walles
> To coþe þe corsed folke   þat hem kepe scholde.
> Þe cors of þe condit   þat comen to toun
> Stoppen, euereche a streem   þer any str[and]e ȝede,
> With stockes and stones   and stynkande bestes
> Þat þey no water myȝt wynne   þat weren enclosed. (685–92)

[Then they choke the ditches with dead bodies, cram them with carrion under all the battlements, so that the stench from that vapor might spread over the walls to infect the cursed folk who should defend them. The course of the canal, every stream where any current went, that came into the town they stop with sticks and stones and rotting beasts so that the inhabitants of the city cannot obtain any water.]

This image both invokes and transforms Guido's illustration of the Xanthus so that the cleansing canal succumbs to the contamination of an imperial siege and enhances the evils and division that plague a city such as Rome. Moreover, the *Siege*-poet's reference to the potential of the ditch to "coþe" the Jewish inhabitants is reminiscent of Guido's suggestion that the *translatio imperii* will infect (*infecerit*) the New Trojan line (11). These scenes and references combine connotatively to conflate the fates of the conquerors and the conquered and recognize the infectious power of sovereignty. Together they create an image of a river flowing into the city of Rome with the floating bodies of the dead king Vitellius and Sir Sabyn and the other rotting corpses that accompany such imperial fantasies. The contamination of imperial currents represents the course of the narrative in which dismembered bodies emerge in gruesome succession, confounding sovereign succession and dooming the birth of Christian imperialism to come. The Romans are now building their own *parvam Troiam* that is a contaminated imitation of the imagined empire of their ancestors.

FOUR

Heraldry

ARTHUR'S ROMAN DRAGON

FOR ADMIRERS of Ernst Kantorowicz's *The King's Two Bodies*, the myth of King Arthur has an irresistible appeal.[1] Arthur's identity as *rex quondam rexque futurus* resonates with Kantorowicz's analysis of the theological character of early modern royal succession, whereby the death of a king (the body natural) is a recurrent episode in the metaphysical life of sovereignty (the body politic). Scholars have identified this juridical insistence on the sempiternity of the sovereign in late medieval incarnations of a King Arthur who never dies or dies and returns in messianic fashion.[2] Yet, as Giorgio Agamben points out, Kantorowicz fails to acknowledge the absolutist nature of sovereignty that this political theology entails. Rather than merely perpetuate the *dignitas* of the kingship, Agamben suggests that "the metaphor of the political body appears . . . as the cipher of the absolute and inhuman character of sovereignty."[3] In other words, the expense of the principle *le roi*

---

1. Ernst Hartwig Kantorowicz, *The King's Two Bodies: A Study in Mediaeval Political Theology* (Princeton: Princeton University Press, 1957; repr. 1997).

2. For a full treatment, see Patricia Clare Ingham, *Sovereign Fantasies: Arthurian Romance and the Making of Britain* (Philadelphia: University of Pennsylvania Press, 2001). See also Stephen Knight, *Arthurian Literature and Society* (New York: St. Martin's Press, 1983); Martin Shichtman and James Carley, eds., *Culture and the King: The Social Implications of the Arthurian Legend* (Albany: State University of New York Press, 1994); Elizabeth T. Pochoda, *Arthurian Propaganda: Le Morte Darthur as an Historical Ideal of Life* (Chapel Hill, NC: University of North Carolina Press, 1971).

3. Giorgio Agamben, *Homo Sacer: Sovereign Power and Bare Life* (Stanford: Stanford University Press, 1998), 91–103 at 101. Cf. Kantorowicz, "Dignitas non moritur," in *The King's Two*

ne meurt jamais is the evacuation of value from human life. By mitigating the impact of a king's death on the political body, sovereignty is simultaneously maintained and dehumanized. In this light, Arthur's legendary sempiternity is demystified as a trace of premodern statecraft.

Optimism about Arthur's return abounds in most Arthurian texts, but resistance to such political theology can be found in the early fifteenth-century alliterative *Morte Arthure*, an intimate portrayal of Arthur as a prideful sovereign. Any enthusiasm for Arthur's virtue, which is called into question throughout the poem, must be attenuated by the concluding lines. In a manner unbecoming of England's greatest king, Arthur orders his knights to track down Mordred's children, kill them, and hurl their bodies into the sea (4320–21).[4] While many readers may forgive Arthur for this cruel act of infanticide, we know that this image of drowning innocent children did not match the chivalric sensibility of Sir Thomas Malory who, despite having drawn much of his material for his "Tale of Arthur and Lucius" from the *Morte*, prefers a more laudatory ending for Arthur and turns to his French sources in describing Arthur's final days.[5] For the *Morte*-poet, the callous extermination of the innocent progeny of an enemy is merely one example of the extensive collateral damage that war produces. The result of this compassion for the victim and condemnation of the sovereign is a poem that expresses great ambivalence about the benefits of war and territorial expansion.

Arthur's decision to execute his enemy's children is especially unsettling because it is also an obliteration of a kinsman's genealogical line, a ramification of Guinevere's adultery with Mordred, who is described as a "Malebranche" (4174).[6] In a poem fraught with invocations of noble heritage and imperial lineage, the extermination of potential contenders to the throne of Britain is more than an act of revenge or self-preservation. Arthur's concern with the progeny produced from Guinevere and Mordred's adulterous union calls attention to the tortuous course of the genealogy of empire that is defined by disruptive and transgressive acts such as Brutus' accidental patricide.

Bodies, 383–450.

4. All citations of the poem refer to Mary Hamel's edition, *Morte Arthure: A Critical Edition* (New York: Garland Publishing, 1984). For different textual readings, I will refer to the following editions: Larry Benson, ed., *King Arthur's Death* (Indianapolis: Bobbs-Merrill, 1974); Valerie Krishna, ed., *The Alliterative 'Morte Arthure': A Critical Edition* (New York: Burt Franklin, 1976); E. Brock, ed., *Morte Arthure*, EETS OS 8 (New York, London, Toronto: Oxford University Press, 1871; rpt. 1961).

5. Hamel, *Morte Arthure*, 4.

6. For a recent treatment of Arthur's execution of Mordred's children, see Edward Donald Kennedy's "Mordred's Sons," in *The Arthurian Way of Death: The English Tradition*, ed. Karen Cherewatuk and K. S. Whetter (Cambridge: D. S. Brewer, 2009), 33–49.

Arthur's dying wish, unsettling in its willful sacrifice of the innocent, is an awakening from the fantasy of empire, a vision of Arthur's return as an imperial messiah. Instead of gesturing toward an ethereal transfer of Arthur's body to Avalon, Arthur dies a tyrant. Such a characterization reflects an ultimate rejection of the *translatio imperii*, which privileges the imagined transfer of sovereignty from Troy to Rome to Britain and interrogates the nature of royal authority. Essentially, Arthur's willingness to sacrifice children for the sake of empire forces readers to ask the following question: is it possible for monarchs to assert their authority without engaging in acts of cruelty and willful violence?

For most readers of this poem, this question strikes a flat note amidst the poem's enthusiasm about war and its investment in Britain's Trojan genealogy. After all, this poem is the most ostentatiously imperialistic of the alliterative genre in that its subject is King Arthur, the legendary champion of British sovereignty. However, as the poem progresses, it becomes evident that the *Morte*-poet is not as interested in praising Britain's greatest king as he is dedicated to critiquing the British fantasy of Arthur, which imagines him as the worthy inheritor and perpetuator of imperial authority that can be traced back to Troy. In the *Morte*-poet's illustration of Arthur's attempt to besiege his Roman heritage and create an empire that surpasses that of Rome, the poem reads as a cautionary tale, as much about the ethics of kingship and Arthurian propaganda as about the nature of warfare and imperialism.

As I have been suggesting in previous chapters, the skepticism about such a transfer of empire is inherent to the alliterative poetry that follows the example of Guido delle Colonne's *Historia destructionis Troiae*. Yet, the *Morte* is unique in its ability to maintain contradictory viewpoints about war and empire by virtue of its intertextual treatment of source material and slippery imperial signifiers. These signs emerge as heraldic symbols that justify Britain's heritage, which is consistently expressed throughout the poem as originating in Troy. Thus, the characteristic figures of the destroyed city of Troy, the conflicted Priam, and the defeated Hector emerge to highlight Britain's ancestral losses and perpetuate the "plague of great destruction" that has afflicted the Trojans, the Romans, and now the Britons. Instead of legitimizing Britain's claims to global sovereignty, the *Morte*-poet presents Britain's Trojan ancestry as a curse and a mode of succession that must be terminated.

Arthur is the natural symbol of sovereignty in the poem by virtue of his intention to reverse the track of the *translatio imperii* and reclaim his Roman heritage. The origin of empire ironically becomes the coveted object of Arthur, who seeks to establish a dominion larger and more powerful than that of the Romans by obliterating his imperial predecessor, thereby expressing a paradoxical desire of Britain to be and not to be Rome. This attempted reclamation of an imperial origin not only inspires self-destruction, but also signifies a recurrent inability to obliterate a spirit of tyranny that runs throughout the poem. The label of "tyraunt" is transferred explicitly from the Roman emperor Lucius and his legions (271, 824) to the Giant of St. Michael's Mount (842, 878, 991) and implicitly to Arthur himself. Just as the Giant's tyranny "tourmentez" (842) people and causes the old widow to mourn the death of the Duchess of Brittany by "wryngande hir handez" (950), Arthur's destruction of Tuscany "turmentez þe pople" (3153) and transforms wives into widows who "wryngene theire handis" (3155). Instead of preserving the *dignitas* of the king, it is as if the greed of the tyrant never dies—when a tyrant is killed, his avaricious spirit fills a new body in the manner of the Virgilian transmigration of souls. As soon as Arthur kills the Giant of St. Michael's Mount, he becomes the Giant—as soon as he defeats the Roman emperor Lucius, he becomes a British "emperor." Rather than promulgate such translations of empire, this poem denounces assertions of authority as translations of tyranny. *Translatio imperii* becomes *translatio tyrannidis*.

I want to suggest that the poem achieves this macabre message of *tyrannus non moritur* primarily through an unstable system of chivalric machinery: the art of heraldry. Alliterative romance is replete with heraldic assertions of nobility, but the *Morte Arthure* is unique in its necrologic interpretation of such chivalric devices. Rather than simply commemorate the deeds of ancestors and confirm the noble blood of the bearers, the heraldic signs of this poem operate as visual necrologies, or lists of the dead. Just as monks would use a liturgical record of the dead in a morning office, knights ritually present the arms of the noble kinsmen who died in battle. Whereas the appropriate heraldic symbol regularly secures the chivalric status of its bearer, such signs in the *Morte* remind onlookers of the death and destruction left in their wake. Consider the following episode after Arthur's victory at Soissons. Arthur commands his heralds, who are normally responsible for recording the details of battle, to act as morticians by embalming the corpses and enclosing them in "kystys" [chests] (2302), which are decorated with "theire baners abowne, theire bagis therevndyre" [their banners above, their badges below] (2303).[7] In this scene, the art of heraldry becomes the art of death,

---

7. I am influenced by D. Vance Smith's reading of this scene in *Arts of Possession: The Middle English Household Imaginary* (Minneapolis: University of Minnesota Press, 2003), 198. For more on the role of heralds, see Anthony Richard Wagner, *Heralds and Heraldry in the Middle Ages: An Inquiry into the Growth of the Armorial Function of Heralds* (Oxford: Oxford University Press, 1939), 33ff; The Chandos Herald, *Vie du Prince Noir*, in *The Life and Campaigns of the*

a striking equivalency that memorializes the dead as it celebrates the living. By transforming heralds into undertakers, the badges and banners become visual reminders of the deaths that accompany all heraldic assertions, from battle standards to coats of arms. Rather than serve as signifiers of the stable system of knighthood and nobility, heraldic devices in this poem emphasize the threat that martial violence poses for the security of chivalric and sovereign identity.[8]

This heraldic signification of death renders such devices indecipherable to their witnesses—they no longer serve as reliable symbols of noble lineage. In the description of Gawain's death, the sight of his heraldic markers that would legitimize his royal blood rise to the fore: "His baners brayden down, betyn of gowlles / His brande and his brade schelde al blody beronen" [His banners struck down, adorned with red / His blade and his broad shield run over completely with blood] (3945). Instead of broadcasting his nobility, his banners and shield signify his death, with his body beaten to the ground and his arms obscured by blood. Without his heraldic symbols to demonstrate his gentility, Arthur consecrates Gawain's blood himself (3991) in a desperate attempt to endow his kinsmen's blood with what Christine Chism calls "the material transcendence of a relic."[9] Such scenes do not suggest, as D. Vance Smith argues, that the "proximity to death" of heraldic gestures renders their signification "impossible."[10] Instead, such devices signify the death that is the necessary consequence of heraldic assertions. The profusion of Gawain's blood, the corporeal manifestation of his nobility, obscures his martial identity and supersedes the heraldic law that would justify his ancestry.

More than any other figure, the image of the dragon, which appears in various forms, embodies the poem's system of heraldic signification. It is through a reading of the dragon that the *Morte*-poet's perspective on war has a particularly alliterative flavor, since the *Morte*-poet draws both the language used to describe the dragon and what I call its "pedagogic" function from the late fourteenth-century alliterative poem, *The Siege of Jerusalem*. The dragon, which is associated with both King Arthur and the Roman Emperor Lucius, is representative of a program of slippery signification throughout the poem, which complicates attempts to fix such signs to their referents. The result of

---

Black Prince, ed. Richard Barber (Woodbridge: Boydell, 1986), 84–139.
    8. Cf. Kenneth J. Tiller, "The Rise of Sir Gareth and the Hermeneutics of Heraldry," *Arthuriana* 17.3 (2007): 74–91, at 78–79; Laurie Finke and Martin Shichtman, *King Arthur and the Myth of History* (Gainesville: University of Florida Press, 2004), 174–78.
    9. Christine Chism, *Alliterative Revivals* (Philadelphia: University of Pennsylvania Press, 2002), 225.
    10. Smith, *Arts of Possession*, 219.

this programmatic slippage is a thoroughgoing critique of heraldic assertions of nobility. The *Morte*-poet attaches multiple meanings to recurring heraldic devices to attenuate martial fervor, obscure distinctions between the conquerors and the conquered, and emphasize the collateral damage of war. By juxtaposing signs of empire with scenes of violence, the relationship between assertions of sovereignty and the indiscriminate extermination of life becomes inseparable.

THE TRAGIC TRADITION

Critics have long acknowledged the poem's ambivalence about war, but most have read its critiques of militaristic overreaching solely in contrast to the poem's primary sources, namely Geoffrey of Monmouth's *Historia regum Britanniae* and its vernacular translations.[11] Even though most critics acknowledge the pessimism of the poem, they read the *Morte*'s unique features as departures and amplifications of Galfridian historiography, rather than the product of alternative influences, such as the Guido-tradition.

Scholars have therefore interpreted the *Morte*'s conflicted representations of violence in three ways.[12] The first reading considers the *Morte* to be essentially pacifistic and/or anti-imperialistic. William Matthews and John Finlayson have claimed that the poem critiques Arthur's offensive military tactics and imperial ambition, while Karl Heinz Göller even goes so far as to claim that "there can be no doubt that the poet is saying that every war

---

11. What many have characterized as the poem's pacifism or ambivalence about empire-building has often been attributed to the poet's own ingenious embellishment of the Galfridian tale. As Maureen Fries has put it, the *Morte Arthure* is "indisputably Galfridian" in its direct use not only of Geoffrey's *Historia*, but also of the later translations by Wace in 1155, Laȝamon at the end of the twelfth century, and Robert Manning *circa* 1338. See "The Poem in the Tradition of Arthurian Literature," in *The "Alliterative Morte Arthure": A Reassessment of the Poem*, ed. Karl Heinz Göller, Arthurian Studies 2 (Woodbridge, Eng.: D. S. Brewer, 1981), 30–43, at 34. For a concise explanation of these chronicle sources, see Hamel, *Morte Arthure*, 34–38. See also Patricia DeMarco, "An Arthur for the Ricardian Age: Crown Nobility, and the Alliterative *Morte Arthure*," *Speculum* 80. 2 (2005): 464–93. In this article on the poem's representations of the conflict between king and noble, DeMarco rehearses the predominant scholarly perception of the relationship between the *Morte* and the Galfridian material: "The *Morte Arthure* departs from that tradition . . . both in its choice of subject matter and its method of handling the material. Amplifying what had been merely the crowning achievement of Arthur's reign in the Galfredian account, the *Morte* focuses on Britain's war against the Romans and . . . produces a lavishly detailed portrait of military life distinguished by its extensive historical topicality and its unparalleled realism" (464).

12. For a brief synopsis of the readings, see pages 466–67 of DeMarco's "An Arthur for the Ricardian Age."

is unjust."[13] In a recent pursuit of this argument, Randy Schiff has suggested that the anti-imperialistic sentiment of the poem—and of two other northern alliterative poems, the *Awyntyrs off Arthure* and *Golagros and Gawan*—emerges from the Anglo-Scottish marches, a "zone that continually bore the brunt of clashing empires."[14] The second reading responds to the arguments made by Matthews and Finlayson: Juliet Vale, Elizabeth Porter, and Rebecca Beal downplay the tragedy of war in the poem and instead focus on the *Morte*-poet's efforts to laud Arthur's heroism, his status as the symbol of British civilization, and his ethical military policies. Vale, at the opposite extreme of readers like Göller, even suggests, "Arthur is very far from the cruel and covetous tyrant that he has been held to be."[15] The more recent third reading, however, follows the trend to deconstruct these competing messages about war, and examine the ambivalence they create. These scholars have recognized the fact that this poem cannot be broken down into set dichotomies or read as justifying one martial discourse over the other.[16] Working from Larry Benson's older claim that the poem unscrupulously maintains contradictory viewpoints, more recent critics such as Lee Patterson, Patricia Clare Ingham, Christine Chism, and Geraldine Heng have focused on the fine line between the poem's legitimizing power and

---

13. Göller, "Reality vs. Romance," 25–29, at 26. For the anti-imperialistic view, see William Matthews, *The Tragedy of Arthur: A Study of the Alliterative "Morte Arthure"* (Berkeley: University of California Press, 1960), 192. Matthews suggests that the emphasis on martial destruction at the end of the poem represented the latter part of Edward III's reign, when "the average Englishman was weary of the tragic futility of his ruler's imperial conquerings." See also Finlayson, "Arthur and the Giant of St. Michael's Mount," *Medium Aevum* 33 (1964): 112–20; "The Concept of the Hero in the *Morte Arthure*," in *Chaucer und seine Zeit: Symposion für Walter F. Schirmer*, ed. Arno Esch, Buchreihe der Anglia: Zeitschrift für englische Philologie 14 (Tübingen: M. Niemeyer, 1968), 249–74. Finlayson claims that even though the *Morte*-poet presents Arthur's original military expedition as justifiable, he condemns his subsequent actions. For extensions of this reading, see Michael W. Twowmey, "Heroic Kingship and Unjust War in the Alliterative *Morte Arthure*," *Acta* 11 (1984): 133–51; and Lesley Johnson, "King Arthur at the Crossroads to Rome," in *Noble and Joyous Histories: English Romances 1375–1650*, eds. Eiléan Ní Cuilleanáin and J. D. Pheifer (Dublin: Irish Academic Press, 1993), 87–112.

14. Randy Schiff, *Revivalist Fantasy: Alliterative Verse and Nationalist Literary History* (Columbus: The Ohio State University Press, 2011), 100–127, at 122.

15. Juliet Vale, "Law and Diplomacy in the Alliterative *Morte Arthure*," *Nottingham Medieval Studies* 23 (1979): 31–46, at 39; Elizabeth Porter, "Chaucer's Knight, the Alliterative *Morte Arthure*, and Medieval Laws of War: A Reconsideration," *Nottingham Medieval Studies* 27 (1983): 56–78; Rebecca S. Beal, "Arthur as the Bearer of Civilization: The *Alliterative Morte Arthure*, Ll. 901–19," *Arthuriana* 5/4 (1995): 32–44; Richard J. Moll, *Before Malory: Reading Arthur in Later Medieval England* (Toronto: University of Toronto Press, 2003), 97–122.

16. A helpful essay on the problem of defining power relationships in broad binaries, particularly between postcolonial treatments of race and gender, is Sara Suleri's "Woman Skin Deep: Feminism and the Postcolonial Condition," in *Women, Autobiography, Theory: A Reader*, ed. Sidonie Smith and Julia Watson (Madison: University of Wisconsin Press, 1998), 116–25.

its expressions of loss to make larger arguments about its relationship to the progression of history, insular colonialism, and chivalric communities.[17] Patterson has been particularly influential in this regard, suggesting that the tragedy of Arthur's demise was integral to its appeal to monarchs: "If kings wanted national heroes to exemplify and authorize their own heroism, they seem also to have wanted them, paradoxically, to have come to tragic ends."[18] According to Patterson, the *Morte* maintains a dialectic between glory and destruction through "historical recurrence," fulfilling the imperial desire for death and its redemption.[19] By deferring the tendency to read the poem as either triumphalist or anti-imperialistic, these readings seek to explain the social work that the poem performs through its ambivalent representations of sovereignty, war, and feudal relationships.

My reading of the poem is deeply indebted to the anti-imperialistic claims of Matthews, Finlayson, and Göller, but it also resonates with the recent focus on the *Morte*-poet's nuanced treatment of war. My interpretation, however, departs from the primary focus on one major avenue of historiographic influence. Despite their best efforts to track down and acknowledge the sources for what Mary Hamel has characterized as the product of a "lifetime's reading," most of these critics restrict their readings of the *Morte* through its comparison to the Galfridian sources.[20] Even James Simpson, who has meticulously tracked the extensive influence of the Guido-tradition, does not perceive the "clerical voice" throughout the *Morte*, which he claims is characteristic of Guido's pessimism.[21] For the majority of the poem, he contends that "there is no critique of war. . . . On the contrary, the poem fairly bristles with militarist confidence and conviction. . . . The disposition of the clerical voice of this text, then, is different from that found in the Guido-tradition. There the reader is made aware of significant errors throughout the text, whose cumulative effect is to produce military disaster;

---

17. Larry Benson, "The Alliterative *Morte Arthure* and Medieval Tragedy," *Tennessee Studies in Literature* 11 (1966): 75–89. See also Lee Patterson, "The Romance of History and the Alliterative *Morte Arthure*," in *Negotiating the Past: The Historical Understanding of Medieval Literature* (Madison: University of Wisconsin Press, 1987), 197–230. Patterson's suggestion that this poem is less about ethics than it is about "tragic submission to the iron law of historical recurrence" (217) has influenced historicist readings such as those of Ingham, *Sovereign Fantasies*; Christine Chism, *Alliterative Revivals*; Geraldine Heng, *Empire of Magic: Medieval Romance and the Politics of Cultural Fantasy* (New York: Columbia University Press, 2003).
18. Patterson, *Negotiating the Past*, 230.
19. Ibid., 217.
20. Hamel, *Morte Arthure*, 34.
21. Simpson, *Reform and Cultural Revolution*, 99. For more on the division between the aristocracy and the clergy, see also Ad Putter, *'Sir Gawain and the Green Knight' and French Arthurian Romance* (Oxford: Clarendon Press, 1995), 197–201.

in the *Morte,* on the contrary, the force of the clerical voice is withheld for one powerful and decisive intervention."[22] Instead, he claims that the *Morte*-poet capitalizes on the weaknesses of the Galfridian material to transform the poem into a tragedy after the Italian campaign.[23] More recently, Dorsey Armstrong has suggested that the poem tells two stories at once: "one narrative confers critique on Arthur and his actions, while the other points to potential positive outcomes that are, tragically, never realized."[24] Rather than argue that a "decisive intervention" emerges, she points to the moment late in the poem when Mordred wields Arthur's sword Clarent, which confirms the allegation that his queen has betrayed him and signals readers to reflect upon the tragic course of the narrative. Armstrong describes this moment, suggesting that "a blinding light is cast on the events of the plot, which encourages the reader to reconsider and rethink how and why the narrative arrives at its ultimate conclusion."[25] Whereas Armstrong turns to the Galfridian chronicle tradition for the origin of this "blinding light," I would suggest that the voice of skepticism comes primarily from the Guido-tradition. While I believe the *Morte*-poet's use of the Guido-tradition to be less explicit than his alliterative predecessors, I want to suggest that Guido's pessimism emerges not only in the "tragic" end of Arthur, but also in many episodes at the beginning of the poem, including the dream of the dragon and the bear. Guido's influence is subtle—it does not emerge as a *deus ex machina* in the guise of Lady Fortune who transforms the poem from a militaristic romance to Aristotelian tragedy. Rather, Guido's skepticism can be perceived throughout the narrative, from Arthur's reproach of Cador's bellicosity in the Giant's Tower war council to Arthur's violent death at the hands of Mordred. Guido's voice once again assumes an alliterative form that is markedly critical of the English praise of Arthur's Trojan heritage, producing a poem whose Galfridian architecture is covered by Guido's dark façade. In the following sections, I demonstrate the way Guido's coloring of the nar-

22. Simpson, *Reform and Cultural Revolution,* 107–110. He also does not share my perspective of the *Siege*-poet's ambivalence about imperialism. In fact, he does not treat the poem as part of the alliterative "tragic" tradition at all. He defends his choice to exclude the poem this way: "One might have thought that it naturally belongs here, since it, too, treats the fall of a city. It resists my case for the generally anti-imperialistic and anti-propagandistic quality of 'fall' narratives of this period. . . . Finally, however, I think it confirms my case, by being the exception to the rule. It is a thoroughly objectionable work of fervid anti-Semitism, unlike almost anything else in the later medieval period in that respect" (116).
23. Ibid., 110.
24. Dorsey Armstrong, "Rewriting the Chronicle Tradition: The Alliterative *Morte Arthure* and Arthur's Sword of Peace," *Parergon* 25.1 (2008): 81–101, at 82.
25. Ibid., 84.

rative builds anti-imperialistic intensity through the figures of the heraldic dragon, King Arthur, and even Hector of Troy.

DEATH WHERE THE DRAGON IS RAISED

Perhaps more than any other aristocratic symbol, the heraldic dragon embodies the *Morte*-poet's departure from Galfridian historiography. Just like Trojan ancestry, the sign of the dragon originates in the East, but in the eyes of the western world the dragon became the quintessential Roman imperial standard by the end of the second century C.E. By the fourth century, it became the chief military ensign and was used both in battles and imperial rituals.[26] As Mary Hamel notes, the Roman dragon symbol is "a distinct oddity" in the *Morte* because, according to the philosophers who interpret Arthur's first dream in the poem, the dragon represents Arthur, not the Romans.

> The dragon þat þow dremyde of   so dredfull to schewe,
> That come dryfande ouer þe deepe   to drynchen thy pople,
> Sothely and certayne   thy seluen it es,
> That thus saillez ouer þe see   with thy sekyre knyghtez. (815–18)

> [The dragon that you dreamed of so dreadful to behold, which came driving over the deep to drown your people, truly and certainly it is you, who thus sails over the sea with your trusty knights.]

The attribution of the dragon to Arthur is natural since it signifies the legacy inherited from his father, Uther Pendragon, who represents the golden dragon in the Galfridian sources. At this point in the poem, the *Morte*-poet clearly follows the genealogical association between the dragon and Arthur, but darkens this inheritance by claiming that Arthur will "drynchen" his people.[27] Arthur's capability to drown his people is confirmed at the end of the poem when he orders Mordred's children to be thrown into "watyrs"

---

26. Vegetius, *Epitoma rei militaris*, ed. M. D. Reeve (Oxford: Clarendon Press, 2004), 1.23, 2.7. For a full discussion of dragons and their British contexts, see J. S. P. Tatlock, "The Dragons of Wessex and Wales," *Speculum* 8.2 (1933): 223–35.

27. This verb could mean "destroy," but in the context of the "deepe" and the "see," it most likely means "drown," the primary MED definition. The variant readings of the two extant manuscripts of *The Wars of Alexander* confirm this definition, at least for the alliterative poets. Whereas the Dublin manuscript, MS 213, olim MS.D.4.12, reads "Þe folez & þe folke þat þe flude drynched" (3072), MS Ashmole 44 reads "þe fooles & þe folke þat þe flode drouned" (3199).

(4321), which indicates that this dream is to be interpreted as a sign not only of his imperial success, but also of the damage he will inflict on his kinsmen. Yet, the philosophers interpret the dream as validation that he and his knights will defeat the "tyrauntez þat tourmentez thy pople" [tyrants who torment your people] (824), that is, the Roman Lucius and his legions, and they make no attempt to explain how or why Arthur's expedition against the Romans will lead to the destruction of his own people.[28] This is the first of many clues in the text that we should not trust this optimistic interpretation of empire-building.

In the earlier description of the dream itself, which the interpreters fail to address, the dragon wields such an infectious power that "Whaym þat he towchede he was tynt for euer" [Whomever he touched was lost forever] (770). Even the symbol of the dragon itself would have inspired fear among medieval readers, since it represented evil, heresy, and even the AntiChrist.[29] Instead of addressing these ominous overtones, however, the philosophers emphasize Arthur's destined role as glorious conqueror of Rome. Even though readers might be tempted to trust these "sage philosophers" and view his march on Rome to be well intentioned and sanctioned by the *Morte*-poet, it becomes clear that the dragon also represents the collateral damage that is an unavoidable consequence of such imperial endeavors.

As the poem proceeds, the dragon transforms from a nightmarish figure to a military standard, rendering the dragon symbol a slippery imperial signifier. Furthermore, in translating the symbol of the dragon from the dream to the battlefield, the *Morte*-poet departs from Galfridian tradition. According to Geoffrey's *Historia*, before his battle with Lucius, "Ipse quoque . . . aureum draconem infixit quem pro uexillo habebat" [He [Arthur] also set up the golden dragon, which he had for a standard] (123).[30] Given his Pendragon legacy and the earlier dream that links Arthur specifically with the dragon, Geoffrey's association is expected, but when the dragon-emblem appears for the first time in battle in the *Morte* it is unexpectedly associated with Lucius and his Roman army. The messengers from the Marshal of France announce Lucius' invasion to Arthur, saying, "He drawes into

---

28. For a discussion of this ambiguous symbol, see John Gardner, ed., *The Alliterative Morte Arthure, The Owl and the Nightingale, and Five Other Middle English Poems* (Carbondale: Southern Illinois University Press, 1971), 254. Hamel finds it "odd that these 'sage philosophers,' subtle doctors of the seven liberal arts (808), do not explain how the Arthur-dragon is to drown his own people." See *Morte Arthure*, 285.

29. Göller, "The Dream of the Dragon and the Bear," in *The "Alliterative Morte Arthure,"* 132.

30. Neil Wright, ed., *The Historia Regum Britannie of Geoffrey of Monmouth, I: Bern, Burgerbibliothek, MS. 568* (Cambridge: D. S. Brewer, 1991). All citations from Geoffrey's *Historia* refer to this edition.

douce Fraunce, as Duchemen tellez, / Dresside with his dragouns, dredfull to schewe" [He draws into sweet France, as Germans tell, dressed with his dragons, dreadful to behold] (1251–52). The dragon's status as a Roman, not an Arthurian, emblem is reaffirmed later in the poem before the battle at Sessye, when Lucius and his army "Dresses vp dredfully the dragone of golde / With egles al ouer, enamelede of sable" [Raise up dreadfully the dragon of gold with eagles on every side, adorned with sable] (2026–27). Geoffrey's account, on the other hand, associates Lucius and his Romans only with a golden eagle: "In medio etiam auream aquilam quam pro uexillo duxerat iussit firmiter poni" [In the middle he [Lucius] also ordered fixed firmly the golden eagle, which he had brought for a standard] (125). Instead of adhering to the example of his Galfridian source, Arthurian tradition, and even Edward III, who appropriated this Pendragon standard for his own marches and battles, the *Morte*-poet renders "auream aquilam" as a "dragone of golde" and "egles . . . enamelede of sable," which transfers the golden feature of the eagles to the dragon, which had earlier been associated with Arthur in his dream.

This use and then later rejection of the Galfridian tradition are manifestations of the *Morte*-poet's heraldic agenda. I support the view that the *Morte*-poet departs from his Galfridian source to borrow the language of another alliterative poem, the *Siege of Jerusalem*, in order to transfer the symbol of the dragon from Arthur to Lucius. It is admittedly difficult to make arguments about "borrowings" when dealing with formulaic poetry, but the *Morte* bears more than what John Finlayson claims are only "superficial resemblances" to its alliterative predecessors.[31] Certainly, many of the verbal parallels between the poems can be attributed to a common wordhoard, but there are undeniable similarities that suggest the direct influence of alliterative poems such as the *Destruction of Troy* and the *Siege of Jerusalem* on the writing of the *Morte*.[32] To date the poem to 1399–1402, Hamel

---

31. John Finlayson, ed., *Morte Arthure*, York Medieval Texts (Evanston, IL: Northwestern University Press, 1967), 11.

32. For a brief discussion of the nature of this "formula" problem, see Hamel, *Morte Arthure*, 46–47. The verbal parallels are so clear that George Neilson actually claims that the same poet composed these poems in *"Huchown of the Awle Ryale," the Alliterative Poet* (Glasgow: James MacLehose & Sons, 1902). J. P. Oakden argues for relationships of dependence in "The Alliterative School," in *Alliterative Poetry in Middle English* (Manchester: Manchester University Press, 1935), 85–111. In critical response to these claims, Thorlac Turville-Petre contends that "tracing verbal parallels between the alliterative poems is a profitless task" and "far from facilitating the tracing of relationships between the poems, the collocational style more often obscures the evidence and makes the process of investigation almost impossible." See *The Alliterative Revival* (Cambridge: D. S. Brewer, 1977), 5.29.

has convincingly argued for a compositional sequence that begins with the *Destruction*'s reference to Geoffrey Chaucer's *Troilus and Criseyde*, and then continues through the *Siege*-poet's use of the *Destruction* and the *Morte*-poet's use of both alliterative poems. Hamel shies away from making a definitive claim that the *Morte*-poet drew material directly from the *Destruction*, but she reveals the numerous correspondences to the *Siege:* these include the shaving of messengers, the vowing on the Vernicle, the description of Lucius' camp, the "arming of the hero," and especially the distinctive use of the dragon-emblem.[33]

The dragon, therefore, plays a significant role in the dating of the *Morte*. The *terminus ad quem* for the *Morte* has been largely accepted as 1402 ever since Larry Benson dated the poem based on the poet's idiosyncratic knowledge of Italian geography and association of the dragon imagery on the Viscount of Rome's shield (2052–27) with the arms of Giangaleazzo Visconti (d. 1402), who fell into ill-repute after his contribution to the defeat of crusaders at Nicopolis in 1396.[34] The hostility expressed toward the Viscount in the poem, which Benson attributes to the late fourteenth-century English enmity toward the Visconti family, combined with other historical allusions to Sir John Montague and Joan of Navarre indicate that this poem was completed no later than 1402.[35] Given the probability that the earliest of the eight copies of the *Siege* dates to the 1390s, the *Morte*-poet would have had the time necessary to consult it extensively. Ralph Hanna and David Lawton even suggest that the *Siege* may predate *Troilus and Criseyde*, a scenario that

---

33. Hamel, *Morte Arthure*, 47, 53–58. See also Neilson, *Huchown of Awle Ryale*, 47–50. He uses these correspondences to identify a common author and notes that the shaving topos also appears in *Ogier le Danois* and II Samuel 10:4. See also Finlayson, "Rhetorical 'Descriptio' of Place in the Alliterative *Morte Arthure*," *Modern Philology* 61 (1963): 1–11; Derek Brewer, "The Arming of the Warrior in European Literature and Chaucer," in *Chaucerian Problems and Perspectives*, eds. Edward Vasta and Zacharias P. Thundy (Notre Dame: Notre Dame University Press, 1979), 221–43, at 233–34. For a discussion of the Vernicle and its relationship to Roman pilgrimages, see Jonathan Sumption, *Pilgrimage: An Image of Mediaeval Religion* (Totowa, NJ: Rowman & Littlefield, 1975), 249–60.

34. Larry Benson, "The Date of the Alliterative *Morte Arthure*," in *Medieval Studies in Honor of Lillian Herlands Hornstein*, eds. Jess B. Bessinger and R. R. Raymo (New York: New York University Press, 1976), 19–40, at 27; George Neilson suggests that this coat of arms was a direct reference to the Visconti family and the Dukes of Milan in "The Viscount of Rome in 'Morte Arthure,'" *Athenaeum* 3916 (1902): 652–53.

35. Benson suggests that the reference to "Mownttagus" (3773) as supporters of Mordred is a pointed attack on the Lollard Sir John Montague, who was lynched for his role in a conspiracy against Henry IV in 1400. See "The Date of the Alliterative *Morte Arthure*," 30–35; Hamel supports this dating by noting the unique reference to the victim of the giant of St. Michael's Mount as the "Duchess of Brittany" (864), a title held by Joan of Navarre, who would have relinquished this title in 1403 when she became Queen of England. See Hamel, *Morte Arthure*, 54.

would allow for nearly twenty years during which the *Morte*-poet could have drawn material from this alliterative predecessor.[36]

In fact, I want to argue that this destabilization of the dragon as a marker of martial authority is a distinctly alliterative technique. The *Morte*-poet does more than simply draw on imagery from the *Siege*—he actualizes the heraldic potential of the *Siege*-dragon, a rhetorical move that complicates not simply the earlier Galfridian attribution of the dragon symbol of imperial power to Arthur, but all heraldic claims to nobility. On the textual level, the peregrination of the dragon from Britain to Rome in the *Morte* is evidence of a switch in source material, namely from Geoffrey's *Historia* to the *Siege*. This is a provocative shift since the *Siege*-dragon appears as a redoubtable sign of the Roman Empire. When Vespasian and his Roman army leave Nero in Rome to exact Christian vengeance upon Jerusalem, they "Lauȝte leue at þat lord, leften his sygne, / A grete dragoun of gold" [took leave of that lord, lifting his insignia, a great dragon of gold] (283–84).[37] And in the later description of the symbols set above Vespasian's tent, the *Siege*-poet juxtaposes the eagle and dragon in a way strikingly similar to the description of Lucius' standard at the battle of Sessye in the *Morte* (2026–27): "A gay egle of gold on gilde appul, / With grete dragouns grym, alle in gold" [a gay eagle of gold on a gilded apple, with terrifying dragons, all in gold] (326–27). Given the prevalence of verbal parallels between the two alliterative poems and their equivalent use of the dragon as a symbol of empire, it is evident that the *Morte*-poet looked to his source in the *Siege* for attribution of the dragon-standard to the Roman imperialists.[38] More importantly, such a broad connotative use of the dragon to represent its destructive capacity places an emphasis on the effect of the signifier rather than the identification of the signified. In other words, whom the dragon represents matters less than the power it wields.

This indicates that the *Morte*-poet gained more than a symbol of the Roman Empire from the *Siege*—he also obtained a pedagogic perspective on visual assertions of sovereignty. The employment of such heraldic symbols as the dragon and eagle calls attention to the cautionary lesson for their observers. To understand this sensibility of imperial signification, we should turn to other references to the golden dragon in the *Siege* that demonstrate a pedagogy of terror consistent with the *Siege*-poet's unapologetic representation of martial violence. The dragon-standard does not simply represent imperial

---

36. Ralph Hanna and David Lawton, eds., *The Siege of Jerusalem*, EETS OS 320 (Oxford: Oxford University Press, 2003), xxxv–xxxvii.
37. All citations from the poem refer to Hanna and Lawton's edition.
38. For a discussion of the literary emergence of the dragon-standard, see Hamel, *Morte Arthure*, 46–52.

power, but actually broadcasts the destruction it will inflict from as far as four miles away. As Vespasian and his army approach the walls of Jerusalem,

> A dragoun was dressed,   drawyn alofte,
> Wyde gapande of gold   [þe] go[llet] to s[che]we,
> With arwes armed in þe mouþe,   and also he hadde
> A fauchyn vnder his feet   with foure kene bladdys . . .
> Þe b[es]t[e] by [his] briȝtnesse   burnes myȝt knowe
> Foure myle þerfro,   so þe feldes schonen.
> + On eche pomel were pyȝt   penseles hyȝe
> Of selke and sendel,   with seluere ybetyn.
> Hit glitered as gled-fure—   ful of gold riche
> Ouer al þe cite to se—   as þe sonne bemys. (393–36, 415–20)

[A dragon of gold was prepared, raised high to behold the wide gaping gullet armed with arrows in the mouth, and also he had under his feet a falchion with four keen blades. . . . Men might recognize the monster by his brightness from four miles away, so much the fields shone. On each pommel were placed high pennons of silk and cendal, beaten with silver. As the sun beamed, it glittered like a glowing fire full of rich gold, visible above the whole city.]

Calling attention to the gaping mouth of the dragon, the *Siege*-poet reveals knowledge of earlier models, such as that of western Roman emperor Otho IV, who at the battle of Bouvines in 1214 displayed a cloth standard that would enlarge when the wind would blow through its open jaws.[39] By constructing the standard this way, the dragon swells to a formidable size as it is carted toward the enemy during a march or siege. The detail of the description of the emblem as well as phrases such as "burnes myȝt knowe / Foure myle þerfro" and "Ouer al þe cite to se" indicate that this dragon is designed to be seen from afar and inspire fear in those who witness its approach. Within the context of an impending siege, the wide-open mouth signifies a subjugation of its victims, in which the restriction of the city's food supply will effect a shift of its inhabitants from eaters to the eaten—this becomes disturbingly literalized in the example of Maria and the eating of her son (1081–88). With the aid of sun-reflecting shields, the Roman army presents a dragon whose golden gaping mouth represents their greedy desire to pillage the city for its legendary riches and exterminate its inhabitants.

39. J. Heller, ed., *Willelmi Chronica Andrensis*, in *Monumenta Germaniae Historica, Scriptores* (Hanover, 1879), 24.684; Tatlock, "The Dragons of Wessex and Wales," 224.

The implication that the raising of the dragon leads to the consumption of human flesh is supported by manuscript evidence. Recent editors Ralph Hanna and David Lawton emend the line that begins with "Wyde gapande of gold" as "[þe] go[llet] to s[che]we," a reading that amplifies the description of the dragon's mouth, because they suspect that the line is a corruption of the original that followed the example of its French source in *La Vengeance de Nostre-Seigneur*.[40] However, previous editors E. Kölbing and Mabel Day read the b-line as "gomes to swelwe" [to swallow men] since this is how it appears in the majority of the manuscripts, which instead identifies the dragon's food of choice and method of human destruction.[41] The juxtaposition of the gold mouth with the act of swallowing is also supported thematically later in the poem, when the Jewish inhabitants of the city resort to eating their gold in order to hide it from the Roman invaders (1165–68).

Read this way, the sign of the dragon communicates more than just impending defeat—it broadcasts comprehensive corporeal annihilation. The raising of this standard is then a sign of its bearers' intent to fight to the death in the same way that Henry III used the dragon-emblem in 1257 to express his imperial resolve in defeating the Welsh.[42] Vespasian's dragon then promises a similar unrelenting *exterminium* to the Jewish inhabitants of Jerusalem.

[On] a bal of brennande gold   þe beste was [a]s[sised],
His taille trayled þeraboute   þat tourne scholde he neuere
Whan he was lifte vpon lofte,   þer þe lord werred
Bot ay lokande on þe londe,   till þat + lauȝte were.
Þerby þe cite myȝt se   no s[agh]tlyng wolde rise
Ne no trete of no trewes,   bot þe toun ȝelde. (401–6)

[The beast was placed on a sphere of burnished gold; his tail trailed around it so that he should never turn when he was lifted up high, ever looking on the land where the lord warred, until it would be taken. Thereby the city might see that no settlement would arise, neither treaty nor truce, unless the town would yield.]

---

40. Hanna and Lawton, *Siege of Jerusalem*, 114.
41. See line 390 of E. Kölbing and Mabel Day's edition, *The Siege of Jerusalem* (Oxford: Oxford University Press, 1932).
42. Hamel, *Morte Arthure*, 49. Matthew Paris in his *Chronica Majora* refers to Henry III's dragon-standard as a sign "qui . . . exterminium generale Walliae minabatur" [which threatened the destruction of the Welsh people]. See Tatlock, "The Dragons of Wessex and Wales," 226; Matthew Paris, *Chronica Majora*, ed. Henry R. Luard, Rolls Series 5 (London, 1880), 648; 1.228.

Again, the emphasis on the display of the standard so that "þe cite myȝt se" indicates the pedagogic function of the sign, but here the message of the dragon is made explicit. As long as the emblem is raised, the Romans will fight to the death and refuse a truce unless the inhabitants plead for mercy and grant the city to their besiegers.[43] This kind of symbolic overkill transgresses the rules of siegecraft and emphasizes the cruelty of those who bear this imperial signifier. The *Siege*-poet's use of the dragon standard is particularly clever: by demonstrating its terrifying potential, he highlights the indiscriminate violence that is the necessary consequence of such assertions of the Roman Empire.

Whereas the association between the sign of the dragon and Roman imperial destruction is vivid in the *Siege,* this heraldic connection in the *Morte* seems to be an afterthought. I want to suggest that this is not the case, however. Whereas the dragon is earlier attributed to Arthur in its battle with the bear and remains consistent in the Galfridian sources, later in the poem when Arthur meets Lucius in battle, the dragon becomes a Roman signifier. Yet, in each appearance of the dragon, it retains its didactic power for its victims by highlighting the consequences of martial violence. In the dream, the *Morte*-poet embellishes his Galfridian sources to claim that the dragon will "drynchen" his own people, and when the dragon appears as a standard in battle, a succession of scenes of the bodily dismemberment of the contending warriors follows. This notion that militaristic aggression leads to an endless cycle of destruction resonates with premodern and modern theories of violence.[44] In a sermon on the feast of St. Laurence, Augustine argues that violence against wrongdoers will beget violence against the righteous.[45] Echoing this sentiment in her famous reflection *On Violence,* Hannah Arendt remarks, "The practice of violence, like all action, changes

---

43. As Hamel notes, such a presentation of this sign of doom "would be superfluous in the normal medieval siege, the laws of which ordinarily proclaimed no quarter to the inhabitants, 'bot þe toun ȝelde.'" See *Morte Arthure,* 49; M. H. Keen, *The Laws of War in the Late Middle Ages* (London: Routledge & Kegan Paul, 1965), 120–21.

44. For a recent discussion of violence in medieval literature, see Albrecht Classen, "Violence in the Shadows of the Court," in *Violence in Medieval Courtly Literature: A Casebook,* ed. Albrecht Classen (New York & London: Routledge, 2004), 1–36.

45. Augustine, *Political Writings,* ed. E. M. Atkins and R. J. Dodaro (Cambridge: Cambridge University Press, 2001), 113. It is also provocative to note that *The Siege of Jerusalem* was likely composed by an Augustinian canon at Bolton Priory. See Ralph Hanna, "Contextualizing *The Siege of Jerusalem,*" *Yearbook of Langland Studies* 13 (1999): 109–21, at 115–16; Elisa Narin van Court, "*The Siege of Jerusalem* and Recuperative Readings," in *Pulp Fictions of Medieval England: Essays in Popular Romance,* ed. Nicola McDonald (Manchester University Press, 2004): 151–70, at 164–65; "*The Siege of Jerusalem* and Augustinian Historians: Writing about Jews in Fourteenth-Century England," *Chaucer Review* 29.3 (1995): 227–48.

the world, but the most probable change is to a more violent world."[46] As a symbol of destruction in both poems, the dragon signifies the reproductive and arbitrary nature of violence, thwarting readings that would valorize any particular military campaign, British or Roman.

The *Morte*-poet's dependence upon the *Siege* is supported further by his use of the dragon's gaping mouth and its consumption of victims. This correspondence of the dragon signifier with violence reaches an interpretive climax in the perplexing *ekphrasis* of the aforementioned shield of the Viscount of Rome:

> He drisside in a derfe shelde   endenttyd with sable,
> With a dragone engowllede,   dredful to schewe,
> Deuorande a dolphin   with dolefull lates,
> In seyne that oure soueraygne   sulde be distroyede
> And all don of dawez   with dynttez of swerddez;
> For thare es noghte bot dede   thare the dragone es raissede. (2052–57)

[He dressed in a strong shield edged with sable, adorned with a dragon with gaping jaws, dreadful to behold, devouring a dolphin with a doleful expression, as a sign that our sovereign should be destroyed and that his days should be ended by dints of swords, for there is nothing but death where the dragon is raised.]

It is important to mention here that Hamel emends Robert Thornton's scribal "engowschede" to "engowllede" (2053), which originates from the heraldic vocabulary of *engoulé de geule,* meaning "with gaping jaws."[47] As Hoyt

---

46. Hannah Arendt, *On Violence* (New York: Harcourt Brace Jovanovich, 1970), 80.
47. See *Morte Arthure,* 49, 316. For more on *engoulé de geule* see Gérard Brault, *Early Blazon: Heraldic Terminology in the Twelfth and Thirteenth Centuries with Special Reference to Arthurian Heraldry* (Oxford: Clarendon Press, 1972), 178–79. Benson and Krishna in their editions do not emend *engowschede,* which the OED defines as "stout, fleshy." The OED claims that *engowschede* derives from the Old French *engoussé,* but, as Hamel notes, forms of this word appear in rare instances. Frédéric Godefroy in his *Dictionnaire de l'ancienne langue française,* 10 vols. (Paris: F. Vieweg, 1880–1902) cites two occurrences of the word. For the mid-fifteenth century instance, see "engousser," III, 176. For the next occurrence, see "engoursé," III, 176. This second instance comes from a modern nineteenth-century edition of fables from the Middle Ages, which defines this word as "gros, gras, bien portant." Adolf Tobler and Erhard von Lomätsch in their *Altfranzösisches Wörterbuch* (Wiesbaden: F. Steiner, 1956) contest this gloss and suggest *engonser* or *engonssier.* Since none of these glosses are relevant in describing the dragon in a heraldic manner, the MED suggests *encowschede,* a relative of the heraldic *couchant,* which means "lying down with head erect." But since no heraldic description includes the notions of both *vorant* and *couchant* as in "deuorande a dolphin," Hamel substitutes *engowllede* because it matches the prototype of the dragon from *Siege,* which describes it as "wyde gapande . . . gomes

Duggan has argued, the alliterating pattern of aa/ax was the rule of alliterative verse, which calls Hamel's emendation of "engowschede" into question. However, as Duggan admits, Robert Thornton's texts of *The Siege of Jerusalem* and *The Parlement of the Thre Ages* demonstrate that he was "an unusually careful copyist" and "content to copy irregularly alliterating lines," which suggests that he reproduced in his *Morte* an irregularity found in his exemplar.[48] Certainly his exemplar could have been corrupt, as Judith A. Jefferson and Ad Putter speculate, but Hamel's emendation is supported further by the fact that it retains the *en-* prefix that accords with the aural context of the word, which is riddled with *en-* modifiers: "enuyous" (2047), "enuerounde" (2051), "and "endenttyd" (2052).[49] The authority of Hamel's emendation of Thornton is confirmed by the fact that the image of the dragon devouring a dolphin thematically evokes the *Siege*'s dragon, which is described as having a gaping mouth that consumes humans. Whereas the open mouth of the dragon surely originates in a tradition of dragon-standards whose gaping jaws caught the wind and inflated their bodies, it is only in the *Siege* and the *Morte* that these dragons are described as possessing the capability to swallow their foes.

The switch from the human to dolphin victim is a curious change that reaffirms the *Morte*-poet's continual employment of subtle connotations, but this alteration also serves to critique the nature of sovereignty and obscure distinctions between the conquerors and the conquered in war. The enigmatic *ekphrasis* of the shield is reminiscent of Aeneas' confusion in deciphering the famous shield he receives in Virgil's *Aeneid*, an episode that has sparked considerable critical comment.[50] The *Morte*-poet provides a

---

to swelwe" (Kölbing and Day, 390). Hamel further suggests that the "sch" may have been used because of its proximity to "schelde" in the line above and "schewe" at the end of the line.

48. Hoyt Duggan, "Alliterative Patterning as a Basis for Emendation in Middle English Alliterative Poetry" *Studies in the Age of Chaucer* 8 (1986): 73–105, at 76.

49. Judith A. Jefferson and Ad Putter, "Alliterative Patterning in the *Morte Arthure*," *Studies in Philology* 102.4 (Fall 2005): 415–33.

50. Interpretations of the scene divided twentieth-century critics into two camps: those who read the shield as an example of Augustan triumphalism and those of the so-called "Harvard School" who identify the darker symbols that connote a more pessimistic view of Roman *imperium*. Whereas critics such as Philip Hardie read the shield as a justification and prophecy of the Roman imperial universe, the Harvard School Virgilians interpret the shield, and the epic as a whole, as representative of the costs of empire both for victor and victim. For an example of the optimistic reading of the future of the Roman Empire in the *Aeneid*, see Philip Hardie, *Virgil's Aeneid: Cosmos and Imperium* (Oxford: Clarendon Press, 1986), 336–76. For the pessimistic perspective of the Harvard School, see S. J. Harrison, "Some Views of the *Aeneid* in the Twentieth Century," in *Oxford Readings in Vergil's Aeneid*, ed. S. J. Harrison (Oxford: Oxford University Press, 1990), 1–20; Adam Parry, "The Two Voices of Virgil's *Aeneid*," *Arion* 2 (1963): 66–80; Wendell Clausen, "An Interpretation of the *Aeneid*," *Harvard Studies in Classical Philology* 68

similarly complex *ekphrasis* of the imperial implications of the dragon on the Viscount's shield that incorporates both antithetical martial ethics and specific historical references. To understand the hermeneutic possibilities of this dragon symbol, we should examine the Viscount's shield within its historical context. In his attempt to date the poem, Benson reveals the poet's extraordinary knowledge of Italian geography. For confirmation, he turns to the chronicle of Adam of Usk, who was intimately familiar with Italian affairs in his exile in Rome. In his chronicle, Adam describes the traditional Visconti shield as one that depicts a snake devouring a man, which suggests that the *Morte*-poet's illustration of the Viscount of Rome's shield points to the Visconti family in Italy.[51] In response to this possibility, Karl Lippe contends, "Although one can argue that 'snake' and 'dragon' are used indiscriminately, various reasons for such alterations can be suggested: either the author did not know the historically correct arms, he wanted to avoid an allusion which he felt was too pointed, or he wanted to ensure a particular interpretation, as is the case here. In this instance the charge functions as a symbol which means 'that our sovereign was to be destroyed.'"[52] The dolphin in particular was commonly known in the fourteenth century as a heraldic sign of the Dauphin, the inheritor of the kingdom of France. By depicting the dolphin's death at the jaws of the dragon and interpreting this scene in the following line as a "seyne that oure soueraygne sulde be distroyede," the shield, representing the dragon as a symbol of imperial destruction and the dolphin as a symbol of the victims of empire, then serves as a warning about the consequences of such assertions of sovereignty over France.[53]

(1964): 139–47; Michael Putnam, *The Poetry of the Aeneid* (Cambridge, MA: Harvard University Press, 1965).

    51. Adam of Usk, *Chronicon Adae de Usk,* Ed. E. M. Thompson, 2nd ed. (London: H. Frowde, 1904), 75. See also Benson, "The Date of the Alliterative *Morte Arthure*," 27.

    52. Karl Lippe, "Armorial Bearings and their Meaning," in *The "Alliterative Morte Arthure": A Reassessment of the Poem,* 96–105, at 100.

    53. Ibid., 100–101. Hamel even goes so far as to suggest that the Viscount's shield points to Edward III, who famously desired the French throne. Is this then the sole reason for the *Morte*-poet's decision to shift the dragon signifier from the Britons to the Romans? Hamel believes this to be the case because "[t]here would have been no particular reason for rejecting his chronicle [i.e. Galfridian] sources in favor of *The Siege of Jerusalem,*" especially while Edward III was in power, since at the battle of Crecy in 1346 he bore the dragon-standard as a symbol of English kingship for the last time before the Tudors took it up a century later (53). She further suggests that the *Morte*-poet may have felt compelled to make a late revision to his poem in 1401 when Owen Glendower, possibly motivated by the Galfridian account, appropriated the sign of the dragon for his emblem. According to this logic, the fact that a rebel to English sovereignty had adopted the dragon for his own would have compelled the *Morte*-poet to turn to his source in the *Siege*, which attributed the dragon to the Romans. She concludes by claiming that this late revision "creates a certain ambiguity that further revision might have clarified." See *Morte Arthure,* 53–54. Ingham disputes Hamel's claim that the dragon-standard "fell into disuse" since there

Numerous interpretive possibilities defy attempts to fix a clear referent for the dragon, and when we consider the multiple uses of the dragon as a night terror, battle standard, and shield symbol, we can conclude that maintaining continuity and clarity was not a value of the *Morte*-poet by any stretch of the imagination. In fact, there are other compelling aspects of the *Siege* and its historiographic perspective that would have provided more than enough reason to reject the Galfridian sources. A literary device of the *Siege* that the *Morte*-poet clearly found attractive was the didactic representation of violence through symbols of destruction such as the dragon. In the *Siege*, the graphic descriptions of dismemberment, mutilation, and cannibalism obscure differences between the Jews and Romans, the besiegers and the besieged, so much so, that even the bodies of the prominent Roman leader Sir Sabyn and Emperor Vitellius end up in ditches (1202–4) and contaminated water (948) that serve as the final resting places for their Jewish victims. The *Siege*-poet's thematic use of death as the great equalizer and graphic descriptions of the casualties of war as a means to terrify his audience affords him a corporeal space on which he can inscribe a warning about the inextricability of violence from imperialism. In the same way, the *Morte*-poet complicates binary oppositions such as Britain/Rome and sovereign/subject through graphic scenes of corporeal violence and signifying play.

For example, if we return to the description of the Viscount of Rome's shield, we find an unsettling message for the one occupying the position of "sovereign." The poet glosses the heraldic symbol, asserting that the dragon eating the dolphin is a sign that "oure soueraygne" should be destroyed. The immediate context gives no clue to whom "oure" refers, which licenses this signifier to attach to several possibilities at once. If we read it as self-reflexive, the sovereign could refer to Lucius; but if we read it in the pedagogic manner of a battle-standard, the symbol is a warning to Arthur. And if we read on, we find a conclusion that confounds a strong interpretation either way: "For thare es noghte bot dede thare the dragone es raissede." In other words, the identification of the actual "soueraygne" is not relevant—rather it is the assertion of sovereignty that causes destruction. Since both Arthur and Lucius in different episodes throughout the poem represent the dragon, then neither can expect anything other than "death where the dragon is raised." And to complicate the matter further, the dragon immediately performs as promised by presaging the violent death of the one who had most recently

---

was a continuous Welsh textual tradition that supported the Galfridian account of the dragon as symbol that "was actively used by those contesting, rather than proclaiming, Plantagenet rule." See *Sovereign Fantasies*, 97–98.

raised the symbol: the Viscount of Rome. Sir Valiant fulfills his vow from the beginning of the poem by piercing the Viscount with a lance

> Abowne þe spayre a spanne   emange þe schortte rybbys,
> That the splent and the spleen   on the spere lengez.
> The blode sprente owtte and spredde   as þe horse spryngez,
> And he sproulez full spakely,   bot spekes he no more. (2060–63)

[a span above the waist between the short ribs so that the armor plate and the spleen hung on the spear. The blood spurts out and spreads as the horse springs, and he sprawls out swiftly, but he speaks no more.]

The forensic detail and description of the course of the lance through the short ribs and the spleen highlights the specifics of the Viscount's destruction and the emphasis on the remains of the spleen lingering on the lance, the spraying blood, and convulsing body intensifies the pedagogic function of the act. On a literal level, the Welsh king Sir Valiant has avenged the wrongs of an old enemy, but the juxtaposition of the sign of the dragon and the extended account of the Viscount's death, which surpasses even that of Lucius (2252–4), reveal the all-encompassing destruction that results from such assertions of sovereignty.

And if we explore the many historical valences of the "Viscount" in the fourteenth century, we can corroborate such a focus on comprehensive and indiscriminate violence. The attribution of the "dolphin" to the "Viscount" confounds historical identifications and reaffirms the *Morte*-poet's predilection for signifying play. As noted above, the "soueraygne" as "dolphin" could refer to the future King of France, but if we examine further the significance of the textual reference to the "Viscount," this sovereign could be the actual King of France, who was the father-in-law of Giangaleazzo Visconti, Sire of Milan. A "Viscount of Rome" did not exist in the fourteenth century, but the title, which was used throughout the Holy Roman Empire, was made famous by the Visconti family, whose name originated in the office of *vice comes* of the emperor.[54] Since Giangaleazzo was also the son-in-law of the King of France, the dolphin on the Viscount's shield gestures toward Giangaleazzo's familial connections to French royalty.[55] For the *Morte*-poet, such a

---

54. Benson, "The Date of the Alliterative *Morte Arthure*," 26. According to the *OED*, the first English use is by John Trevisa in 1387, and the second is in *Morte* around 1400.

55. Neilson was the first to contend that the "Viscount" in the poem actually referred to the Visconti family, which explained the change in his name from "Viscount of Rome" (326) to "Viscount of Valence" (2047). According to Neilson, Valence actually refers to Vallenza, which was

dual identification of the "dolphin" is evidence of his historical awareness and insistence on the unreliability and self-destructive nature of such imperial signifiers. After all, if the Viscount of Rome refers to Giangaleazzo and the dolphin on his shield depicts his father-in-law, the macabre description of the Viscount of Rome's death fulfills what his shield predicts: "es noghte bot dede thare the dragone es raissede." The dolphin, the Viscount of Rome, Giangaleazzo, and the King of France are left dead in the dragon's wake.

Such references to historical figures are compelling, but the poem eludes any definite identifications. As the above analysis demonstrates, such arguments are ultimately circuitous and not provable, which indicates that the *Morte*-poet is not interested in condemning or praising particular sovereigns. For instance, if we follow the Visconti lead even further, we can reaffirm the *Morte*-poet's fetish for contradiction. Even though the Viscontis may have been held in high regard in the 1360s, when the English court was in the midst of marriage negotiations between their prince and a daughter of Galeazzo II, by the end of the fourteenth century, the Viscontis had fallen out of English favor. Giangaleazzo murdered his uncle Bernabó in 1385, an act which English writers, including Geoffrey Chaucer, emphatically condemned. The Monk of the *Canterbury Tales* records the deed this way:

> Thy brother sone, that was thy double allye,
> For he thy nevew was and sone-in-lawe,
> Withinne his prisoun made thee to dye. (2403–5)

His familial treason soon became a martial treason of the kind that caused him to be seen as an Aeneas or Antenor who betrayed Troy. Froissart asserts that in 1396 Giangaleazzo played a significant role in the defeat of the Christian army at Nicopolis because he had informed his allies, the Turks, of the approach of the crusaders. Perplexed that Giangaleazzo "quéroit amour et

---

under Visconti control, and therefore Giangaleazzo Visconti was both the "Viscount of Rome" because he filled the office of *vice comes* for the Emperor and the "Viscount of Valence" because he was the lord of Vallenza. See "The Viscount of Rome in the 'Morte Arthure,'" 652–53. George B. Parks contests this connection because he assumes that *Morte* was composed in the 1360s, noting that it would have been too early for a reference to Vallenza because it did not come under Visconti control until 1382. He further suggests that the reference "would hardly be tactful for the poet to refer to a contemporary ruling family as miscreants and rightfully slain by one of Arthur's knights." See "King Arthur and the Roads to Rome," *Journal of English and Germanic Philology* 45 (1946): 164–70, at 165. Benson notes that if we assume an early composition of the *Morte*, the reference to the Viscount's domain of "Viterbe to Venyse" (2025) would have also been anachronistic since it was not until 1399 that the Viscontis acquired Pisa and expanded their territory south to Viterbo, but if we date the poem to 1400, this identification presents no problems. See "The Date of the Alliterative *Morte Arthure*," 27.

alliance à un roi mescréant" [would seek love or alliance with a miscreant king], Froissart suggests that he "Et tint l'opinion et erreur de son père, car ils disoient et maintenoient que jà ne adoreroient ni creroient (croiroient) en Dieu qu'ils pussent" [held the opinion and error of his father, declaring and maintaining that they should neither worship nor believe in God].[56] His treason had heretical implications that would have incited the ire of the small number of crusaders who had survived the massacre at Nicopolis. Even though Adam of Usk held the Visconti leadership in high regard, Benson suggests that Giangaleazzo's perfidy would have likely inspired the *Morte*-poet's dismemberment of the Viscount: "Our poet, whose attitude towards Lucius' pagan allies indicates that he shared the crusading zeal that led to the disaster at Nicopolis, very likely shared Froissart's opinion of the Visconti."[57] While it is appropriate to posit the *Morte* as well as the *Siege* as contributors to late fourteenth-century crusade polemic, the Viscount's violent death is too symbolically complex to characterize as a fantasized act of Christian vengeance. As Benson admits, the negative perspective of the Viscontis was far from universal and it is not evident that the *Morte*-poet made any connection between the Sire of Milan and the Visconti. To account for this ambiguity, Benson suggests that the *Morte*-poet may have been "simply confused."[58] While Benson's hypothesis is a possibility, the symbolic portability of the dragon, the evocative gloss of "oure soueraygne," and the dissonant use of violence to portray the Viscount's death combine to reveal a pattern of obscurity that denies clear distinctions between conquerors and victims and highlights the death incurred in such assertions of sovereignty. This "confusion" is then a fusing of historiographic voices embodied by the sign of the dragon: the dragon is both Roman and Briton, sovereign and victim, glorious and cruel.

THE BEARDED WIDOW

While the use of the heraldic symbol of the dragon publishes the exterior identity of empire, the *Morte*-poet's treatment of Arthur provides readers with a conflicted figure who reflects the dangers of imperial self-fashioning. The *Morte*-poet's characterization of Arthur as both tyrannical king and victimized widow defies the more nationalistic and iconographic discourses that frequently accompany invocations of Britain's greatest king. In fact, the

---

56. Jean Froissart, *Chroniques de Froissart,* ed. J. A. Buchon, Vol. 13 (Paris, 1825), 333, 339.
57. Benson, "The Date of the Alliterative *Morte Arthure,*" 28–29.
58. Ibid., 29.

Morte-poet's use of violence and signifying play to blur imperial identities is never more apparent than it is in the figure of Arthur. His campaign against Rome calls Britain's Roman and Trojan origins into question in a way consistent with the poem's shifting signifiers. As Gayle Margherita suggests, "The problem of origins . . . is inextricable from the problem of signification."[59] The *Morte*-poet presents an inverted perspective on his alliterative predecessor's translation of the figure Troy, whereby the besieged Trojans in the *Destruction of Troy*, who become the conquering Romans in the *Siege of Jerusalem*, now come under attack by their imperial descendants, the Britons. This enacts the Roman imperial signifier's displacement of the Trojan origin, causing Rome once again to move to the forefront of British concern. Since this imperial impulse leads to the personal and political downfall of Arthur and his court, the translation of Troy is exceedingly self-conscious; the poem acknowledges that an assumption of Roman imperial values means the assumption of the defeated Troy.

This attack of Arthur's inheritance becomes actualized through his defeat of the uncivilized, such as the Giant of Mount St. Michael. The Giant, whom Arthur's philosophers had identified as the bear that would be destroyed by the dragon (825), is fashioned as a barbarous tyrant, who not only rapes and kills the Duchess of Brittany (978–80), but also demands a tribute of beards (1010–4) and feasts on Christian children (1025–8). When he confronts the Giant, it is in reaction to the act of cannibalism that Arthur most ardently expresses his "civilized" disgust:

> Caffe of creatours all,   thow curssede wriche,
> Because that thow killide has   þise cresmede childyre
> Thow has marters made   and broghte oute of lyfe
> Þat here are brochede on bente   and brittenede with thi handez,
> I sall merke þe thy mede,   as þou has myche serfede,
> Thurghe myghte of Seynt Mighell   þat þis monte ȝemes. (1064–69)

[Slave of all creatures, you cursed wretch, because you killed these baptized children and made martyrs and brought out of life those who are skewered here on the field and crushed with your hands, I shall deliver your reward, which you have much deserved, through the might of Saint Michel who reigns over this mount.]

---

59. Gayle Margherita, *The Romance of Origins: Language and Sexual Difference in Middle English Literature* (Philadelphia: University of Pennsylvania Press, 1994), 144.

After characterizing the killing and consumption of baptized children as an act of martyrdom, Arthur launches into an invective filled with the language of Christian vengeance. By claiming that he "sall merke þe thy mede," Arthur claims that he will mete out providential justice in the manner of a crusade. The phrasing of his threat is especially reminiscent of the language in the *Siege* used by Vespasian and the Romans in their justification of the obliteration of the Jews (297–300) and use of the Vernicle (261–64), a relic that appears again in the opening Arthurian council in the *Morte* (309, 348, 386) as a holy object which confirms their vows of Roman conquest. In the second of these instances, Arthur is designated a "conqueror" who proudly proclaims both the nature and course of his imperial project:

> Thereto I make mine avow   devotly to Crist
> And to the holy vernacle,   virtuous and noble;
> I shall at Lamass take leve   to lenge at my large
> In Lorraine or Lumbardy,   whether me leve thinkes;
> Merk unto Meloine   and mine down the walles
> Both of Petersand and of Pis   and of the Pount Tremble;
> In the Vale of Viterbo   vitail my knights,
> Sujourn there six weekes   and solace myselven,
> Send prikers to the pris town   and plant there my sege
> But if they proffer me the pees   by process of time. (347–56)

[To that I make my vow devoutly to Christ and to the holy vernicle, virtuous and noble; I shall on Lammass take leave to live at large in Lorain or Lombardy, wherever I wish; march into Milan and take down the walls of Petra Santa, Pisa, and Pontremoli; in the Vale of Viterbo I will victual my knights, sojourn there six weeks and refresh myself, send horsemen to the prized town, and plant there my siege if they fail to offer me peace in time.]

The combination of his expression of crusading rhetoric, swearing on a holy object, and his articulation of the course of his conquest (a series of sieges in France and Italy) creates an equivalency between the language of crusade and the language of empire. It is through the use of this same kind of crusading polemic that Arthur justifies his attack on the Giant as more than an assertion of imperial glory—it is a fulfillment of God's will.

However, once the battle begins, the violence complicates simple oppositions of civilized/barbarian and Christian/Pagan. If we examine the language used to describe Arthur's battle with the Giant, we find it difficult to distinguish the combatants in a way reminiscent of Beowulf's grappling scuffle with Grendel:

>Wrothely þai wrythyn   and wrystill togederz,
>Welters and walowes ouer   within þase buskez,
>Tumbellez and turnes faste   and terez þaire wedez;
>Vntenderly fro þe toppe   þai tiltin togederz,
>Whilom Arthure ouer   and oþer-while vndyre,
>Fro þe heghe of þe hyll   vnto þe harde roche;
>They feyne neuer are they fall   at þe flode merkes. (1141–47)

[Angrily they writhe and wrestle together, welter and thrash out through the thornbush, swiftly tumble and turn and tear their clothes; roughly from the crest they struggle together, sometimes Arthur on top and other times under, from the height of the hill to the hard rock; they never cease until they fall to the seashore.]

Rather than delineate the specific attacks of each aggressor, the *Morte*-poet conflates their fates, referring to their tumbling as something they do "togederz" and summarizing the action with the indefinite "Whilom" to describe their rolling on the ground as equal foes.

The *Morte*-poet's creation of combative equivalency in this scene differs markedly from his Galfridian sources, particular that of Laȝamon, whose battle includes no grappling or hand-to-hand combat. However, the description of the fight seems to be derived from Laȝamon's version of the wrestling contest between Duke Corineus and the largest of Britain's aborigines, the Giant Gogmagog. The battle is also performed for eyewitnesses and is described in a manner that obscures distinctions between each combatant.

>Oft heo luten adun   alse heo wolden liggen,
>ofte heo up lupan   alse heo fleon wolden.
>Laðliche læches   heo leiteden mid eȝan;
>al was heora gristbatinge   al swa wilde bares eȝe.
>Whil heo weoren blake   and ladliche iburste,
>whil heo weoren ræde   and hehliche wenden,
>heora eiþer wilnada   oðer to wælden
>mid wiȝeleden, mid wrenchen,   mid wunderliche strengðen. (944–49)[60]

---

60. Laȝamon, *Brut*, ed. W. R. J. Barron and S. C. Weinberg (Harlow, Essex: Longman, 1995). Future citations of *Brut* refer to this edition.

[Often they fell as if they would lie down, often they leaped up as if they would fly. They flashed loathly looks with their eyes; they gnashed their teeth like enraged wild boars. Awhile they were blackened and horribly bruised, awhile they were reddened and highly enraged. Each of them tried to conquer the other with trickery, strategy, or wondrous strength.]

Like the *Morte*-poet's consistent use of "þai" in describing the grappling, Laȝamon uses "heo" to illustrate their bending and leaping and to conflate them into one fighter who gnashes his teeth like an angry boar—an animalistic quality that is also used to describe the Giant of St. Michael's Mount. Not only is the structural use of "whil" consistent with the *Morte*'s "Whilom," but also in each fight the winner has his ribs broken, a detail which strengthens the likelihood that the *Morte*-poet drew upon this scene in his own version of Arthur's fight with the Giant. This relationship of dependence causes Chism to conclude, "By echoing the combat of Corineus and Gogmagog, the poet insularizes the Giant, allowing Arthur to redramatize the original conquest of Britain, the ferocious and enjoyable expulsion of its original inhabitants by a captain at least as outsized and appallingly vigorous as they."[61] Chism astutely observes the "civilizing" effect of the *Morte*-poet's use of this aboriginal extraction, but in characterizing the scene's tone as "enjoyable," she effaces its potency as an assertion of sovereignty belied by its proximity to scenes of martial violence.

The *Morte*-poet's use of the Gogmagog episode is a strategic choice of source material because it precedes the invasion of Britain, which is described as an act of good-natured genocide. To the modern reader, such delight in the extermination of the native population is difficult to stomach—and apparently, the *Morte*-poet agreed, because he undercuts these scenes of fantasized violence both by blurring distinctions between conqueror/conquered and circumscribing the imperialism with a thematic critique that suppresses imperial enjoyment. To understand the subtlety of this interrogation, we ought to compare the *Morte*-poet's perspective on corporeal violence with that of his Galfridian sources. After dismembering Gogmagog whereby "al þe feond tobarst" [the fiend completely burst] (962), Laȝamon callously comments on Corineus' victory:

And mid swilce ræde þas eotentes weoren deade.
Nu wes al þis lond iahned a Brutus hond.
Þa hæfde þa Troinische men ouercomen heora teonen,
Þa weoren heo bliðe on heora breost-þonke. (966–69)

61. Chism, *Alliterative Revivals*, 229.

[And with such counsel these giants were killed. Now all of this land was in Brutus' hands. Thus had the Trojan men overcome their sufferings. They were overjoyed in their hearts.]

In this instance Corineus' violent display makes the Trojans feel "bliðe," a clear indication that they not only sanction the killing of the natives, but also enjoy the results of their extermination. The enthusiasm with which the narrative proceeds in its subsequent account of the settlement of Albion, a division of the new kingdoms, and the establishment of the New Troy (970–1018), suggests no discernible effect on the fates of the victims. This enjoyment of imperial violence is distinctively Galfridian in nature, especially when contextualized with Geoffrey's earlier appraisal of Corineus' martial prowess. In the midst of the battle with the Aquitanians, Corineus displays his expertise in wielding a battle axe and his adherence to the Trojan cause by successive acts of dismemberment: "Huic brachium cum manu amputat, illi scapulas a corpore separat. Alii caput ictu truncat, alteri crura dissecat. . . . Quod Brutus aspiciens motus amore uiri cucurit cum una turma ut ei auxilium subuectaret" [Of one he amputates the arm with the hand, of another he separates the shoulders from the body, of another he cuts off the head with one blow, of another he dissects the legs . . . Brutus, beholding this, moved with love of the man, hurried forward with a company to transport aid to him] (11). Through a volley of Latin verbs of mutilation (*amputat, separat, truncat, dissecat*), Geoffrey describes the grotesque fate of Corineus' victims and provides the callous perspective of Brutus on these acts of violence.[62] Brutus is "moved with love of the man" after witnessing Corineus' ability to mutilate his foes, which reflects the sadistic sensibilities of Geoffrey's invading Trojans. In fact, the Galfridian theorization of the origin of the British sovereignty is predicated upon such fantasized violence.

Such is the cruel logic of the *translatio imperii*, whereby native inhabitants of desirable land are callously extricated and replaced by a new *gens*, reaffirming the common conception of a natural cycle of destruction and rebirth that represented the historical progress from Troy to Rome to Britain. If we turn to Gerald of Wales' account of the thirteenth-century English invasion of Wales in his *Descriptio Kambriae*, we find a similar articulation of such a transfer of power through the victimized voice of a Welsh soldier. In response to Henry II's questioning of the Welsh resolve in the

62. For a recent discussion of this violent lexicon, see Siân Echard's essay, "'But here Geoffrey falls silent': Death, Arthur, and the *Historia regum Britannie*," in Cherewatuk and Whetter, eds., *The Arthurian Way of Death*, 17–32.

face of an English invasion, the soldier claims that Wales will be subdued in the same way that the Welsh ancestors, the Trojans, had exterminated the natives upon their arrival to Britain. Yet, in defense of his kinsmen, the soldier adds, "Nec alia, ut arbitror, gens quam haec Kambrica, aliave lingua, in die districti examinis coram Judice supreme . . . pro hoc terrarum angulo respondebit" [I do not believe that on the Day of Direst Judgment in the presence of the Supreme Judge a race other than the Welsh, or any other language, will answer for this corner of the earth] (2.8,10).[63] In the manner evocative of Nietzchean slave morality, the Welsh receive divine possession of the land through their earthly subjugation—secular history runs its recurrent course accumulating losses that are redeemed in the course of salvation history. As Jeffrey Jerome Cohen points out, the mixture of imperial indifference and eschatological optimism may reflect Gerald's own hybrid nature as both Welsh and not Welsh. As the progeny of a mixed marriage between a Norman knight and Welsh woman, Gerald may be using the words of the Welsh soldier to reconcile "all of his identity ambivalence by crossbreeding Christian futurity (the Last Judgment) to secular history (the Welsh as bearers of Trojan *imperium*)."[64] This hybrid mindset seeks solace in the afterlife and perceives martial violence as integral to the translation of imperial power. Any traceable indifference and ambivalence about such assertions of sovereignty are overcome by a fetishized imperial thirst that can only be quenched by blood. Geoffrey's giants are not permitted any nativistic expression of territorial possession—we do not hear their voice or any sympathy for their plight, because such complications would deconstruct a solid basis for any optimistic conception of a unified English nation. This attenuation of imperial ambivalence leads to national fantasies, which understood psychoanalytically become what Kathy Lavezzo calls "a technique of articulating impossible individual psychic desires, whether for wholeness and loving camaraderie or for a grand past punctuated by idealized heroes such as Arthur."[65] Geoffrey's *Historia* and its vernacular translations actively engage in this fantasy, whereby a delight in violence underscores nascent constructions of an English nation.

63. Gerald of Wales, *Descriptio Kambriae* II, *Giraldi Cambrensis Opera*, Volume 6. *Rerum Britannicarum Medii Aevi Scriptores* 21, eds. J. S. Brewer, J. F. Dimock, and G. F. Warner (London: Longmans, 1861–91).

64. For discussion of this passage within the context of postcolonial hybridity and monstrosity, see Jeffrey Jerome Cohen, "Hybrids, Monsters, Borderlands: The Bodies of Gerald of Wales," in *The Postcolonial Middle Ages*, ed. Jeffrey Jerome Cohen (New York: St. Martin's Press, 2000), 85–104, especially 86–89, at 88.

65. See Kathy Lavezzo's editorial introduction to *Imagining a Medieval English Nation* (Minneapolis: University of Minnesota Press, 2004), xv.

In great contrast to this, the *Morte*-poet interrogates such national fantasies and its contiguous graphic accounts of dismemberment, sterilizing any enjoyment that might infect British readers eager to applaud the violence of their imperial predecessors. The detailed descriptions of corporeal destruction also abound in the *Morte*, but they are contextualized with thematic commentary that mollifies any delight in the defeat of enemies and accentuates the inherent horrors of imperialism and war. Any enthusiasm in the destruction of imperial victims is quickly redirected into other martial activities that reflect the unethical behavior of the conquerors. For instance, after the drawn out battle and decapitation of the Giant of St. Michael's Mount, Arthur rejoices in his victory and then proceeds to instruct his knights to plunder the Giant's treasure (1190), which a Templar knight had previously described as more extensive "[t]han in Troye was . . . þat tym þat it was wonn" [than was in Troy . . . the time that it was won] (887). This pillaging of the Giant's goods then momentarily posits Arthur and his knights as crafty Greeks and confuses their identity as Trojan progeny. Instead of praising Arthur's fulfillment of God's will in defeating the heathen giant, Arthur's knights become greedy imperialists, a thematic choice that undercuts their chivalric piety and identifies Arthur with the avaricious tyrant he has just destroyed.

The demise of the Giant is followed by the killing of another tyrant, Lucius, which leads first to plunder and excessive violence and later to the "barbarization" of Arthur and his knights. After Lucius' death, Arthur's knights slaughter thousands (2274) and "tuke whate them likes" [take what they liked] (2282) from the dead bodies that are strewn throughout the battlefield. Then, in an act designed to shame the surviving Romans, Arthur calls forth barbers to shave the two senators who will accompany the coffins back to Rome, which serve as the tribute previously demanded from the Britons (2330–45). This ritual humiliation of the conquered foe is not only an inherited *topos* from the *Siege* (376), but also a gesture that identifies Arthur with the Giant of St. Michael's Mount, who had previously collected beards of subjugated kings as tribute. The old widow, who set the scene of the battle with the "tyraunnt" (991) Giant, even chastises Arthur, saying,

> Bot thowe hafe broghte þat berde,   bowne the no forthire,
> For it es butelesse bale   thowe biddez oghte ells. (1013–4)

[Unless you have brought the beard, go no further. For it is a fruitless endeavor if you have brought anything else.]

To emphasize the barbarous nature of the Giant, she also juxtaposes his means of tribute with his food of choice, "seuen knaue childre / Choppid in a chargour of chalke-whytt syluer" [seven male children chopped in a charger of chalk-white silver] (1025–26). Despite his subsequent condemnation of the Giant's cannibalism and tyranny, Arthur in his victory assumes the trappings of this "savage" by claiming his kirtle of beards and club (1191) and later asserts his sovereignty over the Romans in the same way, shaving the senators, thereby blurring any fine moral distinction between the Giant's sacrifice and consumption of children and Arthur's subjugation of Rome and extermination of Mordred's line. Within the context of Arthur's later enthusiastic imperialism in the poem, his extensive and equalized grappling with the Giant is not the typological assertion of the civilized over the barbarian and instead is an affirmation of the equivalency between the foes that will gradually come to tragic fruition. Even though Arthur does not literally engage in the cannibalism of the Giant, he is complicit in such horrific consumption.

The death of Gawain is the most moving example of the inseparability of sovereignty and corporeal violence in the poem because this scene is described as a moment of hyperbolic and symbolic loss. Through a series of asynchronous references, Arthur transforms into a weeping widow, not in any attempt to redeem or distinguish Gawain's death from any previous victims of empire, but rather to emphasize the extent of the damage that has been incurred from Arthur's campaign. As the following analysis of Arthur's mourning of Gawain demonstrates, the poem reflects little concern with Arthur's own "ambitions" and confounds meaningful distinctions between victims that would set up a hierarchy of corporeal value. In discovering the slain Gawain, Arthur begins his lament and then swoons over the bloodied body:

Than swetes the swete kynge   and in a swoun fallis,
Swafres vp swiftely,   and swetly hym kisses
Til his burliche berde   was blody berown,
Alls he had bestes birtenede   and broghte owt of life. (3969–72)

[Then the stricken king sinks and falls into a swoon, staggers up swiftly, and kisses him sweetly until his burly beard is covered in blood, as if he had killed and slaughtered beasts.]

This touching embrace serves not only as a striking image that challenges exclusive categories of masculinity and femininity within Arthur's chivalric community, but also as a powerful conflation of the identities of conqueror and victim.[66] Arthur's slathering of his beard with Gawain's blood is especially discomfiting because it is both an intimate act of compassion and a physical symbol of imperial self-destruction. This latter connotation is articulated through the image of the bloodied beard since the beard had previously been established as a sign of sovereignty by both the Giant of St. Michael's Mount's tributary exaction and Arthur's humiliation of the Roman senators. Within this context, Arthur's absorption of Gawain's blood reflects the necessary losses that are incurred through assertions of imperial power.

Openly slathering Gawain's blood on his beard does not call his masculinity into question, but rather adds a marker to a symbol of empire, the sovereign's beard, which more accurately reflects the cruel nature of empire building and establishes the sovereign as one of the victims of imperial desires. Arthur's identification with such victims reaches a climax when he begins to grieve like a widow. In fact, the scene subtly connects Gawain's bloodied body to Arthur and the other victims of imperial violence, such as the duchess of Brittany, the christened children, and Mordred's progeny. Within this context, Arthur's excessive mourning identifies him with the old widow who mourns over the corpse of the duchess, "wryngande hir handez" [wringing her hands] (950). His knights also recognize this transformation in their king and castigate him as one who had been emasculated emotionally in the same manner that the Giant had been physically:

It es no wirchipe iwysse,   to wryng thyn hondes;
To wepe als a woman   it es no witt holden.
Be knyghtly of contenaunce,   als a kyng scholde. (3977–79)

[It is surely not honorable to wring your hands; it is not proper to weep as a woman. Be knightly of countenance, is a king should.]

In beseeching Arthur to stop wringing his hands like a woman, they challenge his masculinity and desperately ask him to reassume his patriarchal position as king. Yet, as similar scenes in alliterative romance demonstrate, I would argue that this critique of gender should not to be read as "[w]omen

---

66. It should be noted that the *Morte* is not unique in this respect because, as E. Jane Burns has shown, "masculinity and femininity are not impermeable or mutually exclusive categories" within chivalric culture. See "Refashioning Courtly Love: Lancelot as Ladies' Man or Lady/Man?" in *Constructing Medieval Sexuality,* eds. Karma Lochrie, Peggy McCracken, and James A. Schultz (Minneapolis: University of Minnesota Press, 1997), 111–34, at 127.

weep excessively, while kings bear their grief with 'knightly' demeanor."[67] In fact, such episodes of immoderate male chivalric mourning are ubiquitous in the *Destruction;* for example, Paris weeps so abundantly at the news of the deaths of his brothers that tears burst out through the holes of his helmet (10661–62).[68] Such scenes of grief do not demean masculine knightly identity, but rather blur the line between conqueror and victim and transform victimization into further self-destruction. Rather than maintain a passive posture after this loss, Arthur vows vengeance and returns to battle with a renewed vigor that comes to a climax in his battle with Mordred. After suffering the mortal wound from Mordred, Arthur laments:

> I may helpless one hethe   house be myn one,
> Alls a wafull wedowe   þat wanttes hir beryn;
> I may werye and wepe   and wrynge myn handys,
> For wytt and my wirchipe   awaye es for euer! (4284–87)

> [I may be helpless in my house on the heath, like a woeful widow who wants her husband; I may worry and weep and wring my hands, for truly my honor is lost for ever!]

Confirming his identity as a widow, he expresses the traumatic loss of his brotherhood of knights in the manner that a woman might desire the companionship of her dead husband. By openly wringing his hands, he displays his candid acceptance of the role his knights had criticized him for assuming in bewailing the loss of Gawain and engages in the same ritual of mourning that he observed the foster mother of the duchess of Brittany perform with such poignancy before his battle with Giant of St. Michael's Mount.

Despite his willingness to identify himself with his victims, Arthur's widowing is not a moment of tragic pathos and recognition of his imperial overreaching. Ingham suggests that Arthur's assumption of the widowed identity

---

67. Ingham, *Sovereign Fantasies,* 103. She suggests that the knights' insistence on modest mourning is also evident in the figure of Theseus in Chaucer's *Knight's Tale.* See her article "Homosociality and Creative Masculinity in the *Knight's Tale,*" in *Masculinities in Chaucer: Approaches to Maleness in the Canterbury Tales and Troilus and Criseyde,* ed. Peter G. Beidler (Cambridge: D. S. Brewer, 1998), 23–35. In opposition to this viewpoint, Ruth Mazo Karras contends, "Even if Arthur's grief is seen as excessive, however, it is not so unusual, and it in no way disqualifies him as a king or leader; the audience is not necessarily meant to agree that he has behaved effeminately." See *From Boys to Men: Formations of Masculinity in Late Medieval Europe* (Philadelphia: University of Pennsylvania Press, 2003), 66.

68. John Clerk of Whalley, *The Destruction of Troy: A Diplomatic and Color Facsimile Edition, Hunterian MS V.2.8 in Glasgow University Library,* ed. Hiroyuki Matsumoto (Ann Arbor: University of Michigan Press, 2002). Any future citations are from Matsumoto's edition.

redeems his earlier tyranny in his savage Italian campaign, but there is little indication in the poem that such redemption is possible. In fact, as Ingham also notes, his reaffirmation in the end of the poem of his widowed state both amplifies the castigation of his knights over the body of Gawain, and recalls his earlier deeds of destruction in Tuscany, when his cruelty as conqueror reaches a climax.[69]

> Into Tuskane he tournez,   when þus wele tymede,
> Take townnes full tyte   with towrres full heghe;
> Walles he welte down,   wondyd knyghtez,
> Towrres he turnes   and turmentez þe pople;
> Wroghte wedewes full wlonke,   wrotherayle synges,
> Ofte wery and wepe   and wryngen theire handis,
> And all he wastys with werre   thare he awaye rydez—
> Thaire welthes and theire wonny[n]ges   wandrethe he wrogthe! (3150–57)

[Into Tuscany he turns, and thus he fares well, rapidly takes towns with high towers; he tears down walls, wounds knights, topples towers and torments their inhabitants, makes widows sing with misery, often to curse and weep and wring their hands, and wherever he rides he wastes with war—he turns their wealth and their winnings into sorrow!]

Through the reapplication and layering of alliterative tags, the *Morte*-poet subtly juxtaposes the identities of the bear and Giant of St. Michael who "turmentez þe pople" (824, 842) with the multiple widows throughout the poem who "wryngen theire handis" (950, 3977). Arthur dynamically assumes the respective positions of the tormenting tyrant and the weeping widow throughout the poem to blur distinctions of imperial identities and defy any discrete moment of Aristotelian *peripeteia*. Critics have largely accepted Arthur's destruction of Tuscany as the turning point in the poem, in which Arthur makes the transition from honorable warrior to cruel conqueror, but as the language indicates, the *Morte*-poet challenges his readers to make retrospective connections between seemingly irreconcilable characterizations throughout the poem. The expense of war and imperialism is made manifest not only at the end of the poem when Arthur unabashedly behaves like a tyrant. It is evident throughout the poem through slippery signification, graphic violence, extensive scenes of mourning, and identity crises. Arthur is just as much tyrant and widow as he is king.

69. Ingham, *Sovereign Fantasies*, 105.

HERALDIC HISTORIOGRAPHY

From beards to hands to blood, these bodily markers become chivalric devices that contribute to the *Morte*-poet's heraldic rewriting of British history. In highlighting the sacrifice of the innocent, these corporeal signs join the symbol of the dragon within the *Morte*-poet's heraldic program of translating tyranny. This heraldic hermeneutic consequently evacuates the authority of coats of arms and recitations of lineage in scenes of battle. As the maculation of Gawain's arms makes clear, heraldic symbols fail to legitimize the nobility of their bearers. This interpretive obscurity defies what Smith has noted as the basic function of heraldry, which was to distinguish aristocratic households, a practice that originated in ancient Troy. According to a household treatise in Cambridge University Library MS Dd.10.52, heraldic symbols began to flourish because "ther was so huge a multitude of people that oon might not be knowe from a nothir."[70] If knights could trace their lineage back to Troy through one of these original symbols, their noble heritage could be reasonably assured. A number of contemporary alliterative poems remind their aristocratic readers of this ancient origin, including *Sir Gawain and the Green Knight, Wynnere and Wastoure, St. Erkenwald,* and especially *The Destruction of Troy.* The *Morte* is no exception. Trojan lineage is invoked in multiple ways throughout the poem, from the heraldic assertions of Sir Priamus and Sir Clegis to the dream of the Nine Worthies and the epilogue to Arthur's death. Yet, in each case, the *Morte*-poet reinterprets these heraldic devices, transforming them into signs of death and destruction rather than certificates of nobility and authority.

Gawain's death is the climax of the poem's concern with corporeal violence and the translation of empire. Through its subtle combination of these themes, this episode reflects upon a previous scene that has garnered extensive critical attention: Arthur's dream of the Wheel of Fortune and the Nine Worthies. In particular, Arthur's repeated reference to Gawain as "sakles" or "innocent" (3986, 3989–92) echoes the words of the philosopher who interprets the dream: "Thow has schedde myche blode and schalkes distroyede, / Sakeles, in cirquytrie, in sere kynges landis [Through pride you have shed much blood and killed innocent people in many kings' lands] (3398–89). Given his explicit condemnation of Arthur's shedding of blood and killing of people, it is no mere accident that this is the only other instance of the form of "sakles" in the poem. However, this reference to Gawain as "sakles" does

---

70. I rely on Smith's reading of this household treatise, Cambridge University Library, MS Dd.10.52, fol. I, in *Arts of Possession,* 63.

not exonerate Gawain from his complicity in the deaths of the innocent. In fact, if we turn to a later alliterative romance, the *Awyntyrs off Arthure*, we see that Gawain cannot negate his culpability in what Matthews calls "the sin of imperial war."[71] The ghost that reproves King Arthur for his tyranny speaks this indictment directly to Gawain, who shares Arthur's fate of death on the battlefield after Fortune's Wheel turns (261–99).[72] Within the martial logic of these alliterative romances, the victims of imperial violence are explicitly equalized—no one is accorded special status.

To understand the destructive impetus of what I call the *Morte*-poet's "heraldic historiography," we should turn first to the dream of the Wheel of Fortune and Nine Worthies, an episode that establishes Arthur's imperial lineage. We hear the accounts of not only other doomed conquerors such as Alexander and Julius Caesar, but also Hector of Troy, the glorious ancestor of Arthur.[73] The basic message is the same: those who create empires will suffer from the imperial cycle of violence. Conquerors will experience the fate of the conquered. Hector holds special significance because of his central role in the contemporary alliterative romance, the *Destruction*, a text that emphasizes his death as much as his life.[74] It is then no surprise to readers of

71. Matthews, *The Tragedy of Arthur*, 150.

72. *The Awyntyrs off Arthure* in *Sir Gawain: Eleven Romances and Tales*, ed. Thomas Hahn (Kalamazoo: Medieval Institute Publications, 1995).

73. As Patterson suggests, Fortune's wheel "expresses a historiography of recurrence," whereby Alexander's example is incessantly repeated in figures both pagan and Christian in a way that does not privilege one victim of imperial desire over another. See *Negotiating the Past*, 225.

74. While the Galfridian treatment of Trojan historiography upholds Hector as a great king and virtuous warrior, the Hector who takes center stage in this romance is a corpse that Priam desperately attempts to keep living for Trojan eyewitnesses through a complex method of preservation that incessantly pours balm into his head (8726–32). This macabre machinery ultimately fails to preserve Troy, a result which fashions Hector instead as the ultimate casualty of war and symbol of the destruction that will plague Trojan progeny. Hamel observes that Hector's self-description in the *Morte* departs from the popular tradition of viewing him as a chivalrous knight. Instead, Hector identifies himself as a courtly lover: "On ʒone see hafe I sitten als souerayne and lorde, / And ladys me louede to lappe in theyre armes" [On that seat have I sat as sovereign and lord, and ladies loved to twine me in their arms] (3291–92). The *Morte*-poet likely drew this description from a misreading of the *Destruction*'s illustration of Priam's sons, in which Hector is lauded for both his martial prowess and his popularity among "ledys": "Was neuer red in no Romance of Renke vpon erthe / So well louty with all ledys þat in his lond dwelt" [There was never read in any romance of a man upon the earth, so well loved by all the people that dwelt in his land] (3897–98). Since "ledys" is a translation of Guido's "regnicolis" (86) or "dwellers in his kingdom," it is probable that Clerk did not have "ladies" in mind. See Guido de Columnis, *Historia Destructionis Troiae*, ed. Nathaniel Edward Griffin (Cambridge, Massachusetts: Mediaeval Academy of America, 1936). The reference to "Romance" may have led the *Morte*-poet to misconstrue the context as courtly and substitute the "a" for "e" in "ledys," a common misreading of a cursive hand. Since no other illustration of Hector as a womanizer exists, this error in reading suggests that all of the formulaic parallels between the battle scenes of each poem may not solely originate in a common word hoard and may be evidence of a relationship

alliterative romance that Hector is one of the nine who laments his fall: "And nowe my lordchippes are loste and laide foreuer!" [And now my lordships are lost and laid low forever!] (3293). Even though this comment parallels that of the other eight conquerors, his status would have been of particular interest for an English reading audience, who considered him an historical ancestor. In fact, his position on the wheel encourages readers to view this scene within the context of his previous appearances in the poem, in which he is invoked as a proof of nobility.

For early fifteenth-century readers, an invocation of Trojan heritage was a compelling assertion of gentility, but the *Morte*-poet uses it as a marker of doom. The most striking of these instances occurs during the foraging expedition, often characterized as a romance subplot, in which Gawain meets a foreign knight named Priamus.[75] A fierce battle ensues and Gawain emerges victorious, but not without suffering a grave wound. In the conventional heraldic manner, the strange warrior identifies his noble lineage through his father, who he asserts "es of Alexandire blode, ouerlynge of kynges, / The vncle of his ayele sir Ector of Troye" [is of Alexander's blood, overlord of kings, the uncle of his heir, Sir Hector of Troy] (2603–4). This claim establishes a common bloodline between the combatants and highlights the reflexive nature of the figure of Hector and the name "Priamus"—it is only natural that his name evokes Hector's father Priam. By expressing his lineage in a way that a Priam is a successor of Hector rather than vice versa, the reader is invited to reverse the future-driven track of genealogy and delve into the classical past. As a representative of the ancient Trojan world, Priamus' alterity remains intact, allowing him to speak a lesson that could have been expressed by none other than Hector himself:

---

of dependence. A separate oral tradition may have fostered the image of a licentious Hector, but given the *Morte*-poet's tendency to utilize multiple sources at once, particularly in this scene where he combines the trope of the Nine Worthies with the Boethian Wheel of Fortune, it is more likely that he drew from the *Destruction* extensively to illustrate the horrors of war and capitalize upon the didactic power of the image of Britain's glorious ancestor. See Hamel, *Morte Arthure*, 51–52. For more on the *Morte*-poet's unique use of *Fortuna* and the Nine Worthies, see Anke Janssen, "The Dream of the Wheel of Fortune," in *The Alliterative Morte Arthure: A Reassessment of the Poem*, 140–52; Finlayson, *Morte Arthure*, 13.

75. For a full discussion of this episode, see Patterson, *Negotiating the Past*, 217–29. He suggests that the *Morte*-poet draws on two sources in this scene, the *Fuerres de Gadres* and *Fierabras*. The *Fuerres* is attached to the *Roman d'Alexandre* and can be found in E. C. Armstrong, ed., *The Medieval French Roman d'Alexandre, 2: Version of Alexandre de Paris*, Elliott Monographs 37 (Princeton: Princeton University Press, 1937), 60–127. For *Fierabras* see the edition by A. Kroeber and G. Servois (Paris: F. Viewig, 1860); R. H. Griffith, "Malory, *Morte Arthure*, and *Fierabras*," *Anglia* 32 (1909): 389–98; Finlayson, "The Alliterative *Morte Arthure* and Sir Firumbras," *Anglia* 92 (1974): 380–86.

> I was so hawtayne of herte   whills I at home lengede,
> I helde nane my hippe-heghte   vndire heuen ryche;
> Forthy was I sente hedire   with seuen score knyghttez
> To asaye of this were,   be sente of my fadire.
> And I am for cyrqwitrye   schamely supprisede,
> And be aw[n]tire of armes   owtrayede fore euere. (2612–17)

> [I was so haughty of heart while I lingered at home, I held none as tall as my hip under rich heaven; forth was I sent hither with seventy knights to experience this war, by assent of my father. And I am for pride shamefully captured, and by adventure of arms disgraced forever.]

His pride and insistence on performing chivalric deeds has led to his shame and grievous wound at the hands of an unknown knight. This speech serves as a cautionary tale about such a desire for the possession of "price cetees" (2609), "tresour," and "londes" (2610), but unfortunately its message does not translate into Gawain's chivalric sensibility. Instead he chooses to test Priamus' nobility by calling himself a "knafe" (2621) of Arthur's entourage, a statement that inspires Priamus' exclamation of disbelief:

> Giffe his knaves be syche,   his knyghttez are noble!
> There is no kynge vndire Criste   may kempe with hym on;
> He will be Alexander ayre,   that all þe erthe lowttede,
> Abillere þan euer was   sir Ector of Troye! (2632–35)

> [If his knaves be such, his knights are noble! There is no king under Christ who may battle with him; he will be Alexander's heir, to whom all the world bowed, abler than ever was Sir Hector of Troy!]

Once again he invokes the figure of Hector, but this time, to establish the imperial inheritance of Arthur and assert martial kinship between him and the Round Table. Priamus juxtaposes "knaves" with "knyghttez" and "kynge," a triangular syntax that grammatically lessens the degrees of difference between each. Since the accepted hierarchy of the Round Table and fealty between knights and lords defy such an image of equality, Priamus calls Gawain's bluff, but the trick reminds the reader of the signifying slippage that has occurred throughout the poem—Gawain maintains the oppositional identities of enemy/kinsman and knave/knight just as the dragon is both British/Roman and Arthur is both tyrant/victim.

Priamus' articulation of his heritage establishes common blood and martial intentions with Gawain, an intimacy that is paradoxically obscured and intensified by their mutual wounding. In addition to an emphasis on the violence of this act, the illustration evinces a fetish for armorial bearings and details the destruction of the shoulder piece that is decorated with his coat of arms. Priamus' sword not only damages this genealogical sign, but also cuts into the vein that spurts blood that further obscures it: "his vesturis ryche / With the valyant blood was verrede all ouer" [his rich clothes were spotted all over with the valiant blood] (2572–73). This blow causes Gawain's bodily fluid to efface the symbol of his noble Trojan heritage and equalize him with his wounded foe, whose liver could be observed "with þe lyghte of þe sonne" [with the light of the sun] (2561) after receiving a similar slash from Gawain's sword. For both knights, their mutilated bodies now become the main concern—their armor and their lineage have failed them. Their subsequent conversation in which they discover shared kinship with Hector leads to a revival scene, whereby Priamus assumes the role of his namesake and uses a magical fluid to resurrect their wounded bodies (2686–716). No sooner than Gawain and Priamus are revived, they are propelled into another battle in which they fight on the same side (2990, 2997). This marital violence crescendos throughout Arthur's assault on Metz and Como until it reaches a climax in Tuscany, the moment when Arthur achieves the height of his tyranny. The revivals of Gawain and Priamus reinvigorate the British host, but they employ their new power to pillage towns, tear down city walls, "turmentez þe pople," and cause widows to wring their hands in anguish (3151–55), language that invokes the destructive power of the dragon. Such actions suggest that these Trojan signifiers beget further violence more than they establish nobility.

In fact, the recitation of lineage as a marker of virtue and prowess rings hollow in this poem from beginning to end. For instance, early in the poem when Sir Clegis confronts the King of Syria in battle, the King refuses to engage in battle until Clegis presents his right to bear arms. Insulted, Clegis responds angrily:

> I trowe it be for cowardys   thow carpes thes wordez!
> Myn armez are of ancestrye   enueryde with lordez
> And has in banere bene borne   sen sir Brut tyme,
> At the cité of Troye,   þat tyme was ensegede,
> Ofte seen in asawtte   with certayne knyghttez,
> For þe Brute broghte vs   and all oure bolde elders
> To Bretayne þe braddere   within chippe-burdez. (1693–99)

[I believe it is for cowardice you say these words! My arms of ancestry are acknowledged by lords and have been borne in banners since Sir Brutus' time, at the city of Troy, that time it was besieged, often seen in assault by certain knights, from which Brutus brought us and all our bold elders to Great Britain aboard ships.]

And despite his eloquent account of his ancestry back to Troy, the origin of such heraldry, his justification of nobility falls on deaf ears.[76] The King of Syria retorts, "saye what þe lykez" [say what you like] (1700) and resolves to fight Clegis' forces in mass rather than engage him in a tournament-style battle. Within the historical context of the Scrope Grosvenor trial of 1386 in which such contestations for arms were commonplace, the King of Syria's response demonstrates skepticism of such imperial self-fashionings and claims to Trojan origins. Troy has clearly lost the legitimizing power that provides the structure of Galfridian historiography and approves the creation of British sovereignty out of the ashes of Rome. Trojan blood is no longer an unquestionable marker of virtue—rather it is a shameful inheritance.

FROM THE enigmatic sign of the dragon to the assertions of Trojan heritage, the heraldic claims to nobility and sovereignty in the poem are consistently reconceived as markers of death. Even though the *translatio imperii* ultimately fails and Arthur's pursuit of his Roman inheritance places him as one of many other fallen conquerors such as Julius Caesar, the invocation of lineage retains an influential signifying power. Arthur's tyranny is enhanced through this heraldic recognition that his potential destruction of Rome becomes a metaphorical act of patricidal violence against his own bloodline. During one of the most moving moments in the poem, Arthur mourns Gawain's death as a corporeal expression of the damage inflicted by the *translatio imperii*. This point is exemplified by the fact that at the same time that Arthur's knights view him as a passively weeping widow, Arthur perceives himself as a complicit in the death of Gawain and his royal line. In response to their request that he cease his mourning, Arthur refuses and instead engages in a rhetorical dismemberment of his own body: "'For

---

76. Chism further suggests that "[t]his unreliability of the signs that designate nobility infects the poem as a whole." See *Alliterative Revivals*, 208–9. For extended discussion of the scene's socioeconomic and chivalric implications, see Heng, *Empire of Magic*, 128–46. For the scene's allusion to the Scrope-Grosvenor trial, see M. H. Keen, "Chaucer's Knight, the English Aristocracy, and the Crusade," in *English Court and Culture in the Later Middle Ages*, eds. V. J. Scattergood and J. W. Sherborne (London: Duckworth, 1983), 45–62.

blod' said the bolde kynge 'blynn sall I neuer, / Or my brayne to-briste or my breste oþer!'" ["For blood," said the bold king, "cease shall I never, until my brain or my breast completely burst"] (3981–82). Arthur's unrestrained mourning is his only vehicle to escape the bodily fragmentation, which he perceives as the consequence of his complicity in the violence that has slain his kinsman and innocent victims. The bloodied sovereign's characterization of his kinsman's blood as "ryall rede" (3990) articulates a devastating consequence of his death: the end of a royal line. Arthur combines the unsettling image of his bloodied beard with an imagined dismemberment of his body to express the damage his sovereign fantasies have incurred. Through this ritual of mourning, Arthur's physical and political bodies coalesce into one indivisible entity—the destruction of one entails the destruction of the other. Such an image supports Agamben's reading of the biopolitical nature of the sovereign body. In defiance of Kantorowicz's distinction of the king's two bodies, Agamben suggests that the private and public *corpores* of the king are inseparable.[77] The sovereign body is envisioned as physically reacting to a disruption in the *translatio imperii*. For Arthur, Gawain's death leaves his line to the progeny of his "other" nephew Mordred, the "Malebranche," a genealogical consequence that exemplifies the fragmentation of Arthur's political realm.

As the end of the poem confirms, Arthur's identity as sovereign cannot be interpreted solely with a messianic hermeneutic. After Arthur orders the extermination of Mordred's line, Arthur's body is not translated to the Isle of Avalon—instead he is entombed in a sepulcher before the eyes of grieving witnesses (4332–41). No ethereal transfer of the body politic to future generations is implied or allowed—instead the poem ends with a hollow evocation of his Trojan ancestors (4342–46):

Thus endis Kyng Arthure,   as auctors alleges,
That was of Ectores blude,   the kynge son of Troye,
And of sir Pryamous the prynce,   praysede in erthe:
Fro thethen broghte the Bretons   all his bolde eldyrs
Into Bretayne the brode,   as þe Bruytte tellys. (4342–46)

77. Agamben, *Homo Sacer*, 184; Kantorowicz, *The King's Two Bodies*. For a Lacanian reading of this scene, see Ingham, *Sovereign Fantasies*, 95. She argues that the imagined dismemberment of the body is "aggressive disintegration" and a means of refiguring "aggressive intentions." See Jacques Lacan, *Écrits: A Selection*, trans. Alan Sheridan (New York: Norton, 1982), 4, 11. The *Morte*-poet may have even appropriated such a fusion of the state of the empire with the sovereign body from the *Siege*, in which the biopolitical connection is literalized in Titus' "crippling" reaction to the news of his father Vespasian's ascendancy to the imperial throne (1027–33).

[Thus ends King Arthur, as authorities assert, who was of Hector's blood, the son of the King of Troy, and of Sir Priam the prince, praised on earth. From thence the Britons brought all of his bold elders into Britain the broad, as the *Brut* tells.]

The juxtaposition of Arthur's Trojan heritage with his burial encourages readers to view this heraldic expression of lineage more as a lamentable necrology than the establishment of a future line. A sense of wistful resignation permeates this scene since Arthur has ended his life not as a king to be praised, but as a tyrant who had become a victim of the imperial fantasy that "þe Bruytte tellys" [the *Brut* tells] (4346). As is the case of many of the signifiers throughout this poem, the reference to the "Bruytte" is not to be understood simply as Geoffrey's *Historia*. While it certainly reaffirms its Galfridian source, the tragic ending of the poem encourages readers to grapple with the many histories of Brutus and Troy that express doubt about imperial glory. As I have suggested, this ambivalence can be tracked both through invocations of Trojan origins and the heraldic violence that the *Morte*-poet recasts for chilling effect. As a conduit of antithetical historiographic discourses, the *Morte* demonstrates that assertions of sovereignty, while temporarily glorious, are inextricable from the violence that is inflicted upon victim and aggressor. Rather than delight in the destruction Arthur inflicts upon his Roman imperial predecessor, the *Morte*-poet presents to his British contemporaries a stark representation of empire. The *Morte*-poet justifies Guido's fear. Good cannot emerge from the translation of Troy. Like Arthur's body, it should remain dead and buried.

FIVE

Territory
THE TROJAN PROVINCES OF BRITAIN

AS ERNST RENAN has famously observed, "forgetting is a crucial factor in the creation of a nation."[1] Forgetting treachery that accompanies the foundation of a nation's heritage keeps patriotic metanarratives providential in design, focusing on the ends of nation-formation rather than their means. Such forgetting conveniently obscures the sins of ancestors to maintain the moral and political integrity that inspires movements toward nationalistic unity. In response to Renan, Benedict Anderson influentially suggests that modern conceptions of the "nation" are based on "imagined communities" that "have no clearly identifiable births, and their deaths, if they ever happen, are never natural."[2] Citing the archaeological fascination with finding the body of King Arthur, Anderson emphasizes the way such figures are incessantly imagined in the present moment, which encourages modern nations to fashion a premodern origin that may have never existed.[3] Identifying the influential role that literary criticism has played in such nationalistic ideologies, Randy Schiff has recently argued that the "backward-looking" critical construction of an Alliterative Revival offered a "retrograde" foil for the development of an English national literature, which assumed that south-

---

1. Ernst Renan, "What is a Nation?," trans. Martin Thom, in *Nation and Narration*, ed. Homi Bhabha (New York: Routledge, 1990), 8–22 at 11.
2. Benedict Anderson, *Imagined Communities: Reflections on the Origin and Spread of Nationalism*, rev. ed. (London: Verso, 1991), 205.
3. Ibid.

ern francophone Chaucerian verse thrived while northern Saxon alliterative verse evaporated.[4] Within this fantasized dialectic, one verse form is remembered and canonized while the other is forgotten and disenfranchised.

Sir Gawain and the Green Knight, perhaps the most well-known alliterative poem, complicates this rivalry, not only because the poem is highly francophone, but also because it persists as a representative of the English canon. Its exceptional nature has prompted critics such as Thorlac Turville-Petre, who believes ardently that "the concept of national identity was available to the writers of the fourteenth-century," to suggest that for unique poets, such as the *Gawain*-poet and Chaucer, national identity was not a subject they would "dignify with their attention."[5] Turville-Petre cites the prologue of the poem, which tracks the establishment of New Trojan provinces throughout Europe, as evidence for the *Gawain*-poet's "internationalism," suggesting that the recital of a European heritage and the subsequent chivalric subjects eclipse any pursuit of English nationalism in the poem.[6] While I agree that the poem does not reflect nationalist sentiment, I want to suggest that the Trojan prologue operates more as an expression of provincial contestation than international identification. As I will demonstrate in this chapter, the *Gawain*-poet provincializes Troy by re-imagining insular Trojan provinces as peripheral spaces of critique, which cohere through their attention to treason and surfeit, rather than chivalry and glory. These New Trojan communities are established in defiance of the aristocratic amnesia that emerges most prominently in times of crisis, when the heterogeneity or irregularity of the past threatens the cohesion of the present. Therefore, the remembrance of unsavory acts, such as the Trojan treason in the beginning lines of *Sir Gawain and the Green Knight*, defies the historical forgetting that would have afforded premodern nation-building.

There is no convincing evidence that a modern understanding of the nation or the idea of popular sovereignty existed in fourteenth-century England—rather, "nation" was associated with the Latin *natio*, privileging "birth" or "descent."[7] While English was beginning to come into its own as a lan-

4. Randy Schiff, *Revivalist Fantasy: Alliterative Verse and Nationalist Literary History* (Columbus: The Ohio State University Press, 2011), 4, 161.
5. See Thorlac Turville-Petre, "The Brutus Prologue to *Sir Gawain and the Green Knight*," in *Imagining a Medieval English Nation*, ed. Kathy Lavezzo (Minneapolis: University of Minnesota Press, 2004), 340–46, at 340 and 346. See also his study on medieval English nationalism, *England the Nation: Language Literature, and National Identity, 1290–1340* (Oxford: Clarendon Press, 1996).
6. Turville-Petre, "The Brutus Prologue to *Sir Gawain and the Green Knight*," 341.
7. Liah Greenfeld, *Nationalism: Five Roads to Modernity* (Cambridge: Harvard University Press, 1992), 4, 8. For more on the linguistic origins of "nation" see Guido Zernatto, "Nation: The History of a Word," *Review of Politics* 6 (1944): 351–66.

guage of authority within a highly Latinate and Francophone culture, it was still not a "national" vernacular of the sort it would become in the sixteenth century.[8] Nationhood was not characterized by popular rule or language and instead was primarily defined by the social elite who established their gentility through bloodlines that reached back into antiquity.[9] Therefore, the traces of "nationalism" that appear in fourteenth-century England are merely nascent aristocratic movements that only begin to gain momentum for the commoners in the two succeeding centuries.[10] The English "nation" that is invoked by late medieval writers is essentially a patriotic fantasy of the elite, which seeks justification not in popular rule, but through dynastic inheritance that could be traced back to ancient Troy. Since these genealogical claims could be contested by continental rivals, such as France, England found itself in an extended identity crisis during the Hundred Years War. This state of emergency was especially acute during the reign of the powerful Charles V of France (1364–80), a period which fostered an increasingly nationalist consciousness in a vast number of English literary works such as the prose *Brut*.[11] As a translation and continuation of Geoffrey of Monmouth's prophetic *Historia regum Britanniae*, this English text survives in 166 manuscripts, making it what James Simpson labels "the principal lens through which English readers perceived British history."[12] Such a providential version of history is exemplary in its forgetting and subsequent imagining of a future English nation based on the gentle heritage of their readers.

The alliterative romanciers who adhere to the skeptical historiography of Guido delle Colonne, on the other hand, work against the nationalist impulse of the *Brut* and continually urge their readers *not* to forget the Trojan treachery that caused the destruction of cities and the birth of western empires. In both the alliterative *Morte Arthure* and *Gawain*, this retrospective historiography emerges even at the expense of narratological unity. The British history, which occupies the beginning and/or ending lines of these alliterative romances and other alliterative poems such as *Wynnere and*

---

8. Anderson, *Imagined Communities*, 41.
9. Greenfeld, *Nationalism*, 5.
10. As my argument suggests, I agree with E. J. Hobsbawn's formulation: "Nations do not make states and nationalisms but the other way round." *Nations and Nationalism since 1780: Programme, Myth, Reality* (Cambridge: Cambridge University Press, 1990), 10.
11. For a discussion of Charles' increasing power and its effect on late-fourteenth century understandings of chivalry, see Lynn Staley, "Translating 'Communitas,'" in *Imagining a Medieval English Nation*, 261–303, at 263.
12. James Simpson, *The Oxford English Literary History: Reform and Cultural Revolution*, Volume 2 (Oxford: Oxford University Press, 2004), 76. For more on the manuscripts of the *Brut* see Lister M. Matheson, "The Middle English *Brut*: A Location List of the Manuscripts and Early Printed Editions," *Analytical and Ennumerative Bibliography* 3 (1979): 254–66.

Wastoure, rehearses a Trojan past that appears to bear little relevance to the present plot. In each case, however, aristocratic identity is linked implicitly with Troy. Even in the debate poem *Wynnere and Wastoure*, the Trojan prologue is followed by a conventional heraldic description of Wynnere's army, which is punctuated by the anglicized motto of the Order of the Garter (50–68), a reference famously inscribed at the end of *Gawain*.[13] While these poems often employ playful irony to critique aristocratic practice, the images of a burning Troy, the treacherous Aeneas, and the subjugation of provinces provide a grim historical background for the predominant subjects of the poems. The alliterative romanciers of the Guido-tradition embrace these disjunctures between past and present, history and romance, for a sobering effect, encouraging readers to interpret the romances through the Trojan borderlands that circumscribe the poems. Read this way, these romances satirize the very foundation of English nobility, suggesting that the effacement of their treacherous past has fostered a chivalric amnesia among its aristocratic inheritors.

For the *Gawain*-poet, the symbol of their forgetting is the girdle borne by the knights proudly at the end of the poem, highlighting their refusal to recognize their "untrawþe." The significance of this heraldic misappropriation is considerable since it occurs at the end of the poem, the very border of the text. Because scholarship on the "borders" in *Gawain* has been limited to the geographical borderlands of Cheshire and the Welsh March, I suggest that we expand what we mean when we read the text topographically.[14] In assessing the topographies of this romance, I argue for a reading that transcends the British geographies of the tale, Camelot and Hautdesert, and their fourteenth-century English equivalents, London and Chester. I suggest that the text itself should be read like a map. If read this way, Troy occupies the edges of England's textual world just as Hautdesert and the Northwest Midlands reside on the imaginary outskirts of the Arthurian court and the intellectual periphery of the cultural wealth of the south. As

13. *Wynnere and Wastoure and The Parlement of the Thre Ages*, ed. Warren Ginsberg (Kalamazoo: Medieval Institute Publications, 1992); Citations of *Gawain* refer to *The Poems of the Pearl Manuscript: Pearl, Cleanness, Patience, Sir Gawain and the Green Knight*, ed. Malcolm Andrew and Ronald Waldron (Exeter: Exeter University Press, 2002).

14. For the most recent and definitive study, see Robert W. Barrett, *Against All England: Regional Identity and Cheshire Writing, 1195–1656* (Notre Dame: University of Notre Dame Press, 2009). For other influential "border" readings, see Rhonda Knight, "All Dressed Up with Someplace to Go: Regional Identity in *Sir Gawain and the Green Knight*," *Studies in the Age of Chaucer* 25 (2003): 259–84; Patricia Clare Ingham, *Sovereign Fantasies: Arthurian Romance and the Making of Britain* (Philadelphia: University of Pennsylvania Press, 2001); Michelle R. Warren, *History on the Edge: Excalibur and the Borders of Britain, 1100–1300* (Minneapolis, University of Minnesota Press, 2000).

borderlands, Troy and Cheshire then achieve a topographical interdependency that entices the reader to make thematic and historiographic connections between imperial and provincial identities. The breaking of vows, acts of disloyalty, and aristocratic surfeit inhabit these locales and cast skepticism on Britain's Trojan heritage that serves as the basis for claims to nobility.

This emphasis on textual and geographical borderlands not only identifies the peripheral perspective of the poet, but also destabilizes the development of English fantasies of sovereignty. Being of Trojan descent is neither a justification of nobility nor a guarantee of imperial glory—instead it is a marker of deceit, licentiousness, and pretense. Through what I argue is a focused use of the alliterative romanciers' favorite book, Guido delle Colonne's *Historia destructionis Troiae*, the *Gawain*-poet undercuts his "felicitous" narrative and sets a somber tone for Gawain's journey into the "uncivilized" territory of Hautdesert and the Green Chapel. On the borders of England and the rest of the world, Gawain experiences a chivalric crisis that reminds readers of the Trojan destruction that is rehearsed at the borders of the texts. As the ancient equivalent of fourteenth-century Chester and home of the *Gawain*-poet, Hautdesert becomes a provinicial court that hosts the satiric deconstruction of Arthurian chivalry.

To demonstrate the way Gawain's residence in this border topography becomes the occasion for imperial satire, I juxtapose poetic analyses with the border historiography of the Cheshire and Wales. For the provincial viewpoint of northern England, I turn to Ranulph Higden's *Polychronicon*, which depicts England, and specifically Chester, as occupying the border of the world. Higden expresses pessimism about Arthurian Britain and national integrity that offers a useful corollary to the *Gawain*-poet's description of Gawain's troubled journey to outskirts of "civilization." For the Welsh perspective, I turn to one of Higden's sources, Gerald of Wales, who similarly problematizes such Arthurian nationalism and Trojan identity not only by contesting the English claim to a Trojan heritage, but also by suggesting that a Trojan identity is a mark of vice rather than virtue. Gawain's indulgence in the imperial vice of "surfeit" in this Welsh borderland suggests that he has become Gerald's prototypical "Trojan." Gerald and Higden then join Guido in the borders of the text to append acerbic glosses to the romance, commentary that bleeds into the text at the end of poem to reprove the court's laughter in response to Gawain's pious confession of "untrawþe." By invoking the opening lines of the poem in the last stanza, the *Gawain*-poet admonishes his readership to question such recitations of nobility and to view this failure of chivalry as a failure of national propaganda. England as a New Troy is not a future empire or nation—it is a house of cards.

BLISS AND BLUNDER

Despite the sinister mood of the opening lines, scholars have continued to read them from an optimistic perspective, emphasizing the "blysse" over the "blunder" (18). For instance, if we turn to *A Companion to the Gawain-Poet* and the article by Elisabeth Brewer on "The Sources of *Sir Gawain*," we witness again the overpowering critical influence of Geoffrey of Monmouth. She explains that Geoffrey's *Historia regum Britanniae* had a clear influence on the poem, especially in the characterization of Gawain, his shield, and the British foundation myth, which causes her to conclude that "[i]n consequence of the general acceptance of this tradition in the fourteenth century, London was regarded as a happier Troy."[15] While I do not wish to dispute the general truth of this claim, its emphasis on the optimistic view of an English Troy is not reflected in the illustration of Troy in the opening stanza. To understand this, we only need to examine the first full stanza. While the passage includes positive references to the "high kynde" (5) of the British heritage and the "blysse" (18) that ensues from Brutus' founding of Britain, the references to the destruction of Troy (1–2), Aeneas' "tresoun" (3), and "blunder" (18) paint a negative picture of British sovereignty. As Theodore Silverstein points out, "nearly every figure in it is touched, one or the other, by ambiguity, seeming oddity, apparent irrelevance, or error; some of which, but not all, have been seen by modern editors and, where seen, have bothered critics, though not enough."[16] The key phrase in this apt summary of editing and criticism both before and after his essay is "where seen," since it has not often caught or sustained the attention of readers.

Upon close examination, these opening lines reflect the pessimism of Guido's *Historia*, a fact that has scarcely been addressed by scholars.[17] As I have been suggesting in previous chapters, the alliterative romancers consistently draw upon Guido's *Historia* in expressing skepticism about imperialism. The *Gawain*-poet is no exception. While Geoffrey's *Historia* comprises much of the historiographic borderlands of the narrative, this territory is

---

15. Elisabeth Brewer, "The Sources of *Sir Gawain and the Green Knight*," in *A Companion to the Gawain-Poet*, eds. Derek Brewer and Jonathan Gibson (Cambridge: D. S. Brewer, 1997), 241–55, at 244, 248, and 251.

16. Theodore Silverstein, "*Sir Gawain*, Dear Brutus, and Britain's Fortunate Founding: A Study in Comedy and Convention," *Modern Philology* 62.3 (1965): 189–206, at 192.

17. Malcolm Andrew, "The Fall of Troy in *Sir Gawain and the Green Knight* and *Troilus and Criseyde*," in *The European Tragedy of Troilus*, ed. Piero Boitani (Oxford: Clarendon Press, 1989), 75–93, at 83–84; C. David Benson, *The History of Troy in Middle English Literature*; R. E. Kaske, "*Sir Gawain and the Green Knight*," in *Medieval and Renaissance Studies*, ed. George Mallary Masters (Chapel Hill: University of North Carolina Press, 1984), 24–44.

shared with Guido's *Historia*. The prevalence of Guido's pessimism about this tale of the *translatio imperii* is significant because its presence undercuts the fantasy of empire that has dominated recent criticism on the Trojan frame.[18] For example, in her recent study on Trojan fashionings of nationhood, Sylvia Federico suggests that even though the audience of the poem would have been familiar with the medieval tradition based in the accounts of Dares and Dictys, the stanza's ambivalence about a Trojan origin is reflected in Geoffrey's account of Brutus' "Oedipal drama" involved in his patricide and his position as a "mediator between Rome and Britain."[19] Federico aptly acknowledges the influence of the Dares and Dictys, but the lines do not include any reference to Brutus' accidental killing of his father and instead refer to a particular text of the Dares and Dictys tradition, Guido's *Historia*.

To understand the specific linguistic influence of Guido on these lines, we should first grapple with the problem that the *Gawain*-poet specifies only one "tulk" who betrays Troy. The enigmatic line, "Þe tulk þat þe trammes of tresoun þer wroȝt," has been interpreted by critics as a condemnation of either Antenor or Aeneas for betraying Troy and ensuring victory for the Greeks. While Sir Israel Gollancz in his edition claims that the treasonous "tulk" is Antenor because Dares and Dictys identify him as the leader of the plot, earlier editor Sir Frederic Madden suggests that the tag "[h]it watz Ennias" clearly names the traitor as Aeneas.[20] If we turn to Guido's *Historia*, we find the ultimate traitor to be Aeneas, even though Guido originally condemns Aeneas and Antenor equally: "Troyanis igitur existentibus tantis doloribus anxiosis et inclusis in urbe, Anchises cum eius filio Henea, Anthenor etiam cum eius filio Pollidamas consilium inierunt qualiter uitas eorum possent saluas facere ne perderentur a Grecis, et si aliud facere non possent, prodere ciuitatem" [While the Trojans were experiencing such painful sorrow, and were enclosed in the city, Anchises, with his son Aeneas, and Antenor, with his son Polydamas, conceived a plan how they could make their lives safe so they would not be lost to the Greeks, and if they could do it in no other way, to betray the city] (218).[21] It is no surprise then that the

---

18. See Turville-Petre, "The Brutus Prologue to *Sir Gawain and the Green Knight*," 340–46.

19. Sylvia Federico, *New Troy: Fantasies of Empire in the Late Middle Ages* (Minneapolis: University of Minnesota Press, 2003), 34–35.

20. J. R. R. Tolkien and E. V. Gordon, eds., *Sir Gawain and the Green Knight*, rev. Norman Davis (Oxford: Clarendon Press, 1967), 70; Gollancz, ed., *Sir Gawain and The Green Knight*, Early English Text Society 210 (London: Oxford University Press, 1940); Sir Frederic Madden, ed., *Syr Gawayne* (Bannatyne Club, 1839).

21. Guido de Columnis, *Historia destructionis Troiae*, ed. Nathaniel Edward Griffin (Cambridge, Massachusetts: Mediaeval Academy of America, 1936). Quoted passages are from this edition.

Gawain-poet would associate both Aeneas and Antenor with the treason, but we are left with the question of why Aeneas is singled out among a group that includes not only Antenor, but also Anchises and Polydamas. As Guido's narrative unfolds, the roles of the other traitors, including Antenor, are effaced by the centrality of Hecuba's invective against Aeneas for his responsibility for Troy's destruction. She clearly identifies Aeneas as the "proditor," venting particular disgust for his resolve that allows him to "eius ruinam aspicias... quibus fumat" [behold its [Troy's] ruin... as it goes up in smoke] (234). Her emphasis on his callous gaze invites readers to interpret his observation as an act that certifies Troy's fall and confirms his culpability.[22] The *Gawain*-poet's ambiguous placement of Aeneas' treachery in the "frame" then simultaneously encourages us to condemn this deed and "see" Troy "brent to brondez and askez" through the eyes of Aeneas. Such a perspective requires that readers confront the treasonous circumstances of Britain's foundation and gaze through—a glass darkly—the smoking ashes of Troy to view the rest of the romance.

As the passage continues, the *Gawain*-poet's reliance upon Guido's *Historia* increases. After the establishment of Aeneas as a traitor, the poet tracks Aeneas' exile, which according to the logic of the *translatio imperii* transforms him into a conqueror who "depreced prouinces." The reference to "prouinces" likely depends upon Guido's own explanation for the transfer of empire after Troy's fall: "Et nonnulle alie propterea prouincie perpetuum ex Troyanis receperunt incolatum" [And therefore some other provinces received from the Trojans a lasting settlement] (11). Guido's Aeneas then becomes the original colonizer of the Western Empire, whose Trojans are benignly "received" by *prouincie* such as Rome, Sicily, and Britain. The *Gawain*-poet ironically deploys and belies Guido's representation of the colonized as those good-natured natives who "received" the colonizers through the use of "depreced," a word with the harsher connotations that the *MED* lists as "conquer, subjugate, overthrow, drive out, exclude, and oppress." This negative portrayal of the transfer of empire transforms the subsequent Trojan strongholds from migratory settlements to imperial conquests.

Yet, the *Gawain*-poet engages in a bit of ambiguous wordplay at Guido's expense by using the word "depreced," since it appears again two more times later in the romance during the lady's negotiations with Gawain. In one instance, she "depresed hym so þikke" (1770), literally suggesting that she

---

22. For the way medieval optical theory can be applied in reading the poem, see Richard E. Zeitkowitz, *Homoeroticism and Chivalry: Discourses of Male Same-Sex Desire in the 14th Century* (New York: Palgrave Macmillan, 2003), 93–98; Sarah Stanbury, *Seeing the Gawain-Poet: Description and the Act of Perception* (Philadelphia: University of Pennsylvania Press, 1991), 96.

"pressed him" in her wooing game, but given its use in the colonial language of the frame, the *Gawain*-poet encourages readers to consider the amusing image of the lady as an imperialist who conquers Gawain and seizes his body. Yet, we see a less aggressive connotation of Guido's "receperunt" when we encounter the next instance in which Gawain beseeches the lady to "deprece your prysoun" (1219), which here emerges in an opposite sense, meaning "release your prisoner." Such a use of "deprece" from the French "de(s) presser," also considers the positive implications of Aeneas' imperialism, which demonstrates the *Gawain*-poet's clever use of Guido and preference for ambiguity. Following Arthur Lindley's charge that readers (especially editors) should not "restrict the play of meanings in the text," Turville-Petre suggests that the use of "depreced" in the opening is "deliberately ambiguous."[23] But like many readers of the poem who look for references to Geoffrey's *Historia*, he claims that the opposite valences of the word, "liberate" and "subjugate" can be traced back to the Galfridian account, which describes both Brutus' liberation of the Trojan exiles in Greece (6.20) and his subjugation of Gascony (8.18).[24] While the play on "depreced" is thematically consistent with Geoffrey's history, the *Gawain*-poet's overall pessimism about imperial endeavors, translation of "provinces" from Guido's "provincie," and emphasis on the words themselves evince a particularly skeptical perspective. This polysemic linguistic subtlety suggests that the *Gawain*-poet approaches his Trojan heritage in the manner of the poet of the alliterative *Morte Arthure*, who consistently attends to the underbelly of imperial expansion and undercuts the moral foundation of Arthurian rule.

As the prologue proceeds, the *Gawain*-poet engages in the same kind of semiotic play, transforming a prologue of high seriousness into an epic invocation of amusing proportions through a clever use of Virgil's *Aeneid*. The frenetic course of Aeneas' *translatio* slackens its pace at the enigmatic word, "Ticius," which seemingly refers to nothing recognizable, but actually reaffirms the *Gawain*-poet's ironic use of Guido. Gollancz emends it to read "Tuscus," who was the son of Hercules, Tuscany's first monarch, according to Roman grammarian Paulus Diaconus.[25] This name also appears in Servius' commentary on Virgil in the amplified version known as the Danielis, a text that certainly passed through the British Isles and may have even

---

23. Arthur Lindley, "Pinning Gawain Down: The Misediting of *Sir Gawain and the Green Knight*," *Journal of English and Germanic Philology* 96 (1997): 26–42; Turville-Petre, "The Brutus Prologue to *Sir Gawain and the Green Knight*," 344–45.

24. See Friedrich W. D. Brie, ed., *Anglo-Norman Brut: The Brut, or the Chronicles of England*, Part 1, Early English Text Society o.s. 131 (London: Oxford University Press, 1906).

25. Gollancz, *Sir Gawain and The Green Knight*, 96; Sextus Pompeius Festus, *De verborum significatu*, ed. W. M. Lindsay (Leipzig: Teubner, 1913), 486–87.

been compiled by an Irish clerk.[26] The existence of "Tuscus" in the Danielis would therefore suggest that insular Virgilian commentators accepted it as fact: "cum Tyrrhenus . . . discederet, in mari quod Tyrrhenum ab eo vocatur periit. Cuius filius Tuscus cum populo evasit in regionem Tusciam, quae ab eo nomen accepit" [When Tyrrhenus departed, he perished in the sea, which is called the Tyrrhenian after him. His son Tuscus left with his people in the Tuscan region, which received its name from him] (53).[27] "Ticius" could then refer to "Tuscus" or, as the passage demonstrates, "Tyrrhenus," which is written in the *Aeneid* manuscripts variously as "Tyrrus," "Tirrus," and "Tirius."[28] In the case of the last form, "Tirius," it would have taken only a small scribal error to produce the "Ticius" that appears in the *Gawain* manuscript. Such an identification of "Tirius" as "Tyrrhenus" would have depended upon the *Gawain*-poet's intimate knowledge of both the *Aeneid* and its commentary traditions. If the *Gawain*-poet also composed the other poems of the British Library MS Cotton Nero A.x (*Pearl, Cleanness, Patience*), the use of classical figures and incorporation of translations of Virgil in this corpus demonstrate that he knew the *Aeneid* well, a familiarity he likely gained from grammar books where Virgil was ubiquitous.[29]

It is also clear, however, that the poet's understanding of the *Aeneid* was mediated by Guido's *Historia*, which provides another form of "Tirius" for "Tyrrhenus" and a context that adds to the irony of the lines. At the end of Book 12, Guido rehearses the *translatio imperii* that he had fully articulated in Book 2, explaining that Aeneas left Troy as an exile and "Tirenum nauigando per perlagus" [by sailing through the Tyrrhenian (Tirenum) sea] (109) was able to become prince of the Roman Republic, which he ruled like

---

26. Christopher Baswell, *Virgil in Medieval England: Figuring the Aeneid from the Twelfth Century to Chaucer* (Cambridge: Cambridge University Press, 1995), 37; George P. Goold, "Servius and the Helen Episode," *Harvard Studies in Classical Philology* 74 (1970): 101–68, at 116.

27. E. K. Rand, *Servianorum in Vergilii Carmina Commentariorum Editionis Harvardianae*, Vol. 2 (Lancaster, 1946), 1.67.

28. See Virgil, *Aeneid*, ed. C. G. Heyne (London: T. Rickaby, 1793), 3.75, 7.484n, 9.28 ("Tyrrhidae juvenes"), 9.28n; ed. O. Ribbeck (Leipzig: Teubner, 1895), 3.562–63, 7.484n, 508n; Servius, *Commentary* 7.484, eds. G. Thilo and H. Hagen (Leipzig, 1878–1902), 2.161. "Tirius" also appears in the French *Eneas*, written in the twelfth century. See the edition by Salverda de Grave (Paris, 1925), 3527, 3634, 3656, 3659, 3702, 3720. For more on the connection between "Tyrrhus" and "Tyrrhenus" see Ludwig August Dindorf in Stephanus, *Thesaurus graecae linguae*, eds. Henri Estienne, Charles Benoît Hase, Ludwig August Dindorf, and Wilhelm Dindorf (Leipzig, 1848–54), 7.2611B; August Pauly and Georg Wissowa, *Real-Encyclopädie*, 2^e Reihe, 14er Halbband 2 (1948), 1940–1, *s.n.* "Tyrrhus," especially 1940, lines 64 and following; Wilhelm Roscher, *Ausführliches Lexikon* 5 (Leipzig, 1924), 1468–69, *s.n.* "Tyrrhus pater."

29. Coolidge Otis Chapman, "Virgil and the *Gawain*-Poet," *Proceedings of the Modern Language Association* 60 (1945): 16–23; M. C. Thomas, *Sir Gawayne and the Green Knight* (Zürich: Füssli & Co., 1883).

an emperor. While the form "Tirenum" does not have as strong a philological connection as the "Tirius" of the *Aeneid,* its thematic context suggests that the *Gawain*-poet would have also turned to Guido in tracking the course of empire and likely inherited this form from the *Historia.* The *Gawain*-poet's appetite for irony would have also been sated through Guido's reference to a people's republic being governed like an empire and the additional claim that emperors before Caesar Augustus were called "Aeneases" (109). With this ironic background in place, "Tirius" alters the tone of the opening stanza: the tragic circumstances and itinerary of the Trojan exile that precede Britain's rise to worldly prominence become the focus, not the forgotten means to an end.

The irony that accompanies the *translatio* reaches a climax with the reference to "Felix Brutus," the legendary founder of Britain. Silverstein notes that the "felix" label refers specifically to imperial princes and Roman numismatic formulas for city founders such as Sulla and Commodus, which certainly applies to the case of Brutus, who established the New Troy.[30] The *Gawain*-poet was most likely familiar with this epithet through its traditional association with Aeneas in Tiberius Claudius Donatus' interpretation of the *Aeneid.* In Book 3, Aeneas observes the miniature Troy (*effigiem Troiam*) established by the Trojan refugees at Buthrotum and tells them, "vivite felices, quibus est fortuna peracta / iam sua; nos alia ex aliis in fata vocamur" [Live on blessed ones, whose fortune is accomplished! / As for us, from change to change according to Fate we are called] (493–94).[31] Donatus perceives these lines as an opportunity to discuss Aeneas' position as both "felix" and "infelix" in his exilic wanderings and discernment of his imperial fate.[32] After treating Aeneas' felicity, Donatus paraphrases Aeneas' words to the Trojan exiles: "vivite qui estis a mea infelicitate discreti nec mecum quaeritis Italiam, quae tantum recedit quantum eam nos insistendo persequimur" [Live on, you who are separated from my misfortune and do not seek Italy

---

30. Silverstein, "*Sir Gawain,* Dear Brutus, and Britain's Fortunate Founding," 198; *Thesaurus linguae latinae* 6.1.440, lines 54 and following, *s.v.* "felix": "principium cognomen"; and 6.1.451, lines 67 and following, *s.v.* "feliciter": "speciatim de rebus ad principem pertinentibus." In ancient Rome, the epithetic pairings for founders were "fortis" and "felix," "virtus" and "felicitas," but by the time of Charlemagne, they became "patientia (constantia)" and "felicitas," "prudential" and "felicitas"; see Einhard, *Vita karoli* 7.4, 6–8.3, 12, and 15.1–3, ed. H. W. Garrod and R. B. Mowat (Oxford: Clarendon Press, 1925), 10–12 and 17. For a full numismatic survey of "felix" and "felicitas," see E. Spanheim, *Dissertationes de praestantia et usu numismatum antiquorum* (London: R. Smith, 1706–17), 725–29. It should also be noted that "felix" is commonly used in hagiography.

31. Virgil, *Opera,* ed. R. A. B. Mynors (Oxford: Oxford University Press, 1969).

32. H. George, ed., *Donati Interpretationes Vergilianae* 1 (Leipzig: Teubner, 1905), 330–31.

with me, which recedes as much as we pursue it in our journey].[33] According to Donatus then, Aeneas' imperial itinerary is defined by the fluctuation between the felicity and misfortune, the *Gawain*-poet's "blysse and blunder" (18), that accompanies the founding of cities. Donatus' point is amplified by the fact that Aeneas' speech to the Trojan exiles goes on to express the danger of rebuilding New Troys. This scene serves as a warning to Aeneas that he cannot simply replicate the architecture and authority of his Trojan predecessors. For the *Gawain*-poet, such a reading of the *Aeneid* is consistent with the treason and conflagration that provides the basis for the founding of Britain by "Felix Brutus" in the first stanza. "Felix" then reeks with ironic overtones, which accentuate the misfortune that accompanies imperial designs.

The *Gawain*-poet's sophisticated Virgilianism is confirmed by the juxtaposition and wordplay of "felix" and "with wynne" two lines later. While Donatus may not have been known to Geoffrey of Monmouth, Wace, or the authors of the *Brut* books, he was read in England during the life of Alcuin and then disseminated throughout the continent in the fourteenth and fifteenth centuries.[34] All evidence points to the *Gawain*-poet's knowledge of both the *Aeneid* and its commentaries, which, according to Christopher Baswell, were available "in almost any educational center of the Middle Ages."[35] Most editors read "wynne" as "joy," an interpretation consistent with the enjoyment of imperial expansion, but its proximity to the ironic "felix" presents other compelling possibilities.[36] The Old English "wynn" supports the "joy" reading, but the similar Old English "gewinn," which means "strife, conflict, or labor," presents a provocative alternative. According to the *MED*, the Middle English "wynne," derived from the Old English "wynn," is difficult to distinguish from the Middle English "winn," derived from the Old English "gewinn." This latter reading is therefore a plausible one, undercutting any sense of "joy" with a suggestion of the suffering that inheres to the vacillation of fate of the *(in)felix* conqueror. Silverstein attributes these antithetical connotations to the Galfridian tradition, claiming that the "winn" reading is also

---

33. *Donati Interpretationes Vergilianae* 1, 330–31; see also Servius' comments on *Aeneid* 1.98, "animam hanc": "quasi cum dolore animam hanc, ac si diceret 'infelicem' 'quae ad laborem nata est'" (1.68). Compare also Boethius, *De consolatione philosophiae* 4, ed. H. F. Stewart and E. K. Rand (London, 1918), 334, lines 3–7.

34. Silverstein, "*Sir Gawain*, Dear Brutus, and Britain's Fortunate Founding," 201; *Donati Interpretationes Vergilianae*, xvii ff.

35. Baswell, *Virgil in Medieval England*, 33.

36. For more on the optimism of the Galfridian tradition, see Francisque Michel, ed., *Gestum regum Britanniae* (Cambrian Archeological Association, 1862), 16 (1.458–59); Laȝamon, *Brut*, ed. W. R. J. Barron and S. C. Weinberg (Harlow, Essex: Longman, 1995), 1783–99; Judith Weiss, ed., *Wace's Roman de Brut: A History of the British* (Exeter: University of Exeter Press, 2003), 1058–62; Brie, *The Brut*, 10–11.

"authentic for the Brutus story."[37] As Silverstein admits, however, Geoffrey's narrative is primarily concerned with the "wynn" that ensues from the fertile foundation of Britain.[38] I would suggest that the "winn" connotation is not based in the Galfridian model, but rather in the darker interpretation of the *Aeneid* that is embodied in the Guido-tradition. In fact, if we were to translate "with wynne" into Latin, we would have the adverb "feliciter," a word whose morphology brings us back to the ironic "felix" and Aeneas' conflicted speech to the Trojan exiles. This hyperbolic use of "felix" is corroborated by the alliterative context of *Gawain,* in which "Felix Brutus" sails "fer ouer þe French flod" (13). The *Gawain*-poet's readers would have been amused by the alliteration of "Felix," "fer," "French," and "flod," which conjure the image of a Brutus styled as a Roman conqueror who sails far across a Frankish sea, when in fact the channel between England and France was indeed too *short* a distance for the fourteenth-century English mired in the Hundred Years War. Such a complex and comedic use of "felix" and "wynne" reflects the *Gawain*-poet's philological prowess and remarkable ability to undercut traditional recitations of lineage that seek glory in a Trojan origin.

By satirizing Britain's ancestry in the Trojan "frame," the *Gawain*-poet challenges the legitimacy of the beginnings of a British empire. Moreover, the conflicted Trojan historiography of the textual margin represents the hybridized perspectives of those who inhabited the outskirts of British authority in the Northwest Midlands and the Welsh March. Here we have the other borderland of *Gawain,* which not only is described in Gawain's journey to Hautdesert, but also is the probable residence of the *Gawain*-poet and his alliterative contemporaries, John Clerk and the *Siege of Jerusalem*-poet, who draw extensively from Guido's *Historia.* As I demonstrate in the following section, the *Gawain*-poet's enhancement of the skepticism in his translation of his sources in the first stanza, which interrogates the ethics of imperialist expansion and English nationalism, may have been inspired by the poet's own provincial identity. Geoffrey's *Historia* may have been an unappealing historical source to a provincial such as the *Gawain*-poet, since Geoffrey attends more to Wales and "New Troy" than the English provinces. Jeffrey Jerome Cohen even suggests that, "Geoffrey was profoundly uninterested in the other English towns and cities, granting these locales no place in his history other than as Saxon settlements for British heroes like Arthur to besiege."[39] Given the residence of the *Gawain*-poet in the Northwest

37. Silverstein, "*Sir Gawain,* Dear Brutus, and Britain's Fortunate Founding," 201
38. Ibid.
39. Jeffrey Jerome Cohen, *Hybridity, Identity, and Monstrosity in Medieval Britain: On Difficult Middles* (New York: Palgrave Macmillan, 2006), 111.

Midlands, he must have been disturbed by the Galfridian relegation of the provinces to such conquered states, which were increasingly inhabited by the gentry who had been absorbed into an increasingly nationalistic community.[40] Instead, in the manner of his alliterative contemporaries, he relies on Guido's *Historia* to provide the fodder for his provincial politics.

PROVINCIALIZING TROY

As one of the poets of the alliterative Guido-tradition, it is not surprising that the *Gawain*-poet would engage in such pessimistic political commentary. He was a contemporary of both John Clerk and the *Siege of Jerusalem*-poet, who expressed ambivalence about imperialism through the Guido-tradition and likely composed their works near Whalley and Bolton, locations of monastic houses in northern England. In nearby Cheshire, the dialectical area of the

---

40. The example of Sir Robert Grosvenor is instructive. As Michael Bennett suggests, the *Gawain*-poet was a contemporary and possibly an acquaintance of Grosvenor, who lived in Hulme, just north of the *Gawain*-poet's dialectical zone, and on the road between Chester and the uplands, the place where the Green Chapel may have been located. See "The Historical Background," in *A Companion to the Gawain-Poet*, 71–90, at 72. Grosvenor was involved in a famous heraldic quarrel with Sir Richard Scrope, a dispute in which Geoffrey Chaucer was involved. During the 1380s, Chaucer observed Scrope's arms displayed on a shield hanging outside an inn, but the arms were not Scrope's—they were Grosvenor's. Chaucer did not know Grosvenor or of any claim to Scrope's arms, so he testified on behalf of Scrope in the court of chivalry in October 1386, a trial during which Scrope produced witnesses from the nobility to confirm his charge that Grosvenor had falsified his arms (70–74). While Grosvenor was unsuccessful in his defense, his witnesses testified to his military service in a variety of fourteenth-century campaigns, including Edward III's final tour of France in 1359–60 and the chevauchée of northern France under the command of Sir James Audley, lieutenant to the Black Prince in the late 1360s. He also served Edward III at Sandwich in 1372 and in 1385 even accompanied Richard II during his invasion of Scotland; *Calendar of Close Rolls 1389–92* (London, 1896–1947), 392. Grosvenor was not in fact a career solider and instead remained a typical gentryman in the Northwest Midlands like many of his neighbors in Cheshire or south Lancashire, a region without resident nobles. Many manor-houses, which were likely places of prolific cultural production, populated the region, and by the late fourteenth century the Northwest was experiencing the centripetal force of the powerful and royal South, which was drawing local soldiers or writers into a more national milieu. As Bennett contends, "The paradox is that the conditions for cultural production in the region became more favorable at the time when its regional culture was most under threat. Sir Robert Grosvenor's entanglement with the court of chivalry is symbolic: the local community of honour was being integrated in, and subordinated to, a national one" ("The Historical Background," 77). This type of subordination, destruction of regional identity, and lack of recognition of Grosvenor's aspirations to nobility would have fostered an environment of disenchantment with royal ambitions, at least among some such as Grosvenor who had served his kings faithfully. The *Gawain*-poet reaffirms this regional ambivalence about such movements toward unity through a recitation of lineage, one that does more to undercut rather than bolster England's noble ancestry.

Gawain-poet, monasteries contained collections of Latin works that proved to be attractive sources for alliterative poets. One of these sources was the *Polychronicon*, a universal history composed by Ranulph Higden in the 1330s and 40s, a monk at St. Werbergh's in Chester.[41] This Latin chronicle also expresses skepticism about Britain's imperial progenitors, especially the figure of Arthur, which is consistent with the historiographic mindset of these local alliterative romanciers.

Like Guido, Higden recites the unimaginative facts of history, participates in anti-Galfridian invective, and subverts English pretensions to imperial glory. More importantly, his provincial perspective on Chester as residing on the edge of the world aligns it with *Gawain*'s border-historiography. Scholars have recently addressed Higden's unique contribution to English nationalism, notably the ways he envisions England as peripheral to the rest of the world and critiques Galfridian fantasies of empire.[42] According to Peter Brown, Higden rejects the historicity of Brutus' founding of Britain and privileges "a more factual, ratiocinative, less imaginative but no less fascinating account."[43] This is in direct contrast to most chroniclers of the Hundred Years War, who express a distinct optimism about imperial endeavors and the expansion of English territory.[44]

The *Gawain*-poet and Higden share an interest in the diversity of Englishness that reflects a concomitant disdain for their French counterparts. Higden is especially disgusted by the effect of Danish and French invasions since they resulted in the corruption of his own English tongue, claiming that the language had become reduced to a series of groans ("boatus et garritus").[45] The fragmentation of the English language had become more

---

41. Bennett, "The Historical Background," 77; *Community, Class, and Careerism: Cheshire and Lancashire Society in the Age of Sir Gawain and the Green Knight* (Cambridge: Cambridge University Press, 1983), 7.

42. Andrew Galloway, "Latin England," in *Imagining a Medieval English Nation*, 41–95, at 43; Peter Brown, "Higden's Britain," in *Medieval Europeans: Studies in Ethnic Identity and National Perspectives in Medieval Europe*, ed. Alfred P. Smyth (Houndmills and London: Macmillan; New York: St. Martin's, 1998), 103–18; Lavezzo, *Angels on the Edge of the World*, 71–92.

43. Brown, "Higden's Britain," 106.

44. Galloway, "Latin England," 43; see also Jesse Gellrich, *Discourse and Dominion in the Fourteenth Century: Oral Contexts of Writing in Philosophy, Politics, and Poetry* (Princeton: Princeton University Press, 1995), 134–50. For a study of earlier chronicles, see Monika Otter, *Inventiones: Fiction and Referentiality in Twelfth-Century English Historical Writing* (Chapel Hill and London: University of North Carolina Press, 1996); Gabrielle Spiegel, *Romancing the Past: The Rise of Vernacular Prose Historiography in Thirteenth-Century France* (Berkeley and Los Angeles: University of California Press, 1993).

45. All quotations of Higden and Trevisa's texts refer to *Polychronicon, Together with the English Translation of John of Trevisa and an Unknown Writer of the Fifteenth Century*, ed. Churchill Babington and Joseph R. Lumby (London: Longmans, Green, and Co., 1869).

complex because, according to Higden, English children of nobility were compelled to learn French ("construere Gallice compelluntur") from birth. His invective is especially pointed at the nobility, since the larger effect was that rural people tried to become more "French" ("rurales homines ... francigenare satagunt") in an attempt to appear more acceptable to higher society ("assimilari volentes, ut per hoc spectabiliores videantur") (2.158–61).[46] By referring to the "Frenchified" contexts of Camelot and Hautdesert, the *Gawain*-poet evinces an awareness of this trend of provincial ladder-climbers. This critical perspective on the pretensions to nobility is apparent when the poet characterizes Bertilak's ostentatious display of good manners to Gawain as "Frenkysch fare" (1116). In other words, Bertilak embodies the cultural complexity of the provincial aristocrat, one who is "English" by virtue of his familiarity with all things French.

Higden also implicitly condemns the pervasiveness of French in pretensions to "Englishness" through his complaints about the diversity of English pronunciation:

> Ubi nempe mirandum videtur, quomodo nativa et propria Anglorum lingua, in unica insula coartata, pronunciatione ipsa sit tam diversa; cum tamen Normannica lingua quæ adventitia est, univocal maneat penes cunctos. De prædicta quoque lingua Saxonica tripartita, quæ in paucis adhuc agrestibus vix remansit, orientales cum occiduis tanquam sub eodem coeli climate lineati plus consonant in sermone quam boreales cum austrinis. Inde est Mercii sive Mediterranei Angli, tanquam participantes naturame extremorum, collaterales linguas arcticam et anarcticam melius intelligent quam adinvicem se intelligunt jam extremi. (1.160, 162)

> [It certainly seems a great wonder how the native (*nativa*) and proper (*propria*) language of the English should be so diverse (*diversa*) in pronunciation on one confined island, when yet the language of the Normans, which had arrived [from another land], maintains one sound among all. As of the tripartite language of the Saxons, which scarcely remains now among provincial (*agrestibus*) people, the western people sound more alike in speech to the eastern people under the same climate of heaven than the northern to southern people. Therefore it is that Mercy that people of middle England, as it were, partners of the extremities, understand better the collateral

---

46. For further discussion of these lines and their comparison to Higden's autograph manuscript, San Marino, CA, Huntington Library MS HM 132 see Galloway, "Latin England," 45–46 and 87n7; V. H. Galbraith, "An Autograph Manuscript of Ranulph Higden's *Polychronicon*," *The Huntington Library Quarterly* 23 (1959): 1–18.

languages, northern and southern, than the northern and southern understand each other.]

As if they live in an anglicized Babel, the English-speaking people cannot communicate with each other because of dramatic dialectical differences between the north and the south. Yet, the real rub is that the appropriated French, the language of the invaders, maintains a unity that cannot be found in English. For Higden, the language of the provincials (*agrestibus*) or what John Trevisa in his English translation calls the "tonge" of "vplondisshe men" (1.161), is a dying dialect that regrettably cannot compete with the currency of the French, which pervades the English court. By highlighting the linguistic complexities of the "outlandish" people, Higden displays the uniqueness of the north and its tenuous relationship to southern topographies, while at the same time expressing disdain for the French influence that has achieved unity in the face of English disunity.

Likewise, the *Gawain*-poet's choice to rewrite a French romance in an English alliterative form complicates such francophilia and provides an alternative to the Anglo-Norman spoken in the English court.[47] Moreover, his Northwest Midlands dialect expands and stretches the outer limits of Englishness. As mentioned earlier in this chapter, the *Gawain*-poet even fantasizes about a great distance between England and France, setting Britain's location as "fer ouer þe French flod" (13), positing England as an "outpost" on the edge of the imperial world. When read within a Higdenian context, this reference in the first stanza to Brutus crossing the "French flod," reads as both a *translatio imperii et studii* that tracks the geography of empire and its "frenchifying" effects on English identity.

This shared skepticism about imperial endeavors and linguistic unity suggests the existence of a provincial sensibility that perceived England as remote and peripheral from its imperial past. Higden in his chronicle speaks as a historian who is chronologically distant from the conventional authorities. In the very first sentence of the preface to the *Polychronicon*, he establishes his subservience to his historical predecessors by claiming his belatedness in relation to past recorders of history (1.2).[48] Like Virgil

47. For a succinct assessment of the relationship between *Gawain* and its French antecedents, see Ad Putter, *Sir Gawain and the Green Knight and French Arthurian Romance* (Oxford: Clarendon Press, 1995), 1–9.

48. "Post praeclaros artium scriptores, quibus circa rerum notitiam aut morum modestiam dulce fuit, quo adviverent, insudare, illi merito, velut utile dulci commiscentes, grandisonis sunt praeconiis attollendi, qui magnifica priscorum gesta beneficio scripturae posteris derivarunt" [After the most famous writers of the arts, for whom it was a pleasure to work, as long as they lived, at the knowledge of things and the modesty of morals, they, just as they mixed utility with

or Homer before him, he assumes the difficult task of a compiler who may "quippiam adjiciam laboribus auctorum, nanus residens in humeris giganteis, unde non solum minores ad rudimentum sed et majores ad exercitium provocentur" [as a dwarf sitting on a giant's shoulders, somehow increase the work of authorities, so that not only the lesser but also the greater who are ignorant of the greater volumes may learn from this treatise] (1.14–5). As a historian who combines various accounts for the purpose of teaching the unlearned, this claim is consistent with the vernacular project of John Clerk of Whalley, who relates the history of Dares and Dictys, who had earlier recorded their experiences of the Trojan War:

> of hom þat suet after
> To ken all the crafte how þe case felle,
> By lokyng of letturs þat lefte were of olde. (24–26)[49]

[for those who followed afterwards so that they would know all the causes behind the events through the linking of letters that were left of old.]

These lines are remarkable, not only because of the attention they seem to pay to the sounds of meter and alliteration, but also because they are similar to the ending of the stanza that follows the Trojan "frame" of *Gawain*. In this section, the *Gawain*-poet's voice rises to the forefront, claiming that he will tell his story,

> As it is stad and stoken
> In stori stif and stronge,
> With lel letters loken,
> In londe so hatz ben longe. (33–36)

[As it was set and established in a story stiff and strong, linked with true letters in our land for a long time.]

Even though there is no convincing evidence for a relationship of dependence between Clerk's "lokyng of letturs" and the *Gawain*-poet's "lel letters

---

sweetness, justly ought to be lifted up by high-sounding public criers, who have passed on to the future the noble deeds of the ancients by the benefit of writing]. The phrase "velut utile dulci commiscentes" is remarkably similar to Guido's claim that Ovid mixed truth and falsehood in his books (see Chapter 2, 56–58).

49. John Clerk of Whalley, *The Destruction of Troy: A Diplomatic and Color Facsimile Edition, Hunterian MS V.2.8 in Glasgow University Library*, ed. Hiroyuki Matsumoto (Ann Arbor: University of Michigan Press, 2002).

loken," both phrases suggest that letters or accounts must be combined or translated for the usefulness of their readers/hearers. These and the similar references to the antiquity of the stories, "lefte of olde" and "[i]n londe so hatz ben longe," reflect a distance from their sources that is consistent with Higden's characterization of himself as a dwarfish historian who combines the accounts of his "gigantic" authorities. Given their common residence in the north, their conventional recitations of subservience to the *auctores* of the past may have had a special resonance for a literary community that also perceived itself as synchronically distant from the imperial future of the south.

By specifying his locality in Chester in the northwest, Higden identifies himself as one writing from the geographic borderland not only of the world, but also of England, a sentiment that is expressed both structurally and thematically by the *Gawain*-poet in his Arthurian romance. Higden's notion that he records universal and national history from an "angulo orbis" [corner of the world] is reflected in his discussions of England's geographical distance from the rest of the world, his self-identification as a Chester monk, and even the maps that accompany manuscripts of the *Polychronicon* (2.4). This English marginality is most powerfully expressed in what had been known as the Higden map (British Library Royal MS 14, CIX, iv-2), a mappa mundi that places England (*Anglia*) at the margin of the world. The map is associated with Higden not only because the two-page mappa mundi begins the Ramsey Abbey manuscript of the *Polychronicon,* but also because it visually represents Higden's textual perspective of English identity as being defined by its outlandishness.[50]

Higden's pun on *Anglia* as *angulo orbis* is representative of his overall establishment of England as an outpost on the border, or even outside, of the world. Seven times in book one alone Higden calls attention to England's isolation in comparison to the rest of the world, especially Jerusalem and Rome. He refers to England as "alter orbis" [another world] twice in the opening to the book, even claiming that "Ora Gallici littoris finis foret orbis, nisi Britannia insula nomen pene alterius orbis mereretur" [the border of the French seaside should be the end of the world, if the island of Britain does not nearly merit the name of another world] (2.6). In mapping out the relationship between Britain and France and Spain later in the book (2.10), he asserts that "Britannia intra oceanum quasi extra orbem posita" [Britain is placed within the ocean just as it is placed outside of the world]. And finally in a poem at

---

50. Lavezzo, *Angels on the Edge of the World,* 71. For more on Higden's connection to the map, see Peter Barber, "The Evesham World Map: A Late Medieval English View of God and the World," *Imago Mundi* 47 (1995): 13–33.

the end of his chapter titled "De praerogativis insulae attollendis" [On the Privileges of that Island to be Exalted] he claims that

> Anglia terra ferax et fertilis angulus orbis,
> ... cujus miretur et optet
> Delicias Salomon, Octavianus opes. (2.18–21)

> [England is a fruitful land and a fertile corner of the world ... the delights of which Solomon may admire, the wealth of which Octavian may desire.]

Even though his characterization of England is laudatory, his reference to Octavian's imagined imperial desire (*optet . . . opes*), posits England as an inevitable object of conquest that can only achieve imperial power by virtue of its value to worldly authorities. As Lavezzo suggests, "King Solomon and Emperor Octavian represent the geopolitical might of Jerusalem and Rome, which both appear at or near the center of the world on medieval mappae mundi. England cannot authorize itself, it appears, but requires the legitimizing approval of the center."[51] Without the sanction of the geopolitical core, according to Higden, England is truly an *insula* or *alter orbis* that maintains a tenuous connection to the rest of the world.

Likewise for the *Gawain*-poet, England's marginality is primarily expressed in the frame text by its status as the final destination of the westward movement of the *translatio imperii* from the more central Troy and Rome to the British borderland. Here, too, Britain is described as a desirable object for Rome, but such imperial discourse is belied by the ominous overtones of the burning of cities and consequences of treason. While universal in scope, this recitation of lineage holds legitimizing power that enables nobles and monarchs to claim a particular nationalistic sovereignty separate from other European nations. On the one hand, the *Gawain*-poet stresses affinity with his imperial ancestors that is different from historians such as Geoffrey of Monmouth. This equivalency, which is also embodied in Arthur's tragedy in the alliterative *Morte Arthure,* accords no special status to the English in their imperial pretensions and disastrous consequences of such empire-building—they suffer the same fate as the Trojans and Romans. By claiming that "both blysse and blunder / Ful skete hatz skyfted synne" [both bliss and blunder very swiftly have alternated since] (18–19), the *Gawain*-poet not only acknowledges the tumultuous settlement of Britain, but also confirms the inextricable damage that adheres to achievements of imperial glory.

51. Lavezzo, *Angels on the Edge of the World,* 87.

As much as the poem is international in scope, however, this recitation of ancestry is the heraldic language used to define English nobility, since it establishes a power over the isle that can be traced back to Brutus' foundation. Recall Sir Clegis' description of his arms in the alliterative *Morte*:

> Myn armez are of ancestrye enueryde with lordez
> And has in banere bene borne sen sir Brut tyme,
> At the cité of Troye, þat tyme was ensegede,
> Ofte seen in asawtte with certayne knyghttez,
> For þe Brute broghte vs and all oure bolde elders
> To Bretayne þe braddere within chippe-burdez. (1693–99)

> [My arms of ancestry are acknowledged by lords and have been borne in banners since Sir Brutus' time, at the city of Troy, that time it was besieged, often seen in assault by certain knights, from which Brutus brought us and all our bold elders to Great Britain aboard ships.]

By claiming that his nobility is legitimized by the existence of his arms at the siege of Troy, Clegis asserts a Trojan identity, which could be claimed by other nations, such as France and Spain. However, he specifically asserts that Brutus translated his Trojan arms and "all oure bolde elders" to Britain, which implies that the British could have an exclusive claim to a Trojan identity. This British heraldry becomes an English heraldry in *Gawain* during the arming of Gawain, when we read the description of the pentangle on Gawain's shield. The *Gawain*-poet explains that the pentangle is not only a noble heraldic marker, but also what the "Englych" call the "endeles knot" (629–30). Like Higden's condemnation of social climbers, this pentangle becomes a particularly "Englych" symbol of "cultural chauvinism" that belies the international valuation of the transfer of empire.[52] In the manner of Clegis' claim to a specifically English line of Trojan ancestry, Gawain bears the arms that specifically refer to his English identity.

At the same time that the *Gawain*-poet and Higden distinguish England from continental discourse about imperial authority, they establish a provincial identity distinct from that of the rest of England. For Higden, this primarily means adopting a method of compiling his sources in which he distinguishes his voice from the other authorities through the use of the marker "R" for "Ranulphus."[53] In addition to this very personal method

---

52. Turville-Petre, "The Brutus Prologue to *Sir Gawain and the Green Knight*," 345.
53. This historiographic practice of citing authorities within the text rather than in the margin originates in Vincent of Beauvais' thirteenth-century *Speculum Maius*. See Vincent of Beau-

of critiquing his sources, Higden manipulates the first letters of the first sixty chapters of the longest and last version of the chronicle to announce his name, occupation, and residence in Chester: "PRESENTEM CRONICAM COMPILAVIT FRATER RANULPHUS CESTRENSIS MONACHUS" [Brother Ranulph, monk of Chester, compiled this present chronicle].[54] This acrostic self-definition existed in sermon manuals and Latin poetry, but Higden was the first to use it in a chronicle. The popularity of the *Polychronicon* led to the adoption of the device by not just Latin, but also vernacular writers, including John Clerk of Whalley.[55] Higden's autograph manuscript reflects extensive revision and use through emendations, scrapings, and rewritings, which indicates that the acrostic and much of R's commentary was added in the late 1340s.[56] His identification as a Chester monk is made especially clear during his discussion of various English locales, in which he claims that it is in Chester, "Ubi praesens chronica fuit elaborata, sicut per capitales hujus primi libri apices clarius patet" [where the present chronicle was labored at, as through the initials of the first book stands more fully clear] (2.76–77). This reaffirmation of his provincial perspective is even boldly rubricated and reproduced in the margin by a later hand, which suggests that Higden was concerned with establishing his Chester identity.[57]

Likewise, the *Gawain*-poet expresses his own provincial identity as one from a "town" in the second stanza, claiming that if the audience of the poem will listen, "I schal telle hit astit, as I in toun herde, / With tonge" [I shall hasten to tell it, as I heard it spoken in town] (31–32). Given the poet's residence in the northwest, this "toun" may refer to Chester or a nearby locale, which suggests that his tale has local resonances and had been circulated orally for sometime beforehand. By claiming that "Ay watz Arthur þe hendest, as I haf herde telle" [I have heard it said that King Arthur was the noblest] (26), the *Gawain*-poet not only aligns Arthur with his imperial predecessors, Aeneas

---

vais, *Speculum Maius*, 4 vols (Duacus, 1524; Reprint Graz, Austria: Akademische Druk-u. Verlagenstadt, 1964–5); A. J. Minnis, "Late-Medieval Discussions of *Compilatio* and the Role of the Compilator," *Beiträge zur Geschichte der deutschen Sprache und Literatur* 101 (1979): 385–421, esp. 389.

54. Galloway, "Latin England," 48–49.

55. W. W. Skeat, "Thomas Usk and Ralph Higden," *Notes and Queries*, 10th series, 1 (1904): 205; Galloway, "Latin England," 49, 87n12. Galloway incorrectly claims that "among vernacular writers, only Thomas Usk has been shown to have used the acrostic device." For examples from Latin writers, see Gransden, "Silent Meanings in Ranulph Higden's *Polychronicon* and in Thomas Elmham's *Liber Metricus de Henrico Quinto*," *Medium Ævum* 46 (1976): 231–40.

56. Galloway contends that Galbraith's discovery of the autograph manuscript of Higden's chronicle has allowed scholars to study "Higden's processes of self-definition . . . more closely than those of almost any other major fourteenth-century writer." See "Latin England," 49.

57. Galloway, "Latin England," 49.

and Brutus, but also suggests that he surpasses them in his gentility. Yet, by reporting that he had only "herde telle" of this claim, he does not fashion an "eyewitness" account, in the manner of Dares and Dictys, and instead relegates himself to the status of a recorder of history. The detachment from Arthurian enthusiasm that he implies through this discussion of the tale's oral foundation indicates that he approaches the legitimacy of England's national hero with the trepidation of an outsider. Through these efforts to establish their provincial perspectives, Higden and the *Gawain*-poet address universal themes and concerns from a peripheral standpoint, which affords them the distance to offer substantial critiques of English society at large.

The marginality expressed by Higden and the *Gawain*-poet was likely influenced by their residence in the border city of Chester, whose unique locale between England and Wales fostered a hybrid culture that maintained both Welsh and English sensibilities. Cheshire was not only a geographical borderland, but also legally distant from the rest of England after becoming a palatinate in the thirteenth-century.[58] Because of this local empowerment, Higden expresses an understandable pride in his region throughout the chronicle, especially in his chapter on English towns (2.26–29). Higden punctuates his loyalty to Chester by ending his forty-eighth chapter with an ode of praise to his hometown (2.80–84), which includes the line: "Anglis et Cambris nunc manet urbs celebris" [the city now remains crowded with both the English and Welsh] (2.80). He even questions previous historians in their characterizations of the region. In defense of Chester's natural resources, Higden rejects his source, the Norman historian William of Malmesbury, suggesting that he "somniaverit" [might have dreamed] of the scarcity of the actual wealth of corn, fish, and other necessary sustenance (2.78). Such an allegiance to his diverse city implies that he harbors an especially skeptical view of any exclusive notion of English nobility and fantasized nationhood. He not only perceives England as an *angulo orbis,* but also celebrates the Welsh borderland of his native Chester by locating it "urbs quidem in confinio Angliae ad prospectum Cambriae" [on the border of England looking into Wales] (2.78). His loyalty to his hybrid city accentuates the marginal identity assumed not only by him, but also by his fellow residents in the north. In other words, Higden and the *Gawain*-poet write not only from the edge of the world, but also from the edge of England.

But what exactly are the implications for writing from the outskirts? Were Higden and the *Gawain*-poet attempting to assert some kind of pro-

---

58. As Geoffrey Barraclough maintains, this new independent status "stimulated in Cheshire both a sense of community and a sense of differentiation from the rest of England." See *The Earldom and County Palatine of Chester* (Oxford: Blackwell, 1953), 22.

vincial power in their texts by privileging border spaces? Michel Foucault claims that "space is fundamental in any exercise of power," a formulation which suggests that Higden and the *Gawain*-poet might have drawn on their regional pride to distance and empower themselves separately from England.[59] Cheshire and Lancashire, being heavily militarized regions, were a potential threat to the unity of the England, but as much as the Northwest fostered opportunities for social advancement, they were also perceived by many as exotic outposts on the border of civilization.

The *Gawain*-poet attends to the consequences of such conflicted perspectives of the north to accentuate his wry and satiric reading of Arthurian England. His region's proximity to North Wales is a special concern that emerges in Gawain's journey to Hautdesert in Cheshire (695–701). As he enters the feral Wirral, he observes:

> Wonde þer bot lyte
> Þat auþer God oþer gome with goud hert louied . . .
> Mony klyf he ouerclambe in contrayez straunge.
> Fer floten fro his frendez, fremedly he rydez . . .
> So mony meruayl bi mount þer þe mon fyndez
> Hit were to tore for to telle of þe tenþe dole.
> Sumwhyle with wormez he werrez and with wolues als,
> Sumwhyle with wodwos þat woned in þe knarrez,
> Boþe with bullez and berez, and borez oþerquyle,
> And etaynez þat hym anelede of þe heȝe felle. (701b–2; 713–14; 718–23)

[Very few lived there whom either God or a good-hearted man loved . . . Gawain overcame many cliffs in strange regions. Far removed from his friends, as an alien he rides. . . . So many marvels by the hills there the man encounters, it would be too tedious to tell even a tenth of it. Sometimes he wars with dragons, and also with wolves, sometimes with trolls that lived among rocks, both with bulls and bears, and boars other times, and giants that pursued him from the high fells.]

The references to the dragons, trolls, and giants that haunt this place illustrate a journey from the civilization of King Arthur's court to the wilderness of the Northwest Midlands and Wales. Gawain is specifically characterized as a foreigner to the region in the phrase, "fremedly he rydez," which indicates

---

59. Michel Foucault, *Power-Knowledge: Selected Interviews and Other Writings, 1972–1977* (New York: Pantheon Books, 1980), 144.

his territorial allegiances to the Arthurian lands—for early Britain, these are the residences of Arthur's knights, and for the *Gawain*-poet's readers, these are the estates owned by the nobility to the south.

On one level, it is odd that Gawain, a kinsman of the Welsh Arthur, would feel a stranger in the Welsh March. One would assume that Arthur's status as a distinctly Welsh king and Geoffrey of Monmouth's degradation of the Saxons would have caused some problems for English claims to an Arthurian identity, but this was not the case. Apparently, Arthur's Welsh origin was easily forgotten, for he was readily appropriated within the English court. For Robert Manning in the early fourteenth century, Arthur was even the prototype for all "Englishemen" (1.10973), including Edward I, who failed to live up to his Arthurian heritage in the waning years of his kingship.[60] For Manning, Robert of Gloucester, and their predecessor, Laȝamon, the ancient Britons had prepared the way for the Normans and eventually the "English" people to establish their dominion.[61] And according to Felicity Riddy's examination of English romance, these "Arthurian texts in a sense created a nation."[62] Given this imperial forgetting about the Welsh origin of Arthur, Gawain's position as a foreigner in the Wirral places Arthurian identity squarely in the hands of the English. Or so it seems.

Occupying an uncomfortable position in the wilderness is somewhat expected for an adventuring knight, but the *Gawain*-poet's attention to specific geographical locations of North Wales, the isles of Anglesay, Holy Head, and the Wirral (691–700) suggests that these places not only were known, but also possessed a mystique in the imagination of "civilized" England. However, the disafforestation of the Wirral in 1376 and Richard II's regular habitation of the area in the 1390s demystified its identity as a savage wilderness.[63] When we consider the *Gawain*-poet's satiric perspective on the chivalric journey through this topography, the inaccurate characterization

---

60. Frederick J. Furnivall, ed., *The Story of England by Robert Manning of Brunne, a.d. 1338*, 2 vols., Rolls Series (London, 1887). For Manning's critiques of Edward, see Turville-Petre, "The Brutus Prologue to *Sir Gawain and the Green Knight*," 343.

61. Turville-Petre, *England the Nation*, 82.

62. Felicity Riddy, "Reading for England: Arthurian Literature and National Consciousness," *Bibliographical Bulletin of the International Arthurian Society* 43 (1991): 314–32, at 331.

63. Bennett, "The Historical Background," 73, 76, 86–87; John Bowers, *The Politics of Pearl: Court Poetry in the Age of Richard II* (Cambridge: Brewer, 2001), 71–74; Francis Ingledew, *Sir Gawain and the Green Knight and the Order of the Garter* (Notre Dame, IN: University of Notre Dame Press, 2006), 8–9. Ingledew takes this depiction of the Wirral as anachronistic for a Ricaridan poet and uses this lack of topicality as evidence for an earlier composition of the poem, claiming that "the Cheshire that Richard gravitated toward in the 1390s is hardly the remote and threatening wilderness positioned symbolically against the civilized south of Camelot that *SGGK* presents" (9).

of the Northwest Midlands is precisely the point. After all, this "wilderness" is also inhabited by supernatural beasts and plagued by such severe winter that even the birds, "pitosly þer piped for pyne of þe colde" [piteously piped there for the pain of the cold] (747). Just as a Trojan invocation is a pretentious marker of English nobility, so is the border between England and North Wales a hyperbolic residence of savage beasts.

The separation between the milieu of England's greatest king and these Welsh borderlands is accentuated by the fact that the description of Arthur's court follows hard upon the Trojan prologue, which had seemingly legitimized Britain's potential as an imperial power. In this aristocratic festival of fifteen days, the "sumquat childgered" [somewhat boyish] (86) Arthur presides over a feast worthy of an emperor, filled "[w]ith alle þe mete and þe mirthe þat men couþe avyse" [with all the meat and mirth that men could devise] (45). His court is especially giddy and carefree of any impending threat to the hierarchy that has been carefully established with Arthur at the center seat, the honored guest Bishop Baldwin at his right hand and the queen on his left; Gawain, his nephew, is seated to the left of Guinevere, and his brother Agravain sits at Gawain's left hand. The civilized order of nobility is maintained through this detailed delineation of Arthurian characters, who are all served super-sized portions and limitless beer and wine (106–29) "[t]o emphasize the carefree plenty in a society whose base-line is real hunger."[64] Such an opposition of the supernatural wilderness to Arthur's opulent court amplifies the stereotypical differences between the Welsh marches and the English landed aristocracy. The Trojan paratext, which establishes the conflicted basis of English privilege, condemns the English imagination for contrasting these topographies as representations of civilized and barbaric spaces. Through this Trojan hermeneutic, the *Gawain*-poet criticizes Arthur as an immature sovereign immersed in a world of lavish aristocratic feasts and stereotypes of the Northwest Midlands and Wales, geographies that have been mischaracterized as realms where supernatural beasts roam freely. With these ironies running throughout the poem, the *Gawain*-poet suggests that the distinctions between the English and Welsh are not as hard and fast as they appear on the surface.

The Green Knight demonstrates in his first appearance in the poem that readers should be wary of drawing definite lines between the civilization of the Arthurian court and the barbarity of the Northwest wilderness. When the Green Knight from the wilderness appears in Camelot, on at least one

---

64. For a full discussion of the feasts of the *Gawain*-poet, see Derek Brewer, "Feasts," in *A Companion to the Gawain-Poet*, 131–42, at 137; J. A. Burrow, "Honour and Shame in *Sir Gawain and the Green Knight*," in *Essays on Medieval Literature* (Oxford: Clarendon Press, 1984), 117–31.

level he is the one doing the "civilizing." On the one hand he is a "wild man" covered in the greenness of the natural world, but on the other, he assumes the accoutrements of an aristocrat with his ermine-lined cape, gold ornamentation, silk saddle, and flowing beard (151–86). He is even described as wearing a "kyngez capados" [king's cape] (186) that suggests that his clothes are fit for a king. By contrast, Arthur is merely described as childish and his knights are "bot berdlez chylder" [but beardless children] (280). Within the "civilized" space of the court, the "wild" Green Knight's sartorial splendor performs a noble identity that is glossed by the narrator and Arthur's references to him as a "haþel" [knight] (256, 309, 323). As Susan Crane aptly suggests, the Green Knight's "contained wildness turns out to offer a model from which Gawain and his fellows might learn a superior courtliness."[65] Thus, when the Green Knight assumes his identity as the provincial Bertilak, the transformation is not as abrupt as we might expect. His role as both noble lord and green man and the blurring between civilization and the wilderness is exemplified by Gawain's discovery of Bertilak's residence, Hautdesert, during his journey through the Northwest Midlands:

> Nade he sayned hymself, segge, bot þrye
> Er he watz war in þe wod of a won in a mote,
> Abof a launde, on a lawe, loken vnder boȝez . . .
> A castel þe comlokest þat euer knyȝt aȝte. (763–65, 767)

[No sooner had he signed himself thrice than he was aware in the wood of a dwelling within a moat, above the ground on a mound, locked under boughs . . . the comeliest castle a knight ever owned.]

In the midst of this uncanny space is a nobleman's diamond in the rough. The castle is even described as being shut behind branches, "loken vnder boȝez," which creates an image of civilization imprisoned by wilderness. In contrast to Gawain's earlier experience with the fantastical beasts of the Welsh marches, the very existence of this castle in the wild dispels firm oppositions between Arthur's courtly world and the Cheshire borderland of the Green Knight.

As was beginning to be the case during Higden's life and was finally realized during the time of *Gawain*'s composition, Cheshire obtained a stature that was somewhat unique for a province of its type and location. Because of

---

65. Susan Crane, *The Performance of Self: Ritual, Clothing, and Identity during the Hundred Years War* (Philadelphia: University of Pennsylvania Press, 2002), 169.

its growing prominence, by the late fourteenth century the territory between the Northwest Midlands and Wales, the very space that Gawain treads in his search for Hautdesert, had become valuable political ground, especially for Richard II. When his sovereignty had become open to question and even outright rebellion, Richard retreated to Cheshire and began asserting control over his lands in Wales from this northern location. He confiscated significant portions of Northeastern Wales, which were absorbed into the Cheshire palatinate and given to his supporters in exchange for their loyalty.[66] By 1385, four Welsh castles were under the authority of Cheshire constables, which suggests that Cheshire was beginning to establish a military presence in Wales. During that same time, Richard II drew men from this region to serve in his Scottish campaign. The area of Cheshire and Lancashire in particular assumed a new role as a military stronghold in the Welsh region. Because of their new "border patrol" identities, military men from these regions were empowered through special economic and political privileges to negotiate with Welsh separatists on behalf of the prerogatives of Richard II.[67] Even though a sense of separation between the occupied Welsh and the occupying English clearly existed, Richard II's residence in the Northwest caused the geographical border between England and Wales to become a space for questioning the nature and scope of English sovereignty.

TROJAN SURFEIT

Wales' topographical absorption into Ricardian politics during the period of the composition of *Gawain* points to the larger significance of the Welsh within Britain's imagined history of empire. Because of the tight connections between the Northwest Midlands and Wales, these regions achieve an equivalency in *Gawain* that is expressed through the enigmatic figures of the Green Knight/Bertilak and the mysterious locales of the Green Chapel/ Hautdesert. The result is a hybrid identity of the region that signified both conqueror/conquered and civilized/barbarian. Furthermore, if the region is viewed through the prologue of the poem, the "savage" Welsh March is also the land colonized by Brutus and his fellow Trojan exiles, the bearers of the *translatio imperii*. Whereas the Camelot of Arthur represents the sovereign space endowed by this transfer of empire, the Welsh borderland of the Green Knight represents both a territory absorbed into the English political

---

66. John A. F. Thomson, *The Transformation of Medieval England: 1370–1529* (London: Longmans, 1983), 162–63.
67. Bennett, *Community, Class, and Careerism*, 179–80.

sphere and a hybrid "Other" land to the more homogenous world of southern nobility. The *Gawain*-poet would have known of the complex challenge that the Welsh posed to English sovereignty, not only through Welsh rebellion, but also through their ethnic identity, which according to Geoffrey of Monmouth could be traced back to Troy. In the following section, I want to suggest that the Welsh claim to a Trojan identity not only complicates what it means to be Trojan, but also implies that being "Trojan" means being susceptible to imperial excess.

Through the blurring of the boundary between England and Wales in the description of Gawain's journey to Hautdesert, the *Gawain*-poet interrogates the exclusivity of Trojan lineage. In his subsequent pilgrimage to the Green Chapel nearby, Gawain's guide accentuates the confusion about Trojan identity by comparing the Green Knight to Hector of Troy (2102).[68] While the invocation of the noble Trojan ancestor is on the one hand an emphasis on the sheer girth of the Green Knight, it is on the other a reminder of the Green Knight's aristocratic dress, which suggests that a veritable Welsh wild man has as much a claim to nobility as any in the Arthurian court. This subversion likely originates in the *Gawain*-poet's geographical proximity to the Welsh Marchers, a potentially threatening people who not only lived on the borderland between Northeast Wales and the Northwest Midlands of England, but also claimed Trojan heritage through their mixed identity caused by the intermarriage of the Norman invaders and Welsh natives.[69] Gerald of Wales, a hybrid product of this parentage, expresses the relationship between his people and the *translatio imperii* in his twelfth-century *Expugnatio Hibernica* through the voice of his uncle Robert fitzStephen, commander of the Marchers in their Irish conquest, who states that in addition to their French heritage, they come "Troiano partim ex sanguine" [in part from Trojan blood] (1.9).[70] Such an argument for noble lineage refutes any exclusive claim by the central Anglo-Norman crown to a Trojan identity.

For Gerald, however, a Trojan heritage is subject to the excesses that adhere to empire. According to his *Descriptio Kambriae*, the Welsh Trojan

---

68. The manuscript actually reads "Hestor," which Andrew and Waldron note is "a variant of Hector (of Troy) or less probably a reference to the Arthurian knight Hector de la Mare."
69. For a thorough discussion of the hybridity of the Welsh Marcher, see Cohen, *Hybridity, Identity, and Monstrosity in Medieval Britain*, 77–108; R. R. Davies, *Lordship and Society in the March of Wales* (Oxford: Oxford University Press, 1987), 304–28, 341–47; *The Age of Conquest: Wales, 1065–1415* (Oxford: Oxford University Press, 1991), 97–100, 371–73, 421; *Domination and Conquest: The Experience of Ireland, Scotland, and Wales, 1100–1300* (Cambridge: Cambridge University Press, 1990), 88–89.
70. Citations from *Expugnatio Hibernica* refer to Gerald of Wales, *Expugnatio Hibernica: The Conquest of Ireland*, eds. A. B. Scott and F. X. Martin (Dublin: Royal Irish Academy, 1978).

identity is split between virtue and vice—on the one hand, the Welsh obtain their courage through this inheritance (1.9), but on the other, they are haunted by Trojan sin. Gerald's condemnation of the moral turpitude of the Welsh that they inherited from their Trojan ancestors is strikingly similar to what Guido later calls a "plague of great destruction." Gerald claims, "Praeterea, peccatis urgentibus, et praecipue detestabili illo et nefando Sodomitico, divina ultione tam olim Trojam quam postea Brittanniam amiserunt" [It was because of the urging of their sins, and more particularly the unmentionable and detestable vice of *Sodomitico* that by divine revenge the Welsh so lost first Troy and then Britain] (227).[71] The invocation of "unnatural" sexuality through the word "Sodomitico" suggests that the Trojans have not only transferred imperial power from Troy to Britain, but have also translated sin to their progeny. Gerald's claim that the Trojans and the Welsh are plagued by sin implies that Troy and Britain suffer the same fate as Sodom: condemnation and destruction. The association of Troy with sexual transgression and imperial failure indicates that many readers of Trojan texts such as *Gawain*, especially those with Welsh or provincial loyalties, regarded the justification of empire as a justification of sin.

By virtue of the fact that these locations and identities are circumscribed and defined by the borderland of the Welsh March, we are invited to consider what exactly is at stake for Trojan and English identity. If Gawain, as a representation of the nobility established in the Trojan frame, truly commits such a Trojan sin at a Cheshire palace, what are the implications for British fantasies of empire? If we turn back to Gerald's text, we find a helpful delineation of the relationship between morality and imperialism for exilic cultures such as the Welsh. After condemning the Welsh and Trojans as sodomites, he claims that it has been so long since the Welsh practiced this sexual "enormitas" [irregularity] that few have any memory of it (228).[72] Yet, he does not attribute this change in behavior to any newfound moral fortitude and instead suggests that the Welsh abstain because they are now a subjugated people, no longer carefree conquerors who have the time and means to satisfy their carnal desires. To articulate this view, he addresses

---

71. Citations from *Descriptio Kambriae* refer to Gerald of Wales, *Itinerarium Cambriae seu laboriosae Baldvini Cantuariensis Archiepiscopi per Walliam legationis accurate descriptio, auctore Silv. Giraldo Cambrense*, ed. David Powell (London: Bulmer, 1806); Ingham, *Sovereign Fantasies*, 111. As David Halperin has demonstrated, we should be careful about using our modern term of "homosexuality" to describe same-sex relationships of early cultures. See *One Hundred Years of Homosexuality and Other Essays on Greek Love* (New York: Routledge, 1990), 15–40.

72. "veruntamen multo jam tempore adeo a Britonibus enormitas illa prorsus evanuit, ut ejus etiam memoria jam apud eos vix habeatur" [for a long time now this irregularity has vanished among the Welsh so that hardly anyone can remember it].

the Galfridian prophecy that the Welsh will one day regain their imperial stature:

> Proinde quasi poenitentia jam fere peracta, et quoniam numero praeter solitum et multitudine, viribus et armis, bellorum quoque successibus et terrarum incrementis, nostris plurimum diebus adaucti sunt, gloriantur ad invicem, praedicant et confidentissime jactant, toto (quod mirum est) in hac spe populo manente, quoniam in brevi cives in insulam revertentur, et juxta Merlini sui vaticinia exterorum tam natione pereunte quam nuncupatione antiqua in insula tam nominee quam omine Britones exultabunt. Sed mihi longe aliter visum est . . . paupertati potius in hoc exilio, quo extorres fere facti sunt a regno, attribuenda sit vicii illius, quo in divitiis carere nescierant, illa carentia quam virtuti. (227–28)

> [Since their penance is nearly over, and since, by their successful wars and their seizure of new lands, they have in our own day greatly increased in population, power and arms, the Welsh claim, and most confidently predict, that they will soon reoccupy the whole island. It is remarkable how everyone in Wales abides by this hope. According to the prophecies of Merlin, the foreign nation on the island will disappear, and the Welsh will then be called Britons once more and they will enjoy their ancient privileges. It seems to me otherwise . . . their abstinence from that vice, which in their prosperity they could not resist, must be attributed more to their poverty in this exile, in which they were entirely banished from royal authority, than to virtue.]

For Gerald, immorality is intimately connected with imperial power and excess, a vice that the exiled Welsh do not have the luxury to enjoy. Gerald is therefore explicit about the relationship between empire and morality—sovereignty leads to sin.

This markedly pessimistic view of Galfridian imperialism and Trojan inheritance expressed from the Welsh borderland is important to consider because it is consistent not only with the Trojan prologue of *Gawain,* but also with Gawain's residence at Hautdesert, a series of scenes that implicitly connect aristocratic violence with "surfeit." To understand this association, we should first address the Arthurian identity that Gawain "performs."[73] As a character imprisoned by his role as an Arthurian representative, Gawain

---

73. This reading is informed by Judith Butler's *Gender Trouble: Feminism and the Subversion of Identity* (New York: Routledge, 1990) and *Bodies That Matter: On the Discursive Limits of "Sex"* (New York: Routledge, 1993).

must at all times consider the way his physical appearance and behavior are received by his provincial hosts.[74] And to put even more pressure upon Gawain, the prologue suggests that he is also performing his noble Trojan identity, a source of legitimation that would presumably be bolstered by his individual virtue. However, since this paratext calls our attention to the treason that characterizes this legacy, we find his chivalric *trawþe* constantly being called into question. Once he leaves Arthur's court, he relinquishes the perfection hyperbolically defined by the pentangle on his shield and steps into an "other" world that disrupts his centralized identity as a noble, masculine knight. Shortly after his arrival in this borderland locale, the division of activities is clearly defined: Gawain will eat, rest, and make merry while Bertilak will hunt, kill, and dismember (1088–1109). Settling into his role as a carefree nobleman and allowing Bertilak's retinue to serve him hand and foot, Gawain's chivalric superiority is challenged not only by the lavish trappings of Hautdesert, but also by virtue of the nature of Bertilak's activity and bravado—he engages in the aristocratic activity of hunting and establishes himself as the faithful adherent to the "exchange of winnings" pact. In fact, through these assertions Gawain is transformed into the object of the Lady's sexual quest, a rhetorical siege that is glossed by the adjacent hunting and dismemberment scenes. At the same time that Gawain is implicitly tempted by aristocratic excess, his body is metaphorically torn apart by the hunting sequences. As one of many hunting scenes in the alliterative tradition, it is no surprise that this series of hunts also offers an occasion for a critique of courtly indulgence. In other alliterative poems such as the *Awyntyrs off Arthure, The Parlement of the Thre Ages, De tribus regibus mortuis,* and *Somer Soneday,* the hunt can be interpreted to represent, as Anne Rooney suggests, "the pleasures of courtly life [that] distract men from a proper concern with virtue and their coming fate."[75] Within the context of Gerald's equivalency of Trojanness and vice, the hunt provides a particularly alliterative space wherein Gawain's aristocratic virtue may be dismantled.

Moreover, the juxtaposition of the violence of the hunt and the possibility of sexual transgression associates physical violence with sexual crisis in a way that encourages readers to take a pressing look at the chivalric Trojaness that Gawain represents. Gawain's submissive identity as the "hunted" is con-

---

74. Carolyn Dinshaw explains Gawain's identity crisis best in "A Kiss Is Just a Kiss: Heterosexuality and Its Consolations in Sir Gawain and the Green Knight," *Diacritics* 24, no. 2/3 (1994): 204–26, at 213. For more on the performance and masculinity of knighthood, see Louise Fradenburg, *City, Marriage, Tournament: Arts of Rule in Late Medieval Scotland* (Madison: University of Wisconsin Press, 1991), 201, 203, 212.

75. Anne Rooney, "The Hunts," in *A Companion to the Gawain-Poet,* ed. Brewer, 157–63, at 162.

firmed by the connection of the scenes with conjunctions such as the "[a]nd" in the first transition between the forest and Gawain's bed: "Þus laykez þis lorde by lynde-wodez euez / And Gawayn þe god mon in gay bed lygez" [Thus this lord plays at the edge of the linden-wood and Gawain the good knight lies in the gay bed.] (1178–79). Through these syntactical links, the Lady's disturbance of Gawain's sexuality is directly compared to the killing and preparation of game for a feast. In the first scene, Gawain is associated with a female deer that is cut open, dismembered, eviscerated, and even flayed (1330–52). Even though aristocratic hunters may have relished this detailed account, the fact that the *Gawain*-poet goes to such lengths to include this detail about the breaking of deer in conjunction with the wooing of Gawain, a moment in which his adherence to his vow is tested, indicates that the dismemberment of hunted animals provides an important context for such a moment of sexual and chivalric crisis.

Carolyn Dinshaw remarks that this scene "does seem excessive," but within its genre of alliterative romance, the superfluous violence in the description of the brittling of game is remarkably common.[76] The trope of flaying in particular seems to have been popular among alliterative poets since it is also used by the *Parlement of the Thre Ages*-poet (75–78) and the *Siege*-poet.[77] The latter's use of the image is most pertinent to this discussion, since he includes it in his description of not only the skinning of a deer (991–92), but also the execution of Jewish clerks (697–708).[78] This last instance of flaying Jewish priests is a compelling analogue for the *Gawain*-poet's use of a comparison of human and animal bodies to interpret imperial identities. In describing the Roman killing of Caiaphas and the other Jewish priests, the *Siege*-poet follows a protocol remarkable in its precision and adherence to the conventional skinning of game. Whereas the *Gawain*-poet explains that after the dismemberment, the hind is "rent of þe hyde" (1332), "henged" (1357), and then fed to the "houndes" (1359), the *Siege*-poet relates that the Jewish clerks are "quyk fleyn" (698), "honget . . . hydeles" (700, 702), and then fed to "[c]orres" (703). The fact that both poets follow the same ritual of flaying, hanging, and feeding indicates that they were aiming for similar effects, which, if we follow the trope throughout the *Siege*, suggests that these scenes serve as examples of the

---

76. Dinshaw, "A Kiss Is Just a Kiss," 214.
77. See my discussion of the flaying maxim in chapter 3, 88–93.
78. For the textual references, see Warren Ginsberg, ed., *Wynnere and Wastoure and The Parlement of the Thre Ages* (Kalamazoo, MI: Medieval Institute Publications, 1992) and Ralph Hanna and David Lawton, eds., *The Siege of Jerusalem*, EETS OS 320 (Oxford: Oxford University Press, 2003).

cruelty of imperial resolve and the breaking of chivalric vows. In the other instance of this image in the poem, Sir Sabyn urges Vespasian to relinquish his vow to obliterate Jerusalem and assume the Roman emperorship, suggesting that Vespasian can destroy the holy city by appointing his son Titus to administer the siege, an act of military command by proxy that he compares to the flaying of a deer: "For as fers is þe freke atte ferre ende / Þat offleis þe fel as he þat foot holdeþ" [The man at the far end who flays off the skin is as fierce as he who holds the foot] (991–92). Vespasian may remain fierce in his imperialism even "atte ferre ende," taking the metaphorical position of one flaying a deer from an extremity. The thematic correspondence to *Gawain* is too rich to ignore, since in both instances humans are literally or figuratively skinned within a context in which chivalric *trawþe* is being tested. In the *Siege,* the torture and execution of the priests is even described as a "tokne of tresoun" (725–8) just as the scar on Gawain's neck is a "token of vntrawþe" (2509).

Through such pedagogic effects, Gawain's body becomes a heraldic device that both the Arthurian court and *Gawain*'s readers must interpret. Yet, the interpretation of his body is complicated by the juxtaposition of scenes of animal dismemberment with an examination of Gawain's chivalry, a correlation that compels readers to imagine Gawain's body disaggregated or mutilated. As Jacques Lacan notes, "The image of [man's] body is the principle of every unity he perceives in objects."[79] Gawain's readability is also threatened by his anticipated decapitation, an act that, if consummated, would have made his body difficult to decipher. Instead, Gawain escapes with a scratch, a blemish that invites a reading of its significance within the context of the health of the rest of his body. Through the preceding hunting and wooing sequences that establish a metaphorical relationship between sexual and chivalric conquest and violence, readers are prepared to interpret this botched beheading as one that has consequences for British imperial identity. Even before swinging the axe, the Green Knight implies that it is not just Gawain's virtue, but the integrity of Arthurian knighthood that is at stake: "Halde þe now þe hyȝe hode þat Arþur þe raȝt / And kepe þy kanel at þis kest, ȝif hit keuer may!" [May the noble order, which Arthur bestowed upon you, keep you now and preserve your neck at this stroke, if it is able to accomplish it!] (2297–98). By sarcastically suggesting that only the "hyȝe hode" or the order of chivalry might protect Gawain's neck, the Green Knight chastises

---

79. Jacques Lacan, *The Seminar of Jacques Lacan,* ed. Jacques-Alain Miler, trans. Sylvana Tomaselli, vol. 2 (New York: Norton, 1988), 166.

the Arthurian authority that serves as the perpetuator of English nobility. His subsequent survival from decapitation allows him to be a living symbol of the treachery that preserves the unity of his body and the Arthurian court. The fact that he evades beheading through the breaking of an oath reminds readers of the ancient basis for the Round Table's authority, an act of treason by Aeneas. Within the larger scope of the poem, this means that the Trojan nobility and, to his late medieval English readers, the English nationhood that he represents is not only maintained by such perfidy but also incessantly threatened by violence and fragmentation.

Even though the corporeal blemish represents a small fault for his personal identity, Gawain's hyperbolic lament at the end of the poem indicates that this shortcoming represents a larger problem about the noble identity he embodies. In his repentance to Bertilak about his wearing the girdle for protection he vows not to bear it as sign of glory:

> Bot in syngne of my surfet I schal se hit ofte,
> When I ride in renoun remorde to myseluen
> Þe faut and þe fayntyse of þe flesche crabbed,
> How tender hit is to entyse teches of fylþe. (2433–36)

> [But as a sign of my surfeit I shall see it often when I ride in renown and remember in shame the fault and the frailty of my perverse flesh, how its tenderness entices the filth of sin.]

Thus, Gawain perceives the girdle as a reminder of his corporeal desires that he characterizes not only as a fault but also a "surfet." Gawain's vow to wear it as a sign of sin suggests that the girdle does not simply protect his individual identity as a Christian knight—like his scar, it is a penitential marker for all to see. As my previous analysis indicates, the girdle is a sign of "excess," which, according to Gerald, is a marker of Trojan heritage. However, the Arthurian court recognizes the girdle as a heraldic symbol of renown, much in the style of a Trojan coat of arms. This misappropriation by Arthur's court encourages us to understand the girdle as more than a reminder of vice and to consider the message it projects about the Trojan identity violently deconstructed in the Welsh March. Just as the border between England and Wales in the Northwest Midlands had become a point of contention for assertions of English sovereignty, Hautdesert and the Green Chapel serve as the marginal spaces where Gawain's chivalric pretensions are condemned as excessive.

THE HERALDIC HISTORIOGRAPHY OF THE GREEN GIRDLE

As R. A. Shoaf has suggested, the girdle, as a sign of "surfet" or "excess," represents "both pride and covetousness," sins which caused Gawain to recognize "the excess of his subjectivity."[80] By extension, however, this *syngne of surfet* also characterizes the superfluous ancestral propaganda employed by Arthurian knights and English nobility to indulge their sovereign fantasies. Here we reach the other extremity of the Trojan "frame" in which Gawain reveals the girdle as a token of *vntrawþe* (2505–12). Instead of acknowledging Gawain's penitence however, the knights of Round Table laugh and agree to wear the girdle as a marker of their nobility:

> For þat watz accorded þe renoun of þe Rounde Table
> And he honoured þat hit hade, euermore after,
> As hit is breued in þe best boke of romaunce.
> Þus in Arthurus day þis aunter bitidde—
> Þe Brutus bokez þerof beres wyttenesse. (2519–23)

> [For it was agreed to represent the renown of the Round Table and he who bore it was honored evermore, as it is written in the best book of romance. Thus in Arthur's day this happening befell—the books of Brutus bear witness to this.]

The girdle becomes an heraldic marker whose subtext belies Arthurian hermeneutics that claim its status as a sign of "renoun" (2519). Just as Britain's Trojan heritage is reinterpreted as a justification for nobility, the girdle's girlish nature is recast as a band of brotherhood, or what Geraldine Heng calls a "girdle-become-baldric."[81] What the court fails to realize is that the laugh is on them—by appropriating the girdle they unknowingly acknowledge the treachery that has historically empowered them. This heraldic act unifies the court and momentarily patches holes in their chivalric identity, but the girdle's status as a critique of imperial excess circumscribes, and satirizes, their revelry.

In fact, the *Gawain*-poet's moral distaste for such sovereign fantasies intensifies in this last stanza, where readers are invited to travel from Camelot back to the ashes of Troy—in other words, to remember the past.

---

80. R. A. Shoaf, *The Poem as Green Girdle: Commercium in Sir Gawain and the Green Knight* (Gainesville: University Press of Florida, 1984), 68.

81. Geraldine Heng, "Feminine Knots and the Other *Sir Gawain and the Green Knight*," *PMLA* 106.3 (May 1991): 500–14, at 508.

The court's heraldic appropriation and redefinition of this marker of shame is a *non sequitur* that reminds readers that they are once again in the disjunctive borderlands of the text. Just as the beginning proceeds abruptly from dire destruction to lavish feasting, the end moves from pious repentance to carefree glorification. And just as the ignorant bliss of the Arthurian Christmas feast is darkened by its treasonous heritage, the enthusiasm of the Round Table is undermined by Gawain's sober admission of guilt. The girdle is now worn by knights who do not comprehend its significance. In the same way that Gawain's chivalric identity is tested as the Cheshire/Wales boundary, the legendary origin of British nobility is interrogated at the extremity of the poem.

At the other end of the textual map, the *Gawain*-poet capitalizes on the ambivalence of a border space to undercut popular assumptions and counteract the more optimistic historiographic strains of "the books of Brutus." The dramatic irony of the Round Table's sumptuary ignorance is amplified by an ironic use of source material: the *Gawain*-poet cleverly constructs the following lines in such a way as to cite two types of sources, the "best boke of romaunce" and the "Brutus bokez," as well as identify their precise relationship to the poem. While the book of romance provides the basis for the tale, the Brutus chronicles "beres wyttenesse" to the romance. In other words, the Brutus books are placed on the outside looking in, as if through a lens, to the do the work of history that Dares and Dictys perform in their diaries of the fall of Troy—they verify the truth of the romance through eyewitness testimony. In this way, we are reminded to perceive Gawain's test of *trawþe* through the dark and smoky Trojan lens that had been established at the beginning of the poem. The invocation of the "Brutus bokez" is a direct reference to the Galfridian tradition, a citation that indicates that Geoffrey's *Historia* and its textual descendants provide the material for the "frame." Yet the plural use of "bokez" encourages the reader to think of this Galfridian perspective as multiple and, as we have seen, antithetical, a paradox that is developed in the following lines by the return to the image of the destroyed Troy that began the narrative:

> Syþen Brutus, þe bolde burne, boȝed hider first,
> After þe segge and þe asaute watz sesed at Troye,
>   Iwysse,
>   Mony aunterez herebiforne
>   Haf fallen suche er þis. (2524–28)

[Since Brutus, the bold knight, arrived here first, after the siege and assault was ceased at Troy, truly many exploits of this kind have happened since then.]

The repetition of the opening line, "[a]fter þe segge and þe asaute watz sesed at Troye," is a mnemonic device that brings us back to the beginning stanza and its description of the burning of Troy, Aeneas' treason, the subjugation of provinces, and even the *[in]felix* Brutus' colonization of Britain. The history of empire is recursive, not through its translation of glory upon future cities, but rather through its incessant return to fallen regimes. Therefore, this Arthurian romance, which must be read through the lens of the Brutus books, has ironically been "cast out of the Galfridian structure of meaning."[82] Such a perplexing interpretive situation requires the reader to search for other more marginal historiographic perspectives in the so-called Brutus books. One of these that rely on Geoffrey's structure for its explanation of the birth of Britain is of course none other than Guido's *Historia*, whose influence on the first stanza has already been established. It is therefore likely that the *Gawain*-poet had Guido's *Historia* in mind as one of those "Brutus bokez" that bear witness to the truth about Britain's Trojan ancestry. And once again, Guido's critical perspective emerges in the border of the text to satirize the pretense of centralized assertions of authority.

The mixture of "blysse" and "blunder" produces ambivalence in the text that forces readers to examine England's imperial memory, its Trojan topographies, and ultimately its distinctions between history and romance. This problem of mixing seemingly irreconcilable genres and topographies has prompted many readers to focus exclusively on the beheading game, hunting scenes, and the agency of Bertilak's lady in the romance proper. In establishing such distinctions between the romance and history, however, we should acknowledge that, as Dipesh Chakrabarty suggests, "difference is always the name of a relationship, for it separates just as much as it connects (as, indeed, does a border)."[83] For *Gawain*'s medieval readers, the generic line between romance and history may have been blurry, if not imperceptible.

Ignoring the Trojan "frame," I would conclude, not only restricts readings of the poem, but also misses the poem's heraldic and geographic grounding that evinces provincial literary perspectives on imperialism and constructions of nationhood. Since fourteenth-century readers would have reflected upon Arthur as an historical figure that embodied the origin of Britain's prominence in imperial history, the pessimism about the *translatio imperii* in

82. Federico, *New Troy*, 59.
83. Dipesh Chakrabarty, *Provincializing Europe: Postcolonial Thought and Historical Difference* (Princeton: Princeton University Press, 2000), 110.

the opening and closing lines expresses a peripheral skepticism that may in turn illustrate a broader disunity of Englishness. The critical perspectives on England, as they are expressed through the Cheshire and Welsh historiography of Higden and Gerald, provide an appropriate context for the *Gawain*-poet's use of geographic and historiographic borderlands since they share a provincial distaste for imperial designs, Trojan heritage, and assertions of gentility. In the end, the Trojan paratext of *Gawain*, which interprets and bears witness to the romance, deflates the sovereign fantasies that the English project through the figure of Arthur. Higden articulates this phenomenon best by suggesting that "fortassis mos est cuique nationi aliquem de suis laudibus attollere excessivis" [perhaps it is customary for each nation to elevate one of their own with excessive praise].[84] Likewise, the *Gawain*-poet translates the excessiveness of the English praise of Arthur into the enticing green girdle to represent the *surfet* of imperialism. Given the Round Table's misappropriation and centralization of the sign, the Trojan "frame" attests to the fact that such a critique of English nationhood and nobility can be perceived not only from the Anglo-Welsh geography of Hautdesert, but also from the borders of the text. From the historiographic perspective of the Trojan borderland, Gawain's failure in his test of *trawþe* is yet another "blunder" that England "forgets" in its claims to imperial "blysse."

---

84. For other discussions of this passage, see Galloway, "Latin England," 58–59; Lavezzo, *Angels on the Edge of the World*, 90–91; John E. Housman, "Higden, Trevisa, Caxton, and the Beginnings of Arthurian Criticism," *Review of English Studies* 23 (1947): 209–17, at 212.

Conclusion
ALLITERATING ENGLAND

COMMENTING ON Hilary the Confessor's translation of the Greek Psalms into Latin, Jerome applauds Hilary's translational practice, claiming that, "quasi captiuous sensus in suam linguam uictoris iure transposit" [like some conqueror, he marched the original text, captive, into his own language].[1] For Jerome, translation is an imperial act that captures and reinterprets its object for a superior and, in his case, a Latinate culture. This imperial logic behind translation is the dominant understanding throughout the medieval period for translating Latin texts into the vernacular. Yet, as I have demonstrated in previous chapters, the alliterative romanciers who adhere to the historiography of Guido delle Colonne qualify their translations with caveats for the dangers of the very activity for which they are employed. Their misgivings about nation and empire formation become not only full-scale repudiations of the translations of power (*translatio imperii*) from Troy to Rome to Britain, but also incisive interrogations of the translations of knowledge (*translatio studii*) that accompany them. Their provincial politics resist the machinery of English imperialism, which drives the iteration of textual authority from the clerical and Latinate to the lay and Anglophone. Paradoxically, these alliterative romanciers implicitly

---

1. Jerome, *Epistula 57* in *Sancti Eusebii Hieronymi epistulae,* ed. I. Hilberg, *Corpus Scriptorum Ecclesiasticorum Latinorum* 54 (Vienna-Leipzig: Tempsky, 1910), 512. For a discussion of this comment, see Douglas Robinson, *Western Translation Theory from Herodotus to Nietzsche* (Manchester, UK: St. Jerome Publishing, 1997), 55.

critique the practice of translation in the midst of engaging in that very practice.

In this conclusion, I synthesize my examinations of alliterative romance to characterize what I call a "clerical voice" that runs throughout these texts in opposition to the transfer of imperial authority from Troy to Britain and the movement of textual power from the clergy to the lay aristocracy. Since the alliterative romancers defy precise identification, I turn to the examples of John Trevisa and Geoffrey Chaucer as late-medieval English figures whose perspectives on translation, alliterative poetry, nationalism, empire formation, and the relations between the clergy and the laity more fully contextualize the literary and historiographic projects of alliterative romance. I begin with a reading of Trevisa's translation of Ranulph Higden's *Polychronicon* to demonstrate not only the traditional negotiations between translators and their patrons, but also the way such relationships are theorized and called into question. As a translator committed to the provincial historiography of Higden, Trevisa exhibits a mediated skepticism about the Galfridian praise of Arthur and a surprising preference for the alliterative poetic style, a proclivity which, I conclude, reflects the sensibilities of his clerical class and his educational training in the *ars dictaminis,* the art of letter writing. Trevisa's affinity with the alliterative poets and his ambivalence about Arthurian prophecy make his perspective on empire formation and clerical and lay aristocratic relations as proximate to that of these alliterative romancers as I believe is possible to identify.

In contrast to Trevisa's coded critique of lay aristocratic culture, I address the work of Geoffrey Chaucer and specifically his *Troilus and Criseyde,* since this well known Trojan text plays a significant role in English cultural imperialism. Even though Chaucer draws on Guido's *Historia* in this courtly romance, his engagement with Trojan history is markedly indifferent in comparison to that of the alliterative romancers. The work of courtly love, rather than militaristic history, is the central concern, which makes this poem and his other works more susceptible to absorption within the textual fabrications of the subsequent Lancastrian imperial project. As a poet whose works bolster English claims to literate authority, Chaucer is more readily fashioned by John Lydgate and other fifteenth-century writers into an "imperial author" who possesses the cultural capital capable of elevating the English nation to worldly prominence. Chaucer ultimately satisfies the sensibilities and interests of the aristocracy through his clerical critiques and providential historiography, which differ from the clerical voices and retrospective historiography of these alliterative romancers. Given Chaucer's literary success among the culturally elite, it is no surprise that the work of these alliterative poets fell into relative obsolescence. To the alliterative romanciers, the translation of empire, in its service to aristocratic authority, is a "plague of great destruction" for which there is no remedy besides a recursive awareness of the treacherous origins that belie all such pretensions to sovereignty.

TREVISA'S ALLITERATIVE POLITICS

The notion that translation could be "destructive" defies predominant medieval and modern assumptions about the "universal" nature of translation. To many translators, translation includes rather than excludes and unifies rather than separates. In other words, the translation of language or culture makes that language or culture available and usable to more people. The act of translation accordingly became a valuable tool for ancient conquerors in their communications with and eventual appropriations of conquered peoples and cultures.[2] Early imperial cultures, especially those of Rome, expressed their authority and values through the translation of texts; they even viewed the act of translating as an act of conquering. By translating the ancient vernaculars of Hebrew and Greek into Latin, they made what was once foreign familiar, disseminating another culture's knowledge to a new, and therefore, wider audience. This perspective on translation not only gave the Roman Church in the Middle Ages license to convert Latin from pagan to sacred status, but also firmly established the relationship between the translation of language and the propagation of empire that came to be known as the *translatio imperii et studii*. By making Latin the language of the Western church, Latin assumed a universal identity, which created coherence among cultures and geographies that operated under very different mores. Latin became both the language of empire and the church, making it a vehicle of sovereignty and knowledge that had no equal throughout the Middle Ages.

By the late fourteenth century in England, Latin's role in the "translation of learning and empire" was still embraced in theory, but the rise of English as a language of theological and courtly stature complicated the status of Latin as linguistic conqueror of culture. In the 1380s, Geoffrey Chaucer and John Gower preferred English to the standard languages of poetry, Latin and French, in composing some of their greatest works for courtly audiences.[3] A number of translation projects were also undertaken by clerks such

2. Robinson, *Western Translation Theory from Herodotus to Nietzsche*, 10.
3. Chaucer's *Troilus and Criseyde* is addressed to the court, and may have been specifically written for Richard II's Queen Anne. See John Livingston Lowes, "The Date of Chaucer's *Troilus*

as John Trevisa, who prefaces his rendering of Higden's *Polychronicon* with a dramatization of the conversation that might have (and very well could have) occurred between the clerical translator and his aristocratic patron.[4] This *Dialogue Between a Lord and a Clerk Upon Translation* addresses the tension between Latin and English, clerics and aristocrats.[5] While the Lord's argument for translation emerges victorious, the Clerk's trenchant critiques of aristocratic practice and attempts to translate Latin learning into the vernacular are nonetheless persuasive. To understand the Clerk's argument, it is important to know that Trevisa's rhetorical model for the *Dialogue* derives from another text he translated, the pseudo-Ockham *Dialogus inter clericum et militem*.[6] The fact that both Trevisa's *Dialogue* and this *Dialogus* are appended to every manuscript of the *Polychronicon* solidifies their intimate organizational and thematic relationship. At the literal level, they both not only privilege the voice of the aristocrat, but also express anticlerical views. In the *Dialogus*, the Soldier subdues the Clerk by claiming sovereignty and disendowing clerics who do not merit property. Likewise, in the *Dialogue*, the Lord's victory in the debate suggests that clerics must relinquish their exclusive rights to Latin texts by making them available to secular society. Since the Soldier and the Lord occupy the same power positions, it is clear that Trevisa envisions the clergy as submissive to two interdependent, and possibly indivisible, levels of aristocracy: knights and patrons.

What makes Trevisa's unexceptional equivalency of knights and patrons and degradation of the clerical voice so compelling is the fact that he is translating from a historiographic tradition that resists pretensions of the secular elite. As I established in chapter five, Higden writes from a provincial perspective that remains skeptical about English nationhood, particularly its claim to Arthurian origins. For the alliterative romanciers of this book, both Higden's chronicle and Guido delle Colonne's *Historia destructionis Troiae*

---

and Criseyde," *Proceedings of the Modern Language Association* 23, no. 2 (1908): 285–306. He suggests that "Right as oure firste letter is now an A" is a compliment to Queen Anne. See also J. S. P. Tatlock, "The Date of Troilus: And Minor Chauceriana," *Modern Language Notes* 50, no. 5 (1935): 277–96. Richard II asked Gower to write *Confessio Amantis* in English. See Michael Bennett, "The Court of Richard II and the Promotion of Literature," in *Chaucer's England: Literature in Historical Context*, ed. Barbara Hanawalt (Minneapolis: University of Minnesota, 1992), 3–20, at 7.

    4. For the relationship between Trevisa and his patron Sir Thomas Berkeley, see Ralph Hanna, "Sir Thomas Berkeley and His Patronage," *Speculum* 64. 4 (1989): 878–916, at 891–92.

    5. All subsequent citations of the *Dialogue* and its corresponding epistle refer to the line numbers of the following edition: Jocelyn Wogan-Browne, Nicholas Watson, Andrew Taylor, and Ruth Evans, eds., *The Idea of the Vernacular: An Anthology of Middle English Literary Theory, 1280–1520* (University Park: The Pennsylvania State University Press, 1999).

    6. This text is included with Trevisa's translation in Richard Fitzralph, *Defensio curatorum*, ed. Aaron Jenkins Perry, Early English Text Society 167 (London: Oxford University Press, 1925).

serve as helpful source texts in their critiques of imperialism and warfare.[7] Some of the anti-nationalistic material in the *Polychronicon* would have been difficult for Trevisa to render for a patron who conceived the project as one that would supplement the efforts of such imitable English figures as King Alfred, Cædmon, and the Venerable Bede (100, 103, 105). Yet, in his epistle to Lord Berkeley, he pledges that in his translation "the menyng shal stonde and nought be ychaunged" (148). Such a statement implies that Trevisa will remain faithful to both his source text and the demands of his patron. As I demonstrate below, this pledge proves to be impossible to uphold because of the delicate dance Trevisa must perform in translating an ecclesiastical text for lay aristocratic readers.

In the manner of the alliterative romanciers, Trevisa employs erudition and subtlety to present a text that is both pleasing to his audience and consistent with his clerical viewpoint. While the Lord appears to have egalitarian goals in making the chronicle available to "moo men" (26–27), his desire to translate the *Polychronicon* into English is motivated by the lay aristocratic interest in the elevation of English as a language of authority through manuscript production and the fine book trade. As it turns out, if we follow the reproduction and dissemination of this text, "moo men" actually means "more wealthy men." Six copies of Trevisa's translation appear in finely wrought early fifteenth-century manuscripts that were most likely written and illuminated in London.[8] Ronald Waldron adds, "Their de luxe character suggests that they were designed for a baronial market, . . . [a] restricted circulation . . . among the wealthy and bibliophile."[9] Therefore, the

---

7. Their juxtaposition in monastic libraries is attested by the book owner, Thomas Arnold, who in the 1360s–70s owned both the *Polychronicon* and Guido's *Historia*. A. B. Emden, *Donors of Books to S. Augustine's Abbey Canterbury*, Oxford Bibliographical Society, Occasional Papers no. 4 (Oxford: Oxford Bibliographical Society, 1968), 5–6, 18; Christopher Baswell, "Troy, Arthur, and the Languages of 'Brutis Albyoun,'" in *Reading Medieval Culture: Essays in Honor of Robert W. Hanning*, eds. Robert M. Stein and Sandra Pierson Prior (Notre Dame, IN: University of Notre Dame Press, 2005), 170–97, at 191. For more on the readership and influence of the *Polychronicon*, see Taylor, *The Universal Chronicle of Ranulf Higden*, 140–4; A. S. G. Edwards, "The Influence and Audience of the *Polychronicon*: Some Observations," *Proceedings of the Leeds Philosophical and Literary Society* 17 (1980): 113–19.

8. For a more detailed discussion of the manuscripts, see Ronald Waldron, "John Trevisa and the Use of English," *Proceedings of the British Academy* 74 (1988): 171–202, at 177; MSS London, BL Addit. 24194 (A), Cambridge, St. John's Coll. 204 (J), Aberdeen Univ. Lib. 21 (D), Liverpool Public Lib. f909 HIG (L), Princeton Univ. Lib., Garrett 151 (P), and Formerly Penrose (F). For scribal characteristics of A and J, see A. I. Doyle and M. B. Parkes, "The Production of Copies of the *Canterbury Tales* and the *Confessio Amantis* in the Early Fifteenth Century," in *Medieval Scribes, Manuscripts & Libraries: Essays presented to N. R. Ker*, eds. M. B. Parkes and Andrew G. Watson (London: Scolar Press, 1978), 163–210.

9. Waldron, "John Trevisa and the Use of English," 178.

translation of the *Polychronicon* makes it more accessible and readable not for the entire lay population, but for a new and no less exclusive audience who has the socioeconomic means to produce and circulate books. In other words, the Lord's egalitarianism disguises his push for a transfer of knowledge and literate authority from the clergy to the nobility.

Likewise, the Clerk undercuts his accession to his patron's wishes by privileging his ecclesiastical identity through surprisingly alliterative rhetoric: "Than God graunte us grace graithely to gynne, wit and wisdom wiseliche to worche, myght and mynde of right menyng to make translacioun trusty and trowe, plesyng to the Trinite, thre persones and oon God in mageste, that ever was and ever shal be" (127–30). The language not only establishes a biblical framework, the viewpoint of the church, on the secular history of the chronicle, but also departs from the "more easy and more pleyn" (125–26) prose that the Lord requests. In fact, the crowded syntax of the sentence and its alliterating units transform the requested prose into the alliterative verse so prevalent throughout northern England.[10] And to defy the notion that his interest in alliteration is just a brief anomaly, Trevisa begins his corresponding letter to Lord Berkeley in alliterative prose:

> Welthe and worshipe to my worthy and worshipful lord Sir Thomas, Lord of Berkley. I, John Trevysa, youre prest and youre bedman obedient and buxom to worche youre wille, holde in hert and thenke in thought and mene in mynde youre medeful menyng and speche that ye spake and seide that ye wold have Englissh translacioun of Ranulph of Chestres bokes and cronycles: therefore Y wolde fonnde to take that travail and make Englissh translacion of the same bokes as God grauntith me grace. For blame of bakbiters wol Y not blynne, for envye of enemyes, for evel spighting and speche of evel spekers wol Y nought leve to do this dede, for travayle Y wol nought spare. Comfort Y have in medeful making and plesing to God, and in wityng that Y wote that it is youre wille. (131–41)

In playfully alliterating both the concluding prayer in the *Dialogue* and the salutation to his epistle, Trevisa highlights his interest in England's native verse. Based on the evidence of glosses in manuscripts containing Old English texts, Dorothy Bethurum asserts that "interest in Old English in the West Midlands was not spasmodic antiquarianism but must have run a steady course to the end of the Middle Ages."[11] And given the Lord's invocation of

---

10. Baswell, "Troy, Arthur, and the Languages of 'Brutis Albyoun,'" 180.
11. Dorothy Bethurum, *The Homilies of Wulfstan* (Oxford: Clarendon Press, 1957), 106; A. F. Campbell, "Middle English in Old English Manuscripts," in *Chaucer and Middle English*

King Alfred in the *Dialogue*, Waldron may be correct in characterizing this alliterative prose as Trevisa's nod to the Alfredian tradition in Wessex.[12]

While this acknowledgment of King Alfred's translation program is plausible, I want to suggest that Trevisa's use of the alliterative line is more evocative of the clerical voice of the alliterative poetry of his own era. As Waldron admits, there is no evidence that Trevisa knew Alfred's preface to *Pastoral Care* or the Old English texts that he cites. It would have even been possible for Trevisa to draw exclusively from Higden for his knowledge of the Old English corpus.[13] In fact, Trevisa's alliterative prayer, and specifically the section "God graunte us grace graithely to gynne, wit and wisdom wiseliche to worche" (127–28) is more stylistically and structurally similar to the Middle English alliterative poetry of the north. Compare Trevisa's line to John Clerk's opening prayer in the alliterative *Destruction of Troy:* "Now god of þi grace graunt me þi helpe / And wysshe me with wyt þis werke for to ende" (3–4). The correspondences in vocabulary (God/god, graunte/graunt, grace/grace, wit/wyt, worche/werke) and the organization of the alliterative units suggest that Trevisa's prayer originates in a formula used by alliterative poets.

It is also likely that Trevisa's educational training in Latin prose style directly influenced his employment of alliteration. As David Lawton and Ian Cornelius have argued, the rhythms of alliterative writing are equivalent to the dactylic and spondaic cadences of *dictamen,* the secretarial and bureaucratic practice of letter writing.[14] While the purpose of teaching the *ars dictaminis* was primarily to train future clerks in the rhetorical structures of the letter (such as the salutation, the securing of goodwill, the narration, the petition, and the conclusion), attention was also paid to *cursus* or cadence, a method of rhythmical signature that was described in some

---

Studies in honour of Rossell Hope Robbins, ed. Beryl Rowland (London: George Allen & Unwin, 1974), 218–29, at 226; E. G. Stanley, "Laȝamon's Antiquarian Sentiments," *Medium Ævum* 38 (1969): 23–37.

12. Waldron, "John Trevisa and the Use of English," 177.

13. Ibid. Alfred is the focus in the beginning of Higden's Book 6 and all the other famous "men and moments" in the history of translation cited with Alfred in the *Dialogue* are treated by Higden as well: 2.4,6 (Septuagint), 2.6 (Babel); 4.18 (Aquila, Symachus, Theodocion, and Origen), 4.29 (Jerome); 5.32 (John the Scot). For these and future references to Higden's text, see *Polychronicon, Together with the English Translation of John of Trevisa and an Unknown Writer of the Fifteenth Century,* ed. Churchill Babington and Joseph R. Lumby (London: Longmans, Green, and Co., 1869).

14. David Lawton, "Gaytryge's Sermon, 'Dictamen,' and Middle English Alliterative Verse," *Modern Philology* 76.4 (May 1979): 329–43; Ian Cornelius, "Cultural Promotion: Middle English Alliterative Writing and the *Ars Dictaminis*" (PhD diss., University of Pennsylvania, 2009). See also Lawton's "The Idea of Alliterative Poetry: Alliterative Meter and *Piers Plowman,*" in *Suche Werkis to Werche: Essays on Piers Plowman in Honor of David C. Fowler* (Lansing: Michigan State University Press, 1993), 147–68, especially 158–59 and 168.

dictaminal manuals as a means of authentication.[15] No evidence exists that would convincingly confirm that the stress patterns of alliterative writing directly imitate the *cursus,* but as Cornelius suggests, their rhythmical similarities elevated the prestige of English alliterative texts.[16] In fact, the prologue to the fourteenth-century alliterative devotional treatise, *A Talking of the Love of God,* includes a direct reference to *cursus:* "Men schal fynden lihtliche this tretys in cadence" (16).[17] This description of alliterative rhythm as "cadence," or the "cadentia" of *dictamen,* suggests explicit links between alliterative b-verse patterning and the clause endings of *cursus.*[18] And since this dictaminal training flourished in late fourteenth-century Oxford, when and where Trevisa received his university education, it is no surprise that we see the arts of alliteration and letter writing merge in his epistle to Lord Berkeley.[19]

Trevisa's immersion in the *ars dictaminis* would have likely been accompanied by exposure to a number of literary models of prose style, including that of Guido delle Colonne. As Martin Camargo has shown, an advanced canon of Latin texts, which served as an extension of the standard curricular *Liber Catoniani,* supplemented dictaminal instruction in late-fourteenth century Oxford. This set of literary models included Alain de Lille's *De planctu naturae,* Jean de Limoge's *Morale somnium Pharaonis,* Richard de Bury's *Philobiblon,* and Guido's *Historia destructionis Troiae.* Camargo suggests that "it is highly probable that they clustered together as a set of models from which two or three might be chosen to accompany one or more treatises on prose composition and, optionally, treatises on verse composition as well."[20] This provocative speculation suggests that affinities between Latin prose and alliterative poetry may not have been limited to their concusssive cadences. Indeed, the alliterative romances of this book indicate that Guido's content, his skeptical historiographic model, may have been attractive as well.

If, for example, we consider John Clerk's prologue to his translation of Guido's *Historia,* we find clear evidence of Clerk's own educational training in Latin prose conventions. The typical structures and language of the aca-

---

15. Ian Cornelius, "The Rhetoric of Advancement: *Ars Dictaminis, Cursus,* and Clerical Careerism in Late Medieval England," *New Medieval Literatures* 12 (2010): 287–328, at 314.
16. Cornelius, "Cultural Promotion," 3.
17. *A Talking of the Love of God,* in Wogan-Browne, Watson, Taylor, Evans, eds., *The Idea of the Vernacular,* 223.
18. Cornelius, "The Rhetoric of Advancement," 302.
19. David Fowler, "John Trevisa and the English Bible," *Modern Philology* 58 (1960): 81–98.
20. Martin Camargo, "Beyond the *Libri Catoniani:* Models of Latin Prose Style at Oxford University ca. 1400," *Mediaeval Studies* 56 (1994): 167–87, at 182.

demic *accessus*, formulaic prologues that accompany Latin academic texts, rise to the fore in Clerk's discussion of his sources, his "intent," and the Trojan "matter" at hand.[21] Given the fact that Clerk's poem is a close translation of Guido's popular Latin text, one he likely encountered within an academic context, we might expect his prologue to replicate the *accessus* of his source. As Cornelius points out, however, "John Clerk is here more faithful to the standard Latinate vocabulary of the *accessus* than his Latin source is."[22] After discussing the historical fidelity of poets, Clerk turns to his Trojan material using language specific to the academic prologue: "Now of Troy forto telle is myn entent euyn" (27). The invocation of his "entent" is a direct reference to the conventional *intentio auctoris* or "intention of the author," which does not appear in Guido's text.[23] And to place his prologue firmly within the genre of the academic *accessus*, Clerk prefaces the first book with the rhetorical "Meue to my mater" (98). The English "mater" refers to the *materia libri* or "subject-matter of the book," which serves as a cue to the reader that the crucial textual material or story is about to begin. If Guido's *Historia* had been a central text for Clerk's education, as it likely was for Trevisa, such a treatment of Guido in concert with academic *auctores* would have been a perfectly natural consequence of reading his text alongside those of the *Libri Catoniani*.

When we consider the critiques of imperialism that emerge in Trevisa's translation of Higden's *Polychronicon*, it becomes evident that Trevisa fits the skeptical intellectual profile of these alliterative romanciers. His alliterative epistle and prayer that preface his translation establish a clerical voice so often expressed by John Clerk, the *Siege of Jerusalem*-poet, the alliterative *Morte Arthure*-poet, and the *Gawain*-poet, who embed their critiques of warfare, empire, and nationalism through this rhythmical form. Likewise, Trevisa uses alliteration to assert values of the ecclesiastical class within a translation intended to please the sensibilities of an aristocratic one. Such a deliberate foray into this rhythmic form suggests that if Trevisa were not required to translate the chronicle in prose, he may have chosen alliterative poetry.

After all, just as Trevisa establishes in the preface to the chronicle that he works at the behest of Lord Berkeley, John Clerk identifies an aristocratic patron in the opening folio of the *Destruction of Troy*. He promises that in the thirty-sixth book he will provide both the "nome of the knight þat causet it to

---

21. For a seminal treatment of these academic prologues, see Alastair Minnis, *Medieval Theory of Authorship: Scholastic Literary Attitudes in the Later Middle Ages*, 2nd ed. (Philadelphia: University of Pennsylvania Press, 2010), 9–39.
22. Cornelius, "Cultural Promotion," 77.
23. Minnis, *Medieval Theory of Authorship*, 20–21.

be made / & the nome of hym that translatid it out of latyn in to englysshe." Clerk fulfills his promise to identify himself as the translator, albeit crytically, but leaves out the name of his knightly patron, an interesting and suggestive omission given Trevisa's similar dilemma of translating anti-aristocratic material for an aristocratic audience. As products of the Guido-tradition, John Clerk and Trevisa's texts exhibit what James Simpson has identified as "a division of power between aristocrats and the learned, whom I shall call 'clerics'; this recognized division of power allowed clerics a permissible voice that is trenchantly opposed to aristocratic military, martial, and bureaucratic practice."[24] Because we have no biographical information for the alliterative romanciers, Trevisa and his translation of the *Polychronicon* provide the most analogous information about the respective clerical positions of the alliterative poets and their aristocratic texts. Through an examination of his translation, we can begin to understand the way the alliterative poets negotiated between the desires of their audiences and their own anti-imperialistic tendencies.

Trevisa's momentary indulgence in the alliterative line at the end of the *Dialogue* is the first indication that his translational practice will not adhere to his vow to remain faithful to the text and the intentions of his patron that the text be made "easy" and "plain" (125–26). Instead of vernacularizing the text, as the Lord desires, Trevisa insists on retaining the Latinity of his source by importing Latin words directly into his English translation. For example, he inserts the Latin "fando" to demonstrate its etymological relationship to the English "fable," a clarifying practice that he repeats throughout the translation to ensure that his audience understands a word's meaning and pronunciation (2.18, 2.26). Likewise, he refers to Latin in his explanation of the acrostic that spells out Christ's name in the Sibyl's prophecy: "The heed letters of these thre vers, and of the othere as they beeth i-write in Latyn, speleth this menynge: Ihesus Crist, Goddess one, Savyour" (2.23). This latter use of Latin as an acrostic to disguise a name is also used by Higden to identify himself as the author of the *Polychronicon*, a technique that John Clerk employs in the *Destruction*. Such Latinate erudition does not comply with Lord Berkeley's desire for Trevisa to English the text for a lay population that has little to no Latin, and instead pleases the sensibilities of what Christopher Baswell has called Trevisa's "clerical cohort."[25] Likewise, Trevisa chooses to write section headings in Latin, such as "De quibusdam Romano-

24. James Simpson, *The Oxford English Literary History, Reform and Cultural Revolution*, (Oxford: Oxford University Press, 2004), 98–99. For more on the twelfth-century opposition between the clergy and the military, see Ad Putter, '*Sir Gawain and the Green Knight and French Arthurian Romance* (Oxford: Clarendon Press, 1995), 197–201.
25. Baswell, "Troy, Arthur, and the Languages of 'Brutis Albyoun,'" 181.

rum institutis et observantiis" (1.25) and "De schiris Angliae, siue prouinciis" (1.49), and refers to sources, authors, and important figures in Latin. Virgil is "Virgilius," Isidore is "Isidorus" and Horace is "Horacius"; and when Trevisa cites Isidore's tenth book of the *Etymologies*, he writes "Eth. libro decimo" (1.1). Furthermore, names and places often appear in Latin, as is evident in the following sentence: "at the laste that lond highte Italia of Italus, rege Siculorum, kyng of Sicilia, and is the noblest prouince of al Europa" (1.23). Trevisa's Latin does not overwhelm the text or readers such as the Lord, who know some Latin, but Trevisa's insistence on retaining his clerical language places a Latinate veneer on an Englished text, which reveals his defense of the ecclesiastical possession of textual knowledge.

In addition to the problem of offending clerics opposed to translation, Trevisa faces the difficulty of rendering a diplomatic translation of a text that interrogates the Arthurian heritage of his baronial audience. Higden is famously critical of Geoffrey of Monmouth, particularly in his praise of Arthur, since the Galfridian account does not concur with the Roman, French, and Saxon histories, notably that of William of Malmesbury (5.6). In response, Trevisa interrupts his translation and inserts an objection to his source that likely pleased his aristocratic audience: "Here William telleth a magel tale with oute evidence; and Ranulphus his resouns, that he meveth ayenst Gaufridus and Arthur, schulde non clerke move that can knowe an argument, for it followeth it nought. Seint Iohn in his gospel telleth meny thinges and doynges that Mark, Luk, and Matheu speketh nought of in here gospelles, ergo, Iohn is nought to trowynge in his gospel" (5.6). By equating William and Higden's argument against the existence of Arthur with the argument that Saint John speaks falsely because he addresses matters that do not appear in the other gospels, Trevisa condemns their reasoning as a kind of Arthurian heresy. Clerical readers would have found this analogy humorous, especially since Trevisa presents his objection by shifting into hypotactic syntax and deductive argument characteristic of Latinate sentence structure. While members of the ecclesiastical class may have perceived this irony, it is likely that Trevisa's defense of Arthur would have been accepted by his aristocratic audience, who, as Baswell suggests, "had a real if indirect stake in English territorial ambitions, which were supported by myths of Arthurian empire."[26] Yet, these Arthurian origins were as attractive as they were potentially threatening to the Anglo-Norman nobility, since both the Normans and the Welsh laid claim to this ancestry. For Lord Berkeley, this contention for Arthurian identity would have been particularly acute since

26. Ibid., 183.

he owned territory in Gloucestershire by the Welsh March.²⁷ Trevisa therefore has to take great care to present Arthurian origins in a way that does not privilege one particular ethnic line or promise the future glory of the Britons.

As is the case for the *Morte*-poet, who resists the fantasy of Arthur's return by emphasizing his undignified death, Trevisa prefers a more historical Arthur and critiques the Galfridian prophecy that suggests Arthur will come again to redeem the Britons. Employing the same language that he used to lambaste Higden and William, he claims that it is "a ful magel tale . . . that Arthur schal come aghe, and be eft kyng here of Britayne" (5.6). By arguing for Arthur's existence and arguing against Arthur's return, Trevisa engages in the retrospective historiography of the alliterative romanciers, who both establish Arthur's place in British ancestry and critique Arthurian fantasies of empire. As Baswell suggests, Trevisa's contradictory stance on Arthur either "reject[s] Arthur outright or preserve[s] him as a redeemer of the Britons. Either version cuts into the imperial sentiments or local land tenure of Trevisa's baronial patron and his class."²⁸ Trevisa cleverly belies the Arthurian ambitions of his audience by inserting satiric objections and historical exegesis that are consistent both with his clerical identity and his alliterative politics.

By coupling an examination of Britain's Arthurian identity with the Lord's justification of translation in the *Dialogue*, Trevisa ensures that his audience will recognize the stakes of his Englishing of the *Polychronicon* for both the clergy and the lay aristocracy. Essentially, the Lord's approach to translation is a microcosmic application of the *translatio imperii et studii* that seeks justification and empowerment of English nobility through descent. Just as Higden tells the story of the world from creation up until the English present, the Lord perceives his patronage as the most current moment in the history of translation that stretches back to the earliest translation of scripture. Because of his perception of his authoritative position in universal history, Emily Steiner contends that the Lord both conceives of translation as a cultural operation of the nobility and understands lordship as the theoretical basis for translation. She adds, "This is not just to say that *translatio studii*

---

27. Hanna, "Sir Thomas Berkeley and His Patronage," 880–82.
28. Baswell, "Troy, Arthur, and the Languages of 'Brutis Albyoun,'" 184. As Baswell notes, Trevisa's Cornish heritage may have also caused him to defend the Celtic perspective, despite the fact that he is also Anglo-Norman. See also David Fowler, *The Life and Times of John Trevisa, Medieval Scholar* (Seattle and London: University of Washington Press, 1995), 11–23; Housman, "Higden, Trevisa, Caxton, and the Beginnings of Arthurian Criticism," 209–17; Waldron, "Trevisa's 'Celtic Complex' Revisited," *Notes & Queries* 36 (234) (1989): 303–7.

depends upon and is enabled by *translatio imperii*. It is to say that translation acquires meaning and purpose within the history of aristocratic generation and possession, within a history, which, for the Lord, is a history of Englishness itself."[29] As a deed that both imitates powerful predecessors such as Charles the Bald and Alfred the Great and disseminates knowledge of England's sacred and secular past to the laity, the commissioning of translations expresses and justifies the Lord's lay sovereignty.

Nevertheless, the continuous emergence of Trevisa's clerical voice—manifesting itself in the words of the Clerk, in the Latinate diction of his translation, and in his opposition to Arthurian prophecy—highlights the important part the clergy plays in the textual production and empowerment of the lay aristocracy. As the *Dialogue* suggests, clerks must embrace their roles as academic laborers for the aristocracy to maintain any agency within such a transfer of knowledge and power to the laity. Trevisa's resistant voice, which also characterizes the voices of these alliterative romanciers, reflects the anxiety that he and the rest of his "clerical cohort" might be excluded from the epistemological sphere of textual authority and sacred history, which had previously been their exclusive domain.[30] Hanna claims that this fear of exclusion is especially acute in the *Dialogue*, where "[t]he clerical hope of retaining secular power, of keeping Ranulph Higden's history the exclusive property of a Latinate community, is routed by the Lord's insistence upon the rights of secular readership."[31] The implication of Trevisa's anxiety about the attenuation of the clergy's role is that he writes from a position that belies not only the values of the lay aristocracy, but also vernacularity itself. His defense of Latin as a universal language, which the Clerk makes plain in claiming that it "is so wide iused and iknowe" (33), suggests that he perceives translation as making textual knowledge more, not less, exclusive. Such a stance is counterintuitive, but when we consider the inextricable relationship between the translation of language and the translation of power expressed in the *Dialogue*, Trevisa's Arthurian interpolations, and the fine book trade, the movement of textual authority from all of Latin Christendom to an elite population of lay aristocrats in Northwestern Europe indeed flouts the Lord's claim to disseminate knowledge to "moo men."

---

29. Emily Steiner, "Radical Historiography: Langland, Trevisa, and the *Polychronicon*," *Studies in the Age of Chaucer* 27 (2005): 171–211, at 190.

30. See also Fiona Somerset, *Clerical Discourse and Lay Audience in Late Medieval England* (Cambridge: Cambridge University Press, 1998), 66, 100.

31. Hanna, "Sir Thomas Berkeley and His Patronage," 895; Steiner, "Radical Historiography," 190.

THE CLERICAL VOICE IN ALLITERATIVE ROMANCE

Trevisa's insertion of a clerical voice within the production of an aristocratic text is consistent with the methods of the alliterative poets of the Guido-tradition, who were faced with the same translational project and historiographic viewpoint. For instance, if we turn back to the *Destruction,* we find a consistent privileging of anti-war and anti-imperialistic views characteristic of much clerical discourse. During the Trojan military counsel that Priam convenes to decide whether or not to go to war against the Greeks, two influential voices emerge clearly as those opposed to the campaign. The most prominent is famously that of Hector and the other is that of his brother, the priest Helenus. Using the anachronistic Christian language of the church, John Clerk describes Helenus as if he were an English clergyman, and (possibly an insertion by the scribe Thomas Chetham of the Hunterian MS V.2.8) even labels his anti-war speech as "The counsel of Elinus the Bysshop." In defiance of the earlier calls to war, Helenus boldy advises:

> I know me so konyng in the clene artis
> Thurgh giftes of god . . .
> Therefore puttes of this purpos Let Paris not go.
> (2484–85, 2492, 2499–500)[32]

> [I am versed in the knowledge of the divine arts through gifts of God. . . .
> Therefore, put off this purpose and do not let Paris go.]

By invoking his "giftes of god," Helenus preaches his homily as one endowed with a divine mandate to warn his fellow Trojans about the destruction that will ensue from their bellicosity. The Trojan refusal to follow his counsel and their subsequent defeat retrospectively casts Helenus as a clerical authority who spoke the divine truth and took an ethical stance against war.

Likewise, if we turn to the *Siege of Jerusalem,* we find the clerical voice similarly authorized through a critique of imperialistic excess. In this poem, St. Peter himself appears on the scene as the ecclesiast who converts Vespasian (205–12) and verifies the Vernicle's holiness. Veronica's prostration before his feet best reflects his position of reverence:

---

32. John Clerk of Whalley, *The Destruction of Troy: A Diplomatic and Color Facsimile Edition, Hunterian MS V.2.8 in Glasgow University Library,* ed. Hiroyuki Matsumoto (Ann Arbor: University of Michigan Press, 2002).

> And whan þe womman was ware   þat þe wede owede
> [Of] seint Peter þe pope,   30 platte to þe grounde,
> Vmbefelde his fete   and to þe freke saide:
> 'Of þis kerchef and my cors   þe kepyng Y þe take.' (221–24)[33]

> [And when the woman was aware that the cloth was owned by Saint Peter the Pope, she fell flat on the ground, embraced his feet and said to the man: "I give the protection of this veil and my body to you."]

Such a dramatic acclamation of the "pope" praises Veronica's piety as imitable, but the newly baptized Romans demonstrate no such deference to Peter. In fact, the Romans seek no counsel from Peter in their exaction of the siege of Jerusalem. Rather, as Bonnie Millar puts it, "[e]ssentially St. Peter does the bidding of Vespasian, coming when summoned and responding as he is told."[34] Vespasian irreverent treatment of Peter is significant because, as I have demonstrated, the Roman preference for imperial rather than salvational power is ultimately called into question through the *Siege*-poet's compassion for the fate of the Jews and his condemnation of the Roman cruelty in performing the siege. Like Helenus, Peter's ecclesiastical authority is justified through the lack of respect he is accorded by those with excessive secular interests.

Finally, if we examine the two Arthurian alliterative poems, the *Morte Arthure* and *Gawain,* we again find a preference for the clerical over the aristocratic. After the papacy relinquishes its authority over Rome and agrees to consecrate the imperial sovereignty of King Arthur in the *Morte* (3176–90), Arthur experiences a vision of his downfall during his dream of the Nine Worthies (3218–455) and then reacquaints himself with a knight dressed as a pilgrim, Sir Craddock, who testifies to the reality of Arthur's doom.[35] Sir Craddock's appearance is significant not only because his news turns Arthur's attention back to Britain, but also because Craddock's religious conviction demonstrates the danger of privileging secular over spiritual interests. Before recognizing him as one of his knights, Arthur warns of the danger he faces in passing through this war-strewn region. In response, Craddock says:

---

33. Ralph Hanna and David Lawton, eds., *The Siege of Jerusalem,* EETS OS 320 (Oxford: Oxford University Press, 2003).

34. Bonnie Millar, *The Siege of Jerusalem in Its Physical, Literary and Historical Contexts* (Dublin: Four Courts Press, 2000), 171.

35. All citations of the poem refer to *Morte Arthure: A Critical Edition,* ed. Mary Hamel (New York: Garland Publishing, 1984).

I will noghte wonde for no werrre   to wende whare me likes,
Ne for no wy of this werlde   þat wroghte es on erthe,
Bot I will passe in pilgremage   þis pas vnto Rome,
To purchese me pardonne   of the Pape selfen,
And of the paynes of Purgatorie   be plenerly assoyllede.
Thane sall I seke sekirly   my souerayn lorde,
Sir Arthure of Inglande,   that auenaunt byerne. (3494–500)

[For no war will I turn away from traveling where I wish, nor for no man of this world made on this earth, but I shall pass in pilgrimage at this pace unto Rome to purchase a pardon from the Pope himself, and of the pains of Purgatory be perfectly absolved. Then, shall I seek straightaway my sovereign lord, Sir Arthur of England, that able man.]

By privileging his pilgrimage to Rome and his meeting with the Pope over his loyalty to his lord Arthur, Craddock justifies papal sovereignty. Voicing the clerical perspective of the poem, Craddock's preference for Christian piety reveals Arthur's excessive devotion to empire.

The description and action of the *Morte*-poet's "clerical" knight is consistent with the *Gawain*-poet's characterization of Sir Gawain, who seeks penance in the midst of a court more concerned with heraldic glory. As Ad Putter suggests, Gawain's piety and embodiment of clerical values is a "*translatio* of the traditional *bellator* and his way of life into an ideal of the courtly knight who is pacified, well-mannered, and diplomatic."[36] Moreover, his obsession with somatic mutilation and wholeness, as represented by the sign of his "surfet" (2433) and anxiety about his impending decapitation, cast Gawain as a knight well versed in clerical discourse about the mortification of the flesh and the resurrection of the body.[37] When Gawain displays the "bende of þis blame" [band of this blame] (2506) or scar on his neck to his fellow knights, he not only reveals his own sin, but also reinvokes the sacred power of wounds, which had been earlier represented by the Five

---

36. Putter, *Sir Gawain and the Green Knight and French Arthurian Romance*, 228. For more on the clerical knight see 202–29. See also Jean Frappier, "Vues sur les conceptions courtoises dans les littératures d'oc et de oïl au douzième siècle," *Cahiers de civilization médiévale* 2 (1959): 135–46, at 149; Eugene Vance, "Signs of the City: Medieval Poetry as Detour," *New Literary History* 4 (1973): 557–74, at 571.

37. Citations of the poem refer to *Sir Gawain and the Green Knight* in *The Poems of the Pearl Manuscript*, ed. Malcolm Andrew and Ronald Waldron (Exeter: Exeter University Press, 2002). For a recent discussion of Gawain's Christianity, see Michael W. Twomey, "'Hadet with an alusich mon' and 'britned to noȝt': *Sir Gawain and the Green Knight,* Death, and the Devil," in *The Arthurian Way of Death: The English Tradition*, ed. Karen Cherewatuk & K. S. Whetter (Cambridge: D. S. Brewer, 2009), 73–93.

Wounds of Christ in the pentangle of his shield (642–43). If the *Gawain*-poet shares the Augustinian background of the *Siege*-poet, he may have been particularly influenced by the passage from *The City of God*, which suggests that the wounds of martyrs may be retained in the afterlife: "Non enim deformitas in eis, sed dignitas erit, et quaedam, quamvis in corpore, non corporis, sed virtutis pulchritudo fulgebit" [For in the [wounds] will not be a deformity, but a dignity, and a certain beauty shall shine forth in the body, although it will be of virtue, not of the body].[38] Gawain's wound therefore possesses the potential to instruct its viewers, even if this religious teaching is ultimately lost upon its audience in the Round Table. What matters most to his fellow knights is the retention of his head, proof of his chivalry and a reaffirmation of potential glory of Britain. Unlike their Trojan ancestor Laomedon, who lost his head at the hands of Hercules in the *Destruction* (1339), Gawain has blissfully retained his. The girdle's newfound heraldic identity allows the court to elide the clerical in favor of the aristocratic, a sensibility that is belied by the *Gawain*-poet's return to the ashes of Troy (2525), suggesting that both a historical and clerical lesson have been misinterpreted. The inimitable examples of Sir Craddock and Sir Gawain suggest that even within the realm of secular romance, the alliterative Arthurian voices of reason are markedly clerical.

CHAUCER'S TROJAN HISTORIOGRAPHY

As I have been suggesting, the continuity between past and present that the *translatio imperii* demands is in direct contrast to the clerical perspectives that emerge from the Guido-tradition, which emphasize the ruptures and the dangers of translations of power that occur from Troy to Rome to England. Contrary to the prevalent attacks of avaricious clerics found in the most famous fourteenth-century alliterative poem, William Langland's *Piers Plowman*, these alliterative romancers critique the bellicosity of imperialists such as Arthur and affirm the diplomacy of priests such as Helenus. The thematic link between these alliterative romances is the fall of Troy, a figure that does not appear in *Piers Plowman*. This suggests that like Langland the alliterative romancers perceived the alliterative line as an appropriate medium of social critique, but unlike Langland they interrogated the figure of Troy as an historical subject and aristocratic object.

---

38. Augustine, *De civitate Dei*, ed. Bernhard Dombart and Alfons Kalb, *Corpus Christianorum, Series Latina* 47–48 (Turnhout, 1955), vol. II, 89 (22.19).

What should we then make of Chaucer, a poet who largely eschews alliterative rhythms, but also uses the figure of Troy from Guido's *Historia* as the subject for his own romance *Troilus and Criseyde*?[39] While Chaucer cannot usefully be called an alliterative poet, he does employ alliteration judiciously and exhibits a clear awareness of the vibrant capacity of the alliterative line to replicate the pace and violence of battle scenes. Chaucer provides an alliterative skirmish during "The Legend of Cleopatra" in the *Legend of Good Women* (637–49), but none of these lines follow the standard rule of the regular alliterative line, which dictates that the first three stresses of a four stress line alliterate.[40] In another battle scene in his *Knight's Tale*, however, he adheres to the conventional rhythm in two lines, "Ther shyveren shaftes upon sheeldes thikke" (2605) and "And he hym hurtleth with his hors adoun" (2616), demonstrating an awareness of traditional alliterative formulae and their appropriateness for gritty descriptions of martial conflict. This precise use of alliteration, however, reflects a more aesthetic than political use of the line, the latter of which may be more distinctive of the alliterative poets of the Guido-tradition.

Nevertheless, even Chaucer alliterates Guido's text. As Stephen Barney points out, Chaucer makes a momentary swerve into alliterative verse in his description of Hector and his fellow Trojan warriors in the beginning of Book 4 in *Troilus and Criseyde*:

Ector, and many a worthy wight out wente,
With spere in hond and bigge bowes bente;
And in the herd, with-oute lenger lette,
Hir fomen in the feld anoon hem mette. (4.39–42)[41]

Although the alliteration once again appears within a martial context, it fails to follow the classic formula and instead alliterates haphazardly, stressing three and then two words at either the ending or the beginning of the lines. Since Chaucer likely composed his *Troilus* before many of the alliterative romances of the Guido-tradition, he may have been unfamiliar with their standardized rhythms, but his alliteration of a scene in which Hector and his

39. G. L. Hamilton, *The Indebtedness of Chaucer's Troilus and Criseyde to Guido delle Colonne's Historia Trojana* (New York: Columbia University Press, 1903).
40. References to Chaucer's works are from Larry D. Benson, ed., *The Riverside Chaucer*, 3rd ed. (Boston: Houghton Mifflin, 1987). For a helpful discussion of these passages, see D. Vance Smith, "Chaucer as an English Writer," in *The Yale Companion to Chaucer*, ed. Seth Lerer (New Haven: Yale University Press, 2006), 87–121, at 107–10.
41. Stephen Barney, "Langland's Mighty Line," in *William Langland's Piers Plowman: A Book of Essays*, ed. Kathleen M. Hewett-Smith (New York: Routledge, 2001), 103–17, at 108n14.

band meet the Greeks in battle may have inspired John Clerk, who apparently knew Chaucer's *Troilus,* to render Guido's text in alliterative verse.[42]

It is clear, however, that Chaucer and the alliterative romancers used Guido's *Historia* for divergent purposes. Since Chaucer's main concern is the pain that accompanies courtly love, his Trojan historiography is remarkably ahistorical. When faced with the significance of Troy's fall, he states:

> But how this town com to destruccion
> Ne falleth naught to purpos me to telle;
> For it were a long digression
> Fro my matere, and yow to long to dwelle.
> But the Troian gestes, as they felle,
> In Omer, or in Dares, or in Dite,
> Whoso that kan may rede hem as they write. (1.141–47)

For Chaucer, the writing of history is a digression from the matter at hand that would interrupt his complaint against love. Moreover, he refers readers to authorities whose accounts are either unavailable or contradictory in historical content and methodology. Homer's poems were known by reputation alone and, according to John Clerk, that reputation was not a good one. Homer's epics included material about gods fighting men, an account inconsistent with that of Dares and Dictys, who claimed to have witnessed Troy's fall. At the end of the poem, Chaucer validates the eyewitness account of Dares in yet another evasion of history:

> And if I hadde ytaken for to write
> The armes of this ilke worthi man,
> Than wolde ich of his batailles endite;
> But for that I to writen first bigan
> Of his love, I have seyd as I kan,—
> His worthi dedes, whoso list hem here,
> Rede Dares, he kan telle hem alle ifeere. (5.1765–71)

Once again, Chaucer deflects from his narrative a treatment of the martial material that fascinates the alliterative romancers. Even though Chaucer and these alliterative poets share an interest in Troy, their dedication to Trojan historiography differs greatly.

---

42. C. David Benson, "A Chaucerian Allusion and the Date of the Alliterative *Destruction of Troy*," *Notes & Queries* 219 (1974): 206–7.

In addition to Chaucer's distaste for the historical is his skepticism about the clerical. We could certainly turn to his *Canterbury Tales* for ample evidence to support a Chaucerian critique of the ecclesiastical class, but more germane to the subject at hand is his treatment of the figure of the Trojan cleric. I believe it is appropriate to consider the ways Chaucer critiques the Trojan clerks as English ones since Chaucer has been known to engage in Trojan allegoresis. Most notably, previous scholars have observed that the Trojan Parliament of Book 4 is a political commentary on the Wonderful Parliament of 1386.[43] For Chaucer's clerical commentary in this romance, the most important priest is not Helenus, but Calkas, whose defection to the Greeks creates the eventual dilemma for Criseyde. Calkas is described as a "gret devyn" or augur who foreknew through astronomy and from Apollo that Troy would be destroyed (1.66–70). In contrast to Helenus who gains his divine knowledge in the *Destruction* "from the clene artis / Thurgh giftes of god" (2484–85), Chaucer uses a clever pun to claim that "Calkas knew by calkulynge" (1.71). The suggestion that Calkas dabbled in the "dark arts" to maneuver his way into safety is confirmed just a few lines later where he is condemned as a "traitour" (1.87). Even the Greeks who accept him question his fidelity. Diomede worries that Calkas will

>   lede us with ambages—
> That is to seyn, with double wordes slye,
> Swiche as men clepen a word with two visages—. (5.897–99)

The fear of Calkas' "ambages" or "ambiguities" suggests a greater paranoia about the divine knowledge that such a Trojan cleric possesses.[44] By placing Calkas at the center of the plot of treason, Chaucer expresses ambivalence about such clerical authority.

Chaucer's elusion of a direct engagement with the historical Trojan origins of his aristocratic audience and his acerbic view of clerical knowledge

---

43. Patterson, *Chaucer and the Subject of History,* 158. The connection between the Parliaments was first identified by McCall and Rudisill, Jr., "The Parliament of 1386 and Chaucer's Trojan Parliament," 276–88. D. W. Robertson disagreed in "The Probable Date and Purpose of Chaucer's *Troilus,*" *Medievalia & Humanistica* 13 (1985): 143–71, at 153.

44. As Christopher Cannon notes, Chaucer's use of "ambages" is interesting because it only occurs once in his works and has a telling linguistic history. The word is actually Latin for "winding or circuitous paths" but also has an etymological relationship to "ambiguitas." Both the *Ad Herennium* and Geoffrey of Vinsauf define it as a term that "belies its appearance" (haec vox transvertit visum). "Chaucer's Style," in *The Cambridge Companion to Chaucer,* eds. Piero Boitani and Jill Mann (Cambridge: Cambridge University Press, 1986), 233–50, at 246; Harry Caplan, ed., *Ad Herennium* (Cambridge: Harvard University Press, 1981), 4.53.75ff; Geoffrey of Vinsauf, *Poetria Nova,* trans. Margaret F. Nims (Toronto: Toronto University Press, 1967), 1545–48.

are merely two factors that made *Troilus and Criseyde* and his other works more susceptible to Lancastrian absorption in the fifteenth century. With the exception of his close circle of friends within the servant culture of the court and London, Chaucer did not gain much of a literary reputation during his lifetime, but after 1400 the proliferation of his texts led to his achievement of the Lancastrian title of "the noble rethor Poete of breteine" in Lydgate's "The Life of Our Lady."[45] This newfound popularity meant that Chaucer's circumscription of history ironically led to his direct involvement in it. By deferring history in *Troilus and Criseyde*, Chaucer participates in a forgetting of the past, a crucial act in nation formation that gained fanfare from none other than Henry V. Such a literary amnesia about the tortuous origins of English nobility inspired Henry V to patronize Trojan textual production. In an effort to support his royal lineage and bolster English's claim to literary authority, he not only commissioned John Lydgate to produce a *Troy Book*, a work as dependent upon Chaucer as it is upon Guido, but also commissioned a vellum copy of *Troilus and Criseyde* for his personal library while he was Prince of Wales.[46] The larger result of this patronage of Chaucerian texts was a proliferation of his works; *Troilus and Criseyde* survives in sixteen fifteenth-century codices and *The Canterbury Tales* in fifty-five.[47] Moreover, the fact that Chaucer produced a particularly francophone English poetry made his works more pleasing to the French-speaking elite. Not only did his Hainault wife most likely converse in French both at home and in the company of Queen Philippa of England, who supported such French writers as Jean Froissart, but also Chaucer was conversant with French as a bureaucratic language for state affairs.[48] Chaucer's ability to please the sensibilities of an imperial and francophone culture enabled his works to rise to a state of reverence in the fifteenth-century.

45. Paul Strohm, "Saving the Appearances: Chaucer's *Purse* and the Fabrication of the Lancastrian Claim," in *Chaucer's England*, 21–40, at 35; Caroline Spurgeon, *Five Hundred Years of Chaucer Criticism and Allusion* (Cambridge: Cambridge University Press, 1925), 1:19, 14–19.

46. Henry V's copy of *Troilus* is now known as the Campsell manuscript. See R. K. Root, *The Textual Tradition of Chaucer's Troilus*, Chaucer Society 1st ser., 99 (London: Kegan Paul, Trench, Trübner, 1916), 5. For more on the "power of Trojan precedents," see Patterson, *Chaucer and the Subject of History*, 86–99. For more on the fifteenth-century readership of Chaucer, see Strohm, "The Social and Literary Scene in England," in *The Cambridge Companion to Chaucer*, 1–19; John M. Manly and Edith Rickert, *The Text of the Canterbury Tales*, vol. 1 (Chicago: University of Chicago Press, 1940), 606–20; Robert Kilburn Root, *The Book of Troilus and Criseyde* (Princeton: Princeton University Press, 1926), liii–lxi.

47. Strohm, "The Social and Literary Scene in England," 13.

48. John Bowers, "Chaucer After Smithfield: From Postcolonial Writer to Imperialist Author," in *The Postcolonial Middle Ages*, ed. Jeffrey Jerome Cohen (New York: Palgrave, 2000), 53–66, at 54; Rolf Berndt, "Period of Final Decline," in *Cambridge History of the English Language*, vol. 1: 1066–1476, ed. Norman Blake (Cambridge: Cambridge University Press, 1992), 352–59.

The imperial and linguistic currency of Chaucerian works among the elite contrasts greatly with the northern verse of the alliterative romanciers, whose formulaic rhythms and provincial historiography fell into relative obscurity. Even though Richard II may have participated in an effort to empower the Northwest Midlands and the Cheshire dialect, the belated movement was no match for Chaucer's London idiom, which was used extensively within the city's populace, government, and commerce.[49] The fact that Chaucer did not participate in the so-called Alliterative Revival or translate earlier Anglo-Saxon works displays a lack of interest in native folklore, provincial literature, and ethnic Englishness.[50] Rather than engage in bold critiques of the *translatio imperii,* Chaucer even went so far as to participate in such Lancastrian fabrications of lineage and royalty.[51] For instance, in his last stanza of *To His Purse,* Chaucer asserts Henry's sovereignty through the invocation of his Trojan heritage:

O conqueror of Brutes Albyon,
Which that by lyne and free eleccion
Been verray king, this song to yow I sende. (22–24)

In addition to the gratuitous claim that Henry had been elected by the people, Chaucer affirms Henry's place in the "lyne" of "conqueror[s]" occupied by "Brutes" and his Trojan ancestors. Chaucer's disciple John Lydgate echoes this argument for lineage in the prologue to the *Troy Book:*

The eldest sone of the noble Kyng
Henri the Firthe, of knyghthood welle and spryng . . .
In sothefastnesse, this no tale is,
Callid Henry ek, the worthy prynce of Walys,
To whom schal longe by successioun
For to governe Brutys Albyoun. (95–96, 101–4)

---

49. Bowers, "Chaucer After Smithfield," 54; "Pearl in Its Royal Setting: Ricardian Poetry Revisited," *Studies in the Age of Chaucer* 17 (1995): 111–55; Bennett, "The Court of Richard II and the Promotion of Literature," 3–20; Bernard Guenée, *States and Rulers in Later Medieval Europe,* trans. Juliet Vale (Oxford: Blackwell, 1985), 126–34.

50. Bowers, "Chaucer After Smithfield," 56; "Chaucer's Canterbury Tales—Politically Corrected," in *Rewriting Chaucer: Culture, Authority, and the Idea of the Authentic Text, 1400–1602,* eds. Thomas A. Prendergast and Barbara Kline (Columbus: Ohio State University Press, 1999), 13–44; Edward Said, "Yeats and Decolonization," in *Nationalism, Colonialism, and Literature,* ed. Seamus Deane (Minneapolis: University of Minnesota Press, 1990). Said argues, "Nativism, alas, reinforces the distinction by revaluating the weaker or subservient partner" (82).

51. For a full analysis of Chaucer's contribution to Lancastrian claims, see Strohm, "Saving the Appearances," 21–40.

The replication of Chaucer's characterization of Henry as the rightful inheritor of "Brutys Albyoun" confirms Chaucer's centrality within a larger movement of English cultural imperialism in the fifteenth century.

The return to Lydgate is apt since my analysis of alliterative romance began with a comparison of his translation of Guido's *Historia* with that of John Clerk. This comparison situates Lydgate within an imperial program relatively distant from John Clerk's provincial skepticism, a sensibility shared by his northern contemporaries, the *Siege*-poet, the *Morte*-poet, and the *Gawain*-poet. Their anonymity is a mystery that will likely never be solved, but it is nevertheless striking how their resistance to the *translatio imperii* remains consistent throughout their poems. In each case, Troy appears either literally or figuratively as an origin recuperated for imperial fabrications, a revival that incurs great losses for the sovereigns and their victims. Even though Chaucer shares this obsession with Troy, his engagement with its destruction is indifferent and tangential to his concern with the trials of courtly romance. His agenda is by no means imperialist, but his affirmation of triumphalist historiography in *To His Purse* suggests that his commitment to the ethics of warfare and empire-building is lukewarm, at best. We cannot conclude that Chaucer disliked the rough sound of the alliterative line, but we may be able to say that he avoided the unsavory message that it often bore.

THE MANUSCRIPT EVIDENCE, the clues within the texts themselves, the dependence on Latin sources, and Trevisa's representative example suggest that these alliterative romanciers were clerics who produced texts for noble patrons or readers with aristocratic pretensions. They realized that English translation empowered the laity and disenfranchised the clergy, but they resisted this call for clerical reform. By undercutting aristocratic claims to empire, these alliterative romanciers called the logic of the *translatio imperii et studii* into question, suggesting instead that such a transfer of power from Troy to Rome to England and the concomitant transfer of knowledge from Latin to English would result in Guido's "plague of great destruction." Within an imperial culture that continually looked into the future to prophesy England's greatness, these alliterative romanciers attended to the treachery, destruction, and sacrifice of the innocent that served as the origin for English claims to empire. The result is a Trojan genre of alliterative romance that not only expresses great ambivalence about warfare, imperialism, and English nationhood, but also quietly implies that the rise of English as a language of authority may come at a great cost.

WORKS CITED

Abray, Lorna Jane. "Imagining the Masculine: Chistine de Pizan's Hector, Prince of Troy," in *Fantasies of Troy: Classical Tales and the Social Imaginary in Medieval and Early Modern Europe.* Eds. Alan Shepard and Stephen D. Powell. Toronto: Centre for Reformation and Renaissance Studies, 2004. 133–48.
Abulafia, Anna Sapir. "Bodies in the Jewish-Christian Debate," in *Framing Medieval Bodies.* Eds. Sarah Kay and Miri Rubin. Manchester: Manchester University Press, 1994. 123–37.
Abulafia, Anna Sapir, ed. *Religious Violence Between Christians and Jews: Medieval Roots, Modern Perspectives.* New York: Palgrave, 2002.
Adam of Usk. *Chronicon Adae de Usk.* Ed. E. M. Thompson. 2nd ed. London: H. Frowde, 1904.
Ad Herennium. Ed. Harry Caplan. Cambridge: Harvard University Press, 1981.
Agamben, Giorgio. *Homo Sacer: Sovereign Power and Bare Life.* Trans. Daniel Heller-Roazen. Stanford: Stanford University Press, 1998.
———. *State of Exception.* Trans. Kevin Attell. Chicago: University of Chicago Press, 2005.
The Alliterative 'Morte Arthure': A Critical Edition. Ed. Valerie Krishna. New York: Burt Franklin, 1976.
The Alliterative Morte Arthure, The Owl and the Nightingale, and Five Other Middle English Poems. Ed. John Gardner. Carbondale: Southern Illinois University Press, 1971.
Anderson, Benedict. *Imagined Communities: Reflections on the Origins and Spread of Nationalism.* Rev. ed. London: Verso, 1991.
Andrew, Malcolm. "The Fall of Troy in *Sir Gawain and the Green Knight* and *Troilus and Criseyde*," in *The European Tragedy of Troilus.* Ed. Piero Boitani. Oxford: Clarendon Press, 1989. 75–93.
Angeli, Giovanna. *L'Eneas e I primi romanzi volgari.* Milan: Riccardo Ricciardi, 1971.
Anglo-Norman Brut: The Brut, or the Chronicles of England. Ed. Friedrich W. D. Brie. Part 1. Early English Text Society o.s. 131. London: Oxford University Press, 1906.
Arendt, Hanna. *On Violence.* New York: Harcourt Brace Jovanovich, 1970.
Armstrong, Dorsey. "Rewriting the Chronicle Tradition: The Alliterative *Morte Arthure* and Arthur's Sword of Peace." *Parergon* 25.1 (2008): 81–101.
Asad, Talal. *Genealogies of Religion.* Baltimore: Johns Hopkins University Press, 1993.
Augustine of Hippo. *Confessions.* Ed. Lucas Berheijeni. *Corpus Christianorum. Series Latina* 27. Turnholt, 1981.
———. *De civitate Dei.* Ed. Bernhard Dombart and Alfons Kalb. *Corpus Christianorum. Series Latina* 47–48. Vol. II. Turnhout, 1955.

———. *Political Writings*. Ed. E. M. Atkins and R. J. Dodaro. Cambridge: Cambridge University Press, 2001.

The Awyntyrs off Arthure in *Sir Gawain: Eleven Romances and Tales*. Ed. Thomas Hahn. Kalamazoo: Medieval Institute Publications, 1995.

Barber, Peter. "The Evesham World Map: A Late Medieval English View of God and the World." *Imago Mundi* 47 (1995): 13–33.

Barber, Richard, ed. *The Life and Campaigns of the Black Prince*. Woodbridge: Boydell, 1986.

Barker, Juliet R. V. *The Tournament in England, 1100–1400*. Woodbridge: Boydell, 1968.

Barney, Stephen. "Langland's Mighty Line," in *William Langland's Piers Plowman: A Book of Essays*. Ed. Kathleen M. Hewett-Smith. New York: Routledge, 2001. 103–17.

Barnie, John. *War in Medieval English Society; Social Values and the Hundred Years War*. London: Weidenfeld and Nicolson, 1974.

Barraclough, Geoffrey. *The Earldom and County Palatine of Chester*. Oxford: Blackwell, 1953.

Barrett, Robert W. *Against All England: Regional Identity and Cheshire Writing, 1195–1656*. Notre Dame: University of Notre Dame Press, 2009.

Barron, W. R. J. *English Medieval Romances*. London: Longman, 1987.

Barrow, G. W. S. "Wales and Scotland in the Middle Ages." *Welsh Historical Review* 10 (1980–1): 305.

Baswell, Christopher. "Troy, Arthur, and the Languages of 'Brutis Albyoun,'" in *Reading Medieval Culture: Essays in Honor of Robert W. Hanning*. Eds. Robert M. Stein and Sandra Pierson Prior. Notre Dame, Indiana: University of Notre Dame Press, 2005. 170–97.

———. "*Troy Book*: How Lydgate Translates Chaucer into Latin," in *Translation Theory and Practice in the Middle Ages*. Ed. Jeanette Beer. Kalamazoo: Medieval Institute Publications, 1997. 215–37.

———. *Virgil in Medieval England: Figuring the Aeneid from the Twelfth Century to Chaucer*. Cambridge: Cambridge University Press, 1995.

Baumgartner, W. "Zu den vier Reichen von Dan 2." *Theologische Zeitschrift* 1 (1945): 17–22.

Baumstark, Anton. *Aristoteles bei den Syrern vom V.–VIII. Jahrhundert*. Leipzig: B. G. Teubner, 1900.

Beal, Rebecca S. "Arthur as the Bearer of Civilization: The *Alliterative Morte Arthure*, Ll. 901–19." *Arthuriana* 5/4 (1995): 32–44.

Beckwith, Sarah. "Making the World in York and the York Cycle," in *Framing Medieval Bodies*. Eds. Sarah Kay and Miri Rubin. Manchester: Manchester University Press, 1994. 254–76

Benjamin, Walter. *Selected Writings, Vol. 1, 1913–1926*. Trans. Edmund Jephcott. Eds. Marcus Bullock and Michael W. Jennings. Cambridge: Harvard University Press, 1996.

———. "Zur Kritik der Gewalt," in Rolf Tiedemann and Hermann Schweppenhäuser. *Gesammelte Schriften* 2.1. Suhrkamp, 1921.

Bennett, H. "Sacer esto." *Transactions of the American Philological Association* 61 (1930): 5.

Bennett, Michael J. *Community, Class, and Careerism: Cheshire and Lancashire Society in the Age of Sir Gawain and the Green Knight*. Cambridge: Cambridge University Press, 1983.

———. "The Court of Richard II and the Promotion of Literature," in *Chaucer's England: Literature in Historical Context*. Ed. Barbara Hanawalt. Minneapolis: University of Minnesota, 1992. 3–20.

———. "The Historical Background," in *A Companion to the Gawain-Poet*. Eds. Derek Brewer and Jonathan Gibson. Cambridge: D. S. Brewer, 1997. 71–90.

Benoît de Sainte-Maure. *Le Roman de Troie*. Ed. Leopold Constans. Paris: Firmin Didot, 1904–12.

Benson, C. David. "A Chaucerian Allusion and the Date of the Alliterative *Destruction of Troy*." *Notes & Queries* 219 (1974): 206–7.

———. *The History of Troy in Middle English Literature: Guido delle Colonne's Historia destructionis Troiae in Medieval England*. Woodbridge, Suff.: D. S. Brewer, 1980.

———. "'The Matter of Troy' and its Transmission through Translation in Medieval Europe," in

Übersetzung: Ein internationales Handbuch zur Übersetzungsforschung. Vol. 2. Eds. Harald Kittel, Juliane House, Brigitte Schultze. Berlin and New York: Walter de Gruyter, 2007. 1337–1340.

———. "'O Nyce World': What Chaucer Really Found in Guido Delle Colonne's History of Troy." *The Chaucer Review* 13.4 (1978–9): 308–15.

Benson, Larry D. "The Alliterative *Morte Arthure* and Medieval Tragedy." *Tennessee Studies in Literature* 11 (1966): 75–89.

———. "The Date of the Alliterative *Morte Arthure*," in *Medieval Studies in Honor of Lillian Herlands Hornstein*. Eds. Jess B. Bessinger and R. R. Raymo. New York: New York University Press, 1976. 19–40.

Berndt, Rolf. "Period of Final Decline," in *Cambridge History of the English Language, vol. 1: 1066–1476*. Ed. Norman Blake. Cambridge: Cambridge University Press, 1992. 352–59.

Bethurum, Dorothy. *The Homilies of Wulfstan*. Oxford: Clarendon Press, 1957.

Bezzola, Reto R. *Les Origines et la formation de la littérature cortoise en Occident, 500–1200*. 3 vols. Paris: Champion, 1963.

Birns, Nicholas. "The Trojan Myth: Postmodern Reverberations," *Exemplaria* 5.1 (1993): 45–78.

Blake, N. F. "Chaucer and the Alliterative Romances." *The Chaucer Review* 3.3 (Winter 1969): 163–69.

———. "Middle English Alliterative Revivals." *Review* 1 (1979): 205–14.

Bloch, R. Howard. *Etymologies and Genealogies: A Literary Anthropology of the French Middle Ages*. Chicago: University of Chicago Press, 1983.

Bloom, Harold. *The Anxiety of Influence*. New York: Oxford University Press, 1973.

Blumenfeld-Kosinski, Renate. "Old French Narrative Genres: Towards the Definition of the *Roman Antique*." *Romance Philology* 34 (1980): 143–59.

Blurton, Heather. *Cannibalism in High Medieval English Literature*. New York: Palgrave MacMillan, 2007.

Boethius. *De consolatione philosophiae*. Eds. H. F. Stewart and E. K. Rand. London, 1918.

Bowers, John. "Chaucer After Smithfield: From Postcolonial Writer to Imperialist Author," in *The Postcolonial Middle Ages*. Ed. Jeffrey Jerome Cohen. New York: Palgrave, 2000. 53–66.

———. "Chaucer's Canterbury Tales—Politically Corrected," in *Rewriting Chaucer: Culture, Authority, and the Idea of the Authentic Text, 1400–1602*. Eds. Thomas A. Prendergast and Barbara Kline. Columbus: Ohio State University Press, 1999. 13–44.

———. "Pearl in Its Royal Setting: Ricardian Poetry Revisited." *Studies in the Age of Chaucer* 17 (1995): 111–55.

———. *The Politics of Pearl: Court Poetry in the Age of Richard II*. Cambridge: D. S. Brewer, 2001.

Brault, Gérard. *Early Blazon: Heraldic Terminology in the Twelfth and Thirteenth Centuries With Special Reference to Arthurian Heraldry*. Oxford: Clarendon Press, 1972.

Brewer, Derek. "The Arming of the Warrior in European Literature and Chaucer," in *Chaucerian Problems and Perspectives*. Eds. Edward Vasta and Zacharias P. Thundy. Notre Dame: Notre Dame University Press, 1979. 221–43.

———. "Feasts," in *A Companion to the Gawain-Poet*. Ed. Derek Brewer and Jonathan Gibson. Cambridge: D. S. Brewer, 1997. 131–42.

Brewer, Derek and Jonathan Gibson, eds. *A Companion to the Gawain-Poet*. Cambridge: D. S. Brewer, 1997.

Brewer, Elisabeth. "The Sources of *Sir Gawain and the Green Knight*," in *A Companion to the Gawain-Poet*. Derek Brewer and Jonathan Gibson, eds. Cambridge: D. S. Brewer, 1997. 241–55.

Brooke, Christopher. "Geoffrey of Monmouth as a Historian," in *Church and Government in the Middle Ages*. Eds. C. Brooke, D. E. Luscombe, G. H. Martin, and Dorothy Owen. Cambridge: Cambridge University Press, 1976. 77–91.

Brown, Peter. "Higden's Britain," in *Medieval Europeans: Studies in Ethnic Identity and National*

Perspectives in Medieval Europe. Ed. Alfred P. Smyth. Houndmills and London: Macmillan; New York: St. Martin's, 1998. 103–18.

Brundage, James. "Intermarriage Between Christians and Jews in Medieval Canon Law," in *Sex, Law, and Marriage in the Middle Ages.* Aldershot, Hampshire: Variorum, 1993. XIII: 25–40.

Burnley, J. D. "*Sir Gawain and the Green Knight,* lines 3–7." *Notes & Queries* 218 (1973): 83–84.

Burns, E. Jane. "Refashioning Courtly Love: Lancelot as Ladies' Man or Lady/Man?," in *Constructing Medieval Sexuality.* Eds. Karma Lochrie, Peggy McCracken, and James A. Schultz. Minneapolis: University of Minnesota Press, 1997. 111–34.

Burrow, J.A. "Honour and Shame in *Sir Gawain and the Green Knight,*" in *Essays on Medieval Literature.* Oxford: Clarendon Press, 1984. 117–31.

———. *Ricardian Poetry: Chaucer, Gower, Langland, and the 'Gawain' Poet.* New Haven: Yale University Press, 1971.

Butler, Judith. *Bodies That Matter: On the Discursive Limits of "Sex."* New York: Routledge, 1993.

———. *Gender Trouble: Feminism and the Subversion of Identity.* New York: Routledge, 1990.

Bynum, C. Walker. *The Resurrection of the Body in Western Christianity, 200–1336.* New York: Columbia University Press, 1995.

Calendar of Close Rolls 1389–92. London, 1896–1947.

Camargo, Martin. "Beyond the *Libri Catoniani*: Models of Latin Prose Style at Oxford University ca. 1400." *Mediaeval Studies* 56 (1994): 167–87.

Campbell, A.F. "Middle English in Old English Manuscripts," in *Chaucer and Middle English Studies in honour of Rossell Hope Robbins.* Ed. Beryl Rowland. London: George Allen & Unwin, 1974. 218–29.

Cannon, Christopher. "Chaucer's Style," in *The Cambridge Companion to Chaucer.* Eds. Piero Boitani and Jill Mann. Cambridge: Cambridge University Press, 1986. 233–50.

A Catalogue of the Manuscripts preserved in the Library of the University of Cambridge. Cambridge, 1980.

Chakrabarty, Dipesh. *Provincializing Europe: Postcolonial Thought and Historical Difference.* Princeton: Princeton University Press, 2000.

Chapman, Coolidge Otis. "Virgil and the *Gawain*-Poet." *Proceedings of the Modern Language Association* 60 (1945): 16–23.

Chaucer, Geoffrey. *The Riverside Chaucer.* Ed. Larry Benson. 3rd ed. Boston: Houghton Mifflin, 1987.

Chism, Christine. *Alliterative Revivals.* Philadelphia: University of Pennsylvania Press, 2002.

———. "The Siege of Jerusalem: Liquidating Assets." *Journal of Medieval and Early Modern Studies* 28 (1998): 309–40.

Christine de Pizan. *Book of the City of Ladies.* Trans. Earl Jeffrey Richards. New York: Persea, 1982.

———. *Le Livre de la Mutacion de Fortune.* Ed. Suzanne Solente. Paris: A&J Picard, 1959.

———. *Oeuvres poétiques de Christine de Pisan.* Ed. Maurice Roy. 1896 ; repr., London: Johnson, 1975.

Clark, John. "Trinovantum—the Evolution of a Legend." *Journal of Medieval History* 7 (1981):135–51.

Classen, Albrecht, ed. *Violence in Medieval Courtly Literature: A Casebook.* New York & London: Routledge, 2004.

Clausen, Wendell. "An Interpretation of the *Aeneid.*" *Harvard Studies in Classical Philology* 68 (1964): 139–47.

Clerk, John. *The Destruction of Troy: A Diplomatic and Color Facsimile Edition, Hunterian MS V.2.8 in Glasgow University Library.* Ed. Hiroyuki Matsumoto. Ann Arbor: University of Michigan Press, 2002.

Clogan, Paul M. "New Directions in Twelfth-Century Courtly Narrative: *Le Roman de Thèbes.*" *Mediaevistik* 3 (1990): 55–70.

Cohen, Jeffrey Jerome. *Hybridity, Identity, and Monstrosity in Medieval Britain: On Difficult Middles*. New York: Palgrave Macmillan, 2006.
———. "Hybrids, Monsters, Borderlands: The Bodies of Gerald of Wales," in *The Postcolonial Middle Ages*. Ed. Jeffrey Jerome Cohen. New York: Palgrave, 2000. 85–104.
Cohen, Jeremy. *Living Letters of the Law: Ideas of the Jew in Medieval Christianity*. Berkeley: University of California Press, 1999.
Cokayne, George E. *The Complete Peerage* 3. London: St. Catherine's Press, 1910–59.
Cooper, Helen. *The English Romance in Time: Transforming Motifs from Geoffrey of Monmouth to the Death of Shakespeare*. Oxford: Oxford University Press, 2004.
Coopland, G. W., ed. *Philippe de Mézières: Letter to King Richard II*. Liverpool: Liverpool University Press, 1975.
Cormier, Raymond. *One Heart One Mind: The Rebirth of Virgil's Hero in Medieval French Romance*. University, MS: Romance Monographs, 1973.
Cornelius, Ian. "Cultural Promotion: Middle English Alliterative Writing and the *Ars Dictaminis*." PhD diss. University of Pennsylvania, 2009.
———. "The Rhetoric of Advancement: *Ars Dictaminis, Cursus,* and Clerical Careerism in Late Medieval England." *New Medieval Literatures* 12 (2010): 287–328.
Crane, Susan. *The Performance of Self: Ritual, Clothing, and Identity during the Hundred Years War*. Philadelphia: University of Pennsylvania Press, 2002.
Creed, Barbara. *The Monstrous-Feminine: Film, Feminism, Psychoanalysis*. London: Routledge, 1993.
Crick, Julia C. *The 'Historia regum Britannie' of Geoffrey of Monmouth, 3: A Summary Catalogue of the Manuscripts*. Cambridge, Eng.: D. S. Brewer, 1989.
Cripps-Day, F. H. *The History of the Tournament in England*. London: Quaritch, 1918.
Curtius, Ernst Robert. *European Literature and the Latin Middle Ages*. Trans. Willard R. Trask. New York: Pantheon Books, 1953.
Daretis Phrygii De Excidio Troiae Historia. Ed. Ferdinand Meister. Leipzig: Teubner, 1873.
Davies, R. R. *The Age of Conquest: Wales, 1065–1415*. Oxford: Oxford University Press, 1991.
———. *Domination and Conquest: The Experience of Ireland, Scotland, and Wales, 1100-1300*. Cambridge: Cambridge University Press, 1990.
———. *Lordship and Society in the March of Wales*. Oxford: Oxford University Press, 1987.
Davis, Charles T. *Dante and the Idea of Rome*. Oxford: Clarendon Press, 1957.
de Boer, S. "Rome, the 'Translatio Imperii' and the Early-Christian Interpretation of Daniel II and VII." *Rivista di storia e letteratura religiosa* 21 (1985): 181–218.
DeMarco, Patricia. "An Arthur for the Ricardian Age: Crown Nobility, and the Alliterative *Morte Arthure*." *Speculum* 80.2 (2005): 464–93.
Derrida, Jacques. "From *Des Tours de Babel*," in *Theories of Translation: An Anthology of Essays from Dryden to Derrida*. Trans. Joseph F. Graham. Eds. Rainer Schulte and John Biguenet. Chicago: University of Chicago Press, 1992. 218–27.
Desmond, Marilynn. *Reading Dido: Gender, Textuality, and the Medieval Aeneid*. Medieval Cultures 8. Minneapolis: University of Minnesota Press, 1994.
Dictys Cretensis Ephemeridos Belli Troiani Libri. Ed. Werner Eisenhut. Leipzig: Teubner, 1973.
Dinshaw, Carolyn. "A Kiss Is Just a Kiss: Heterosexuality and Its Consolations in Sir Gawain and the Green Knight." *Diacritics* 24.2/3 (1994): 204–26.
Dobson, R. B. *The Jews of Medieval York and the Massacre of March 1190*. Borthwick Papers 45. York: St. Anthony's Press, 1974.
Donati Interpretationes Vergilianae 1. Ed. H. George. Leipzig: Teubner, 1905.
Doyle, A. I. and M. B. Parkes. "The Production of Copies of the *Canterbury Tales* and the *Confessio Amantis* in the Early Fifteenth Century," in *Medieval Scribes, Manuscripts & Libraries: Essays presented to N. R. Ker*. Eds. M. B. Parkes and Andrew G. Watson. London: Scolar Press, 1978. 163–210.

Duggan, Hoyt N. "Alliterative Patterning as a Basis for Emendation in Middle English Alliterative Poetry." *Studies in the Age of Chaucer* 8 (1986): 73–105.
Dunger, Hermann. *Die Sage vom troyanischen Kriege in den Bearbeitungen des Mittelalters und ihre antiken Quellen.* Leipzig, 1869.
Ebin, Lois A. *John Lydgate.* Boston: Twayne Publishers, 1985.
Echard, Siân. "'But here Geoffrey falls silent': Death, Arthur, and the *Historia regum Britannie,*" in *The Arthurian Way of Death: The English Tradition.* Ed. Karen Cherewatuk and K. S. Whetter. Cambridge: D. S. Brewer, 2009. 17–32.
Eddy, S. K. *The King is Dead.* Lincoln: University of Nebraska Press, 1961.
Edwards, A. S. G. "The Influence and Audience of the *Polychronicon*: Some Observations." *Proceedings of the Leeds Philosophical and Literary Society* 17 (1980): 113–19.
Einhard. *Vita karoli.* Eds. H. W. Garrod and R. B. Mowat. Oxford: Clarendon Press, 1925.
Emden, A. B. *Donors of Books to S. Augustine's Abbey Canterbury.* Oxford Bibliographical Society. Occasional Papers no. 4. Oxford: Oxford Bibliographical Society, 1968.
Eneas. Ed. Salverda de Grave. Paris, 1925.
Estienne, Henri, Charles Benoît Hase, Ludwig August Dindorf, and Wilhelm Dindorf, eds. *Thesaurus graecae linguae.* Leipzig, 1848–54.
Evangelia apocrypha. Ed. Constantin Tischendorf. Leipzig, 1876.
Everett, Dorothy. *Essays on Middle English Literature.* Ed. Patricia Kean. London: Oxford University Press, 1959.
Faral, E. *Les arts poétiques du xiie et du xiiie siècle, Bibliothèque de l'École des Hautes Études* 238. Paris: É. Champion, 1923.
———. *La Légende Arthurienne.* Paris: Champion, 1929.
Federico, Sylvia. *New Troy: Fantasies of Empire in the Late Middle Ages.* Medieval Cultures 36. Minneapolis, University of Minnesota Press, 2003.
Festus, Sextus Pompeius. *De verborum significatu.* Ed. W. M. Lindsay. Leipzig: Teubner, 1913.
Fierabras. Ed. A. Kroeber and G. Servois. Paris: F. Viewig, 1860.
Finke, Laurie and Martin Shichtman. *King Arthur and the Myth of History.* Gainesville: University of Florida Press, 2004.
Finlayson, John. "The Alliterative *Morte Arthure* and Sir Firumbras." *Anglia* 92 (1974): 380–86.
———. "Alliterative Narrative Poetry: The Control of the Medium." *Traditio: Studies in Ancient and Medieval History, Thought, and Religion* 44 (1988): 419–51.
———. "Arthur and the Giant of St. Michael's Mount." *Medium Aevum* 33 (1964): 112–20.
———. "The Concept of the Hero in the *Morte Arthure*" in *Chaucer und seine Zeit: Symposion für Walter F. Schirmer.* Ed. Arno Esch. Buchreihe der Anglia: Zeitschrift für englische Philologie 14. Tübingen: M. Niemeyer, 1968. 249–74.
———. "Guido de Columnis' *Historia Destructionis Troiae*, The 'Gest Hystorial' of the Destruction of Troy, and Lydgate's *Troy Book*: Translation and the Design of History." *Anglia* 113.2 (1995): 141–62.
———. "Rhetorical 'Descriptio' of Place in the Alliterative *Morte Arthure*." *Modern Philology* 61 (1963): 1–11.
Fisher, John H. "A Language Policy for Lancastrian England." *Proceedings of the Modern Language Association* 107. 5 (1992): 1168–80.
Fitzralph, Richard. *Defensio curatorum.* Ed. Aaron Jenkins Perry. Early English Text Society 167. London: Oxford University Press, 1925.
Flint, Valerie I. J. "The *Historia Regum Britanniae* of Geoffrey of Monmouth: Parody and its Purpose. A Suggestion." *Speculum* 54 (1979): 447–68.
Flusser, D. "The Four Empires in the Fourth Sibyl and in the Book of Daniel." *Israel Oriental Studies* 2 (1972): 148–75.
Folz, Robert. *The Concept of Empire in Western Europe.* Trans. S. A. Ogilvie. London: Edward Arnold, 1969.

Foucault, Michel. *The Archaeology of Knowledge and The Discourse on Language.* Trans. A. M. Sheridan Smith. New York: Pantheon Books, 1972.
———. *History of Sexuality, Volume I: An Introduction.* Trans. Robert Hurley. New York: Random House, 1978.
———. *Power-Knowledge: Selected Interviews and Other Writings, 1972–1977.* New York: Pantheon Books, 1980.
Fowler, David C. "John Trevisa and the English Bible." *Modern Philology* 58 (1960): 81–98.
———. *The Life and Times of John Trevisa, Medieval Scholar.* Seattle and London: University of Washington Press, 1995.
Fradenburg, Louise. *City, Marriage, Tournament: Arts of Rule in Late Medieval Scotland.* Madison: University of Wisconsin Press, 1991.
Frappier, Jean. "Vues sur les conceptions courtoises dans les littératures d'oc et de oïl au douzième siècle." *Cahiers de civilization médiévale* 2 (1959): 135–46.
Fries, Maureen. "The Poem in the Tradition of Arthurian Literature," in *The "Alliterative Morte Arthure": A Reassessment of the Poem.* Ed. Karl Heinz Göller. Arthurian Studies 2. Woodbridge, Eng.: D. S. Brewer, 1981. 30–43.
Froissart, Jean. *Chroniques de Froissart.* Ed. J. A. Buchon. Vol. 13. Paris, 1825.
Fuchs, H. "Zur Verherrlichung Roms und der Römer in dem Gedichte des Rutilius Namatianus." *Basler Zeitschrift für Geschichte und Altertumskunde* 42 (1943): 49–51.
Galbraith, V. H. "An Autograph Manuscript of Ranulph Higden's *Polychronicon.*" *The Huntington Library Quarterly* 23 (1959): 1–18.
Galloway, Andrew. "Latin England," in *Imagining a Medieval English Nation.* Ed. Kathy Lavezzo. Minneapolis: University of Minnesota Press, 2004. 42–45.
Gellrich, Jesse. *Discourse and Dominion in the Fourteenth Century: Oral Contexts of Writing in Philosophy, Politics, and Poetry.* Princeton: Princeton University Press, 1995.
Geoffrey of Monmouth. *The Historia Regum Britannie of Geoffrey of Monmouth, I: Bern, Burgerbibliothek, MS. 568.* Ed. Neil Wright. Cambridge: D. S. Brewer, 1991.
Geoffrey of Trani. *Summa super titulis Decretalium.* Aalen: Scientia Verlag, 1968.
Geoffrey of Vinsauf. *Poetria Nova.* Trans. Margaret F. Nims. Toronto: Toronto University Press, 1967.
Gerald of Wales. *Descriptio Kambriae* II. *Giraldi Cambrensis Opera, Volume 6. Rerum Britannicarum Medii Aevi Scriptores* 21. Eds. J. S. Brewer, J. F. Dimock, and G. F. Warner. London: Longmans, 1861–91.
———. *Expugnatio Hibernica: The Conquest of Ireland.* Eds. A. B. Scott and F. X. Martin. Dublin: Royal Irish Academy, 1978.
———. *Itinerarium Cambriae seu laboriosae Baldvini Cantuariensis Archiepiscopi per Walliam legationis accurate descriptio, auctore Silv. Giraldo Cambrense* Ed. David Powell. London: Bulmer, 1806.
Gerould, G. H. "King Arthur and Politics." *Speculum* 2 (1927): 33–51.
Gervais of Melkley. *Ars poetica.* Ed. H. J. Gräbener. *Forschungen zur romanischen Philologie* 17. Münster, 1965.
The Gest Hystoriale of the Destruction of Troy. Ed. G. A. Panton and David Donaldson. Early English Text Society 39, 56. New York, Greenwood Press, 1869 and 1874.
Gestum regum Britanniae. Ed. Francisque Michel. Cambrian Archeological Association, 1862.
Gillingham, John. *The English in the Twelfth Century: Imperialism, National Identity, and Political Values.* Woodbridge, U.K.: The Boydell Press, 2000.
Ginzburg, C. *Ecstasies: Deciphering the Witches' Sabbath.* New York: Pantheon Books, 1991.
Given-Wilson, Chris. *The Royal Household and the King's Affinity: Service, Politics and Finance in England 1360–1413.* New Haven: Yale University Press, 1986.
Godefroy, Frédéric. *Dictionnaire de l'ancienne langue française.* 10 vols. Paris: F. Vieweg, 1880–1902.

Goez, Werner. *Translatio Imperii: Ein Beitrag xtlr Gedichte des Geschichtsdenkens und der politischen Theorien im Mittelalter und in der frühen Neuzeit.* Tübingen, 1958.
Gollancz, Sir Israel, ed. *Sir Gawain and The Green Knight.* Early English Text Society 210. London: Oxford University Press, 1940.
Göller, Karl Heinz, ed. *The "Alliterative Morte Arthure": A Reassessment of the Poem.* Arthurian Studies 2. Woodbridge, Eng.: D. S. Brewer, 1981.
Goold, George P. "Servius and the Helen Episode." *Harvard Studies in Classical Philology* 74 (1970): 101–68.
Gorra, Egidio. *Testi Inediti di Storia Trojana.* Turin: C. Trevirio, 1887.
Gower, John. *The Complete Works of John Gower: Volume 4.* Ed. G. C. Macaulay. Oxford: Clarendon Press, 1901.
———. *The Major Latin Works of John Gower: The Voice of One Crying and The Tripartite Chronicle.* Ed. Eric W. Stockton. Seattle: University of Washington Press, 1962.
Gransden, Antonia. *Historical Writing in England c. 550 to c. 1307.* Ithaca: Cornell University Press, 1974.
———. "Silent Meanings in Ranulph Higden's *Polychronicon* and in Thomas Elmham's *Liber Metricus de Henrico Quinto.*" *Medium Ævum* 46 (1976): 231–40.
Gray, Sir Thomas. *Scalacronica.* Ed. J. Stevenson. Edinburgh, 1836.
Greenfeld, Liah. *Nationalism: Five Roads to Modernity.* Cambridge: Harvard University Press, 1992.
Griffith, R. H. "Malory, *Morte Arthure*, and *Fierabras.*" *Anglia* 32 (1909): 389–98.
Grundmann, H. "Sacerdotium, Regnum, Studium." *Archiv für Kulturgeschichte* 34 (1952): 5–21.
Guddat-Figge, G., ed. *Catalogue of the Manuscripts containing Middle English Romances.* Munich: W. Fink, 1976.
Guenée, Bernard. *States and Rulers in Later Medieval Europe.* Trans. Juliet Vale. Oxford: Blackwell, 1985.
Guido de Columnis. *Historia Destructionis Troiae.* Ed. Nathaniel Edward Griffin. Cambridge, MA: Mediaeval Academy of America, 1936.
Guido delle Colonne. *Historia Destructionis Troiae.* Trans. Mary Elizabeth Meek. Bloomington: Indiana University Press, 1974.
Halperin, David. *One Hundred Years of Homosexuality and Other Essays on Greek Love.* New York: Routledge, 1990.
Hamel, Mary. "*The Siege of Jerusalem* as a Crusading Poem," in *Journeys Toward God: Pilgrimage and Crusade.* Ed. Barbara N. Sargent-Baur. Kalamazoo: University of Michigan Press, 1992. 177–94.
Hamilton, G. L. *The Indebtedness of Chaucer's Troilus and Criseyde to Guido delle Colonne's Historia Trojana.* New York: Columbia University Press, 1903.
Hampton, Timothy. *Writing from History: The Rhetoric of Exemplarity in Renaissance Literature.* Ithaca: Cornell University Press, 1990.
Hanna, Ralph. "Alliterative Poetry," in *The Cambridge History of Medieval English Literature.* Ed. David Wallace. Cambridge: Cambridge University Press, 1999. 488–512.
———. "Contextualizing *The Siege of Jerusalem.*" *Yearbook of Langland Studies* 13 (1999): 109–21.
———. *London Literature, 1300–1380.* Cambridge: Cambridge University Press, 2005.
———. *Pursuing History: Middle English Manuscripts and their Texts.* Stanford: Stanford University Press, 1997.
———. "Sir Thomas Berkeley and His Patronage." *Speculum* 64.4 (1989): 878–916.
Hanning, Robert W. *The Vision of History in Early Britain.* New York: Columbia University Press, 1966.
Hardie, Philip. *Virgil's Aeneid: Cosmos and Imperium.* Oxford: Clarendon Press, 1986.
Harrison, S. J. "Some Views of the *Aeneid* in the Twentieth Century," in *Oxford Readings in Vergil's Aeneid.* Ed. S. J. Harrison. Oxford: Oxford University Press, 1990. 1–20.

Hartman, L. G. and A. A. di Lella. *The Book of Daniel.* New York, 1978.
Hay, Denys. *Europe in the Fourteenth and Fifteenth Centuries.* London: Longman, 1989.
Hebron, Malcolm. *The Medieval Siege: Theme and Image in Middle English Romance.* Oxford: Clarendon Press, 1997.
Heng, Geraldine. *Empire of Magic: Medieval Romance and the Politics of Cultural Fantasy.* New York: Columbia University Press, 2003.
———. "Feminine Knots and the Other *Sir Gawain and the Green Knight.*" *PMLA* 106.3 (May 1991): 500–14.
Herrtage, S. J. H. and H. B. Wheatley, eds. *Catholicon Anglicum: An English-Latin Wordbook.* Early English Text Society 75, 1881; reprint 1987.
Higden, Ranulph. *Polychronicon, Together with the English Translation of John of Trevisa and an Unknown Writer of the Fifteenth Century.* Eds. Churchill Babington and Joseph R. Lumby. London: Longmans, Green, and Co., 1869.
Higgins, Iain. *Writing East: The "Travels" of Sir John Mandeville.* Philadelphia: University of Pennsylvania Press, 1997.
Hobsbawn, E. J. *Nations and Nationalism Since 1780: Programme, Myth, Reality.* Cambridge: Cambridge University Press, 1990.
Housman, John E. "Higden, Trevisa, Caxton, and the Beginnings of Arthurian Criticism." *Review of English Studies* 23 (1947): 209–17.
Hsia, R. P. *The Myth of Ritual Murder.* New Haven: Yale University Press, 1988.
Hulbert, J. R. "A Hypothesis Concerning the Alliterative Revival," *Modern Philology* 28 (1931): 405–22.
Ingham, Patricia Clare. "Homosociality and Creative Masculinity in the *Knight's Tale*," in *Masculinities in Chaucer: Approaches to Maleness in the Canterbury Tales and Troilus and Criseyde.* Ed. Peter G. Beidler. Cambridge: D. S. Brewer, 1998. 23–35.
———. *Sovereign Fantasies: Arthurian Romance and the Making of Britain.* Philadelphia: University of Pennsylvania Press, 2001.
Ingham, Patricia Clare and Michelle Warren. "Introduction: Postcolonial Modernity and the Rest of History," in *Postcolonial Moves: Medieval Through Modern.* Eds. Ingham and Warren. New York: Palgrave Macmillan, 2003. 1–15.
Ingledew, Francis. "The Book of Troy and the Genealogical Construction of History: The Case of Geoffrey of Monmouth's *Historia regum Britanniae.*" *Speculum* 69.3 (1994): 665–704.
———. *Sir Gawain and the Green Knight and the Order of the Garter.* Notre Dame, IN: University of Notre Dame Press, 2006.
Jacobs, N. "Alliterative Storms: A Topos in Middle English." *Speculum* 47 (1972): 695–719.
Jacobus de Voragine. *Legenda Aurea.* Ed. T. Graesse. Dresden, 1846.
Jaeger, C. Stephen. *The Origins of Courtliness.* Philadelphia: University of Pennsylvania Press, 1985.
Janssen, Anke. "The Dream of the Wheel of Fortune," in *The Alliterative Morte Arthure: A Reassessment of the Poem* Ed. Karl Heinz Göller. Arthurian Studies 2. Woodbridge, Eng.: D. S. Brewer, 1981. 140–52.
Jefferson, Judith A. and Ad Putter. "Alliterative Patterning in the *Morte Arthure.*" *Studies in Philology* 102.4 (Fall 2005): 415–33.
Jerome. *Sancti Eusebii Hieronymi epistulae.* Ed. I. Hilberg. *Corpus Scriptorum Ecclesiasticorum Latinorum* 54. Vienna-Leipzig: Tempsky, 1910.
John Clerk of Whalley. *The Destruction of Troy: A Diplomatic and Color Facsimile Edition, Hunterian MS V.2.8 in Glasgow University Library.* Ed. Hiroyuki Matsumoto. Ann Arbor: University of Michigan Press, 2002.
John of Garland. *Poetria.* Ed. G. Mari. *Romanische forschungen* 13 (1902).
Johnson, Lesley. "King Arthur at the Crossroads to Rome," in *Noble and Joyous Histories: English Romances 1375–1650.* Ed. Eiléan Ní Cuilleanáin and J. D. Pheifer. Dublin: Irish Academic Press, 1993. 87–112.

Johnson, W. R. *Darkness Visible: A Study of Vergil's Aeneid*. Berkeley: University of California Press, 1976.
Johnston, Michael. "Robert Thornton and *The Siege of Jerusalem*." *Yearbook of Langland Studies* 23 (2009): 125–62.
Joly, Aristide. *Benoît de Sainte-More et le Roman de Troie ou les Métamorphoses d'Homére et L'Épopée Gréco-Latine au Moyen Age*. Paris: F. Vieweg, 1870–1.
Jones, Michael. "'Mon Pais et Mon Nation': Breton Identity in the Fourteenth Century," in *War, Literature, and Politics in the Late Middle Ages*. Ed. C. T. Allmand. Liverpool: Liverpool University Press, 1976. 144–45.
Joseph of Exeter. *Trojan War*. Ed. A. K. Bate. Wiltshire, England: Aris & Phillips, 1986.
Josephus, Flavius. *The Jewish Wars*. Trans. H. St J. Thackeray. Cambridge: Harvard University Press, 1928; rpt. 1990.
Kantorowicz, Ernst Hartwig. *The King's Two Bodies: A Study in Mediaeval Political Theology*. Princeton: Princeton University Press, 1957; repr. 1997.
Karras, Ruth Mazo. *From Boys to Men: Formations of Masculinity in Late Medieval Europe*. Philadelphia: University of Pennsylvania Press, 2003.
Kaske, R. E. "*Sir Gawain and the Green Knight*," in *Medieval and Renaissance Studies*. Ed. George Mallary Masters. Chapel Hill: University of North Carolina Press, 1984. 24–44.
Kassel, Rudolf. *Aristotelis de Arte Poetica Liber*. Oxford: Clarendon Press, 1965.
Keen, M. H. "Chaucer's Knight, the English Aristocracy, and the Crusade," in *English Court and Culture in the Later Middle Ages*. Eds. V. J. Scattergood and J. W. Sherborne. London: Duckworth, 1983. 45–62.
———. *The Laws of War in the Late Middle Ages*. London: Routledge & Kegan Paul, 1965.
Kellogg, Judith L. "Christine de Pizan as Chivalric Mythographer: *L'Epistre Othea*," in *The Mythographic Art: Classical Fable and the Rise of the Vernacular in Early France and England*. Ed. Jane Chance. Gainesville: University of Florida Press, 1990. 100–24.
Kendrick, T. D. *British Antiquity*. London: Methuen, 1950.
Kennedy, Edward Donald. "Mordred's Sons," in *The Arthurian Way of Death: The English Tradition*. Ed. Karen Cherewatuk and K. S. Whetter. Cambridge: D.S. Brewer, 2009. 33–49.
Kershaw, Ian. *Bolton Priory: The Economy of a Northern Monastery, 1286–1325*. Oxford: Oxford University Press, 1973.
King Arthur's Death. Ed. Larry D. Benson. Indianapolis: Bobbs-Merrill, 1974.
Knight, Rhonda. "All Dressed Up with Someplace to Go: Regional Identity in *Sir Gawain and the Green Knight*." *Studies in the Age of Chaucer* 25 (2003): 259–84.
Knight, Stephen. *Arthurian Literature and Society*. New York: St. Martin's Press, 1983.
Lacan, Jacques. *Écrits: A Selection*. Trans. Alan Sheridan. New York: Norton, 1982.
———. *The Seminar of Jacques Lacan*. Ed. Jacques-Alain Miler. Trans. Sylvana Tomaselli. Vol. 2. New York: Norton, 1988.
Langmuir, Gavin. "Thomas of Monmouth: Detector of Ritual Murder." *Speculum* 59 (1984): 820–46.
———. *Toward a Definition of Antisemitism*. Berkeley: University of California Press, 1990.
Laud Troy Book. Ed. J. Ernst Wulfing. London: Early English Text Society, 1902.
Lavezzo, Kathy. *Angels on the Edge of the World: Geography, Literature, and English Community, 1000–1534*. Ithaca: Cornell University Press, 2006.
Lavezzo, Kathy, ed. *Imagining a Medieval English Nation*. Minneapolis: University of Minnesota Press, 2004.
Lawton, David. "*The Destruction of Troy* as Translation from Latin Prose: Aspects of Form and Style." *Studia Neophilologica* 52 (1980): 259–70.
———. "The Diversity of Middle English Alliterative Poetry." *Leeds Studies in English* 20 (1989): 143–72.

———. "Gaytryge's Sermon, 'Dictamen,' and Middle English Alliterative Verse." *Modern Philology* 76.4 (May 1979): 329–43.
———. "The Idea of Alliterative Poetry: Alliterative Meter and *Piers Plowman*." *Suche Werkis to Werche: Essays on Piers Plowman in Honor of David C. Fowler*. Lansing: Michigan State University Press, 1993. 147–68.
———. "Titus Goes Hunting and Hawking: The Poetics of Recreation and Revenge in *The Siege of Jerusalem*," in *Individuality and Achievement in Middle English Poetry*. Ed. O. S. Pickering. Woodbridge, UK: D. S. Brewer, 1997. 105–17.
———. "The Unity of Middle English Alliterative Poetry." *Speculum* 58 (1983): 72–94.
Lawton, Lesley. "The Illustration of Late Medieval Secular Texts, with Special Reference to Lydgate's *Troy Book*," in *Manuscripts and Readers in Fifteenth-Century England: The Literary Implications of Manuscript Study*. Cambridge: D. S. Brewer, 1983. 41–69.
Laʒamon. *Brut*. Eds. W. R. J. Barron and S. C. Weinberg. Harlow, Essex: Longman, 1995.
Lefebvre, Henri. *The Production of Space*. Trans. Donald Nicholson-Smith. Malden, MA: Blackwell, 1991.
Legge, M. Dominica. *Anglo-Norman Literature and Its Background*. Oxford: Clarendon Press, 1963.
Lindberg, Carter. *The European Reformations*. Oxford: Blackwell, 1996.
Lindenbaum, Sheila. "The Smithfield Tournament of 1390." *Journal of Medieval and Renaissance Studies* 20 (1990): 1–20.
Lindley, Arthur. "Pinning Gawain Down: The Misediting of *Sir Gawain and the Green Knight*." *Journal of English and Germanic Philology* 96 (1997): 26–42.
Lippe, Karl. "Armorial Bearings and their Meaning," in *The "Alliterative Morte Arthure": A Reassessment of the Poem*. Ed. Karl Heinz Göller. Arthurian Studies 2. Woodbridge, Eng.: D. S. Brewer, 1981. 96–105
Lloyd, J. E. *A History of Wales* 2. London: Longmans, Green & Company, 1912.
Lowes, John Livingston. "The Date of Chaucer's *Troilus and Criseyde*." *Proceedings of the Modern Language Association* 23 no. 2 (1908): 285–306.
Luttrell, C. A. "Three North-West Midland Manuscripts." *Neophilologus* 42 (1958): 38–50.
Lydgate, John. *Troy Book: Selections*. Ed. Robert R. Edwards. Kalamazoo, MI: Medieval Institute Publications, 1998.
MacCormack, Sabine. *The Shadows of Poetry: Vergil in the Mind of Augustine*. Berkeley: University of California Press, 1998.
Malory, Sir Thomas. *The Works of Sir Thomas Malory*. Ed. Eugène Vinaver. Oxford: Clarendon Press, 1967.
Manly, John M. and Edith Rickert. *The Text of the Canterbury Tales*. Vol. 1. Chicago: Chicago University Press, 1940.
Manning, Robert. *The Story of England by Robert Manning of Brunne, A.D. 1338*. Ed. Frederick J. Furnivall. 2 vols. Rolls Series. London, 1887.
Margherita, Gayle. *The Romance of Origins: Language and Sexual Difference in Middle English Literature*. Philadelphia: University of Pennsylvania Press, 1994.
Maselli, Vito. "Tradizione e cataloghi delle opere aristoteliche." *Rivista italiana di filologia e istruzione classica* 34 (1956): 337–63.
Matheson, Lister M. "The Middle English *Brut*: A Location List of the Manuscripts and Early Printed Editions." *Analytical and Enumerative Bibliography* 3 (1979): 254–66.
Matthews, William. *The Tragedy of Arthur: A Study of the Alliterative "Morte Arthure*." Berkeley: University of California Press, 1960.
McCall, John P. and George Rudisill, Jr. "The Parliament of 1386 and Chaucer's Trojan Parliament." *Journal of English and Germanic Philology* 58 (1959): 276–88.
McIntosh, A. "A New Approach to Middle English Dialectology." *English Studies* 44 (1963): 1–11.

The Medieval French Roman d'Alexandre, 2: Version of Alexandre de Paris. Ed. E. C. Armstrong. Elliott Monographs 37. Princeton: Princeton University Press, 1937.

Mendels, Daniel. "The Five Empires: A Note on a Propagandistic Topos." *American Journal of Philology* 102 (1981): 330–37.

The Middle English Prose Translation of Roger d'Argenteuil's Bible en françois: Edited from Cleveland Public Library, MS Wq091.92-C.468. Ed. Phyllis Moe. Middle English Texts 6. Heidelberg: Winter, 1977.

Millar, Bonnie. "The Role of Prophecy in the *Siege of Jerusalem* and its Analogues." *The Yearbook of Langland Studies* 13 (1999): 153–78.

———. *The Siege of Jerusalem in Its Physical, Literary and Historical Contexts*. Dublin: Four Courts Press, 2000.

Minnis, A. J. "Late-Medieval Discussions of *Compilatio* and the Role of the *Compilator*." *Beiträge zur Geschichte der deutschen Sprache und Literatur* 101 (1979): 385–421.

———. *Medieval Theory of Authorship: Scholastic Literary Attitudes in the Later Middle Ages*. 2nd ed. Philadelphia: University of Pennsylvania Press, 2010.

Moll, Richard J. *Before Malory: Reading Arthur in Later Medieval England*. Toronto: University of Toronto Press, 2003.

Mommsen, Theodor E. "Orosius and Augustine," in *Medieval and Renaissance Studies*. Ed. Eugene F. Rice, Jr. Ithaca: Cornell University Press, 1959.

Monumenta Germaniae Historica, Scriptores. Hanover, 1826–1934.

Mooney, Linne. "Two Fragments of Lydgate's *Troy Book* in the Bodleian Library." *Journal of the Early Book Society* 4 (2001): 259–66.

Moraux, Paul. *Les listes anciennes des ouvrages d'Aristote*. Louvain: Editions Universitaires de Louvain, 1951.

Morte Arthure. Ed. E. Brock. Early English Text Society OS 8. New York, London, Toronto: Oxford University Press, 1871; rpt. 1961.

Morte Arthure. Ed. John Finlayson. York Medieval Texts. Evanston, IL: Northwestern University Press, 1967.

Morte Arthure: A Critical Edition. Ed. Mary Hamel. New York: Garland Publishing, 1984.

Narin van Court, Elisa. "*The Siege of Jerusalem* and Augustinian Historians: Writing about Jews in Fourteenth-Century England." *Chaucer Review* 29.3 (1995): 227–48.

———. "*The Siege of Jerusalem* and Recuperative Readings," in *Pulp Fictions of Medieval England: Essays in Popular Romance*. Ed. Nicola McDonald. Manchester University Press, 2004. 151–70.

Neilson, George. *"Huchown of the Awle Ryale," the Alliterative Poet*. Glasgow: James MacLehose & Sons, 1902.

———. "The Viscount of Rome in 'Morte Arthure.'" *Athenaeum* (1902): 652–3.

Nicholson, Roger. "Haunted Itineraries: Reading *The Siege of Jerusalem*." *Exemplaria* 14.2 (2002): 470–84.

Nietzsche, Friedrich. *The Gay Science*. Trans. Walter Kaufmann. New York: Vintage Books, 1974.

Oakden, J. P. *Alliterative Poetry in Middle English*. Manchester, 1935.

Otter, Monika. *Inventiones: Fiction and Referentiality in Twelfth-Century English Historical Writing*. Chapel Hill and London: University of North Carolina Press, 1996.

Palmer, J. J. N. *England, France, and Christendom, 1377–99*. Chapel Hill: University of North Carolina Press, 1972.

Paris, Matthew. *Chronica Majora*. Ed. Henry R. Luard. Rolls Series 5. London, 1880.

Parks, George B. "King Arthur and the Roads to Rome." *Journal of English and Germanic Philology* 45 (1946): 164–70.

Parry, Adam. "The Two Voices of Virgil's *Aeneid*." *Arion* 2 (1963): 66–80.

Partner, Nancy. *Serious Entertainments: The Writing of History in Twelfth-Century England*. Chicago: University of Chicago Press, 1977.

Patterson, Lee. *Chaucer and the Subject of History.* Madison: University of Wisconsin Press, 1991.
———. "The Historiography of Romance and the Alliterative *Morte Arthure.*" *Journal of Medieval and Renaissance Studies* 13.1 (1983): 1–32.
———. *Negotiating the Past: The Historical Understanding of Medieval Literature.* Madison: University of Wisconsin Press, 1987.
Patrologiae Cursus Completus. Ed. J. P. Migne. Vol. 31. Paris, 1846.
Pauly, August and Georg Wissowa. *Real-Encyclopädie.* 2^e Reihe. 14er Halbband 2, 1948.
Pearl. Ed. E. V. Gordon. Oxford: Clarendon, 1953.
Pearsall, Derek. "The Alliterative Revival: Origins and Social Backgrounds" in *Middle English Alliterative Poetry and its Literary Background.* Ed. David Lawton. Cambridge: D. S. Brewer, 1982. 34–53.
———. *John Lydgate.* Medieval Authors: Poets of the Later Middle Ages. London: Routledge and Kegan Paul; Charlottesville: University Press of Virginia, 1970.
———. *Old and Middle English Poetry.* London: Routledge & K. Paul, 1977.
———. "The Origins of the Alliterative Revival," in *The Alliterative Tradition in the Fourteenth Century.* Eds. Bernard S. Levy and Paul E. Szarmach. Kent, OH: Kent State University Press, 1981. 1–24.
———. "Rhetorical *Descriptio* in *Sir Gawain and the Green Knight.*" *Modern Language Review* 50 (1955): 129–34.
Plato. *Republic.* Trans. Paul Shorey. The Loeb Classical Library. London: Heinemann, 1930.
Pochoda, Elizabeth T. *Arthurian Propaganda: Le Morte Darthur as an Historical Ideal of Life.* Chapel Hill, N.C.: University of North Carolina Press, 1971.
The Poems of the Pearl Manuscript: Pearl, Cleanness, Patience, Sir Gawain and the Green Knight. Eds. Andrew, Malcolm and Ronald Waldron. Exeter, Devon: University of Exeter Press, 2002.
Porter, Elizabeth. "Chaucer's Knight, the Alliterative *Morte Arthure,* and Medieval Laws of War: A Reconsideration." *Nottingham Medieval Studies* 27 (1983): 56–78.
Preminger, Alex, O. B. Hardison Jr., and Kevin Kerrane, eds. *Classical and Medieval Literary Criticism: Translations and Interpretations.* New York: Frederick Ungar, 1974.
Price, Merrall Llewelyn. "Imperial Violence and the Monstrous Mother: Cannibalism at the Siege of Jerusalem," in *Domestic Violence in Medieval Texts.* Eds. Eve Salisbury, Georgiana Donavin, and Merrall Llewelyn Price. Gainesville: University Press of Florida, 2002. 272–98.
Putnam, Michael. *The Poetry of the Aeneid.* Cambridge, MA: Harvard University Press, 1965.
———. *Virgil's Aeneid: Interpretation and Influence.* Chapel Hill: University of North Carolina Press, 1995.
Putter, Ad. Review of Hanna and Lawton, eds., *The Siege of Jerusalem. Speculum* 81.2 (April 2006): 524–26.
———. *'Sir Gawain and the Green Knight' and French Arthurian Romance.* Oxford: Clarendon Press, 1995.
Putter, Ad, Judith Jefferson, and Myra Stokes. *Studies in the Metre of Alliterative Verse.* Oxford: The Society for the Study of Medieval Languages and Literature, 2007.
Quint, David. *Epic and Empire: Politics and Generic Form from Virgil to Milton.* Princeton: Princeton University Press, 1993.
Rand, E. K. *Servianorum in Vergilii Carmina Commentariorum Editionis Harvardianae.* Vol. 2. Lancaster, 1946.
Raymond of Penyafort. *Summa de paenitentia.* Eds. X. Ochoa and A. Díez. Universa bibliotheca iuris. Vol. 1.4.3. Rome, 1976.
Renan, Ernst. "What is a Nation?" Trans. Martin Thom. *Nation and Narration.* Ed. Homi Bhabha. New York: Routledge, 1990. 8–22.
Riddy, Felicity. "Reading for England: Arthurian Literature and National Consciousness." *Bibliographical Bulletin of the International Arthurian Society* 43 (1991): 314–32.

Rigg, A. G. *A History of Anglo-Latin Literature, 1066–1422.* Cambridge: Cambridge University Press, 1992.
Roberts, Brynley F. "Geoffrey of Monmouth and the Welsh Historical Tradition." *Nottingham Medieval Studies* 20 (1976): 29–40.
Robertson, D. W. "The Probable Date and Purpose of Chaucer's *Troilus.*" *Medievalia & Humanistica* 13 (1985): 143–71.
Robinson, Douglas. *Western Translation Theory from Herodotus to Nietzsche.* Manchester, UK: St. Jerome Publishing, 1997.
Rollo, David. "Benoît de Sainte-Maure's *Roman de Troie:* Historiography, Forgery, and Fiction." *Comparative Literature Studies* 32.2 (1995): 191–225.
Rooney, Anne. "The Hunts," in *A Companion to the Gawain-Poet.* Ed. Derek Brewer and Jonathan Gibson. Cambridge: D. S. Brewer, 1997. 157–63.
Root, Robert Kilburn. *The Book of Troilus and Criseyde.* Princeton: Princeton University Press, 1926.
———. *The Textual Tradition of Chaucer's Troilus.* Chaucer Society 1st ser., 99. London: Kegan Paul, Trench, Trübner, 1916.
Roscher, Wilhelm. *Ausführliches Lexikon* 5. Leipzig, 1924.
Rubin, Miri. "Desecration of the Host: The Birth of an Accusation." *Studies in Church History* 29 (1992): 169–85.
———. "The Person in the Form: Medieval Challenges to Bodily 'Order,'" in *Framing Medieval Bodies.* Eds. Sarah Kay and Miri Rubin. Manchester: Manchester University Press, 1994. 100–22.
Said, Edward W. "Yeats and Decolonization," in *Nationalism, Colonialism, and Literature.* Ed. Seamus Deane. Minneapolis: University of Minnesota Press, 1990. 82.
Saint Erkenwald. Ed. Ruth Morse. Cambridge: D. S. Brewer, 1975.
Schiff, Randy. "The Instructive Other Within: Secularized Jews in *The Siege of Jerusalem,*" in *Cultural Diversity in the British Middle Ages: Archipelago, Island, England.* Ed. Jeffrey Jerome Cohen. New York: Palgrave-Macmillan, 2008. 135–51.
———. *Revivalist Fantasy: Alliterative Verse and Nationalist Literary History.* Columbus: The Ohio State University Press, 2011.
Schirmer, Walter F. and Ulrich Broich. *Studien zum literarischen Patronat in England des 12. Jahrhunderts.* Cologne: Westdeutscher Verlag, 1962.
Schmitt, Carl. *Political Theology: Four Chapters on the Concept of Sovereignty.* Trans. George Schwab. Chicago: University of Chicago Press, 2005.
Servius. *Commentary.* Eds. G. Thilo and H. Hagen. Leipzig, 1878–1902.
Shichtman, Martin and James Carley, eds. *Culture and the King: The Social Implications of the Arthurian Legend.* Albany: State University of New York Press, 1994.
Shoaf, R. A. *The Poem as Green Girdle: Commercium in Sir Gawain and the Green Knight.* Gainesville: University Press of Florida, 1984.
The Siege of Jerusalem. Ed. E. Kölbing and Mabel Day. Oxford: Oxford University Press, 1932.
The Siege of Jerusalem. Ed. Michael Livingston. Kalamazoo, MI: Medieval Institute Publications, 2004.
The Siege of Jerusalem. Ed. Ralph Hanna and David Lawton. Early English Text Society OS 320. Oxford: Oxford University Press, 2003.
Silverstein, Theodore. "*Sir Gawain,* Dear Brutus, and Britain's Fortunate Founding: A Study in Comedy and Convention." *Modern Philology* 62.3 (1965): 189–206.
Simpson, James. "The Other Book of Troy: Guido delle Colonne's *Historia destructionis Troiae* in Fourteenth and Fifteenth Century England." *Speculum* 73. 2 (1998): 397–423.
———. *The Oxford English Literary History, Volume 2. 1350–1547: Reform and Cultural Revolution.* Oxford: Oxford University Press, 2002.

———. "Poetry as Knowledge: Dante's Paradiso XIII." *Forum for Modern Language Studies* 25 (1989): 329–43.
Sir Gawain and the Green Knight. Ed. J. R. R. Tolkien and E. V. Gordon. Rev. Norman Davis. Oxford: Clarendon Press, 1967.
Sir Perceval of Galles and Ywain and Gawain. Ed. Mary Flowers Braswell. Kalamazoo, MI: Medieval Institute Publications, 1995.
Skeat, W. W. "Thomas Usk and Ralph Higden." *Notes and Queries*, 10th series, 1 (1904): 205.
Smith, D. Vance. *Arts of Possession: The Middle English Household Imaginary.* Minneapolis: University of Minnesota Press, 2003.
———. "Chaucer as an English Writer," in *The Yale Companion to Chaucer.* Ed. Seth Lerer. New Haven: Yale University Press, 2006. 87–121.
Somerset, Fiona. *Clerical Discourse and Lay Audience in Late Medieval England.* Cambridge: Cambridge University Press, 1998.
Spanheim, E. *Dissertationes de praestantia et usu numismatum antiquorum.* London: R. Smith, 1706–17.
Spearing, A. C. *Readings in Medieval Poetry.* Cambridge: Cambridge University Press, 1987.
Spiegel, Gabrielle M. "Genealogy: Form and Function in Medieval Historical Narrative." *History and Theory* 22 (1983): 43–53.
———. *Romancing the Past: The Rise of Vernacular Prose Historiography in Thirteenth-Century France.* Berkeley and Los Angeles: University of California Press, 1993.
Spivak, Gayatri. "Subaltern Studies: Deconstructing Historiography," in *The Spivak Reader.* Ed. Donna Landry and Gerald Maclean. New York: Routledge, 1996.
Spurgeon, Caroline. *Five Hundred Years of Chaucer Criticism and Allusion.* Cambridge: Cambridge University Press, 1925.
Staley, Lynn. "Translating 'Communitas,'" in *Imagining a Medieval English Nation.* Ed. Kathy Lavezzo. Minneapolis: University of Minnesota Press, 2004. 261–303.
Stanbury, Sarah. *Seeing the Gawain-Poet: Description and the Act of Perception.* Philadelphia: University of Pennsylvania Press, 1991.
Stanley, E. G. "Laȝamon's Antiquarian Sentiments." *Medium Ævum* 38 (1969): 23–37.
Steiner, Emily. "Radical Historiography: Langland, Trevisa, and the *Polychronicon*." *Studies in the Age of Chaucer* 27 (2005): 171–211.
Stow, Kenneth. *Alienated Minority: The Jews of Medieval Latin Europe.* Cambridge: Harvard University Press, 1992.
Strohm, Paul. "Saving the Appearances: Chaucer's *Purse* and the Fabrication of the Lancastrian Claim," in *Chaucer's England: Literature in Historical Context.* Ed. Barbara Hanawalt. Minneapolis: University of Minnesota, 1992. 21–40.
———. "The Social and Literary Scene in England," in *The Cambridge Companion to Chaucer.* Eds. Piero Boitani and Jill Mann. Cambridge: Cambridge University Press, 1986. 1–19.
———. *Social Chaucer.* Cambridge, MA: Harvard University Press, 1989.
Suleri, Sara. "Woman Skin Deep: Feminism and the Postcolonial Condition," in *Women, Autobiography, Theory: A Reader.* Ed. Sidonie Smith and Julia Watson. Madison: University of Wisconsin Press, 1998. 116–25.
Sumption, Jonathan. *Pilgrimage: An Image of Mediaeval Religion.* Totowa, NJ: Rowman & Littlefield, 1975.
Sundwall, McKay. "*The Destruction of Troy*, Chaucer's *Troilus and Criseyde*, and Lydgate's *Troy Book*." *Review of English Studies* 26 (1975): 313–7.
Suzuki, Mihoko. *Metamorphoses of Helen: Authority, Difference, and the Epic.* Ithaca: Cornell University Press, 1989.
Swain, J. W. "The Theory of the Four Monarchies Opposition History Under the Roman Empire." *Classical Philology* 35 (1940): 1–21.

Syr Gawayne. Ed. Sir Frederic Madden. Bannatyne Club, 1839.
A Talking of the Love of God in *The Idea of the Vernacular: An Anthology of Middle English Literary Theory, 1280–1520*. Ed. Jocelyn Wogan-Browne, Nicholas Watson, Andrew Taylor, and Ruth Evans. University Park: The Pennsylvania State University Press, 1999.
Tatlock, J. S. P. "The Date of Troilus: And Minor Chauceriana." *Modern Language Notes* 50.5 (1935): 277–96.
———. "The Dragons of Wessex and Wales." *Speculum* 8.2 (1933): 223–35.
Taylor, John. *The Universal Chronicle of Ranulph Higden*. Oxford: Clarendon Press, 1966.
Teutonicus, Johannes. *Glossa Ordinaria* to the *Decretum*. Venice, 1605.
Thomas, M. C. *Sir Gawayne and the Green Knight*. Zürich: Füssli & Co., 1883.
Thomas, Richard F. "Dido and Her Translators" in *Virgil and the Augustan Reception*. Cambridge: Cambridge University Press, 2001. 154–89.
Thomson, John A. F. *The Transformation of Medieval England: 1370–1529*. London: Longman, 1983.
Tigerstedt, E. N. "Observations on the Reception of the Aristotelian *Poetics* in the Latin West." *Studies in the Renaissance* 15 (1968): 7–24.
Tiller, Kenneth J. "The Rise of Sir Gareth and the Hermeneutics of Heraldry." *Arthuriana* 17.3 (2007): 74–91.
Tischendorf, Constantin, ed. *Evangelia apocrypha*. Leipzig: Mendelssohn, 1876.
Tkatsch, Jaroslaus. *Die arabische Übersetzung der Poetik des Aristoteles*, I–II. Vienna: Holder-Pichler-Tempsky 1928–32.
Tobler, Adolf and Erhard von Lomätsch. *Altfranzösisches Wörterbuch*. Wiesbaden: F. Steiner, 1956.
Trachtenberg, J. *The Devil and the Jews*. New York: Jewish Publication Society of America, 1943.
The Trojan War: The Chronicles of Dictys of Crete and Dares the Phrygian. Ed. R. M. Frazer. Bloomington: Indiana University Press, 1966.
Turville-Petre, Thorlac. *Alliterative Poetry of the Later Middle Ages: An Anthology*. Washington D.C.: Catholic University of America Press, 1989.
———. *The Alliterative Revival*. Cambridge: D. S. Brewer, 1977.
———. "The Author of *The Destruction of Troy*." *Medium Ævum* 57 (1988): 264–69.
———. "The Brutus Prologue to *Sir Gawain and the Green Knight*," in *Imagining a Medieval English Nation*. Ed. Kathy Lavezzo. Minneapolis: University of Minnesota Press, 2004. 340–46.
———. *England the Nation: Language, Literature, and National Identity, 1290–1340*. Oxford: Clarendon Press, 1996.
———. "The 'Pearl'-Poet in his 'Fayre Regioun,'" in *Essays on Ricardian Literature in Honour of J. A. Burrow*. Ed. A. J. Minnis, Charlotte C. Morse, and Turville-Petre. Oxford: Clarendon, 1997. 276–94.
Twowmey, Michael W. "'Hadet with an alusich mon' and 'britned to noȝt': *Sir Gawain and the Green Knight*, Death, and the Devil," in *The Arthurian Way of Death: The English Tradition*. Ed. Karen Cherewatuk & K. S. Whetter. Cambridge: D. S. Brewer, 2009. 73–93.
———. "Heroic Kingship and Unjust War in the Alliterative *Morte Arthure*." *Acta* 11 (1984): 133–51.
Tyerman, Christopher. *England and the Crusades, 1095–1588*. Chicago: University of Chicago Press, 1988.
Tyson, Diana B. "Patronage of French Vernacular History Writers in the Twelfth and Thirteenth Centuries." *Romania* 100 (1979): 180–222, 584.
Vale, Juliet. *Edward III and Chivalry: Chivalric Society and its Context, 1270–1350*. Woodbridge: Boydell Press, 1982.
———. "Law and Diplomacy in the Alliterative *Morte Arthure*." *Nottingham Medieval Studies* 23 (1979): 31–46.
Vance, Eugene. "Signs of the City: Medieval Poetry as Detour." *New Literary History* 4 (1973): 557–74.

Van den Baar, H. "Translatio Imperii Romani." *Analecta Gregoriana* 78 (1956): 45–47.
Vegetius. *Epitoma rei militaris*. Ed. M. D. Reeve. Oxford: Clarendon Press, 2004.
La Vengeance de Nostre-Seigneur: The Old and Middle French Prose Versions. 2 vols. Ed. Alvin Ford. Studies and Texts 63, 115. Toronto: Pontifical Institute of Mediaeval Studies, 1984–93.
Vincent of Beauvais. *Speculum Maius*. 4 vols. Duacus, 1524. Reprint Graz, Austria: Akademische Druk-u. Verlagenstadt, 1964–5.
Virgil. *Aeneid*. Ed. C. G. Heyne. London: T. Rickaby, 1793.
———. *Aeneid*. Ed. O. Ribbeck. Leipzig: Teubner, 1895.
———. *Opera*. Ed. R. A. B. Mynors. Oxford: Oxford University Press, 1969.
Wace. *Wace's Roman de Brut: A History of the British*. Ed. Judith Weiss. Exeter: University of Exeter Press, 2003.
Wagner, Anthony Richard. *Heralds and Heraldry in the Middle Ages: An Inquiry into the Growth of the Armorial Function of Heralds*. Oxford: Oxford University Press, 1939.
Waldron, Ronald A. "John Trevisa and the Use of English." *Proceedings of the British Academy* 74 (1988): 171–202.
———. "Oral-Formulaic Technique and Alliterative Poetry." *Speculum* 32.4 (1957): 792–804.
———. "Trevisa's 'Celtic Complex' Revisited." *Notes & Queries* 36 (234) (1989): 303–7.
Warren, Michelle R. *History on the Edge: Excalibur and the Borders of Britain, 1100–1300*. Minneapolis: University of Minnesota Press, 2000.
The Wars of Alexander. Ed. Hoyt N. Duggan and Thorlac Turville-Petre. Oxford: Oxford University Press, 1989.
Watkins, John. *The Specter of Dido: Spenser and Virgilian Epic*. New Haven and London: Yale University Press, 1995.
Watson, Nicholas. "Censorship and Cultural Change in Late-Medieval England: Vernacular Theology, the Oxford Translation Debate, and Arundel's Constitutions of 1409." *Speculum* 70.4 (1995): 822–64.
Wigginton, Waller Bimster. "The Nature and Significance of the Late Medieval Troy Story: A Study of Guido Delle Colonne's Historia Destructionis Troiae." PhD diss. Rutgers University, 1964.
William of Newburgh. *Historia rerum Anglicarum* in *Chronicles of the Reigns of Stephen, Henry II, and Richard I*. Ed. Richard Howlett. London: Longman, 1856.
Wilson, Edward. "John Clerk, Author of *The Destruction of Troy*." *Notes and Queries* 235 (1990): 391–96.
Winston, D. "The Iranian Component in the Bible, Apocrypha and Qumran." *History of Religions* 5 (1966): 189–92.
Wogan-Browne, Jocelyn, Nicholas Watson, Andrew Taylor, and Ruth Evans, eds. *The Idea of the Vernacular: An Anthology of Middle English Literary Theory, 1280–1520*. University Park: The Pennsylvania State University Press, 1999.
Wolfson, Harry A. "Revised Plan for the Publication of a Corpus Commentariorum Averroïs in Aristotelem." *Speculum* 38 (1963): 88–104.
Wood, Gordon R. "A Note on the Manuscript Source of the Alliterative *Destruction of Troy*." *Modern Language Notes* 67 (1952): 145–50.
Wynnere and Wastoure and The Parlement of the Thre Ages. Ed. Warren Ginsberg. Kalamazoo, Michigan: Medieval Institute Publications, 1992.
Yeager, Suzanne. *Jerusalem in Medieval Narrative*. Cambridge: Cambridge University Press, 2008.
Young, John and P. Henderson Aitken. *A Catalogue of the Manuscripts in the Library of the Hunterian Museum in the University of Glasgow*. Glasgow: James Maclehose and Sons, 1908.
Zeitkowitz, Richard E. *Homoeroticism and Chivalry: Discourses of Male Same-Sex Desire in the 14th Century*. New York: Palgrave Macmillan, 2003.
Zernatto, Guido. "Nation: The History of a Word." *Review of Politics* 6 (1944): 351–66.

INDEX

Abulafia, Anna, 82n4, 101
Achilles, 1, 3, 68, 69–70, 73–74
Adam of Usk, 143, 147, 188n55
Aeneas, 1, 6, 14, 17, 23, 29, 31–32, 35, 36n54, 62–63, 66, 75, 77, 116–19, 122, 142, 146, 170, 172–79, 188, 201, 204
Aeneid (Virgil), 23, 29, 31–32, 36n54, 50n19, 62–63, 74, 117–18, 142–43, 175–79
Agamben, Giorgio, 8–9, 81–82, 84–86, 91, 100, 124, 165
Albion, 45, 50, 79, 152, 227–28
Alexander the Great, 4, 12, 28, 69, 73n59, 93, 133n27, 160–62
Alfred the Great, 210, 212, 218
alliterative poetry, 1–2, 4–15, 17–18, 38–43, 68–69, 80–81, 93–95, 97–98, 109–10, 125–28, 135–37, 158–61, 167–72, 179–81, 183–84, 186–87, 198–99, 206–20, 222–24, 227–28; formulaic nature of, 10, 47, 94, 135, 212, 223, 227; meter of, 1, 3–5, 10, 47–62, 184; rhythm of, 10, 49, 212–14, 223, 227
Alliterative Revival, 5–7, 9–11, 14–15, 56–57, 68, 167–68, 227
ancestry. *See* genealogy
Anchises, 32, 63, 173–74
Andrew, Malcolm, 56, 90n30, 195n68
Andromache, 68, 117
Angevins, 21, 23–24
Anglo-Norman, 20n3, 54n29, 183, 195, 216–17
Anglo-Saxon verse, 5, 11, 54n29, 56–57, 72, 227. *See also* English; Old English

Anglo-Welsh, 18, 205
Antenor, 35, 64, 66–68, 75, 77, 118–19, 146, 173–74
antisemitism, 16, 82, 88–89, 93, 99, 106, 108, 110, 112
Arendt, Hannah, 140–41
aristocratic culture, 1–4, 7–8, 10–15, 17–18, 37–38, 49–50, 91–92, 104–5, 127–29, 161–64, 168–71, 186–89, 191–93, 195–203, 207–11, 214–20, 225–28; and patronage, 11–12, 18, 46, 50, 60, 79, 207, 209–11, 214–15, 217, 226, 228
Aristotle, 51–52, 116, 132, 158
ars dictaminis, 207, 212–13
Arthur, King, 4, 7, 9, 14–15, 17, 20, 26, 28, 38n59, 69, 94, 113–14, 124–67, 169–71, 175, 179, 181, 185–95, 197–98, 200–205, 207, 209–11, 214–18, 220–22
Augustine of Hippo, 19–20, 27, 30–31, 34–35, 110–15, 140, 222
authority. *See* sovereignty
Avalon, 126, 165
Awyntyrs off Arthure, 4, 130, 160, 198

Baswell, Christopher, 61n41, 178, 210–11, 215–17
Bede, Venerable, 113–14, 210
Bennett, Michael J., 38, 180–81,
Benoît de Sainte-Maure, 33–34, 36–37, 51n20, 54n29, 58n36, 61n42, 67, 98
Benson, C. David, 34, 40n1, 44–46, 54, 60n39, 64

246

Benson, Larry, 130–31, 136, 141n47, 145–47
Berkeley, Sir Thomas, 114n97, 210–11, 213–18
Bertilak, 90n30, 182, 193, 194, 198, 201, 204
biopolitics, 8, 84, 99–110, 165. *See also* body
Blake, Norman, 5, 56, 68
Blurton, Heather, 90, 104
body, 7–10, 14–16, 81–91, 139–40, 142–45, 154–56, 158–59, 163–67, 220–22; as a city, 2–3, 7–9, 14–15, 42, 71–72, 74–75, 118–23, 175; mutilated, 8–9, 15–16, 22, 69, 74–75, 82, 85–86, 88, 97, 99, 106, 109–10, 114, 120, 123, 140, 144, 147, 151–52, 154, 163–65, 198–201, 204, 221; politic, 8–9, 72–73, 84–86, 90, 99–110, 124–25, 165; revived, 15, 68–69, 71–75, 83, 99–103, 221; sovereign, 8–9, 84, 101, 119, 124–28, 164–66. *See also* biopolitics
Bolton, 92, 111, 115, 119, 140n45, 180
borderlands, 17, 181, 205; geographic, 96, 170–71, 179, 185–86, 189–90, 192–98, 201; textual, 170–72, 203–4. *See also* margins
Brembre, Nicholas, 36–37
Britain, 10–11, 18–22, 24–30, 44–45, 49–50, 125–27, 147–48, 150–53, 166–67, 171–74, 177–79, 185–87, 191–92, 194–96, 206–7
Britons, 147–48, 165–66, 196–97. *See also* Welsh
Brut, narratives, 4, 22, 150, 165–66, 169, 175, 178; *Brut* (Laʒamon), 22, 150–51, 178n36; *Roman de Brut* (Wace), 22, 178n36
Brutus, 14, 19, 24, 26, 29, 44, 75, 125, 151–52, 164, 166, 172–73, 175, 177–81, 183, 187, 189, 194, 202–4
Buthrotum, 36n54, 117, 177

Caesar Augustus, 75, 177
Caiaphas, 16, 88–90, 105, 108, 110, 119, 199
Calkas, 35, 225
Camelot, 170, 182, 191–92, 195, 202
cannibalism, 10, 17, 89–90, 104–8, 119, 144, 148, 155. *See also* Maria, cannibalistic mother
Canterbury Tales (Chaucer), 146, 225–27
Cassandra, 68, 78
Chakrabarty, Dipesh, 7, 204
Charlemagne, 21, 177n30

Charles V, 95–96, 169
Chaucer, Geoffrey, 3–6, 9–10, 18, 26–27, 35–36, 40n1, 46–47, 61n41, 64n46, 73, 79, 105n71, 130n15, 136, 146, 157n67, 164n76, 168, 180n40, 207–9, 222–28
Chester, 114–15, 170–71, 180–81, 185, 188–89
Cheshire, 170–71, 180–81, 189–91, 193–94, 196, 203, 205, 227
Chetham, Thomas, 43, 66, 219
Chism, Christine, 9, 56n35, 68–69, 73n59, 82, 88, 100–1, 109, 111n86, 128, 130–31, 151, 164n76
chivalry, 4, 7, 14, 17, 70, 91, 96, 103, 125, 131, 154, 157, 159, 162, 168, 191, 222; and heraldry, 127–28; and memory, 170–71; and sexual identity, 198–203; and vows, 2, 14, 91, 99, 103, 108, 136, 145, 149, 157, 171, 199–201, 215
Christ, 16, 38, 81–83, 85–92, 96, 105–6, 109–11, 134, 149, 162, 215, 222
Christendom, 21, 96, 101, 218
Christianity, 96, 221n37
Christians, representations of, 82–85, 87–88, 90–92, 100–103, 105–7, 110–12, 146–49
Christine de Pizan, 37, 79
Cité des dames (Christine de Pizan), 37, 79
city, 1–3, 7–9, 28–29, 37–38, 44–45, 71–72, 74–79, 84–85, 101–4, 116–20, 138–40, 163–64, 177–79, 186–87; siege of a, 4, 14–16, 73, 81–84, 87, 89, 91, 99–101, 103–4, 108–9, 111–12, 115, 118–20, 122, 126, 138, 140, 144, 148–49, 164, 179, 187, 198, 200, 203, 220. *See also* body; as a city
Cleanness, 100n61, 176
Clegis, 159, 163–64, 187
clerics, 88–91; skeptical voice of, 131–32, 207–12, 214–22
Cohen, Jeffrey Jerome, 153, 179, 195n69
Colchis, 2, 11–12, 28
colonialism, 7, 131, 174–75, 194, 204
Confessions (Augustine), 31n39–40, 34
Constantinople, 95, 116n100
Cooper, Helen, 20, 22
Corineus, 150–52
Cornelius, Ian, 212–14
Cornelius Nepos, 33, 49, 54, 58n36
corporeality. *See* body
Craddock, 220–22

Criseyde, 18, 35, 46n13, 73, 136, 207–9, 223–26
crusades, 9, 95–96, 136, 146–47, 149

Dares, 24, 27, 33–34, 49, 51n20, 54–55, 57–58, 61, 78, 113, 173, 184, 189, 203, 224
Day, Mabel, 46n13, 83n8, 94, 139, 142n47
De Excidio Troiae Historia (Dares), 34, 54
Descriptio Kambriae (Gerald of Wales), 152–53, 195–96
destruction, themes of, 3–4, 6–11, 14–16, 21–23, 28–29, 31–32, 35–37, 44–45, 66–69, 73–75, 78–80, 83–88, 90–91, 95–96, 103–4, 116–21, 126–27, 137–41, 143–46, 156–60, 163–66, 171–72. *See also* plague, themes of
Destruction of Troy (John Clerk of Whalley), 2–4, 10–12, 14–17, 40–80, 93–99, 102–3, 118–20, 135–36, 159–61, 214–15, 224–25
Dialogue Between a Lord and a Clerk Upon Translation (Trevisa), 209, 211–12, 215, 217–18
Diana, 24, 26, 30, 75
dictamen. *See ars dictaminis*
Dictys, 24, 27, 33–34, 49, 51n20, 54–55, 57–58, 61, 78, 113, 173, 184, 189, 203, 224
Dido, 23–24, 37, 62n43
Dinshaw, Carolyn, 198–99
diplomacy, 4, 7, 15–16, 35, 64, 78, 96, 216, 221, 222
dismemberment. *See* body; mutilated
Donaldson, David, 12, 41, 43, 50n18, 66n47
Donatus, Claudius Tiberius, 177–78
Duchess of Brittany, 127, 136n35, 148, 156–57
Duggan, Hoyt N., 73n59, 141–42

East, representations of the, 10, 38, 109, 116n100, 133, 182
Edward I, 29n35, 191
Edward III, 130n13, 135, 143n53, 180n40
England, 1–4, 18–20, 22–24, 34–35, 37–38, 82–84, 92–93, 95–96, 168–71, 175–76, 178–83, 185–92, 204–6, 208–9, 221–22; Northern, 2, 4–7, 15–17, 114, 130, 168, 170–71, 179–80, 182–83, 185, 188–95, 201, 211–12, 218, 227–28; Southern, 5, 10, 92, 167–68, 170, 182–83, 185, 191, 195
English, 26–28, 38–42, 47–51, 56–62, 80–84, 167–72, 178–79, 205–19; dialects of, 4, 6–7, 94, 180, 183, 227; Middle English, 5–6, 56n35, 72n56, 83n9, 89n28, 94, 97–98, 178, 212; Old English, 5, 11, 94n41, 178, 211–12. *See also* Anglo-Saxon verse
Ephemeris Belli Troiani (Dictys), 34, 55
Eucharist, 85, 87, 89–90, 105
excess. *See* surfeit

fantasies, 8–9, 33–35; of empire, 115–16, 165–66, 168–69; of violence, 151–54
Federico, Sylvia, 10, 35, 173
Finlayson, John, 41n4, 129–31, 135–36, 161n75
flaying, as a hunting metaphor, 16, 88–93, 99, 109, 199–200
Fortune, 37, 42, 44, 63, 65–66, 79, 132, 159–61, 177–78; Wheel of, 159–61
Foucault, Michel, 8, 100, 121, 190
France, 79, 134–35, 143, 145–46, 149, 169, 179–81, 183, 185, 187
French, 60–61, 175–76, 181–83, 185
Froissart, Jean, 146–47, 226

Galfridian history, 19–30, 34–35, 113–15, 131–35, 143–44, 150–52, 178–81, 203–4, 216–17. *See also* Geoffrey of Monmouth
Gawain, 4, 6–7, 14–15, 17, 19, 29–30, 38, 55–57, 69, 73, 90n30, 98n56, 128, 131n21, 155–65, 167–205, 214–15, 220–22, 228
genealogy, 3–4, 79–80, 111–12, 153–54, 186–87, 195–97, 216–17, 226–28; and imperial heritage, 6–39, 44–46, 49–50, 116–17, 159–67, 169–70; and kinship, 125–28
Geoffrey of Monmouth, 19–30, 36–37, 49–50, 75–76, 111–14, 134–35, 152–53, 172–73, 178–80, 203–4. *See also* Galfridian history
Gerald of Wales, 25, 112, 152–53, 171, 195–98, 201, 205

Germans, 21, 106, 135
Giant of St. Michael's Mount, 68, 127, 136n35, 148–51, 154–58
Gildas, 113–14
Gogmagog, 150–51
Golden Fleece, 2, 28
Gollancz, Sir Israel, 173, 175
Göller, Karl Heinz, 129–31
Gorra, Egidio, 29n35, 34
Gower, John, 10, 36, 76–77, 208–9
Greece, 38, 64, 68, 74, 175
Greeks, 1–3, 11–12, 66–67, 73–75, 119–20, 224–25
Green Chapel, 19, 171, 180n40, 194–95, 201
Green Knight, 4, 6, 14–15, 17, 55, 68–69, 90n30, 98n56, 131n21, 159, 168, 170n14, 183n47, 191–95, 198n74, 200, 215n24, 221n37
Guido delle Colonne, 3–4, 6–7, 11–12, 14–17, 26–38, 40–55, 57–70, 72, 75, 77–80, 84, 93–99, 101, 106, 110–11, 113–18, 120–22, 126, 129, 131–32, 160n74, 166, 169–77, 179–81, 184n48, 196, 204, 206–7, 209–10, 213–15, 219, 222–24, 226, 228
Guinevere, 125, 192

Hamel, Mary, 94–96, 98, 129n11, 131, 133–37, 139–43, 160–61
Hanna, Ralph, 5, 46n13, 82–84, 89n28, 91–95, 97, 115, 136, 139, 209n4, 218
Hanning, Robert, 25n25, 27, 210n7
Hautdesert, 17, 170–71, 179, 182, 190, 193–94, 194–95, 197–98, 201, 205
Hebron, Malcolm, 84, 120
Hector, 1, 4, 15–16, 42, 62–75, 78–80, 99, 102–3, 126, 133, 160–63, 166, 195, 219, 223
Hecuba, 32, 174
Hegisippus, 106–7
Helen of Troy, 1, 3, 23, 35
Helenus, 36n54, 68, 78, 117, 219–20, 222, 225
Heng, Geraldine, 9–10, 19, 25–26, 28, 38n59, 116n100, 130–31, 164n76, 202
Henry II, 11, 24, 152
Henry IV, 92, 136n35
Henry V, 3, 45, 50, 60, 79, 226–27
heraldry, 3, 14, 170, 187, 200–5, 221–22; and the dragon symbol, 17, 124–66; and the green girdle, 17, 170, 201–5, 222
Hercules, 2, 8, 11–12, 175, 222
Higden, Ranulph, 83, 111, 114–15, 171, 181–83, 185–90, 193, 205, 207, 209–10, 212, 214–18
Histoire ancienne jusqu'à César, 24, 37
Historia de preliis Alexandri Magni, 93, 97
Historia destructionis Troiae (Guido delle Colonne), 3, 6, 14–15, 19, 22, 26, 28–29, 31–32, 34–37, 40–43, 45, 47, 50, 54, 58n36, 61, 84, 93–94, 97–99, 111, 113, 116–17, 126, 160n74, 171–74, 176–77, 179–180, 204, 207, 209–10, 213–14, 223–24, 228.
Historia rerum Anglicarum (William of Newburgh), 84, 111, 113, 115
Historia regum Britanniae (Geoffrey of Monmouth), 19–27, 29–30, 36–37, 49–50, 69n52, 75–76, 112–14, 116–17, 129, 134, 137, 152–53, 166, 169, 172, 175, 179, 203
history, 3–4, 9–15, 17–18, 41–43, 47–51, 54–62, 68–69, 145–46, 152–53, 168–70, 183–86, 216–18; and historiography, 6–7, 14–17, 19–39, 78–80, 84–85, 110–16, 159–64, 171–72, 202–7, 222–28
Holy Land, 95–96
Homer, 3, 16, 23, 27, 33–34, 36n54, 51–55, 59–60, 62, 113, 184, 224
Huchown of the Awle Ryale, 43, 94n43, 135–36
Hundred Years War, 169, 179, 181

Iliad (Homer), 3, 52
imperialism, 2–3, 6–14, 42–47, 75–80, 82–88, 90–93, 96–101, 125–27, 139–40, 143–49, 171–81, 185–88, 194–97, 199–200, 226–28; critiques of 16–32, 34–38, 68–69, 112–18, 120–23, 129–31, 133–35, 151–60, 164–66, 214–22; and memory, 191–92, 204–8; Roman, 61–63, 103–4, 107–10
Ingham, Patricia Clare, 7, 9, 25, 30, 38n59, 124n2, 130–31, 143n53, 157–58, 165n77, 170n14
Ingledew, Frances, 25–28, 34–35, 191n63
Islam, 96, 117n200

Italy, 26, 31–32, 63, 132, 136, 143, 149, 158, 177, 216

Jacobs, Nicholas, 41n4, 97–98
Jacobus de Voragine, 102–3
Jason and the Argonauts, 2, 11–12, 28
Jefferson, Judith, 92n35, 142
Jerome, Saint, 206, 212n13
Jerusalem, 14–16, 81–85, 87–97, 100–103, 108–12, 114–16, 118–22, 137–40, 142–43, 179–80, 185–86, 199–200, 219–20
Jewish War (Josephus), 83, 101, 105–6, 112
Jews, 15–16, 81–85, 88–93, 101–12, 118–20, 139–40
John Clerk of Whalley, 2, 4, 8–10, 14–15, 18, 28, 40–51, 53–59, 61–66, 68–71, 73–79, 84, 95, 98, 99n58, 102, 115, 118, 120–21, 157n68, 160n74, 179–80, 184, 188, 212–15, 219, 224, 228
Joseph of Exeter, 11, 24, 58n36
Josephus, Flavius, 16, 83, 101–9, 112
Judaism, 81–82, 111–12
Julius Caesar, 29, 160, 164

Kantorowicz, Ernst, 8n21, 124, 165
Knight's Tale (Chaucer), 6, 73, 157n67, 223
Kölbing, E., 46n13, 83n8, 139, 141–42

Lacan, Jacques, 25, 165n77, 200
Lady Bertilak, 174–75, 198–99, 204
Laʒamon, 22, 129n11, 150–51, 178n36, 191
Lancashire, 180–81, 190, 194
Lancaster (House of), 3, 10, 40n1, 92, 207, 226–27
Langland, William, 10, 222
Laomedon, 2–3, 8–9, 11, 35, 43, 64, 74, 83, 222
Latin, 10–11, 40–42, 47–49, 58–61, 97–98, 168–69, 208–9, 212–16
Laud Troy Book, 40, 44
Lavezzo, Kathy, 153, 186, 205n84
Lawton, David, 41n4, 46n13, 57n35, 59, 83n8, 89n28, 91–95, 97, 115, 136–37, 139, 199n78, 212
Lefebvre, Henri, 71–72
Legenda Aurea (Jacobus de Voragine), 102–3
Legend of Good Women (Chaucer), 6, 223
Liber Catoniani, 213–14

Livingston, Michael, 86–87, 89n28, 94n43, 121n108
Livre de la Mutacion de Fortune, Le (Christine de Pizan), 37, 79
Lollards, 92–93, 136n35
London, 7, 10, 22, 30, 36, 76–77, 92, 170, 172, 210, 226–27
Lucius, Roman emperor, 125, 127–28, 134–37, 140, 144–45, 147, 154
Lydgate, John, 3, 11n31, 15, 28, 35, 40–42, 44–47, 49–50, 54–55, 57, 60–66, 69–70, 73, 75, 79, 207, 226–28

Macedonia, 12, 21, 113
Malebranche, 125, 165. *See also* Mordred
Malory, Sir Thomas, 28, 72n56, 125
Manning, Robert, 129, 191
manuscripts, 10, 22, 24–26, 30, 98, 139, 169, 176, 185, 188, 209–11, 228; Cambridge University Library MS Mm.v.14, 92–93, 97; Hunterian MS V.2.8, 11–12, 41, 43–47, 59, 66
margins, 17, 179, 201, 204; and marginalia, 47, 188; and marginalization, 7, 38, 185–86, 189. *See also* borderlands
Maria, cannibalistic mother, 16, 87, 103–6, 108, 110
Matsumoto, Hiroyuki, 40–41, 43, 50n18, 66
Matthews, William, 129–31, 160
Meek, Mary, 3n2, 29n35, 34, 58n36
Merlin, 30, 112–13, 197
Milan, 136n34, 145, 147, 149; Sire of, 145, 147
Millar, Bonnie, 97n54–55, 100n61, 102–3, 109n83, 220
Mordred, 125, 132–33, 136n35, 155–57, 165. *See also* Malebranche
Morte Arthure, alliterative, 4, 9, 14–15, 17, 20n4, 28, 38n59, 69, 94, 116n100, 124–66, 169, 175, 186–87, 214, 217, 220–21, 228

Narin van Court, Elisa, 82–83, 108, 111–12, 115, 140n45
nationalism, 153–54, 167–69, 173–74, 179–81, 185–87, 204–7, 209–10
Neilson, George, 43, 94n43, 135–36, 145n55
Nero, 16, 83, 91, 101, 137
Nicholson, Roger, 88n27, 95–96

Nicopolis, 95, 136, 146–47
Nietzsche, Friedrich, 51, 54
Nine Worthies, 159–61, 220
Normans, 20–21, 30, 153, 182–83, 189, 191, 195, 216–17
Northwest Midlands, 4, 15–17, 170, 179–80, 183, 190, 192–95, 201, 227. *See also* England; Northern

Odyssey (Homer), 3, 36n54
Old Testament, 110–11
On Violence (Arendt), 140–41
Orosius, 19–20, 27, 30–32, 113
Other, representations of the, 3n2, 26–35, 106, 195
Ovid, 23n15, 53, 57, 60, 62, 113, 184n48

pagans, representations of, 16, 38, 52, 83, 101, 147, 149, 160n73, 208
Pallas, 23, 62n43
Panton, G. A., 11–12, 41, 43, 50n18, 66n47
Paris of Troy, 23, 68, 74, 157, 219
Parlement of the Thre Ages, 4, 142, 198–99
Patience, 97–98, 176
Patterson, Lee, 20n4, 23–24, 35–36, 130–31, 160–61, 225–26
Pearl, 7, 176
Pearsall, Derek, 57, 60, 82n5, 98n56
Pendragon, 133–35
Peter, Saint, 91, 219–20
Piers Plowman (Langland), 10, 222
Pilate, Pontius, 88, 90
plague, themes of, 11–12, 28, 30, 35, 42, 44, 64, 78, 80, 120, 122, 126, 196, 208, 228. *See also* destruction, themes of
Plato, 52, 58
Poetics (Aristotle), 51–52
Polychronicon (Higden), 83, 111, 114–15, 171, 181–83, 185, 188, 207, 209–12, 214–15, 217–18
Polydamas, 173–74
Polyxena, 73–74
Priam, 1, 9, 14, 16, 32, 35, 42, 63–71, 73–75, 83, 118–19, 126, 160–61, 165–66, 219
Priamus, 68, 159, 161–63
prophecies, 11, 21, 23, 29, 63, 77–78, 118, 120, 215, 228; biblical, 87, 91; Galfridian, 24, 26, 30, 112–13, 169, 207, 217–18
providence, 18–19, 29, 44, 115, 149; and history, 26, 31, 45, 86, 110, 167, 169, 207; and transfers of power, 22, 63–66, 77–78
provincial politics, 4, 11–14, 17–18, 168, 170–71, 179–94, 196, 198, 204–7, 209, 227–28; defined, 6–7; of Guido delle Colonne, 28–29, 174–75
Psalms, 111, 206
Putter, Ad, 92n35, 131n21, 142, 183n47, 215n24, 221

Quint, David, 36n54, 117

Richard II, 7, 46n13, 76, 92, 95–96, 180n40, 191, 194, 208–9, 213, 227
Rollo, David, 33–34
Romans, 3–4, 14–17, 20–22, 32–33, 81–93, 99–101, 107–13, 115–16, 118–20, 122–24, 126–29, 133–45, 147–49, 154–56, 175–77, 199–200; and imperialism, 3, 16–17, 21, 32, 63, 81, 83–85, 90–91, 110, 116, 118, 120, 137, 140, 142n50, 145
romance, alliterative, 7–15, 67–69, 160–61; and Chaucer, 222–25, 227–28; clerical voice of, 219–22; defined, 4; and fantasy, 25–26; and history, 17–22, 169–72, 202–10, 213–15
Roman d'Eneas, 21n5, 23, 176n28
Roman de Troie (Benoît de Sainte-Maure), 21n5, 33–34, 36, 51n20, 61n42, 67, 98
Rome, 3–4, 10–11, 21–23, 31–32, 100–101, 115–23, 126–27, 136–37, 143–46, 154–55, 173–74, 185–86, 220–22; Augustan, 23, 142n50; Old, 83, 90, 101
Round Table, 162, 201–3, 205, 222

Sabyn, Titus Flavius Sabinus, 121–22
Sabyn of Syria, 91–92, 108–9, 121–22, 143, 200
sacrifice, themes of, 7, 17, 23, 74, 84–87, 107, 110–11, 119, 126, 155, 159, 228
Saint Erkenwald, 4, 76, 159
Sallust, 33, 58n36
Schiff, Randy, 5n7, 6, 9, 56, 68, 82, 130, 167–68
Schmitt, Carl, 84–85
Scotland, 41, 130, 194
Scrope Grosvenor trial, 164, 180n40

Servius, 175–76, 178n33
Sicily, 3, 174, 216
Siege of Jerusalem, 4, 10, 14–17, 43, 46n13, 69, 81–123, 128, 132n22, 135–44, 147–49, 154, 165n77, 179–80, 199–200, 214, 219–20, 222, 228
Simpson, James, 3n2, 28, 58, 69n52, 71, 74, 78, 131–32, 169, 215
Sir Gawain and the Green Knight, 4, 6–7, 14–15, 17, 19, 29–30, 38, 55–57, 69, 90n30, 98n56, 131n21, 159, 167–205, 214–15, 220–22, 228
Sessye, 135, 137
Silverstein, Theodore, 172, 177–79
Smith, D. Vance, 127–28, 159, 223n40
Socrates, 52–54
sovereignty, 7–10, 194–95, 201–2, 208–9, 220–21; and biopolitics, 99–110; fantasies of, 14–15, 122–26, 171–72; and Galfridian history, 24–25, 164–66, 227–28; and tyranny, 155–57; and violence, 81–82, 84–86, 128–29, 141–47, 151–53
Spain, 185, 187
surfeit, 4, 16, 71, 82, 101–3, 112, 154, 156–57, 168, 171, 195–99, 201–2, 205, 219–21
Syria, 91, 108, 121, 163–64

territory, 14, 17–18, 30, 38, 79, 125, 153, 167–205, 216–17
Thames, 30, 75
Thornton, Robert, 93n40, 141–42
Tiber, 116–18, 121–22
Titus, 16, 83–84, 87, 91, 96, 99–110, 119–21, 165n77, 200
To His Purse (Chaucer), 227–28
translatio imperii, 6–8, 16–22, 29–30, 36–38, 43–47, 76–77, 115–16, 126–27, 164–65, 173–77, 194–95, 217–18, 221–22, 227–28; defined, 3; *et studii*, 18, 27, 183, 206, 208, 217, 228
translation, 2–3, 14–15, 21–22, 26–27, 32–34, 39–42, 44–47, 49–51, 53–62, 64–66, 71–72, 83–84, 98–99, 116–18, 165–66, 175–76, 204–19, 227–28; of bodies, 32, 71, 165; of language, 3, 10, 14–15, 18, 22, 24, 26–27, 33–34, 40–42, 44–47, 49–51, 53–62, 64–66, 72, 95, 98–99, 106, 112, 114, 117, 129, 134, 148, 153, 162, 169, 175–76, 179, 183, 185,
206–19, 227–28; of power, 2, 10, 21–22, 39, 80, 83–84, 92, 101, 116–18, 120, 127, 148, 153, 159, 166, 187, 196, 204–6, 208, 218, 222. See also *translatio imperii*
treason, themes of, 14–15, 29–30, 68–70, 89–90, 117–19, 146–47, 167–70, 173–74, 201–4
Trevisa, John, 18, 83n9, 114, 145n54, 183, 207–19, 228
Troilus, 18, 46n13, 62, 73–74, 136, 207–9, 223–66
Troilus and Criseyde (Chaucer), 18, 46n13, 73, 136, 207–9, 223–26
Trojans, 1–4, 6–12, 14–29, 31–38, 41–42, 44–45, 49–52, 61–72, 74–80, 116–118, 132–33, 152–54, 159–61, 163–71, 173–75, 177–79, 186–87, 194–98, 201–5, 222–28; and the Trojan War, 64, 184
Troy, 1–4, 6–12, 14–17, 19–29, 31–38, 40–47, 49–52, 58–64, 68–72, 74–80, 83–85, 93, 112–13, 115–23, 159–66, 168–74, 176–79, 186–87, 195–96, 202–4, 206–7, 210–12, 214–15, 222–28; First, 1, 3, 9, 11, 28–29, 66, 69, 74–75, 83; Little (Parva Troia), 36, 117, 123; New, 4, 7–10, 12, 15–16, 22, 25, 29, 35, 35–39, 42, 44–45, 75–78, 116, 118, 122, 152, 168, 171, 177–79
Troy Book (Lydgate), 3, 11n31, 15, 35, 40–41, 44–45, 61, 69, 79, 226–27
Troynovant. See Troy; New
Turks, 96, 146
Turville-Petre, Thorlac, 4–7, 41, 43, 46n13, 56n35, 92n34, 110, 115n99, 135n32, 168, 175
Tuscany, 127, 158, 163, 175
Tuscus, 175–76

Vengeance de Nostre-Seigneur, La, 89n28, 139
vernacularity, 10–11, 14–15, 59–61, 208–9
Vernicle, 136, 149, 219
Veronica, 219–20
Vespasian, 4, 9, 16, 83–84, 89, 91–93, 96, 99–101, 103, 105, 109, 121–22, 137–39, 149, 165n77, 200, 219–20
Vindicta Salvatoris, 95, 107
violence, themes of, 8–10, 16–18, 81–123, 128–29, 140–41, 144–45, 147–49, 151–56, 158–60, 163–66, 197–201
Virgil, 19, 22–23, 26–27, 29, 31, 34, 36n54,

50n19, 55, 59–60, 62–66, 73–75, 113, 117–18, 127, 142, 175–78, 183, 216
Visconti family, 136, 143, 145–47; and Giangaleazzo Visconti, 136, 145–47
Viscount of Rome, 136, 141, 143–47
Vitellius, 121–22, 143
Vox Clamantis (Gower), 36, 76

Wace, 22, 24, 54n29, 129n11, 178
Waldron, Ronald, 56, 90n30, 94–95, 195n68, 210, 212, 217n28
Wales, 25, 112, 152–53, 171, 179, 189–92, 194–97, 201, 203, 226; and its border with England, 190–92, 194, 195
war, 2–4, 9–10, 40–80; and Chaucer, 223–24; and chivalric identity, 14–18; clerical critiques of, 219–21; and empire-building, 82–83, 103–4, 113–14; and violence, 125–26, 128–34, 139–44, 151–54, 160–63, 214–15
Wars of Alexander, 4, 28, 69, 73n59, 93, 133n27

Welsh, 17–18, 144–45, 152–53, 170–71, 191–97, 216–17. *See also* Britons
Welsh March, 17, 119, 170, 179, 191–96, 201, 217
West, representations of the, 7, 10, 21–22, 38, 51, 60, 116, 133, 138, 169, 174, 182, 186, 208, 218
Whalley, 2, 4, 15, 40–41, 43, 46n13, 92, 95, 99n58, 115, 157n68, 180, 184, 188, 219n32
William of Malmesbury, 25, 112, 114, 189, 216–17
William of Newburgh, 25, 84, 111–15
Wirral, 190–91
Wynnere and Wastoure, 4, 159, 169–70

Xanthus, 116–18, 122

Yorkshire, 92, 95, 111–12; and York, 93, 111–12

INTERVENTIONS: NEW STUDIES IN MEDIEVAL CULTURE
Ethan Knapp, Series Editor

Interventions: New Studies in Medieval Culture publishes theoretically informed work in medieval literary and cultural studies. We are interested both in studies of medieval culture and in work on the continuing importance of medieval tropes and topics in contemporary intellectual life.

Scribal Authorship and the Writing of History in Medieval England
MATTHEW FISHER

Fashioning Change: The Trope of Clothing in High- and Late-Medieval England
ANDREA DENNY-BROWN

Form and Reform: Reading across the Fifteenth Century
EDITED BY SHANNON GAYK AND KATHLEEN TONRY

How to Make a Human: Animals and Violence in the Middle Ages
KARL STEEL

Revivalist Fantasy: Alliterative Verse and Nationalist Literary History
RANDY P. SCHIFF

Inventing Womanhood: Gender and Language in Later Middle English Writing
TARA WILLIAMS

Body Against Soul: Gender and Sowlehele *in Middle English Allegory*
MASHA RASKOLNIKOV